# Programmer's Supplement for Release 6

*of the X Window System, Version 11*

**R6 UPDATE**

# Programmer's Supplement for Release 6

## *of the X Window System, Version 11*

### Edited by Adrian Nye

O'Reilly & Associates, Inc.
103 Morris Street, Suite A
Sebastopol, CA 95472

# Programmer's Supplement for Release 6 of the X Window System

Copyright © 1995 O'Reilly & Associates, Inc. All rights reserved.
Printed in the United States of America.

**Editor:** Adrian Nye
**Production Editor:** Nicole Gipson

**Printing History**

September 1995: First Edition.

This book is printed on acid-free paper with 85% recycled content, 15% post-consumer waste. O'Reilly & Associates is committed to using paper with the highest recycled content available consistent with high quality.

ISBN: 1-56592-089-9

# Table of Contents

## CHAPTER 7: Other Changes in X11R6 ............................................... 193

# PART III: X Toolkit Reference

# *Preface*

Release 6 of the X Window System includes useful features in addition to those of previous releases, not drastic changes to X's basic features. With session management, multithreading, font rotation, extension event handling, practical internationalization, an imaging extension, and more, Release 6 has something useful for almost any X programmer.

This book provides a complete tutorial to programming with the new features and includes reference pages for the new Xt and Xlib functions.

## How to Use This Manual

Part I contains the chapters and appendix. First read Chapter 1 for an overview of the new features of the release. Then read any chapters that cover subjects you need or want to know about. These chapters can be read as a tutorial and consulted for reference later. Parts II and III contain reference pages for Xlib and Xt, respectively. Use these two sections whenever you need reference pages for the new functions. Here is an overview of each chapter:

Chapter 1, *Introduction to X11R6*, gives you an overview of all the other chapters and a context in which to read them.

Chapter 2, *Xt Session Management*, describes how to write a session-manager-compliant Xt application, so that users can save and restart your application as part of their sessions.

Chapter 3, *Other New Features in Xt*, describes all the miscellaneous changes in Xt.

Chapter 4, *Multithreading*, tells you how to use Multithreading to acheive better interactivity for your GUI.

Chapter 5, *New Font Technology*, shows you how to use scaled or rotated fonts and other new R6 font features.

Chapter 6, *Internationalization*, is a guide to writing an internationalized X program, including how to set up a test environment.

Chapter 7, *Other Changes in X11R6*, provides an overview of the capabilities of this newly standardized imaging extension.

Chapter 8, *An Introduction to the X Image Extension*, covers the remaining bits and pieces of R6.

Appendix A, *Release 6 Release Notes*, is the official release notes for R6.

Part II, *Xlib Reference*, includes reference pages for all new X11R6 functions in Xlib.

Part III, *X Toolkit Reference*, includes reference pages for all new X11R6 functions in Xt.

## *Getting the Example Programs*

The example programs in this book are available electronically by FTP, *ftpmail*, BITFTP, and UUCP. The cheapest, fastest, and easiest ways are listed first. If you read from the top down, the first one that works for you is probably the best. Use FTP if you are directly on the Internet. Use *ftpmail* if you are not on the Internet, but can send and receive electronic mail to Internet sites (this includes CompuServe users). Use BITFTP if you send electronic mail via BITNET. Use UUCP if none of the above works.

### FTP

To use FTP, you need a machine with direct access to the Internet. A sample session is shown, with what you should type in **boldface**.

```
% ftp ftp.uu.net
Connected to ftp.uu.net.
220 FTP server (Version 6.21 Tue Mar 10 22:09:55 EST 1992) ready.
Name (ftp.uu.net:joe): anonymous
331 Guest login ok, send domain style e-mail address as password.
Password: joe@ora.com   (use your user name and host here)
230 Guest login ok, access restrictions apply.
ftp> cd /published/oreilly/xbook/r6update
250 CWD command successful.
ftp> binary    (You must specify binary transfer for compressed files.)
200 Type set to I.
ftp> get r6update.tar.Z
200 PORT command successful.
150 Opening BINARY mode data connection for r6update.tar.Z.
226 Transfer complete.
ftp> quit
221 Goodbye.
%
```

The file is a compressed *tar* archive; extract the files from the archive by typing:

```
% zcat r6update.tar.Z | tar xvf -
```

System V systems require the following *tar* command instead:

```
% zcat r6update.tar.Z | tar xof -
```

If *zcat* is not available on your system, use separate *uncompress* and *tar* or *shar* commands.

```
% uncompress r6update.tar.Z
% tar xvf r6update.tar.Z
```

## ftpmail

*ftpmail* is a mail server available to anyone who can send electronic mail to, and receive it from, Internet sites. This includes any company or service provider that allows email connections to the Internet. Here's how you do it.

You send mail to *ftpmail@online.ora.com*. In the message body, give the FTP commands you want to run. The server will run anonymous FTP for you and mail the files back to you. To get a complete help file, send a message with no subject and the single word "help" in the body. The following is a sample mail session that should get you the examples. This command sends you a listing of the files in the selected directory and the requested example files. The listing is useful if there's a later version of the examples you're interested in.

```
% mail ftpmail@online.ora.com
Subject:
reply-to janetv@xyz.com        Where you want files mailed
open
cd /published/oreilly/xbook/r6update
dir
mode binary
uuencode
get r6update.tar.Z
quit
.
```

A signature at the end of the message is acceptable as long as it appears after "quit."

## BITFTP

BITFTP is a mail server for BITNET users. You send it electronic mail messages requesting files, and it sends you back the files by electronic mail. BITFTP currently serves only users who send it mail from nodes that are directly on BITNET, EARN, or NetNorth. BITFTP is a public service of Princeton University. Here's how it works.

To use BITFTP, send mail containing your *ftp* commands to *BITFTP@PUCC*. For a complete help file, send HELP as the message body.

The following is the message body you send to BITFTP:

```
FTP   ftp.uu.net   NETDATA
USER  anonymous
PASS  myname@podunk.edu    Put your Internet email address here (not your BITNET address)
```

```
CD     /published/oreilly/xbook/r6update
DIR
BINARY
GET    r6update.tar.Z
QUIT
```

Once you've got the desired file, follow the directions under FTP to extract the files from the archive. If you are not on a UNIX system, you may need to get versions of *uudecode, uncompress, atob,* and *tar* for your system. VMS, DOS, and Mac versions are available. The VMS versions are on *gatekeeper.dec.com* in */pub/VMS*.

Questions about BITFTP can be directed to Melinda Varian, *MAINT@PUCC* on BITNET.

## UUCP

UUCP is standard on virtually all UNIX systems and is available for IBM-compatible PCs and Apple Macintoshes. The examples are available by UUCP via modem from UUNET; UUNET's connect-time charges apply.

You can get the examples from UUNET whether you have an account there or not. If you or your company has an account with UUNET, you have a system somewhere with a direct UUCP connection to UUNET. Find that system, and type (on one line):

```
uucp uunet\!~/published/oreilly/xbook/r6update/r6update.tar.Z
     yourhost\!~/ yourname/
```

The backslashes can be omitted if you use the Bourne shell (*sh*) instead of *csh*. The file should appear some time later (up to a day or more) in the directory */usr/spool/uucppublic/yourname*. If you don't have an account, but would like one so that you can get electronic mail, contact UUNET at 703-204-8000.

It's a good idea to get the file */published/oreilly/ls-lR.Z* as a short test file containing the filenames and sizes of all the files available.

Once you've got the desired file, follow the directions under FTP to extract the files from the archive.

# *Compiling the Example Programs*

Once you've got the examples and unpacked the archive as described above, you're ready to compile them. The easiest way is to use *imake*, a program supplied with the X11 distribution that generates proper Makefiles on a wide variety of systems.) *imake* uses configuration files called Imakefiles which are included. If you have *imake*, you should go to the top-level directory containing the examples, and type:

```
% xmkmf -a
% make Makefiles
% make
```

All the application-defaults files are in the main examples directory. The application-defaults files are not automatically installed in the system application-defaults directory (usually *usr/lib/X11/app-defaults* on UNIX systems). If you have permission to write to that directory, you can copy them there yourself. Otherwise, you can set the XAPPLRES-DIR environment variable to the complete path of the directory where you installed the examples. The value of XAPPLRESDIR must end with a / (slash). (Most of the examples will not function properly without the application-defaults files.)

## Assumptions

Readers should be proficient in the C programming language and should be familiar with the features of X11 Release 5.

## Font Conventions Used in This Manual

*Italic* is used for:

- UNIX pathnames, filenames, program names, user command names, and options for user commands.

- New terms where they are defined.

`Typewriter Font` is used for:

- Anything that would be typed verbatim into code, such as examples of source code and text on the screen.

- The contents of include files, such as structure types, structure members, symbols (defined constants and bit flags), and macros.

- Xlib functions.

- Names of subroutines of the example programs.

*`Italic Typewriter Font`* is used for:

- Arguments to Xlib functions, since they could be typed in code as shown but are arbitrary.

## Related Documents

The following documents are included on the X11 source distribution:

- *Xt Toolkit Intrinsics* by Paul Asente and Ralph Swick

- *Xlib — C Language X Interface* by Jim Gettys and Robert Scheifler

The following other books on the X Window System are available from O'Reilly & Associates, Inc.:

- Volume Zero — *X Protocol Reference Manual*

- Volume One — *Xlib Programming Manual*

- Volume Two — *Xlib Reference Manual*

- Volume Three — *X Window System User's Guide*

- Volume Four — *X Toolkit Intrinsics Programming Manual*

- Volume Five — *X Toolkit Intrinsics Reference Manual*

- Volume Six A — *Motif Programming Manual*

- Volume Six B — *Motif Reference Manual*

- Volume Seven — *XView Programmer's Guide*

- Volume Eight — *X Administrator's Guide*

- *Motif Tools: Streamlined GUI Design and Programming with the Xmt Library*

- *PHIGS Programming Manual*

- *PHIGS Reference Manual*

- *Pexlib Programming Manual*

- *Pexlib Reference Manual*

- Quick Reference — *The X Window System in a Nutshell*

## We'd Like to Hear From You

We have tested and verified all of the information in this book to the best of our ability, but you may find that features have changed (or even that we have made mistakes!). Please let us know about any errors you find, as well as your suggestions for future editions, by writing:

> O'Reilly & Associates, Inc.
> 103 Morris Street, Suite A
> Sebastopol, CA 95472
> 1-800-998-9938 (in the US or Canada)
> 1-707-829-0515 (international/local)
> 1-707-829-0104 (FAX)

You can also send us messages electronically. To be put on the mailing list or request a catalog, send email to:

> `info@ora.com`     (*via the Internet*)
> `uunet!ora!info`     (*via UUCP*)

To ask technical questions or to comment on the book, send email to:

> `bookquestions@ora.com`   (*via the Internet*)

# Acknowledgments

This book is a cooperative endeavor by many hands. I'd like to thank all the authors for sharing their expertise with me (and the reader). Paula Ferguson of O'Reilly & Associates did her usual fine job on Chapters 1, 3, and 7. John Vergo of Vertechs Consulting wrote Chapter 2 on Session Management. Ajay Vohra (then of Sun Microsystems) wrote Chapter 4 on Multithreading. Nathan Meyers of Hewlett Packard wrote Chapter 5 on the new font features. Hideki Hiura of Sun Microsystems wrote Chapter 6 on Internationalization. Ben Fahy (then of AGE Logic) wrote Chapter 8 on the X Image Extension.

The information contained in this manual is based in part on various specifications developed by the X Consortium and its member organizations. We owe a great debt to the X Consortium for its policy allowing others to build on their work.

I'd also like to thank the X Consortium for their careful review. Any remaining errors should be blamed on the authors and editor.

— *Adrian Nye, Editor*

# Chapters and Appendix

This part consists of tutorial chapters that explain how to use the various major features of Release 6. The appendix is a reprint of the X Consortium's Release Notes for Release 6.

# CHAPTER 1

# Introduction to X11R6

*Paula Ferguson*

This chapter contains a brief introduction to each of the major new components of X11R6. It also provides a roadmap to the rest of this book. You can use it to decide which of the following chapters you need to read, as well as the order in which you want to read them.

Release 6 of the X Window System contains a wealth of new features. Except in very isolated cases, the libraries, protocols, and servers in R6 are upward compatible with R5, so R5 applications should port to R6 with few, if any, difficulties. Some of the major new features in X11R6 include support for session management and multithreading in Xt, enhanced internationalization capabilities, support for image handling with the X Image Extension, and enhanced font capabilities. Although these features are all important additions to X, they are also optional, which means that you don't have to use them if they are not relevant to your applications.

All developers should know about the session management capabilities in Xt, so that they can make their applications session-aware. However, most of the major components of X11R6 satisfy specialized needs. For example, the X Image Extension is of primary interest to developers of image processing systems. If you plan to market your application in many different countries, especially in Asia, you will be interested in the enhanced internationalization functionality.

The new capabilities in R6 are independent of one another, so you may read about them in any order. We have tried to organize the chapters by importance and frequency of use, but of course this order cannot work for everyone. Since the new features are optional, you may even skip some chapters. Keep in mind, however, that these features have been included in X based on industry demand, so there is a strong feeling that the technology is important. Even if you don't have an immediate need to

**Paula Ferguson** is author of the *Motif Programming Manual* and *Motif Reference Manual* and editor of *The X Resource*, all published by O'Reilly & Associates, Inc.

use the new functionality, you may want to be familiar with the concepts behind it. The sections that follow provide an overview of the new features in X11R6 and the structure of this book.

## 1.1    Session Management in Xt

R6 introduces support for session management. A session is the group of applications the user is running. Session management enables the user to log out and log back in to find the same set of applications running, all in the same states.

The session manager is a separate program analogous to the window manager. It communicates with the applications to keep track of how to restart them in their current states, and it provides a user interface for logging out that allows the user to interact with each program to save work. R6 comes with a session manager, but it's designed to prove that the underlying support works, not to manage the real sessions.

The session manager communicates with the applications using a new X Consortium standard, the Session Management (SM) protocol. This protocol is based on another new standard, the InterClient Exchange (ICE) protocol. ICE (and therefore SM) does not use the X protocol at all. The session manager and applications communicate with each other directly using ICE, not through the X server. This means that non-X programs can be part of a session and can be managed by the session manager.

Xt provides the new SessionShell widget class to support communication between an application and a session manager. The SessionShell supports communication with the session manager through the use of various callback lists and other new routines. Chapter 2, *Xt Session Management,* describes the session management features in Xt and shows how to create session-aware Xt applications.

## 1.2    Writing Multithreaded Xt Applications

Threads are lightweight processes supported by some operating systems. The entire Xt library is thread-safe in X11R6. Only one thread at a time is allowed to enter the library and global data is protected as necessary from concurrent use. Multithreading makes it possible to develop Xt applications that demonstrate improved interactivity, or even real-time program concurrency. The development of multithreaded applications also requires the use of widgets that are thread-safe. Chapter 4, *Multithreading,* presents programming techniques for writing multithreaded Xt applications and offers guidelines for writing widgets that can be used safely in multithreaded applications.

# 1.3    Additional Features in Xt

The Intrinsics library has several new pieces of functionality in R6 besides support for session management and multithreading. A number of these features deal with event management. Xt now provides a way to register selectors and event handlers for events generated by X protocol extensions and to dispatch those events to the appropriate widgets. Prior to this release, extension events had to be handled at the Xlib level or in a custom main event loop, which made working with them quite cumbersome. A mechanism has also been added for dispatching events for non-widget drawables, such as pixmaps used within a widget, to a particular widget. POSIX signals and other asynchronous notifications can now be handled safely through the use of signal callbacks. This mechanism makes it possible to mix signals with Xt applications without having to worry about breaching the X protocol. In R6, an application can also ask to be notified when the Intrinsics event manager is about to block in an operating system call pending some input (which provides another way to use idle time).

The *Inter-Client Communication Conventions Manual* (ICCCM) has been updated to Version 2.0 in X11R6. Several new resources have been added to WMShell widgets to make Xt compliant with the new ICCCM. There is also a new API to support the parameterized selection targets described by the new ICCCM. When a client requests a selection, it can specify target parameters that are then retrieved by the selection owner and used in converting the selection. The MULTIPLE target has always used parameterized targets, but now it uses the new, generalized API. Xt provides additional support for the economical use of property atom names, so that they can be used as parameters.

Other changes in Xt include two new widget methods in the Object class: instance allocation and instance deallocation. These methods allow widgets to be treated as C++ objects in a C++ environment. Another new interface allows bundled changes to the set of managed children of a Composite widget, which can be used to reduce the inefficiency and visual disruption of multiple changes to a geometry layout. The resource file search path syntax has been extended to make it easy to prepend and append to the default search path that controls resource database construction. External agents that wish to track application activity can register callbacks on a per-display basis for notification about a large variety of operations in the X Toolkit. These hooks make it possible for an external agent to communicate with and instrument an application for the purpose of accessibility, testing, or customization. Chapter 8, *An Introduction to the X Image Extension*, describes all of the miscellaneous changes in Xt in R6. It also presents some examples of the use of various features.

# 1.4    Internationalization

Internationalization, which was introduced in X11R5, has been improved significantly in R6. The R6 internationalization architecture is still based on the locale model used in ANSI-C and POSIX, with most of the internationalization capability provided by Xlib. R5 introduced a fundamental framework for internationalized text input and output; it supported basic localization for languages with left-to-right, non-context-sensitive, and 8-bit or multi-byte encodings. R6 still does not support all possible languages and cultural conventions, but it does contain substantial new Xlib interfaces to support future internationalization enhancements such as additional language support and more practical localization.

The new functionality is mainly in the area of text output. In order to support multi-byte encodings, the concept of a `FontSet` was introduced in R5. Xlib expands this concept in R6 to include the more generalized notion of output methods and output contexts. Just as input methods and input contexts support complex text input, output methods and output contexts support complex and more intelligent textual displays that deal with multiple fonts as well as with context dependencies. The result is a general framework that enables bidirectional, context-sensitive text output.

Another substantial change in internationalization functionality in R6 involves input methods. Some languages require a complex pre-editing input method; such an input method is typically implemented separately from applications in a process called an Input Method (IM) server. The IM server handles the user's input operations and the display of pre-edit text. The new IM protocol in R6 standardizes the communication between the IM library and the IM server, so that the user can choose his favorite IM server that supports the IM Protocol to use with all applications. The IM protocol is a completely new protocol, based on experience with the sample implementations of input methods in R5. Some of the new features of the IM protocol include a mechanism for temporal escape from and return to pre-editing, enhanced IM server error and restart handling, and the ability for a client to initiate string conversion.

Chapter 5, *New Font Technology*, covers all of the new internationalization features in X11R6.

## 1.5    New Font Capabilities

The X Logical Font Description (XLFD) specification has been enhanced in R6 to include general 2-dimensional linear transformations, character set subsets, and scalable aliases. Font names can specify a 2D linear transformation matrix in the pixel or point size fields by using square brackets. The matrix enhancement permits many special effects, such as sheared or rotated text, that were not possible previously using core X functionality. However, these effects require clients that know how to position the transformed characters. Since such effects may require opening many fonts only to use a few characters in each, they can be expensive. Efficiency may be improved if a client can tell the font source which characters it needs, so the XLFD now allows a subsetting hint at the end of the font name. Character values and ranges in square brackets tell the font source which characters the client actually needs. The notion of a font alias has been extended to support scalable aliases. If an alias specifies scalable fonts as both the source and destination names, the alias applies to all sizes of the font. Previously, all fields in the names of the alias and the replacement font had to be specified exactly.

The sample implementation of font support in R6 has also been modified to support deferred glyph loading and an authorization protocol. In R5, when the X server opened a font from a font server, it immediately requested all of the bitmaps for that font. In R6 there is an option that allows the X server to request glyphs only as it needs them and then cache the glyphs for future use. This technique can be particularly effective with large Asian fonts, in which only a fraction of the glyphs typically are used. A sample font authorization protocol based on host names is also provided. The protocol makes it possible to build font licensing systems, but none are included in R6.

Chapter 6, *Internationalization,* discusses all of the font enhancements in X11R6.

## 1.6    The X Image Extension

The X Image Extension (XIE) facilitates efficient and robust image display on X Window System servers. XIE provides tools for rapidly transferring images between client and server and for converting image formats to match server hardware characteristics. Since XIE handles compressed images and permits images to be stored in the server for redisplay, it can significantly reduce network traffic. Without XIE, full images must be transferred using the core X protocol, which made X too slow for most image-intensive applications. Although XIE is not intended to be a general purpose image processing engine, it does provide a rich set of image rendition and enhancement operations. Moving these computationally-intensive image rendition primitives to the server relieves the burden on the host system. In addition, XIE expands the virtual hardware model of X so hardware manufacturers can incorporate accelerators for these tasks.

While XIE offers considerable power and flexibility, not all applications require XIE's full functionality. The Document Imaging Subset (DIS) of XIE caters to the needs of the document imaging market; DIS supports the decoding of compressed bitonal images, but it removes all of the processing elements except those required to scale an image and convert pixel values to a format compatible with X drawables. DIS is a proper subset of full XIE, so DIS applications run, without change, on any server that provides full XIE functionality.

X11R6 includes a sample implementation of a hardware-independent XIE server, the XIElib client library, and a test/demo program called *xieperf.* XIElib is an X Consortium standard C subroutine library that provides a low-level C binding for all of the features defined by Version 5 of the XIE protocol. Chapter 7, *Other Changes in X11R6,* provides a more complete overview of the features and functionality of XIE. XIE is too complex for a complete tutorial to fit in this book.

## 1.7    Other Changes in X11R6

X11R6 has a number of additional modification. For example, several of Xlib's limitations have been removed in ways transparent to programmers: a form of asynchronous replies improves performance of XInternAtoms; and clients can reuse resource IDs and make protocol requests that are longer that what is supported by the standard X protocol. Version 2.0 of the ICCCM contains a large number of minor but significant changes in the areas of window management, selections, session management, and resource sharing, and has been rewritten for clarity. The new Inter-Client Exchange (ICE) protocol provides a framework on which to build protocols, while the X Session Management Protocol (XSMP) enables network-based session managers to communicate with client applications. ICElib and SMlib are implementations of these protocols that may be useful in some applications.

The set of operating systems on which the client-side sample implementation code runs now includes Microsoft Windows NT. All of the base libraries are supported, including multithreading in Xlib and Xt, but some of the more complicated clients, such as *xterm* and *xdm*, are not supported. There are some additional rough edges in the implementation, including lack of support for non-socket file descriptors as alternate Xt inputs and not using the registry for configurable parameters like system filenames and search paths.

R6 also provides some functionality that is considered work-in-progress by the X Consortium. Fresco, Low Bandwidth X (LBX), the Record extension, and the X Keyboard extension (XKB) are neither standards nor draft standards as shipped in R6. The versions in R6 all need implementation work and will not be compatible with any final standard should such a standard evolve. The functionality is being made available in an early form in order to gather feedback about potential standards. (The Record Extension is nearing standardization as this book goes to press.)

All of these changes, as well as other miscellaneous changes are described in Chapter 8, *An Introduction to the X Image Extension.*

In addition, there has been progress on standardizing several extensions before and since R6. O'Reilly & Associates is working on a book of documentation of these extensions, including Shape, Synchronization, Shared Memory, XTest, Record, Double buffering, and Input. To find out about its release, see our Web server at *http://www.ora.com* or subscribe to the ora-news mailing list by sending mail to *listserv@ora.com.*

## 1.8    Reference Pages

The second section in this book is the reference section. It contains manual pages for all of the new X11R6 Xt and Xlib functions. With these and the man pages in the Release 5 editions of Volumes Two and Five of the O'Reilly X series, you have a complete set of R6 man pages for these libraries.

# Xt Session Management

*John Vergo*

A major new feature of X11R6 is session management. Session management allows users to pick up their applications at the same place they were when they last stopped their session (usually, by logging out).

This chapter describes how to write a session manager compliant Xt application, utilizing the new facilities provided in the Release 6 version of Xt, specifically the `Session-Shell` widget.

## 2.1 Session Management Architectural Overview

In order to clearly present the rationale for many of the session-management-related features of Xt, we need to discuss aspects of session management as they exist outside of Xt. These areas include the X Session Management Protocol, the X Session Management Library (SMlib), and the InterClient Exchange (ICE) library, all of which are defined as X Consortium Standards in Release 6. In general, I will minimize references to these topics, except where it is necessary to clarify how or why Xt implements certain session-manager-related features.

SMlib and ICElib are both completely independent of Xlib. Neither library makes any Xlib calls, or includes any Xlib header files. However, SMlib does depend on and use many features of ICElib. Figure 2-1 shows the relationship between the various libraries. Communication between the session manager and the session manager client is via the ICE protocol. This means that clients do not need to be X clients in order to participate in session management and that clients which connect to multiple X displays can be unambiguously managed by one session manager. For the reader who needs to write a non-X session managed client, refer to literature that covers SMlib, the X Session Management library.

---

**John Vergo** is an X programming consultant.

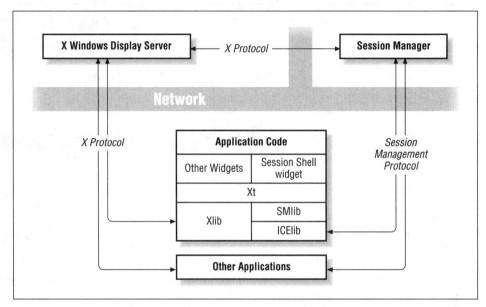

**Figure 2-1:** Architecture of a session-aware Xt application

## 2.1.1 What Is a Session?

A session, as defined in the X Session Management Protocol, is "a group of clients, each of which has a particular state." When a client starts up, it registers itself with a network service known as a session manager. Once a client has done this, it becomes part of a session and is known as a *session client.* The session manager and client communicate directly with each other (via the ICE protocol, not using the X protocol).

In principle, sessions exist so that they can be re-created at a later time. For example, assume that you initiate a session manager function to log out of the system. If all of the applications that are running at log out time are robust session manager clients, they will be terminated gracefully, with each one saving its state. The state is saved in a way that allows for restarting each program and restoring the program's state at a later time. The task of restarting each client is performed by the session manager when the session is restarted. Each client is responsible for restoring its own state based on information it is given when it is restarted.

We can break up the topic of session management into a series of progressively more sophisticated features and interactions between the session manager and the session client. At the simplest level, we may want our client to be restarted from scratch if our session is terminated and then restarted. In this simple scenario, we choose to ignore the state of the client when the session is shut down, and hence we do not attempt to restore that state when the session (and subsequently, the client) is restarted.

The next level of complexity involves saving and restoring the state of the client, in addition to restarting it. For example, if the client is an editor with certain files in its buffers, we would like the program to be restarted in the same state as when the session was terminated, including the identical files in the buffers.

From here, the topic of session management branches out to include a number of ancillary topics. These topics include:

- How and when the session client may interact with the user when the client is told to save its state

- How sessions and session clients are shutdown

- Cancelling the shutdown of a session

- How to delay session participation until after the SessionShell widget has been created

- Transferring session management control to the session shell widget

- Cleaning up after a session client has exited (i.e., deleting working files)

All of these topics will be discussed in detail later in the chapter.

## 2.1.2    The Release 6 Session Manager and Session Client

Some aspects of session management are fully implemented in Release 6, and others are considered to be "work in progress." The work that was fully completed in Release 6 includes the session management protocol, the ICE library, the session management library and the SessionShell widget. The sample session manager, *xsm*, is a work in progress. It was designed only to test the underlying layers of software, not to be usable as a real session manager.

Since Release 6, work has continued on *xsm* so that it is now considered fully usable. You can apply all public patches (at least through patch 8) to the Release 6 source code to get the latest session manager, or you can get a fairly recent version from the source archive for this book. We describe the archive version in this section.

The session testing client, *xsmclient*, was designed only for testing the original Release 6 version of *xsm*. *xsmclient* includes a minimal implementation of the code that should be in all session clients. For example it does not save and restore any state information. A more complete example of a session client is presented at the end of this chapter.

### 2.1.2.1    The xsm session manager

A sesson manager's basic purpose is to save and restore the programs that make up a session, and to shut down a session. *xsm* provides a simple interface to these functions. We'll first discuss how to set up and start *xsm*, and then describe its features. Figure 2-2 shows the main window of *xsm*. We'll structure its description by describing what each of the four buttons do.

**Setting Up xsm.** *xsm* is designed to be started automatically when the user logs in. It should be the only program listed in the user's *.xsession* file (the file that lists programs started by *xdm*, the X display manager). Users probably have a list of applications in *.xsession* now. The old contents of *.xsession* should be moved to *.xsmstartup*, which will be used only the first time that user logs in with *xsm* in action. Remove all the ampersands (&) from the lines and add a line to *.xsmstartup* that says:

```
smproxy
```

Note that *smproxy* has no x at the beginning. It is an intermediary between the session manager and some applications that haven't been ported to be session-manager aware. These might be Release 5 X programs or non-X programs. The proxy can only mediate for clients that confrom to earlier ICCCM (Interclient Communication Conventions Manual) standards for environment variables such as WM_COMMAND and WM_CLIENT_MACHINE. Also, proxied clients cannot save or restore state. The proxy just allows them to be restarted as part of the session.

Now that you've got *.xsession* and *.xsmstartup* ready, you can save any work in current applications, then log out and log back in. All the applications listed in *.xsmstartup* should then be running. If any are not running, it means *xsm* could not start them.

Once *xsm* is running, you'll see the window shown in Figure 2-2. This is the interface you'll use to control most aspects of the session, although you can also start and kill applications from *xterm* windows as you did before using *xsm*.

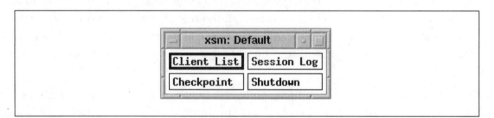

**Figure 2-2:** The main window of xsm

**The client list.** The first thing to check is that *xsm* is managing all the clients. The client list button brings up the dialog box shown in Figure 2-3.

The top half of the client list dialog lists the clients that *xsm* knows about either directly or by communicating with *smproxy*. These are the applications you can kill or clone (duplicate) using the buttons at the top of the dialog. You can also view the *xsm* properties (not X properties) associated with each client, which is useful for testing session management code in your application, and can also tell you which clients are session management compliant and which are not but are using the *smproxy*.

The Restart Hint button brings up a menu that controls how the selected client will be started the next time the session starts. There are four settings:

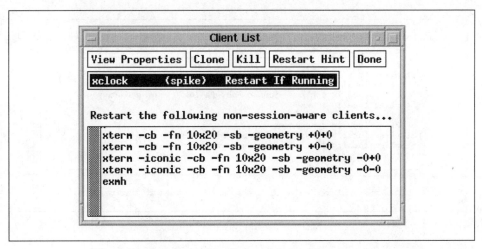

**Figure 2-3:** The Client List dialog of xsm

Restart If Running
> Restart the client only if it was running at session shutdown. This is the default setting and the right one for most clients.

Restart Anyway
> Restart client even if the client was not running when the session was shut down.

Immediately
> Try to restart the client even if it dies during this session, and also at session startup. This is a good setting for *smproxy*.

Never
> Never restart the client.

The bottom half of the client list window provides a way to hand-configure *xsm* to start clients that can't communicate with *xsm* directly and can't use *smproxy*. This includes non-X applications that haven't been made session aware. The done button simply dismisses the dialog box.

**The session log.** The session log button simply displays a list of the clients *xsm* thinks it started at the beginning of the session. (We say "thinks" because the log doesn't indicate whether or not startup of each application succeeded.) The log also does not record clients cloned or killed during the session. Figure 2-4 shows the session log window.

**Checkpointing.** The Checkpoint button displays a dialog that allows you to tell the applications to save themselves, and at the same time tell *xsm* to save the session with a certain name. When you log out and log back in, you'll be allowed to choose from these named sessions. Figure 2-5 shows the checkpoint dialog.

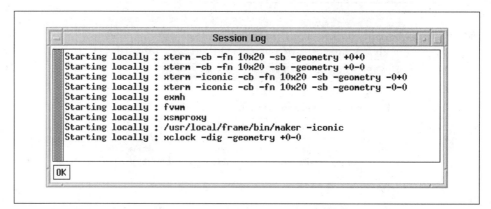

**Figure 2-4:** The Session Log of xsm

---

Session name

Save Type    Local   Global   **Both**
Interact Style   None   Errors   **Any**

Checkpoint   Help   Cancel

**Figure 2-5:** The Checkpoint dialog of xsm

The first time you issue a checkpoint, you're required to fill in the session name. Use any name you want. The help button at the bottom brings up a description of the choices for the save type and interact style. We won't repeat them here since they're covered elsewhere in this chapter.

When you issue a checkpoint using *xsm*, what actually happens is that *xsm* sends a SaveYourself message to each session client. Each client receiving a SaveYourself message may elect to interact with the user (assuming the interact style is not None). A real-life application may want to interact with the user if the application is "dirty." For example, if the application is an editor, it may pop up a dialog saying "Edit buffer has been modified. Do you want to save it?" During the interaction, the client usually gives the user the option of cancelling the shutdown.

Multiple clients may want to interact with the user. These user interactions proceed one at a time, coordinated by the session manager. For example, assume two session clients are registered with *xsm*. The user, using *xsm*, sends a SaveYourself message, starting a shutdown, to both of the session clients. Each client requests permission from the session manager to interact with the user. The session manager grants permission to the first session client. The first client pops up a dialog that allows the user to proceed with the shutdown process or to cancel the shutdown. If the user proceeds with the shutdown, the first client sends a message to the session manager indicating that the interaction is complete, and the session manager grants permission to the second client to begin an interaction. If the user cancels the shutdown during the interaction with the first client, the session manager sends a message to all of the clients, indicating that the shutdown has been cancelled (the ShutdownCancelled message). This indicates to the second client that there is no need to perform user interaction.

**Shutdown.** The Shutdown button is a menu that gives you the choice of a session shutdown with a checkpoint, or an immediate shutdown without checkpoint. If you select with checkpoint, you get the dialog shown in Figure 2-5. The only difference is that the checkpoiont button in that dialog now says shutdown. If you've set up *xsm* correctly, shutting down the session should log you out.

### 2.1.2.2    The Sample Session Client

The original Release 6 sample session manager has a button to start *xsmclient* (a client used only for testing *xsm*) from the main window. The new version of *xsm* is a real session manager so it has no need to start this particular client in a special way.

With either the old or new versions of *xsm* you can start any session manager compliant Xt application from the command line, and automatically connect to the session manager if the SESSION_MANAGER environment variable is set properly, as in the section called "The SESSION_MANAGER environment variable". Figure 2-6 shows *xsmclient*.

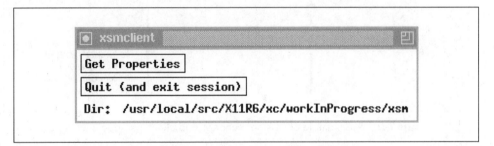

**Figure 2-6:**   The xsmclient on the screen

### 2.1.3    Session Messages and Properties

To understand Xt's session manager interface, you need to understand the types of messages that are passed between the session manager and the session client. These messages implement a controlled handshaking that governs how the state of the client is to be saved and re-started at a later time. In addition to exchanging messages, the client will set, get, or delete properties in the session manager. Properties are just named data areas, just like X properties, but stored in the session manager, not with the X server. There is a set of predefined properties in the session manager that a typical client uses. For example, the session client tells the session manager how to restart the client by setting the `RestartCommand` property. This property contains the command needed to restart the client.

Figure 2-7 illustrates a simple (but common) exchange of messages and information between a session manager and a session client. A description of all session management message types and properties is given in the section called "Session manager/client messages and properties". Figure 2-7 is presented in order to give you the flavor of what goes on between a session manager and a session client. It is not intended to be a complete overview of the protocol, and you should not get hung up on the low level details of this exchange.

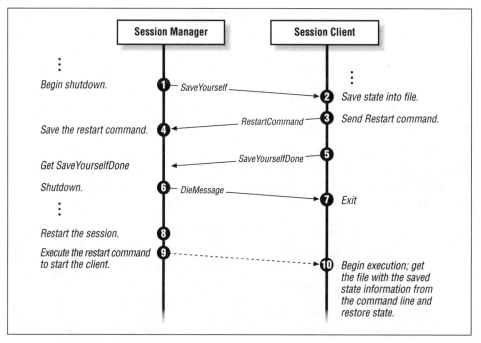

**Figure 2-7:**  An example of session manager and client message exchange

Here's what is happening in Figure 2-7:

1. The session manager, probably at the request of the user, starts to initiate a shutdown of the session. It sends a `SaveYourself` message to the client.

2. The client, in response to the `SaveYourself` message, writes a file that contains its current state information.

3. The client sets the `RestartCommand` property in the session manager. This property contains the command that the session manager will use to restart the client in its current state. The command will probably contain a reference to the state file that was created in step 2. (Or state information could be entirely in the command-line arguments.)

4. The session manager saves the restart command for this client.

5. The client, after sending the `RestartCommand` property, sends a `SaveYourself-Done` message, indicating to the session manager that the client is through with its checkpoint processing.

6. The session manager tells the client to terminate itself by sending a Die message.

7. The session client now exits.

8. At a later time, the session manager restarts the session.

9. The session manager executes the `RestartCommand` (saved in step 4), restarting the client.

10. The client is restarted. Once started, it restores its own state with the information saved in step 2.

### 2.1.4    The SessionShell Widget

The X11R6 intrinsics provide a new widget class called `SessionShell` that encapsulates many of the responsibilities of a session client. This new widget class is a subclass of the `ApplicationShell`. It makes the `ApplicationShell` widget class obsolete (i.e., you should no longer directly instantiate an `ApplicationShell`). `SessionShell` is intended to be the main window of an application, and it has the responsibility of interacting with the session manager. The application writer is responsible for ensuring that there is only one `SessionShell` per application instance. Applications with multiple primary windows should use `TopLevelShells` for additional primary windows beyond the first. You can refer to the `SessionShell` reference page of this book for information on the `SessionShell` class record, the class record pointer, and the `SessionShellPart`.

Understanding the usage of `SessionShell` resources is the key to writing Xt-compliant session-managed applications. The `SessionShell` reference page gives a complete listing and brief explanation of all the new resources that are associated with the `SessionShell` widget. The following section describes how to use all of these resources.

## 2.2    Session Support in Xt Applications

Adding session capability to an Xt application is primarily a matter of adding state-saving and restoring ability (if it's not already supported) and creating a few callback functions. This section outlines the steps.

## 2.2.1    Joining a session for the first time

The Xt `SessionShell` widget makes it quite simple to have a client participate in a session. In order to become a session client, these guidelines should be followed:

- A `SessionShell` widget should be created as the top level widget of your application by calling `XtAppInitialize()`.

- Let the `SessionShell` resources default.

The Xt initialization for a simple session client looks like this:

```
main(argc, argv)
int  argc;
char **argv;
{
XtAppContext appContext;
Widget     rootwid;

    /*
     * rootwid is the primary window of the application
     */
    rootwid = XtOpenApplication(&appContext, "mySessionClient",
                          NULL, 0,
                          &argc, argv, NULL,
                          sessionShellWidgetClass, NULL, 0);
    .
    .
    .
    XtAppMainLoop(appContext);
}
```

The `argv` argument is imported because it is passed to the session manager as the default restart command.

## 2.2.2    The SESSION_MANAGER environment variable

By way of analogy, the SESSION_MANAGER environment variable is to SMlib as the DISPLAY environment variable is to Xlib. The SESSION_MANAGER environment variable is set by the session manager, when it is run. The intent is that the session manager is run when the user logs in. It then forks all the applications the user will run, passing the SESSION_MANAGER environment variable to each application. Applications such as window managers and terminal emulators, which will launch applications themselves, have the variable set and are ready to start other session clients.

In POSIX environments, the `SessionShell` widget looks at the SESSION_MANAGER environment variable and uses it to determine how to connect to a session manager. The SESSION_MANAGER environment variable contains a comma-separated list of network id's for session managers. The format for network id's are as follows:

```
tcp/<hostname>:<portnumber>

decnet/<hostname>::<objname>

local/<hostname>:<path>
```

SMlib attempts to use the first network id in the list and continues down the list if an attempt fails.

### 2.2.3   SessionShell creation - An inside look

When a `SessionShell` widget is first created, it sends a `RegisterClient` message to the session manager. This action is what actually initiates session participation by a client.

The session manager responds to the client's `RegisterClient` message with a `RegisterClientReply` message. This message contains a unique client ID, which `SessionShell` stores in its `XtNsessionID` resource. This ID remains with this client until the client resigns from the session. Client ID's can be passed between different machines, users, and session managers; the session manager constructs the client ID's in a way that ensures they are globally unique—by combining the following pieces of information:

- The session management protocol version number
- The IP address of the machine the session manager is running on
- A time stamp
- The process id of the session manager
- A sequence number (generated by the session manager for each new client)

After a connection between the session client and session manager is established, the `SessionShell` goes through these steps:

1. If the `XtNrestartCommand` resource is `NULL`, it is set using the value of `argv`. This resource is a string containing the command the session manager should use to restart the client in the next session.

2. If there is no appearance of "-*xtsessionID* <*session id*>" in the `XtNrestartCommand`, it is added.

3. If the `XtNcloneCommand` is `NULL`, it is set with the value of the `XtNrestartCommand`, minus the "-*xtsessionID* <*session id*>" option.

4. If the `XtNprogramPath` is `NULL`, it is initialized with the first element of the *restart* command.

5. The widget calls `XtAppAddInput()` with the file descriptor for the session connection, thereby setting up the handling of session manager messages.

6. The `SessionShell` widget sets the `XtNconnection` resource with the connection handle.

## 2.2.4 Saving application state

When the session manager wants the client to save its state, it sends the client a `Save-Yourself` message. The `SessionShell` widget handles the incoming messages and informs the application that it has received these messages by calling the callbacks on the `XtNsaveCallback` list. The process of saving state is known as a *checkpoint*.

As we've said, the most common scenario in which the session manager has its clients save their state is when the session manager is shutting down the session. Shutdowns are broken down into two phases. The first phase consists of each client being sent a `SaveYourself` message. After all of the clients have received and processed the phase one `SaveYourself` message in their `XtNsaveCallbacks`, clients that have expressed interest in phase 2 save callbacks (usually just the window manager) have their `XtNsaveCallbacks` called a second time. A client expresses interest in receiving `SaveYourselfPhase2` messages by sending a `SaveYourselfPhase2Request` message after receiving a `SaveYourself` message.

The following sections describe the structure used to pass data in and out of `Save-Yourself` callbacks and how to handle it.

### 2.2.4.1 The XtCheckpointToken

The `call_data` parameter that Xt passes to some of the `SessionShell` callbacks (including the save callbacks) is of type `XtCheckpointToken`. It is defined as follows:

```
typedef struct
{
        int         save_type;
        int         interact_style;
        Boolean     shutdown;
        Boolean     fast;
        Boolean     cancel_shutdown;
        int         phase;
        int         interact_dialog_type;     /* Return */
        Boolean     request_cancel;           /* Return */
        Boolean     request_next_phase;       /* Return */
        Boolean     save_success;             /* Return */
}XtCheckpointTokenRec, *XtCheckpointToken;
```

The following table gives the legal values for each of these members:

| Member | Possible Values |
|---|---|
| save_type | SmSaveLocal<br>SmSaveGlobal<br>SmSaveBoth |
| interact_style | SmInteractStyleNone<br>SmInteractStyleErrors<br>SmInteractStyleAny |
| shutdown | True<br>False |
| fast | True<br>False |
| cancel_shutdown | True<br>False |
| phase | 1<br>2 |
| interact_dialog_type | SmDialogNormal<br>SmDialogError |
| request_cancel | True<br>False |
| request_next_phase | True<br>False |
| save_success | True<br>False |

The first six members of the checkpoint token, data passed to the client by the session manager, are described further in the section called "XtCheckpointToken read-only members". The remaining four members provide a way for the application to return data back to Xt and the session manager and are covered in the section called "XtCheckpointToken return values".

## 2.2.4.2   *XtCheckpointToken read-only members*

The information in the save_type, interact_style and shutdown, fast and phase members of XtCheckpointToken is set by the SessionShell widget and can be read but not modified in your XtNsaveCallbacks. These members are explained in detail in the following list:

save_type
  The save_type can have one of the following three values:

`SmSaveLocal`

Saves enough information to restore the state as seen by the user.

`SmSaveGlobal`

Saves data to permanent, globally accessible storage.

`SmSaveBoth`

Does both operations.

An editor, for example, that received a `SaveYourself` message with a `save_type` of `SmSaveGlobal` would simply write out the current contents of the file. If the save type was `SmSaveLocal`, it would create a temporary file and save the contents of the editor, plus any other aspects of the current editing session (editor parameters like layout information, fonts, current cursor position, etc.).

A client-server database application is another good example for understanding how local versus global saves should operate. If the application receives a `SaveYourself` message from the session manager with a `save_type` of `SmSaveGlobal`, then you must update the database. If the `save_type` is `SmSaveLocal`, the state of the application must be saved locally, without updating the database. Obviously, `SmSaveBoth` means that both operations should take place.

After the state is saved in a file, the client should update the `RestartCommand` property in the session manager by setting the `XtNrestartCommand` resource to a string that contains enough information so that the temporary file that was created can be used in restoring the state of the application. Finally, the client should set the `XtNdiscard-Command` resource such that the temporary file can be cleaned up by the session manager.

`interact_style`

`interact_style` member tells the application if interaction with the user is allowed, and what kind. If the `interact_style` has been set to `SmInteract-StyleNone`, the client should refrain from any user interaction during the checkpoint. If the `interact_style` has been set to `SmInteractStyleErrors`, then user interaction is only allowed if an error condition arises. If the `interact_style` is `SmInteractStyleAny`, the application may initiate any user interaction it deems appropriate. The

`shutdown`

The `shutdown` member indicates whether a system shutdown is in progress.

The client should handle save callbacks differently if a shutdown is in progress, by saving its state (based on the `save_type`, above) and then disallowing user interaction until it receives either a Die message (`XtNdieCallback`) or a `ShutdownCancelled` message (`XtNsaveCallback` with the `cancel_shutdown` member of the `XtCheckpointToken` structure set to `True`).

If the `shutdown` member is `False`, it must comply with the `interact_style` regarding user interactions.

fast
> A `True` setting for the `fast` member of the `XtCheckpointToken` tells the application to do its checkpoint as quickly as possible. The session manager sometimes toggles the setting to `True` when responding to a power loss condition. A client that was monitoring the power supply would send a `SaveRequest` message to the session manager, which would send a `SaveYourself` request to all session clients.

phase
> The `phase` member indicates whether the client is in phase 1 or phase 2 of a shutdown. See the section below on `request_next_phase` for more information.

cancel_shutdown
> When the `SessionShell` knows that a pending shutdown has been cancelled, any tokens passed to callbacks have this field set to `True`. See the section called "Cancelling a Shutdown" for a full discussion of the topic.

### 2.2.4.3    XtCheckpointToken return values

The `XtCheckpointToken` has four members that serve as return fields. In other words, you can set them in your `XtNsaveCallbacks`, and they are passed back to the session manager by the `SessionShell` widget when the `XtNsaveCallbacks` return. These members are the `save_success`, `request_next_phase`, `request_cancel`, and `interact_dialog_type` fields.

save_success
> The `save_success` return field, initially `True`, indicates whether the `XtNsave-Callback` was able to complete its mission successfully. The course of action taken by the session manager if a save was not successful is not defined. The session manager implementor could choose to ignore the failure, inform the user, etc. The save callback should set the value of this field to `False` if the checkpoint operation fails for some reason, such as a full file system.

> If there are no callbacks registered on the save callback list, the `SessionShell` sends a message back to the session manager that the save operation was unsuccessful.

request_next_phase
> A client expresses its interest in phase 2 callbacks by setting the `request_next_phase` member of the `XtCheckpointToken` to `True` when the `XtNsaveCallback` is called the first time. A common example of a session client that would need to employ this technique is a window manager. When a window manager saves its state, it needs to be sure that the other clients have reached a

quiescent state (i.e., they have already gone through their phase 1 save, and they are not allowing user interactions). This action would ensure that window placement, size, and stacking order are all stable before the window manager takes a snapshot of the state.

request_cancel

The request_cancel member of the XtCheckpointToken is examined by the SessionShell only when an XtNinteractCallback has been called. It is not used for XtNsaveCallbacks.

interact_dialog_type

The interact_dialog_type member is initialized to SmDialogNormal. The legal values for this member are SmDialogNormal and SmDialogError. Set the value based on the type of user interaction the application wants to engage in.

### 2.2.4.4    Handling the XtCheckpointToken

The application gets a XtCheckpointToken as an argument of each XtNsaveCallback. These are implicitly returned to Xt when the callback procedure returns to Xt. This means that the XtNsaveCallback should not explicitly return the XtCheckpointToken (i.e., it shouldn't call XtSessionReturnToken).

As mentioned above, the XtCheckpointToken contains four members that serve as return values: interact_dialog_type, request_cancel, request_next_phase, and save_success. The values are initialized by the SessionShell. If the callback procedure changes one of the values, the changed value is retained through all subsequent callbacks on the callback list. The SessionShell examines the values only after executing all of the callback procedures on the callback list.

If the application receives a SaveYourself message and needs to defer indicating whether it has successfully completed a save, it should request an additional XtCheckpointToken from Xt. This is done by calling XtSessionGetToken(), using the following format:

```
XtCheckpointToken XtSessionGetToken(widget)
Widget widget;
```

The widget argument must be the SessionShell widget.

The application must keep this token until the save operation is completed, at which time it must return the token. Tokens that were explicitly gotten with XtSessionGet-Token() should be returned with XtSessionReturnToken(). The prototype for XtSessionReturnToken() is:

```
void XtSessionReturnToken(token)
XtCheckpointToken token;
```

The application may get as many tokens as it needs. The SessionShell does not indicate completion of the checkpoint processing to the session manager until all of the tokens have been returned to Xt. XtSessionReturnToken() is also used to return tokens passed to XtNinteractCallbacks (see the section called "Interacting with the user—the Protocol").

## 2.2.5    Interacting with the user—the Protocol

When a session is shutting down, and multiple applications wish to interact with the user, this series of interactions needs to be coordinated so the user is not inundated with simultaneous dialog boxes. When an application is in the process of saving itself, and it wishes to interact with the user, it should issue an InteractRequest message to the session manager. It must not engage in any user interaction until the session manager responds with an Interact message.

The session manager issues Interact messages one at a time when multiple clients request interactions. The session manager waits for an InteractDone message from the client that is currently interacting with the user before issuing the next Interact message to the next client (if a request has been made).

The client sends the InteractDone message in response to an Interact message after all its interactions with the user are completed. The exception to this rule is when a ShutdownCancelled message has been received. The application must not interact with the user if a shutdown is cancelled (see the section called "How to interact with the user—Xt implementation").

## 2.2.6    How to interact with the user—Xt implementation

The user interaction protocol described above is encapsulated nicely by the SessionShell widget. When Xt calls the XtNsaveCallbacks with the interact_style set to allow user interaction, the client requests interaction by adding a callback procedure to the XtNinteractCallback list. At the completion of processing the XtNsaveCallbacks, if the XtNinteractCallback list is not empty, the SessionShell issues an InteractRequest message to the session manager on behalf of the application. When the session manager issues an Interact message to this application, Xt calls the XtNinteractCallbacks. Each callback creates and pops up a dialog box.

The types of interactions that your client can request are SmDialogError or SmDialogNormal, and are specified in the XtNsaveCallbacks using the interact_dialog_type member of the XtCheckpointToken.

Please note that the handling of XtCheckpointTokens in XtNinteractCallbacks is different than in XtNsaveCallbacks. The XtCheckpointToken is not implicitly returned when the XtNinteractCallback returns to Xt; it is the application's responsibility to return the checkpoint token first. This sequence is due to the event-driven nature of X applications. When the application wants to interact with the user, it usually pops up a dialog in the `XtNinteractCallback` and returns to `XtAppMainLoop()`. Since we typically want to defer sending the `InteractDone` message to the session manager until the interaction has been completed, the `XtCheckpointToken` is not implicitly returned when the `XtNinteractCallback` completes. The application should save the token and return it when user interaction completes, using `XtSessionReturnToken()`. Usually the token is returned in a callback for the OK or similar button in the dialog box.

In addition to deferring the transmission of the `InteractDone` message, the `SessionShell` uses the `XtCheckpointToken` to control the execution of additional callbacks on the `XtNinteractCallback` list. The `SessionShell` calls the first procedure on the `XtNinteractCallback` list and removes it from the list. The `SessionShell` then waits until the `XtCheckpointToken` is returned before proceeding to process the next callback on the list. In this manner, the `XtNinteractCallbacks` are executed one at a time, with each callback being deferred until the one preceding it has returned its token. This serial order would, for example, allow an editor to use a separate dialog and `XtNinteractCallback` for each buffer that could be saved into a separate file. Note that the application is not responsible for removing the `XtNinteractCallbacks` from the callback list; the `SessionShell` removes them after each one is executed.

An application may request that the session manager cancel a pending shutdown by setting the `request_cancel` member of the `XtCheckpointToken` to `True` in the `XtNinteractCallback`. The session manager only looks at this member of `XtCheckpointToken` if the shutdown member is `True` and the `cancel_shutdown` member is `False`. Any subsequent `XtNinteractCallbacks` on the list will still be called, but the `request_cancel` member of the `XtCheckpointToken` token passed to them will be `True`. At the completion of all `XtNinteractCallbacks`, the `InteractDone` message will be sent to the session manager, passing along the request to cancel the shutdown.

### 2.2.6.1    Checkpoint completion

As stated above, a checkpoint operation is completed when all of the `XtCheckpointTokens` have been returned to Xt. When a checkpoint does not involve user interaction, the checkpoint process is complete when all of the `XtNsaveCallbacks` have been executed and all of the `XtCheckpointTokens`, acquired with a `XtSessionGetToken()`, have been returned. To reiterate an important point, if the application does not get any additional `XtCheckpointTokens` and does not request any user interaction, then the checkpoint is complete after all the `XtNsaveCallbacks` have been called. It is not necessary to return the `XtCheckpointTokens` passed to the `XtNsaveCallbacks` because they are returned implicitly.

If the application requests user interactions, a checkpoint is complete when the above conditions are met, all of the `XtNinteractCallbacks` have been called, and all of the `XtCheckpointTokens` passed to the `XtNinteractCallbacks` have been returned with `XtSessionReturnToken()`.

For clients such as window managers that process phase 2 save operations, the above conditions must be met for both phases.

At the completion of a checkpoint operation, the `SessionShell` widget sends a `Save-YourselfDone` message to the session manager. After all clients have responded to the session manager with a `SaveYourselfDone` message, the session manager sends `Save-Complete` messages to the clients. The `SessionShell` widget then calls any callbacks registered on the `XtNsaveCompleteCallback` list. The `XtNSaveCompleteCallback` should allow the user to begin changing the application state (i.e., normal, non-session related application processing should resume).

### 2.2.6.2  When a session is shutting down

As was shown in Figure 2-6, the final step in a shutdown is the Die message.

When all applications have checkpointed themselves during a shutdown (both phase 1 and phase 2), the session manager sends a Die message to each session client. If the client has a `SessionShell` managing the connection, the `SessionShell` calls all the on the `XtNdieCallback` list. The `call_data` is `NULL` in an `XtNdieCallback`. The die callback resigns from the session and exits the application (see the section called "Resigning from a session").

The `SessionShell` cleans up session-related issues prior to calling the `XtNdieCall-backs`. The cleanup procedure includes breaking the connection to the session manager by sending a `ConnectionClosed` message, and removing the file descriptor that was added to `XtAppAddInput()` to get session manager protocol messages. If the client set the `XtNshutdownCommand` resource, the session manager executes the command it specifies. A client would typically set this resource if it always runs when the session is restarted, and it has persistent side-effects after it has exited. For example, a multimedia application that uses a video camera and microphone to get real-time video and audio may turn this equipment on when the session is started (the application probably has its `RestartStyle` set to `RestartAnyway`). The persistent side-effects would be to leave the equipment on after the client application has exited and resigned from the session. The `ShutdownCommand` could be used to turn off the equipment. Note that the `ResignCommand` is not appropriate in this case, because the session client could resign from the session well before it desired that the equipment be turned off.

### 2.2.6.3  Cancelling a session shutdown

A session manager doesn't know what kinds of applications are running and when it might be inconvenient to terminate them. Therefore, the protocol allows individual applications to cancel a shutdown. If an application contains work that the user has not saved yet, the application may want to give the user the option to either save the work or cancel the entire shutdown. On the other hand, if you are writing an application that can be safely killed at any time, then you might want to forego giving the user the option to cancel a shutdown.

As stated in the section called "XtCheckpointToken return values", an application can cancel a shutdown by setting the `request_cancel` member of the `XtCheckpointToken` to `True`. The session manager will respond to the shutdown cancellation by sending a `ShutdownCancelled` message to all clients. The `SessionShell` widget detects the message and calls the `XtNcancelCallbacks`, if any were registered.

The `ShutdownCancelled` message could be received while the application is:

- Executing save callbacks

- Interacting with the user

- Waiting for permission to interact with the user

- Waiting for a Die or `SaveComplete` message, after saving its state

If there are save or interact callbacks to be executed when a `ShutdownCancelled` message is received, the callbacks are still executed. Save callbacks should do their normal processing. The `SessionShell` sets the `interact_style` member of the `XtCheckpointToken` to `SmInteractStyleNone` before calling any of the interact callbacks. The interact callbacks should check this member and refrain from any user interactions if it is set to `SmInteractStyleNone`.

## 2.2.7    Resigning from a session

An application which terminates before the session is ended should resign from the session. Whether the program ends because the user chooses to quit, or the program simply completes its work, the goal is a graceful resignation in which the application lets the session manager know that the program should not be restarted when the session is ultimately resumed. The client can send a `ConnectionClosed` message to the session manager prior to exiting. The `SessionShell` neatly handles session manager notification in most cases by sending a `ConnectionClosed` message while executing its destroy method. Remember, a widget's destroy method is not called immediately when `XtDestroyWidget()` is called. `XtDestroyWidget()` only marks the widget as "being destroyed." The actual destruction (and execution of the destroy method) happens when execution reverts back to Xt (in phase 2 destroy). If the application destroys the `SessionShell` and waits for the phase 2 destroy to complete, it need not take any explicit action to resign from a session. If the application doesn't wait (i.e., the application calls `exit()` in a callback) the application should set the `XtNjoinSession` resource to `False`, resulting in a `ConnectionClosed` message being sent to the session manager.

If an application wishes to stop having its session managed, but wants to maintain a connection to the session manager, it can set its `XtNconnection` resource to `NULL`.

If the client sets the `XtNresignCommand` resource before it resigns from a session, the session manager executes the command stored in the resign property. This can be a useful tool to undo certain effects that are "persistent," that is, effects that continue after the client has exited. An example of this might be a client that runs *xmodmap*, modifying the keyboard mapping. The resign command could set the keyboard mapping back to its original mapping when the client exits.

## 2.3   Miscellaneous techniques

This section is presented for completeness. The techniques described give the application developer flexibility in managing the session connection, but will not be needed in most applications.

### 2.3.1   Transferring session management to a SessionShell

A client may already have an existing connection to the session manager when the session shell is created. The client could create this setup by opening a session connection using the `SmcOpenConnection()` function provided by SMlib prior to creating the `SessionShell` widget. `SmcOpenConnection()` returns a `SmcConn` session connection handle. In this case, it may be desirable to hand over the management responsibilities to the `SessionShell` widget by setting the `XtNconnection` resource with the existing session handle when creating the `SessionShell` widget.

### 2.3.2   Delayed session participation

The application design may call for the ability to place the decision whether to participate in session management in the hands of the application user. If we want the user to make this decision at run time (e.g., via a menu choice or command), we would want to defer session participation until the user asks for it.

To accomplish this, the `SessionShell` widget should be created with `XtNjoinSession` set to `False`, so that the widget does not initiate a session manager connection when it is created. The session connection can be made at a later time by setting (via `XtVaSet-Values()` or its equivalent) `XtNjoinSession` to `True` or `XtNconnection` to an existing `SmcConn` connection handle. If `XtNjoinSession` is changed from `False` to `True` and `XtNconnection` is `NULL`, the `SessionShell` widget will get the SESSION_MANAGER environment variable and make the connection to the session manager. If `XtNconnection` is a connection handle, the widget will assume management responsibility for the connection.

### 2.3.3    Relieving the SessionShell of session management responsibilities

If the application wants to take over session management responsibilities from the
`SessionShell` widget, it should get the connection handle by calling `XtGetValues()`
on the `XtNconnection` resource. It should then set the `XtNconnection` resource to
`NULL`. The application could then manage the connection using straight SMlib techniques. The `SessionShell` widget could be destroyed, if it were no longer needed by
the application.

# 2.4    Example application

Our example client uses the `SessionShell` widget to do session management. The
program only allows the user to change the background color of the application. The
color is the state of the program. When this client is told to save itself, it creates a state
file that contains the current background color. The `RestartCommand` property in the
session manager is then altered so that the client is passed the state file on the command line when it is restarted by the session manager. This client also engages in simple user interaction during a checkpoint by putting up a dialog. The dialog title
indicates if a shutdown is in progress, and whether the interact style is `SmInteract-`
`StyleAny` or `SmInteractStyleNone`. The program is presented in sections. The complete code is available in the book's code archive, as described in the preface.

The command to compile and link the program is:

```
% cc -o xtsmclient xtsmclient.c -lXaw -lXmu -lXt -lX11 -lXext -lSM -lICE
```

The example uses the Athena widget set, libXaw, which requires libXmu and libXext.
The `SessionShell` widget uses libSM, which in turn requires libICE. The Xt and X
libraries, libXt and libX11, are required for all X toolkit applications. We recommend
that you get the code as described in the preface and play with the application.

### 2.4.1    The module header section

The first part of the program includes header files for the widgets and functions we
need and declares the application data structure and command-line arguments.

```
#include <X11/Intrinsic.h>
#include <X11/Xlib.h>
#include <X11/Shell.h>
#include <X11/StringDefs.h>
#include <X11/Xaw/Form.h>
#include <X11/Xaw/Command.h>
#include <X11/Xaw/Dialog.h>
#include <X11/Xaw/Toggle.h>
#include <stdio.h>

#include <unistd.h>

#ifndef PATH_MAX
#ifdef MAXPATHLEN
```

```
#define PATH_MAX MAXPATHLEN
#else
#define PATH_MAX 1024
#endif
#endif

/*
 * This application data is declared in main(), and passed
 * around to routines that need access to it.
 */
typedef struct
{
    Widget              sessionShell;
    Widget              mainWindow;
    Widget              dialog;
    XtCheckpointToken   cp_token;
    Pixel               current_color;
    Pixel               red;
    Pixel               green;
    Pixel               blue;
}ApplicationDataRec, *ApplicationData;


static XrmOptionDescRec options[] =
{
    {
    "-sessionFile",
    "*sessionFile",
    XrmoptionSepArg,
    (XPointer) NULL
    },
};

/* application resources */
static struct resources
{
    char*session_file;
}appResources;

static XtResource Resources[] =
{
    {
        "sessionFile",
        "SessionFile",
        XtRString,
        sizeof(String),
        XtOffsetOf(struct resources, session_file),
        XtRImmediate,
        NULL
    },
};
/*
 * The restart command is global to the module.
 */
String restart_command[6];
```

## 2.4.2    The SaveState() routine

The `SaveState()` routine is called from `SaveCB()` and `OKCB()`. `SaveCB()` is called when the session manager wants the application to save its state. `OKCB()` is called when the user presses the OK button on the interact dialog. The `SaveState()` routine saves the state of the application, and then sets the appropriate session shell widget resources so that the session manager knows how to restart the application in the current state. Note particularly how the state file name is generated.

```
static Boolean SaveState(ad)
ApplicationData ad;
{
        String      str;
        Arg         args[10];
        Cardinal    n;
        String      session_id;
        char        session_file[256];
        FILE        *sf;
        String      color;
        String      discard_command[4];
        String      resign_command[3];
        String      shutdown_command[3];

    /*
     * Get the session ID, and use it to construct the filename of the
     * state file (the file that will hold the state information for this
     * client). Using the sessionID will make sure the filename is unique
     * for multiple instantiations of this application.
     */
    XtVaGetValues(ad->sessionShell, XtNsessionID, &session_id, NULL);
    sprintf(session_file, "%s/.session.%s", getenv("HOME"), session_id);

    /*
     * Complete the construction of the restart command. Note that
     * restart_command[0] and restart_command[2] were filled out in
     * main() (below).
     */
    restart_command[1] = "-xtsessionID",
    restart_command[3] = "-sessionFile",
    restart_command[4] = session_file;
    restart_command[5] = NULL;

    /*
     * Construct the discard command (remove state file)
     */
    discard_command[0] = "rm";
    discard_command[1] = "-f";
    discard_command[2] = session_file;
    discard_command[3] = NULL;

    /*
     * Construct the resign command
     */
    resign_command[0] = "echo";
    resign_command[1] = "resigning";
    resign_command[2] = NULL;
```

```
/*
 * Construct the shutdown command
 */
shutdown_command[0] = "echo";
shutdown_command[1] = "shutdown";
shutdown_command[2] = NULL;

/*
 * Write the state of the application (in this case, the color) to
 * the state file.
 */
if(ad->current_color == ad->red)
    color = "red";
else if(ad->current_color == ad->green)
    color = "green";
else if(ad->current_color == ad->blue)
    color = "blue";
else
    color = "white";

sf = fopen(session_file, "w");
fwrite(color, sizeof(char), strlen(color), sf);
fclose(sf);

/*
 * Get the current working directory
 */
str = getcwd((char *)NULL, PATH_MAX+2);

/*
 * Set the various properties in the session manager
 */
XtVaSetValues(ad->sessionShell,
              XtNcurrentDirectory,      str,
              XtNrestartCommand,        restart_command,
              XtNdiscardCommand,        discard_command,
              XtNresignCommand,         resign_command,
              XtNshutdownCommand,       shutdown_command,
              NULL);

/*
 * Return a status indicating success or failure in saving state.
 */
return True;
}
```

## 2.4.3   The Interact Callback

InteractCB() is called when the session manager gives us permission to interact with
the user during a checkpoint operation. Getting here indicates that we were told to
save ourselves, and we requested permission to interact with the user before saving the
program state. It is possible that this process was started as a result of a session manager shutdown. The shutdown may have since been cancelled by another session
client. In this case, we will return a checkpoint token that indicates the save operation

failed. An alternative would be to complete the checkpoint and set the save_success field of the XtCheckpointToken to True. This decision can be made on an application by application basis.

```
static void InteractCB(sessionShell, client_data, call_data)
Widget sessionShell;
XtPointer client_data, call_data;
{
    ApplicationData ad = (ApplicationData) client_data;
    XtCheckpointToken token = (XtCheckpointToken) call_data;
    Position x, y;
    String label;
    Widget cancel;
    /*
     * If a shutdown has been cancelled, or we are not allowed to
     * interact with the user, indicate we have not saved our state,
     * and return the token. Returning the token tells the session
     * manager that we are done.
     */
    if (token->cancel_shutdown || token->interact_style == None)
    {
        token->save_success = False;
        XtSessionReturnToken(token);
        return;
    }

    /*
     * We have received permission to interact.
     *
     * Save the XtCheckpoint token. We will return it later, when we have
     * completed the user interaction.
     */
    ad->cp_token = token;

    /*
     * If we are not in the process of shutting down, make the cancel
     * button insensitive.
     */
    cancel = XtNameToWidget(ad->dialog, "dialogCancelButton");
    XtSetSensitive(cancel, token->shutdown);

    /*
     * Set the dialog label to indicate the interact style, and whether a
     * shutdown is in progress. This is for demonstration purposes only.
     */
    if (token->interact_style == SmInteractStyleAny)
    {
        if (token->shutdown)
            label = "Shutdown in progress: Normal dialog";
        else
            label = "Normal dialog";
    }
    else
    {
        if (token->shutdown)
            label = "Shutdown in progress: Error dialog";
        else
            label = "Error dialog";
```

```
        }
        XtVaSetValues(ad->dialog, XtNlabel, label, NULL);

        /*
         * Make the dialog pop up over this client (so it is less likely to be
         * confused with other instantiations of this client, or other
         * session clients).
         */
        XtVaGetValues(ad->sessionShell, XtNx, &x, XtNy, &y, NULL);
        XtVaSetValues(XtParent(ad->dialog), XtNx, x, XtNy, y, NULL);
        XtPopup(XtParent(ad->dialog), XtGrabNone);
}
```

## 2.4.4    The Save Callback

SaveCB() is called when the session manager wants the application to save state. If
user interactions are not allowed, or if a shutdown has been initiated, user interactions
with the application are halted by making the session shell widget (the top level widget
of the application) insensitive. This makes all children of the session shell insensitive
also.

If the interact_style member of the XtCheckpointToken indicates that we are not
allowed to interact with the user, then SaveState() is called. If user interaction is
allowed, we ask the session manager to be put on the list of clients wanting to interact
by adding a callback to the XtNinteractCallback list. When the session manager
decides to allow this application to interact with the user, the InteractCB() routine
will be called.

```
static void SaveCB(sessionShell, client_data, call_data)
Widget sessionShell;
XtPointer client_data, call_data;
{
    ApplicationData ad = (ApplicationData) client_data;
    XtCheckpointToken token = (XtCheckpointToken) call_data;

    /*
     * If the session manager is shutting down the session, or if the
     * interact_style is SmInteractStyleNone, disallow user interaction.
     */
    if (token->shutdown || token->interact_style != SmInteractStyleNone)
        XtSetSensitive(ad->sessionShell, False);

    /*
     * If we are not allowed to interact with the user, simply save the
     * state.
     */
    if (token->interact_style == SmInteractStyleNone)
    {
        token->save_success = SaveState(ad);
    }
    else
    {
        /*
         * If we get here, we are allowed to interact with the user. Set
         * the interact_dialog_type to be SmDialogNormal or SmDialogError,
```

```
          * depending on the type of interaction allowed.
          */
         if (token->interact_style == SmInteractStyleAny)
             token->interact_dialog_type = SmDialogNormal;
         else
             token->interact_dialog_type = SmDialogError;

         /*
          * When an XtNinteractCallback is added, the sessionShell widget
          * will send an InteractRequest message to the session manager,
          * requesting permission for us to interact with the client. The
          * session manager will ensure that user interactions take place in
          * an orderly fashion.
          *
          * This callback is removed automatically after InteractCB has been
          * called.
          */
         XtAddCallback(sessionShell, XtNinteractCallback, InteractCB,
                       client_data);
    }
}
```

## 2.4.5    The Die Callback

The session manager terminates the application as the last step of the shutdown process by sending a Die message. The `DieCB()` routine is called in response to receiving the Die message.

```
    static void DieCB(sessionShell, client_data, call_data)
    Widget sessionShell;
    XtPointer client_data, call_data;
    {
        ApplicationData ad = (ApplicationData) client_data;


        XtDestroyWidget(sessionShell);
        exit(0);
    }
```

Destroying the session shell widget before exiting assures a graceful resignation from the session, because the session shell destroy method performs the resignation.

## 2.4.6    The SaveComplete and ShutdownCancelled Callbacks

In this example application, the `SaveCompleteCB()` routine is set up to respond to both `SaveComplete` and `ShutdownCancelled` messages from the session manager. In either case, the required action is to re-enable user interactions with the application (the application was de-sensitized in the `SaveCB()` routine).

```
    static void SaveCompleteCB(sessionShell, client_data, call_data)
    Widget sessionShell;
    XtPointer client_data, call_data;
    {
        ApplicationData ad = (ApplicationData) client_data;
```

```
    /*
     * Resume normal operation.
     */
    XtSetSensitive(ad->sessionShell, True);
}
```

## 2.4.7    Setting the background color

The SetColor() routine is called whenever the user presses the "Red," "Green," or "Blue" buttons on the main window. The widget name is used to determine what button was pressed, and the background color is set according to the user's selection.

```
static void SetColor(w, client_data, call_data)
Widget      w;
XtPointer      client_data, call_data;
{
    ApplicationData ad = (ApplicationData) client_data;
    Pixel pix;

    /*
     * Get the widget name, and set the parent's background color
     * accordingly.
     */
    if(strcmp(XtName(w), "redButton") == 0)
        ad->current_color = pix = ad->red;
    else if(strcmp(XtName(w), "greenButton") == 0)
        ad->current_color = pix = ad->green;
    else if(strcmp(XtName(w), "blueButton") == 0)
        ad->current_color = pix = ad->blue;

    XtVaSetValues(XtParent(w), XtNbackground, pix, NULL);
}
```

## 2.4.8    Resigning from the session

The QuitCB() routine is called in response to the user pressing the "Quit" button on the main window. The user is terminating the application, and hence the application ceases to be part of the session. If the application quits without resigning from the session, the application will be restarted the next time the session is restarted.

```
static void QuitCB(w, client_data, call_data)
Widget      w;
XtPointer      client_data, call_data;
{
    ApplicationData ad = (ApplicationData) client_data;

    /*
     * A well-behaved session client closes the session connection before
     * exiting.
     */
    XtVaSetValues (ad->sessionShell, XtNjoinSession, False, NULL);/*
     * Do the exact same thing we'd do if we just received a Die message
     * by calling DieCB().
     */
    XtCallCallbacks(ad->sessionShell, XtNdieCallback, NULL);
}
```

## 2.4.9    Completing a user interaction

This callback routine is called when the OK button on the interact dialog is pressed. Since the interact dialog is popped up during a checkpoint, the pressing of the OK button indicates that the user has completed the interaction. The XtCheckpointToken is returned to the session manager to indicate that the checkpoint is complete.

```
static void OKCB(button, client_data, call_data)
Widget        button;
XtPointer        client_data, call_data;
{
    ApplicationData ad = (ApplicationData) client_data;
    XtCheckpointToken token = ad->cp_token;

    /*
     * Assume the user interaction indicates we should save state
     */
    token->save_success = SaveState(ad);

    XtPopdown(XtParent(ad->dialog));

    /*
     * Returning the XtCheckpointToken tells the session manager we are
     * done with the checkpoint.
     */
    XtSessionReturnToken(token);
    ad->cp_token = NULL;
}
```

## 2.4.10    Cancelling a Shutdown

This callback is invoked when the user presses the "Cancel Shutdown" button on the interact dialog. This routine tells the session manager to cancel the shutdown by setting the request_cancel member of the token to True and returning the token.

```
static void CancelCB(button, client_data, call_data)
Widget          button;
XtPointer    client_data, call_data;
{
    ApplicationData ad = (ApplicationData) client_data;
    XtCheckpointToken token = (XtCheckpointToken) ad->cp_token;

    /*
     * If we get here, the user pressed the 'Cancel Shutdown' button. We
     * pass that request on to the session manager by setting the
     * request_cancel member of the XtCheckpointToken to True
     */
    token->request_cancel = True;

    /*
     * Indicate that we have not saved state
     */
    token->save_success = False;

    /*
     * Return the token to Xt when done interacting
```

```
        */
        XtSessionReturnToken(token);
        ad->cp_token = NULL;

        XtPopdown(XtParent(ad->dialog));
}
```

## 2.4.11   Creating the interact dialog

This is routine Xt programming.

```
static void CreateInteractDialog(ad)
ApplicationData ad;
{
    Widget okay, cancel;
    Widget dialogPopup;

    dialogPopup = XtVaCreatePopupShell (
                "dialogPopup", transientShellWidgetClass, ad->sessionShell,
                XtNtitle,               "Dialog",
                XtNallowShellResize,    True,
                XtNancestorSensitive,   True,
                NULL);

    ad->dialog = XtVaCreateManagedWidget (
                "dialog", dialogWidgetClass, dialogPopup,
                XtNresizable,           True,
                NULL);

    okay = XtVaCreateManagedWidget (
                "dialogOkButton", commandWidgetClass, ad->dialog,
                XtNlabel,               "OK",
                NULL);

    XtAddCallback(okay, XtNcallback, OKCB, ad);

    cancel = XtVaCreateManagedWidget (
                "dialogCancelButton", commandWidgetClass, ad->dialog,
                XtNlabel,               "Cancel Shutdown",
                NULL);

    XtAddCallback(cancel, XtNcallback, CancelCB, ad);
}
```

## 2.4.12   Creating the main windows

```
static void CreateMainWindow(ad)
ApplicationData ad;
{
    Widget quitButton, redButton, greenButton, blueButton;

    ad->mainWindow = XtCreateManagedWidget (
                "mainWindow", formWidgetClass, ad->sessionShell, NULL, 0);

    redButton = XtVaCreateManagedWidget (
                "redButton", commandWidgetClass, ad->mainWindow,
                XtNlabel,        "Red",
                NULL);
```

```
        XtAddCallback(redButton, XtNcallback, SetColor, ad);

        greenButton = XtVaCreateManagedWidget (
                    "greenButton", commandWidgetClass, ad->mainWindow,
                    XtNlabel,       "Green",
                    XtNfromVert,    redButton,
                    NULL);

        XtAddCallback(greenButton, XtNcallback, SetColor, ad);

        blueButton = XtVaCreateManagedWidget (
                    "blueButton", commandWidgetClass, ad->mainWindow,
                    XtNlabel,       "Blue",
                    XtNfromVert,    greenButton,
                    NULL);

        XtAddCallback(blueButton, XtNcallback, SetColor, ad);

        quitButton = XtVaCreateManagedWidget (
                    "quitButton", commandWidgetClass, ad->mainWindow,
                    XtNlabel,       "Quit",
                    XtNfromVert,    blueButton,
                    NULL);

        XtAddCallback(quitButton, XtNcallback, QuitCB, ad);

    }
```

## 2.4.13    The example program main()

```
main(argc, argv)
    int  argc;
    char **argv;
{
    XtAppContext appContext;
    ApplicationDataRec adr;
    FILE *sf;
    char readbuf[256];
    XColor screen, exact;
    String smcid;

    adr.sessionShell = XtOpenApplication(&appContext, "Xtsmclient",
                    options, XtNumber(options),
                    &argc, argv, NULL,
                    sessionShellWidgetClass, NULL, 0);
    /*
     * Set up the callbacks for the session manager messages.
     */
    XtAddCallback(adr.sessionShell, XtNsaveCallback,
                    SaveCB, &adr);
    XtAddCallback(adr.sessionShell, XtNcancelCallback,
                    SaveCompleteCB, &adr);
    XtAddCallback(adr.sessionShell, XtNsaveCompleteCallback,
                    SaveCompleteCB,&adr);
    XtAddCallback(adr.sessionShell, XtNdieCallback,
                    DieCB, &adr);

    XtGetApplicationResources(adr.sessionShell, (XtPointer)&appResources,
```

```
                    Resources, XtNumber(Resources), NULL, 0);

    CreateMainWindow(&adr);
    CreateInteractDialog(&adr);

    XtVaGetValues(adr.sessionShell, XtNsessionID, &smcid, NULL);

    /*
     * Save the program name and the session ID for the restart command
     */
    restart_command[0] = argv[0];
    restart_command[2] = XtNewString(smcid);

    /*
     * Get the colors we will need (red, green, and blue)
     */
    XAllocNamedColor(XtDisplay(adr.sessionShell),
            DefaultColormap(XtDisplay(adr.sessionShell), 0),
            "red", &screen, &exact);
    adr.red = screen.pixel;

    XAllocNamedColor(XtDisplay(adr.sessionShell),
            DefaultColormap(XtDisplay(adr.sessionShell), 0),
            "green", &screen, &exact);
    adr.green = screen.pixel;

    XAllocNamedColor(XtDisplay(adr.sessionShell),
            DefaultColormap(XtDisplay(adr.sessionShell), 0),
            "blue", &screen, &exact);
    adr.blue = screen.pixel;

    /*
     * If we were passed a session file, open it and restore the state of
     * the program.
     */
    if (appResources.session_file)
    {
        sf = fopen(appResources.session_file, "r");
        fread(readbuf, sizeof(char), 256, sf);
        if(strcmp(readbuf, "red") == 0)
            adr.current_color = adr.red;
        else if(strcmp(readbuf, "green") == 0)
            adr.current_color = adr.green;
        else if(strcmp(readbuf, "blue") == 0)
            adr.current_color = adr.blue;

        XtVaSetValues(adr.mainWindow,
                    XtNbackground, adr.current_color,
                    NULL);
    }

    XtRealizeWidget(adr.sessionShell);
    XtAppMainLoop(appContext);
}
```

## 2.5  Session manager/client messages and properties

This section provides a reference for the various types of messages and properties that are exchanged between a session client and a session manager.

### 2.5.1  Messages

ConnectionClosed

Sent from the session client to the session manager, resigning the client from the session.

Die

Sent by the session manager to the client, usually when the session is being shutdown. The client should answer this message by sending a `ConnectionClosed` message and then exiting.

GetProperties

Sent by the client to query the session manager about the current values of all properties it has for the client.

GetPropertiesReply

Sent by the session manager when it gets a `GetProperties` message. It sends all the properties that have been set for the requesting client.

Interact

Sent by the session manager to the client, indicating to the client it may proceed with user interactions.

InteractDone

Sent by the client to the session manager when the client has finished interacting with the user.

InteractRequest

Sent by the client to the session manager during a checkpoint operation, requesting permission to engage in interaction with the user.

RegisterClient

Sent by a client to the session manager, initiating session participation. If this client is being restarted, `RegisterClient` should contain the client's old ID.

RegisterClientReply

Sent by the session manager to the client in response to a `RegisterClient` message. This message contains a client ID. A new ID is assigned by the session manager if this client is joining a session for the first time. Otherwise, it uses the ID passed in with the `RegisterClient` message.

`SaveComplete`

> Sent by the session manager when it has completed a checkpoint operation. This is a signal that the client may now change its state.

`SaveYourself`

> Sent by the session manager to the client, instructing the client to save its state in such a way as to allow it to be restarted later. When a client is joining a session for the first time, it receives a `SaveYourself` message immediately after getting the `RegisterClientReply` message.

`SaveYourselfPhase2Request`

> A message from the client to the session manager asking to be notified when all of the other clients have settled down and completed their `SaveYourself` processing. (WINDOW MANAGER would probably use this.)

`SaveYourselfPhase2`

> Passed to a client that has made a `SaveYourselfPhase2Request`, indicating that all SM clients have saved themselves.

`SaveYourselfRequest`

> Sent from a client to the session manager. The session manager replies by sending a `SaveYourself` back to the client, effectively allowing the client to checkpoint itself. Additionally, the client may indicate that the `SaveYourself` message should be sent to ALL SM clients, causing them all to save their state. A system administrator that is going to bring down a central file server on a network may want to write a simple client that performs this function prior to the shutdown.

`SaveYourselfDone`

> After a client has received a `SaveYourself` or `SaveYourselfPhase2` message and updated the appropriate properties in the session manager, it should respond with a `SaveYourselfDone` message. The client should then refrain from any actions that would result in a change of state until it receives a `SaveComplete` message from the session manager.

`SetProperties`

> Used by the client to set properties in the session manager.

`ShutdownCancelled`

> Sent by the session manager to the client, indicating that the current shutdown operation has been cancelled. The client may interpret this as approval to resume normal operations.

## 2.5.2  Properties

Command properties are set by the client and are executed by the session manager at the appropriate time.

**CloneCommand**

Same as the `RestartCommand`, except the client ID is not supplied.

**CurrentDirectory**

The directory the client is running in. It is restored by the session manager when restarting the client.

**DiscardCommand**

When executed, cleans up any files used as state information by the client. This allows the session manager to clean up when a client resigns from the session.

**Environment**

The POSIX environment of the client, restored by the session manager prior to restarting a client.

**ProcessID**

The OS-specific process ID.

**Program**

Name of the program that is running.

**RestartCommand**

Contains the command to restart the client when a session resumes. The command should have enough information encoded in it to allow the client to restart in its original state.

**ResignCommand**

Executed by the session manager when a client resigns from the session. The client must have set the `RestartStyleHint` to `RestartAnyWay`.

**RestartStyleHint**

Indicates to the session manager when the client would like to be restarted. The possible values are `RestartIfRunning`, `RestartAnyway`, `RestartImmediately`, and `RestartNever`.

**ShutdownCommand**

Executed by the session manager when the session is shutting down. Each client may specify a shutdown command.

**UserID**

The user's POSIX ID, as given in the `pw_name` field of the passwd struct.

# CHAPTER 3

# Other New Features in Xt

*Paula Ferguson*

X11R6 includes the following changes to the X Toolkit Intrinsics (the section where each feature is described is in parentheses):

- A new convenience procedure, `XtOpenApplication()`, to initialize the toolkit, create an application context, open an X display connection, and create the root of the widget instance hierarchy. (Section 3.1)

- New routines to register event handlers for events generated by X protocol extensions. (Section 3.2.1)

- Support for dispatching events for a non-widget drawable, such as a pixmap used within a widget, to a particular widget. (Section 3.2.3)

- Signal callbacks that support the safe handling of POSIX signals and other asynchronous notifications. (Section 3.2.2)

- A mechanism that allows applications to be notified when the Xt event manager is about to block pending input. This provides another way for applications to detect and use idle time. (Section 3.2.4)

- New resources for the `WMShell` widget to make it compliant with the new ICCCM.

- New routines that support parameterized selection targets. When a client requests a selection, it can specify target parameters that are then retrieved by the selection owner and used in converting the selection. (Section 3.3)

- Support for temporary property names that can be used as selection parameters, to reduce the number of unique atoms that need to be created in the server. (Section 3.3.3)

**Paula Ferguson** is author of the *Motif Programming Manual* and *Motif Reference Manual* and editor of the *X Resource*, all published by O'Reilly & Associates, Inc.

- A new routine for simultaneously managing and unmanaging a group of children of a composite widget. (Section 3.4)

- New resource converters for window gravity and resource types associated with session participation. (Section 3.5)

- Two new widget methods in the object class that support instance allocation and deallocation. These methods allow widgets to be treated as C++ objects in a C++ environment. (Section 3.6.1)

- Clarification of the textual description of the processes of widget creation and destruction to aid widget writers. (Section 3.6.5)

- A new routine to locate a widget class extension record in a linked list. (Section 3.6.4)

- A new exposure compression flag that widgets can use to indicate that they don't use exposure region information. (Section 3.6.3)

- The addition of hook callbacks that allow an external agent to track application activity. (Section 3.7)

- An extended file search path syntax that makes it easy to prepend and append path elements to the default search path. (Section 3.8)

- Support for the NumLock modifier in the default key translator. (Section 3.8)

The Release 6 Xt implementation requires the Release 6 version of Xlib. An application that links with Xt also needs to link with the Session Management library (SMlib) and the Inter-Client Exchange library (ICElib). The XTOOLLIB *make* variable and the XawClientLibs *imake* variable cause automatic linking with these libraries.

# 3.1  XtOpenApplication

XtOpenApplication() is a new convenience procedure in X11R6 that supercedes XtAppInitialize(). It initializes the toolkit, creates an application context, opens an X display connection, and creates the root of the widget instance tree. The only difference between the two routines is that XtOpenApplication() takes an additional argument that specifies the widget class of the root shell widget to be created.

Alternatively, an application can use XtVaOpenApplication() for initialization purposes. This routine is like XtOpenApplication(), except that it takes a NULL-terminated variable-length argument list of resources instead of the args and num_args parameters.

XtOpenApplication() and XtVaOpenApplication() are now the recommended interface for application initialization, so that clients can easily become session participants. The recommended value for the widget_class argument is SessionShellWidgetClass. See Chapter 2, *Xt Session Management*, for a complete discussion of session management in Xt.

## 3.2    Event Management

The new event management capabilities of the Xt library fill in gaps that existed in previous releases, making it possible to handle X protocol extension events and POSIX signals at the Xt level. The Release 6 event manager can also dispatch events for non-widget drawables to a particular widget and notify an application when Xt is about to block in an operating system call pending input.

With Release 6 you can now retrieve the event from the most recent call to `XtDis-patchEvent()` for a specific display with `XtLastEventProcessed()`. If there is no such event, the routine returns `NULL`. This routine is mostly useful for Xt selection handling routines, when it is necessary to extract the time from the event that triggered a selection request.

### 3.2.1    Handling Extension Events

Prior to Release 6, Xt applications had to handle events generated by X protocol extensions at the Xlib level or in a modified main event loop, because Xt did not provide a way to dispatch extension events. Now it is possible to register event handlers for extension event types using `XtInsertEventTypeHandler()`. Although an application can use this routine to register event handlers for both core and extension events, it is easier to handle core X protocol events using the simpler `XtAddEventHandler()`.

`XtInsertEventTypeHandler()` is passed six arguments: a widget, an integer that specifies the event type, a `select_data` parameter that Xt uses to request events of the specified type from the server, an event handler procedure, optional client data, and the position of the event handler. We'll explain how `select_data` is used shortly, when we describe what's involved in selecting extension events from the server. As with all Xt `client_data` parameters that pass data to the event handler procedure, the position parameter specifies the order in which the handler is called relative to other registered event handlers for the same event. To have the event handler called first, use `XtListHead`. If the order is not important, use `XtListTail`, which causes the handler to be registered after any other handlers.

One extension that really benefits from this new functionality is the `InputExtension`, as it is now possible to handle events from other input devices using Xt. Example 3-1 shows a code fragment that registers event handlers on a drawing area that react to motion and button events from a Spaceball.

**Example 3-1:** Registering event handlers for extension events

```
#include <X11/extensions/XInput.h>

XEventClass sb_motion_class,
            sb_button_press_class,
            sb_button_release_class;

main (argc, argv)
```

**Example 3-1:** Registering event handlers for extension events (continued)

```
int     argc;
char    **argv;
{
    Widget toplevel, drawing_area;
    XtAppContext  app_context;
    Display *display;
    XID device_id;
    XDevice *sb;
    int sb_motion_type, sb_button_press_type, sb_button_release_type;

    .
    .
    .

    sb = XOpenDevice (display, device_id);

    /* Use device macros to get the event types and classes for
     * motion, button press, and button release events.
     */
    DeviceMotionNotify (sb, sb_motion_type, sb_motion_class);
    DeviceButtonPress (sb, sb_button_press_type, sb_button_press_class);
    DeviceButtonRelease (sb, sb_button_release_type, sb_button_release_class);

    /* Register the sb_handler event handler for motion, button press,
     * and button release events.
     */
    XtInsertEventTypeHandler (drawing_area, sb_motion_type,
        sb_motion_class, sb_handler, NULL, XtListTail);
    XtInsertEventTypeHandler (drawing_area, sb_button_press_type,
        sb_button_press_class, sb_handler, NULL, XtListTail);
    XtInsertEventTypeHandler (drawing_area, sb_button_release_type,
        sb_button_release_class, sb_handler, NULL, XtListTail);

    .
    .
    .

    XtRealizeWidget (toplevel);
    XtAppMainLoop (app_context);
}

/* sb_handler() -- Event handler for spaceball events.
 */
void sb_handler (widget, client_data, event, continue_to_dispatch)
Widget widget;
XtPointer client_data;
XEvent *event;
Boolean *continue_to_dispatch;
{
    /* Do what needs to be done with events from the space ball */
}
```

The event handler, sb_handler(), is registered for motion, button press, and button release events from the Spaceball. This event handler functions just like an event handler registered for core events with XtAddEventHandler(). Each widget has a single event handler list; there is just one list for both core and extension events. To remove an event type handler, use XtRemoveEventTypeHandler().

When the specified events occur in the drawing area, we want the event handler to be invoked with the specified `client_data` as one of its arguments. However, because we are dealing with extension events, there are a few other steps we need to perform to actually make this happen.

### 3.2.1.1   Registering an Event Selector

When an event handler is registered for core X protocol events, Xt automatically requests the events from the X server using the Xlib function `XSelectInput()`. Extensions to the X protocol define their own event selection mechanisms, however, so Xt needs to be told how to request extension events from the server. A *selector* is a function that selects (requests) extension events from the server. An application uses `XtRegisterExtensionSelector()` to register a selector function.

`XtRegisterExtensionSelector()` takes five arguments: a display pointer, minimum and maximum event type values for the extension, an extension event selector procedure, and optional client data. The selector procedure is of type `XtExtensionSelectProc`. This procedure is called in two situations. After a widget is realized, Xt checks to see if it has any event handlers with an event type in the range specified for an extension selector. If so, the selector procedure is called. Whenever an event type handler is added or removed, if the event type for the handler falls in a specified range, Xt also calls the appropriate selector.

An `XtExtensionSelectProc` is passed as arguments the widget for which events are being selected, a list of event types specified in calls to `XtInsertEventTypeHandler()`, a list of the `select_data` parameters also from calls to `XtInsertEventTypeHandler()`, the number of items in the lists, and the optional client data. The `event_types` and `select_data` lists always have the same number of elements, because each event-type/select-data pair corresponds to a single call to `XtInsertEventTypeHandler()`.

The actual `select_data` values vary depending on how a particular extension selects events. Some extensions, such as the Shape Extension and the Doublebuffering Extension, use event masks, so the `select_data` values would be event masks that correspond to the different event types. In this case, the selector procedure would combine the masks to create a single event mask that would be passed to the event selector function for the extension. In the case of the Input Extension, events are selected using an array of `XEventClass` pointers. In Example 3-2 we passed an `XEventClass` pointer for each event type in our calls to `XtInsertEventTypeHandler()`. Continuing with this example, we can register an extension selector for the Spaceball events as shown in Example 3-2.

**Example 3-2:** Registering an event selector for extension events

```
#include <X11/extensions/XInput.h>

#define NUM_INPUT_EVENTS 15

XEventClass sb_motion_class,
            sb_button_press_class,
            sb_button_release_class;

void select_cb_events;

main (argc, argv)
int     argc;
char    **argv;
{
    Widget toplevel, drawing_area;
    XtAppContext app_context;
    int event_base, error_base, opcode;
    Boolean ext_exists;
    Display *display;

    ext_exists = XQueryExtension (display, "XInputExtension", &opcode,
        &event_base, &error_base);
    .
    .
    .
    /* Register the extension event selector for the Input Extension.
     */
    XtRegisterExtensionSelector (display, event_base,
        event_base + NUM_INPUT_EVENTS - 1, select_sb_events, NULL);
    .
    .
    .
    XtRealizeWidget (toplevel);
    XtAppMainLoop (app_context);
}

/* select_sb_events() -- Extension event selector for spaceball events.
 */
void select_sb_events (widget, event_types, select_data, count, client_data)
Widget widget;
int *event_types;
XtPointer *select_data;
int count;
XtPointer client_data;
{
    XEventClass *xcp = (XEventClass *) select_data;

    XSelectExtensionEvent (XtDisplay (widget), XtWindow (widget),
        xcp, count);
}
```

In the call to XtRegisterExtensionSelector(), we need to pass the minimum and maximum event types values for the Input Extension. Since the X server dynamically assigns event codes to extensions, these values cannot be determined until runtime. The minimum event type is returned by the call to XQueryExtension().

We have to be more creative to figure out the maximum event type, as extensions are not required to provide this information. The solution is to check the extension documentation or header files to figure out how many events the extension supports. In the case of the Input Extension, in the *<X11/extensions/XIproto.h>* header file, the constant IEVENTS is defined to be 15. Event codes increase monotonically within an extension, so we can use this value to calculate the maximum event type value.

In the actual extension selector, select_sb_events(), we cast the array of select_data values to an array of XEventClass values and then call XSelectExtensionEvent(). We select the events for the window of the *widget* passed to the selector.

Most protocol extensions select events by passing an event mask to a requesting function. As a result, an extension selector procedure needs to work for all event types in an extension. Any time an event type handler is added or removed, the extension selector is passed an array of all events that should be selected, not just the single event added or removed. An application that handles events from multiple extensions needs a separate event selector for each extension because extension event types are assigned dynamically by the X server.

If an application does not register an event selector for a particular extension event, Xt cannot select those extension events automatically. As an alternate technique, an application can explicitly request the event for specific windows. As long as the application has registered event handlers for the event and set up a dispatching mechanism as described in the next section, Xt can still handle the extension event for the application.

### 3.2.1.2    *Dispatching Extension Events*

The final step in setting up extension event handling is to register procedures to dispatch the specific event types. By default, Xt's event dispatcher handles all of the core X protocol events, but it discards all extension events. To make extension event handlers work, an application customizes the default event dispatcher by registering dispatch procedures for the specific event types, using XtSetEventDispatcher(). This routine provides a way for an application to modify the default event dispatching mechanism, as shown in Figure 3-1.

XtSetEventDispatcher() takes three arguments: the display, the event type, and the event dispatch procedure. Once the event dispatch procedure is registered, whenever Xt calls XtDispatchEvent() with the specified event type, it invokes the dispatch procedure to deal with the event. To remove an event dispatch procedure and restore the default behavior (throw away the events), pass NULL as the third argument in a call to XtSetEventDispatcher().

It is possible to write a single event dispatch procedure to handle any or all of the event types for an extension. In this case, an application still needs to call XtSetEventDispatcher() for each event type to be supported. If an application works with multiple

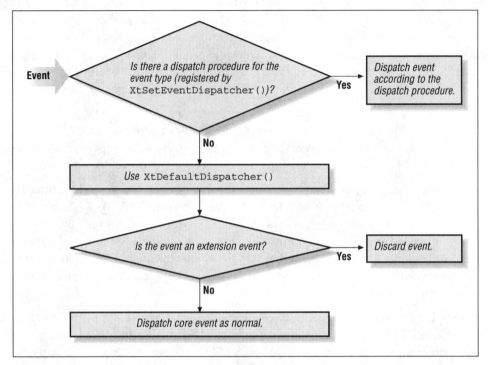

**Figure 3-1:** Event dispatching in Xt

displays, it should call the routine once for each event type for each display. Use `XtGetDisplays()` to get all of the open displays for an application context.

An event dispatch procedure is of type `XtEventDispatchProc`. The procedure is passed a single argument, a pointer to the `XEvent` that is to be dispatched. The procedure should return `True` if it successfully dispatches the event and `False` otherwise. The dispatch procedure first needs to determine if the event should be dispatched to a widget, which in most simple cases it should. To determine the appropriate widget, call `XtWindowToWidget()` using the `window` field of the event structure.

Next the procedure should call `XFilterEvent()` to allow any internationalization Input Method that might be running the opportunity to process the event. If `XFilterEvent()` returns `True`, the input method has processed the event, so the event dispatcher is done and can return `True`.

If `XFilterEvent()` returns `False`, the dispatch procedure should continue to dispatch the event by calling `XtDispatchEventToWidget()`. `XtDispatchEventToWidget()` checks the list of registered event handlers for the specified widget and calls each handler that has been registered for the current event type. If an event handler returns `False` as its `continue_to_dispatch` parameter, `XtDispatchEventToWid-`

get() stops calling event handlers. XtDispatchEventToWidget() returns True if it calls an event handler and False otherwise, so the event dispatch procedure can simply return this value.

Example 3-3 shows the final piece of our Input Extension example, where we register an event dispatch procedure for Spaceball motion, button press, and button release events.

**Example 3-3:** Registering an event dispatch procedure for extension events

```
#include <X11/extensions/XInput.h>

XEventClass sb_motion_class,
            sb_button_press_class,
            sb_button_release_class;

main (argc, argv)
int     argc;
char    **argv;
{
    Widget toplevel, drawing_area;
    XtAppContext app_context;
    Display *display;
    XID device_id;
    XDevice *sb;
    int sb_motion_type, sb_button_press_type, sb_button_release_type;

    .
    .
    .
    sb = XOpenDevice (display, device_id);

    /* Use device macros to get the event types and classes for
     * motion, button press, and button release events.
     */
    DeviceMotionNotify (sb, sb_motion_type, sb_motion_class);
    DeviceButtonPress (sb, sb_button_press_type, sb_button_press_class);
    DeviceButtonRelease (sb, sb_button_release_type, sb_button_release_class);
    .
    .
    .
    /* Set up event dispatchers for each extension event type.
     */
    XtSetEventDispatcher (display, sb_motion_type, sb_dispatch);
    XtSetEventDispatcher (display, sb_button_press_type, sb_dispatch);
    XtSetEventDispatcher (display, sb_button_release_type, sb_dispatch);

    XtRealizeWidget (toplevel);
    XtAppMainLoop (app_context);
}

/* sb_dispatch() -- Dispatch extension events to the appropriate widget.
 */
Boolean sb_dispatch (event)
XEvent *event;
{
```

```
    Widget w;
    XAnyEvent *xany = (XAnyEvent *) event;

    w = XtWindowToWidget (xany->display, xany->window);

    if (!XFilterEvent (event, (w == NULL) ? None : w))
      return (XtDispatchEventToWidget (w, event));
    else
      return True;
}
```

When XtDispatchEventToWidget() is called, Xt behaves as though event handlers for Expose, NoExpose, GraphicsExpose, and VisibilityNotify events are registered at the head of the list of event handlers. Xt uses the exposure events to invoke the widget's expose procedure according to the exposure compression rules, and uses the visibility event to update the widget's visible field if visible_interest is True.

A dispatch procedure for extension events may want to forward an event to another widget according to Xt's keyboard focus mechanism. In this case, the procedure can call XtGetKeyboardFocusWidget() to get the widget that is the end result of keyboard event forwarding.

## 3.2.2  Signal Handling

POSIX signals and other asynchronous notifications have always posed a problem at the Xt level: it has been difficult to handle signals safely in an Xt application without potentially breaching the X protocol. The addition of signal callbacks in Release 6 now makes it possible to deal with signals without running this risk.

Under the UNIX operating system, signals are delivered to an application (a process) when an abnormal condition occurs. These signals may be generated by the user at the keyboard, by another process using the kill() system call (which sends a signal to a process ID), or by the operating system itself. For example, job control typically involves one signal that indicates when the process has stopped (SIGTSTP) and another that indicates when the process has continued (SIGCONT). Another signal is generated when an application has spawned a new process with fork(), and this child process dies. The operating system notifies the parent about the child's process death, so that the parent can reap the child. In this case, the operating system delivers a SIGCHLD (SIGCLD for System V) to the parent. Still another signal is SIGFPE (floating point exception), which indicates a division by zero error.

In all these cases, the programmer has the ability to specify how these signals should be serviced by trapping them using *signal handlers*. A signal handler is a function installed for a signal type using the signal() system call, which takes the following form:

```
    signal(sig_number, function)
```

The sig_number is the signal identifier, which is a defined symbol like those described above, while *function* is a routine written by the programmer. If the signal is delivered (called *raised*), the routine is called automatically. What the signal handler function actually does is decided by the programmer. For example, if a program traps the SIGCHLD signal, when a previously forked process terminates, the signal handler should probably call the wait() system to reap the child.

The problem with mixing signals and an X application is that a UNIX signal can interrupt communication with the X server via the X protocol. When a UNIX signal is delivered, the operating system immediately branches to the signal handler without notice. If the program is in the middle of an X protocol message (an Xlib call) at the time of the signal delivery, and the signal handler also calls an Xlib routine that generates another protocol message, the X server is sent a garbled message. The result is an X protocol error.

To respond to a signal safely, an application should call XtAppAddSignal() to establish a signal callback before it sets up a signal handler with signal(). XtAppAddSignal() is passed an application context, a signal callback procedure, and optional client data. XtAppAddSignal() returns a signal ID that uniquely identifies the signal callback. This identifier must be stored so that it is accessible to the actual signal handler, so it is typically kept in a global variable.

Now the application can establish a signal handler using signal() or a related routine. This signal handler needs to call XtNoticeSignal() to notify Xt that the signal has been handled. XtNoticeSignal() is the only Xt routine that can be called safely from a signal handler. It takes a single argument, the signal ID returned by XtAppAddSignal(). If Xt is blocking for input when XtNoticeSignal() is called, it wakes up and calls the signal callback immediately. Otherwise, if Xt is dispatching an event, the signal callback is invoked as soon as control returns to the main event loop.

In an Xt application, the actual signal handler should not do any work other than call XtNoticeSignal(). The signal callback (as opposed to the handler), of type XtSignalCallbackProc, does the actual processing for the signal and can call any Xt or Xlib routine safely. This callback is passed the optional client data that is registered with XtAppAddSignal() and the signal ID returned by that routine. Figure 3-2 shows the signal handling process in Xt.

Example 3-4 shows a simple application that handles the SIGCHLD signal. The application provides a button that, when activated, forks an *xterm* process. Once the button has been pressed, it is set insensitive so that it cannot be used again while the *xterm* process is running. When the child process is terminated, the program handles the SIGCHLD signal by resetting the sensitivity of the button.

**Example 3-4:** Handling the SIGCHLD signal using a signal callback

```
/* signal.c -- make a button that, when activated, starts an xterm process.
 * When the program is running, the button is insensitive.  When the
 * program dies, reactivate the button so the user can select it again.
 */
#include <X11/Intrinsic.h>
```

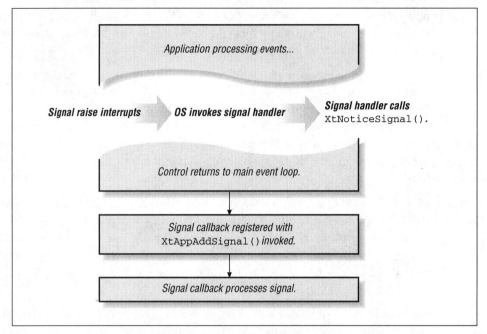

**Figure 3-2:** Signal handling in Xt

**Example 3-4:** Handling the SIGCHLD signal using a signal callback (continued)

```
#include <X11/StringDefs.h>
#include <X11/Shell.h>
#include <X11/Xaw/Command.h>
#include <signal.h>

#ifndef SYSV
#include <sys/wait.h>
#else
#define SIGCHLD SIGCLD
#endif /* SYSV */

static XtSignalId sigchld_id;

/* sigchld_handler() -- the UNIX signal handler that is registered
 * with signal(). It uses XtNoticeSignal() to tell the Intrinsics
 * to invoke the signal callback associated with the signal ID.
 */
void sigchld_handler ()
{
    XtNoticeSignal (sigchld_id);
}

/* sigchld_callback() -- the signal callback that we want to be
 * called in response to the signal. Xt invokes this callback
 * when it is safe to do so, so we can make Xt and X calls.
 * We simply reset the sensitivity of the button so the user
 * can press it again.
```

```
    */
void sigchld_callback (client_data, id)
XtPointer client_data;
XtSignalId *id;
{
    Widget button = (Widget) client_data;

    XtSetSensitive (button, True);
}

/* exec_prog() -- when the button is pressed, fork() and call
 * execlp() to start xterm. If this succeeds, set the button's
 * sensitivity to False to prevent the user from pressing it
 * again.
 */
void exec_prog (widget, client_data, call_data)
Widget widget;
XtPointer client_data;
XtPointer call_data;
{
    int pid;

    switch (pid = fork ()) {
        case 0:  /* child */
            execlp ("xterm", "xterm", (char *)0);
            perror ("xterm"); /* command not found? */
            _exit (255);
        case -1:
            printf ("fork() failed.\n");
    }

    /* The child is off executing program... parent continues */
    if (pid > 0)
        XtSetSensitive (widget, False);
}

main(argc, argv)
int argc;
char *argv[];
{
    XtAppContext app;
    Widget toplevel, button;
    Pixmap pixmap;
    int width, height, xhot, yhot;

    XtSetLanguageProc (NULL, NULL, NULL);

    toplevel = XtVaOpenApplication (&app, "Signal",
        NULL, 0, &argc, argv, NULL, sessionShellWidgetClass, NULL);

    XReadBitmapFile (XtDisplay (toplevel),
        RootWindowOfScreen (XtScreen (toplevel)),
        "/usr/include/X11/bitmaps/terminal",
        &width, &height, &pixmap, &xhot, &yhot);

    button = XtVaCreateManagedWidget ("button",
        commandWidgetClass, toplevel,
```

**Other New Features
in Xt**

```
            XtNbitmap, pixmap,
            NULL);

    /* Register the signal callback with Xt and get the signal ID
     * for use in the signal handler. Notice this is done before
     * we register the signal handler.
     */
    sigchld_id = XtAppAddSignal (app, sigchld_callback, button);

    /* Register the signal handler so that we are notified
     * when child programs die.
     */
    signal (SIGCHLD, sigchld_handler);

    XtAddCallback (button, XtNcallback, exec_prog, NULL);

    XtRealizeWidget (toplevel);
    XtAppMainLoop (app);
}
```

Logically, Xt maintains a "pending" flag for each registered signal callback. The flag is False initially; it is set to True by XtNoticeSignal(). During event processing, all registered signal callbacks with this flag set to True are invoked and the flags are reset to False.

What this process means in terms of signal handling is that if XtNoticeSignal() is called multiple times before Xt is able to invoke the signal callback, the callback is typically invoked only once. If the functionality of the signal callback depends on knowing how many times the signal has been raised, the signal handler should use a counter to keep track of signal raises and the signal callback can then access this counter to handle multiple signal raises. Due to timing issues, it is also possible for a signal callback to be invoked even though all signal raises have already been handled in previous callbacks. The signal handler and signal callback can also use a counter to handle this case if it is important.

An application can remove a signal callback by calling XtRemoveSignal() and passing the signal ID of the call back to it. The source of a signal should be removed by calling signal() with the function value SIG_DFL before the signal callback is removed, to avoid missing signal raises.

## 3.2.3 Dispatching Events to Non-widget Drawables

In some cases, an application may need to handle events for drawables that are not associated with widgets in its widget hierarchy. For example, an application may need to handle GraphicsExpose and NoExpose events generated by drawing to a pixmap. Or, if an application wanted to provide complex graphical behavior in its icon window, it would need to handle Expose events for the associated pixmap. Another example of handling events to non-widget drawables occurs with various ICCCM protocols. In this case, an application may need to handle `PropertyNotify` events on the root window or other client windows.

In Release 6, the `XtRegisterDrawable()` routine provides a way for an application to register a drawable with Xt's event manager. This routine takes three arguments: a display pointer, a drawable, and a widget. `XtRegisterDrawable()` associates the drawable with the widget. After the call, if the drawable is passed in a call to `XtWindowToWidget()`, the associated widget is returned. Furthermore, the event manager dispatches events for the drawable to the widget as though the event specifies the widget's window. However, the actual event is not changed in any way when it is passed to an event handler or action procedure.

If a drawable is already registered with a widget, the results of calling `XtRegisterDrawable()` with that drawable and another widget are undefined. The behavior of the routine is also undefined if an application calls it with a drawable that is the window of a widget in that application's widget hierarchy. In other words, don't do these things even if you know what one particular Xt implementation does in these cases.

An application can remove the association between a drawable and a widget by calling `XtUnregisterDrawable()`. This routine simply takes a display pointer and a drawable. When a drawable is unregistered, the event manager no longer dispatches events for that drawable to an associated widget. If an application calls `XtUnregisterDrawable()` with a drawable that is the window of a widget in that application's widget tree, the results are, again, undefined.

## 3.2.4    Blocking Notification

In some situations, an application may find it desirable to be notified when the Xt event manager is about to block in an operating system call, waiting for events. The Release 6 routine `XtAppAddBlockHook()` registers a procedure that is called once immediately before event blocking occurs. The block hook procedure is useful for flushing log files and other tasks you want done before the application waits for events, possibly for a long time if it is obscured or iconified. (By contrast, work procs are called while the apllication is waiting for events.)

`XtAppAddBlockHook()` are passed to an application context, a procedure, and optional client data. The routine returns a "block hook" ID that identifies the procedure and can be used to remove it. The procedure passed to `XtAppAddBlockHook()` is of type `XtBlockHookProc` and takes a single `client_data` parameter. Once a hook procedure is registered, it is called at any time when the Xt event manager detects no pending input from file sources or from X server event sources and is about to block waiting for input.

An application can remove a hook procedure by calling `XtRemoveBlockHook()` with the ID returned by `XtAppAddBlockHook()`.

# 3.3    Selections

The *Inter-Client Communications Conventions Manual* (ICCCM) has been updated to Version 2.0 in X11R6. Three new resources have been added to WMShell widgets to make Xt compliant with the new ICCCM. These new resources specify various attributes of session management, so they are described in detail in Chapter 2, *Xt Session Management.*

Xt also provides a new API to support parameterized selection targets, as described by the new ICCCM. The basic idea behind parameterized targets is that when a client requests a selection, it can specify both a target and target parameters. These parameters are then retrieved by the selection owner and used in converting the selection. The MULTIPLE target has always used parameterized targets, but it did so behind the scenes. Now the functionality has been generalized into an API so that it can be used for other targets.

For example, use of the LENGTH target is discouraged because of the ambiguity around which target it is supposed to return the length of. With parameterized selections, it is possible to define a BYTE_LENGTH_OF target. When a client requests the BYTE_LENGTH_OF target, the client passes as a parameter the target that it wants the length of. Now the selection owner can return the length in bytes of the appropriate target.

## 3.3.1    Setting and Retrieving Target Parameters

When an application requests that the value of a selection be converted to a particular target, it may also need to specify additional information to be used in the conversion. This additional information is stored in a property on the requesting client's window. The actual type and format of the property depends on the specific target type that is being requested. None of the current standard selection targets use parameters, but you could use parameters with custom target types for communication between related clients.

To specify target parameters for a selection request that has a single target, use XtSet-SelectionParameters() before requesting the selection value. This routine takes arguments that specify both the widget making the request and the atom that names the selection being requested. The rest of the arguments provide information about the parameters. Four arguments are passed to the routine: an atom that specifies the type of the property that contains the parameters, a pointer to the parameters, the number of data items in the parameters, and the size of the data items. The specified parameters are copied and stored in a new property of the specified type and format on the requestor's window.

*3. Other New Features in Xt*

To initiate a selection request using the parameters specified with XtSetSelectionPa-rameters(), a client simply makes a subsequent call to XtGetSelectionValue() or XtGetSelectionValueIncremental(). This call needs to specify the same requestor widget and the same selection atom as... In this case, the call generates a ConvertSe-lection request that refers to the property that contains the parameters. If a client calls XtSetSelectionParameters() multiple times with the same widget and selection atom without requesting the selection, the most recently specified parameters are used when the selection is requested.

This example uses the BYTE_LENGTH_OF target described earlier. The code fragment in Example 3-5 shows the use of XtSetSelectionParameters():

**Example 3-5:** Setting selection target parameters

```
Atom BYTE_LENGTH_OF, xa_STRING, xa_ATOM, xa_INTEGER, xa_PRIMARY;

main(argc, argv)
int argc;
char *argv[];
{
    .
    .
    .
    BYTE_LENGTH_OF =
        XInternAtom (XtDisplay (toplevel), "BYTE_LENGTH_OF", False);
    xa_STRING = XInternAtom (XtDisplay (toplevel), "STRING", False);
    xa_ATOM = XInternAtom (XtDisplay (toplevel), "ATOM", False);
    xa_INTEGER = XInternAtom (XtDisplay (toplevel), "INTEGER", False);
    xa_PRIMARY = XInternAtom (XtDisplay (toplevel), "PRIMARY", False);
    .
    .
    .
}

void
get_selection_CB(widget, client_data, call_data)
Widget widget;
XtPointer client_data;
XtPointer call_data;
{
    Atom *paramp, params;

    params = xa_STRING;
    paramp = &params;

    XtSetSelectionParameters (widget, xa_PRIMARY, xa_ATOM,
        (XtPointer) paramp, 1, 32);

    XtGetSelectionValue (widget, xa_PRIMARY, BYTE_LENGTH_OF, targetCB,
        NULL, XtLastTimestampProcessed (XtDisplay (widget)));
}
```

In the call to XtSetSelectionParameters(), we pass the parameter XA_STRING to indicate that we want the length of the selection when it is encoded as a character string.

`XtSetSelectionParameters()` cannot be used to specify parameters for individual targets in a `MULTIPLE` request created with `XtGetSelectionValues()` or `XtGetSelectionValuesIncremental()`. As we explain in the next section, creating `MULTIPLE` selection requests that include parameterized targets requires using `XtCreateSelectionRequest()` and `XtSendSelectionRequest()`.

After the requesting client has requested a selection that has target parameters, the client that owns the selection needs to retrieve the parameters. The selection owner calls `XtGetSelectionParameters()` to perform this task. This call can only be made from within an `XtConvertSelectionProc` or in the first call to an `XtConvertSelectionIncrProc`.

`XtGetSelectionParameters()` takes arguments that specify the widget that owns the selection, the atom that names the selection, and the requestor ID in the case of an incremental transfer. If the transfer is atomic, the requestor ID argument should be `NULL`. The four remaining arguments, which are pointers that return information about the selection parameters, include the following: the atom that specifies the property type of the parameters, a pointer to the parameters, the number of data items in the parameters, and the format of the data items.

Example 3-6 shows a fragment of an `XtConvertSelectionProc` that handles the BYTE_LENGTH_OF target.

**Example 3-6:** Getting selection target parameters

```
Boolean convertCB (w, selection, target, type, value, length, format)
Widget w;
Atom *selection;
Atom *target;
Atom *type;
XtPointer *value;
unsigned long *length;
int *format;
{
    .
    .
    .
    if (*target == BYTE_LENGTH_OF) {

        Atom *ptype;
        XtPointer *pvalue;
        unsigned long *plength;
        int *pformat;

        XtGetSelectionParameters (w, *selection, NULL, &ptype, &pvalue,
            &plength, &pformat);

        if (ptype == xa_ATOM) {
            if (*pvalue == xa_STRING) {
                tmp_length = (int *)XtMalloc(sizeof(int));
                *tmp_length = last_select_char - first_select_char;
                *value = (XtPointer)tmp_length;
                *length = 1;
```

**Example 3-6:** Getting selection target parameters  (continued)

```
                *type = xa_INTEGER;
                *format = 32;
                return True;
        }
        /* handle length of other targets */
    }
}
        .
        .
        .
```

`XtGetSelectionParameters()` is called in the `XtConvertSelectionProc` to get the value of the multiplier. The value of `select_value` is assumed to be the value of the PRIMARY selection.

## 3.3.2   Generating MULTIPLE Requests

Prior to Release 6, the only way to create a MULTIPLE target selection request was to call `XtGetSelectionValues()` or `XtGetSelectionValuesIncremental()`. These routines take a list of target atoms and ensure that all of the conversions use the same selection. The same callback procedure is called for each target, although a different `client_data` value can be specified for each target. However, as we mentioned earlier, these routines do not allow parameters to be specified for the individual targets within the MULTIPLE request.

Release 6 provides a new API for bundling selection requests into a MULTIPLE request that supports individual parameterized targets. To initiate the bundling process, a client calls `XtCreateSelectionRequest()`, passing the widget that is making the request and the atom that names the selection. After this call, subsequent calls to `XtGetSelectionValue()`, `XtGetSelectionValues()`, `XtGetSelectionValueIncremental()`, and `XtGetSelectionValuesIncremental()` that specify the same widget and selection atom are bundled into a single request with multiple targets. If an individual target has parameters, the request can be preceded by a call to `XtSetSelectionParameters()`.

When selection requests are bundled in this manner, the actual requests are deferred until the client calls `XtSendSelectionRequest()`. This routine is passed the requesting widget, the selection atom, and the timestamp from the event that initiated the selection request. When this routine is called with a widget and selection atom that match the arguments in a previous call to `XtCreateSelectionAtom()`, a selection request is actually sent to the selection owner.

If multiple targets are queued, they are bundled into a single request using the MULTI-PLE target. As the values are returned by the selection owner, the callbacks specified in the various selection request calls are invoked. Another advantage to this approach over just using `XtGetSelectionValues()` or `XtGetSelectionValuesIncremental()` is that different callback routines can be specified for different targets.

multithreaded applications should lock the application context before calling XtCreateSelectionRequest() to ensure that the thread that assembles the request is protected from interference by another thread assembling a different request using the same widget and selection atom. Once XtSendSelectionRequest() is called, the application can release the lock. See Chapter 4, *Multithreading*, for more information about writing multithreaded Xt applications.

A client can also decide to stop assembling a MULTIPLE request by calling XtCancelSelectionRequest(). This routine discards all of the requests that have been queued for the specified widget and selection atom. A subsequent call to XtSendSelectionRequest() does not result in a request. Subsequent calls to XtGetSelectionValue(), XtGetSelectionValues(), XtGetSelectionValueIncremental(), and XtGetSelectionValuesIncremental() are not deferred, so they result in immediate selection requests.

### 3.3.3    Using Temporary Property Names

Certain uses of parameterized selections require clients to name other properties within a selection parameter. To permit reuse of temporary property names in these circumstances and thereby reduce the number of unique atoms created in the server, Xt maintains a cache of reusable "scratch" atoms. The MULTIPLE request has always used scratch atoms internally; now it is possible to use them with other targets.

To get a temporary property name for use in a selection request, a client calls XtReservePropertyAtom(). This routine returns an atom that may be used as a property name for selection requests that involve the specified widget. As long as the atom remains reserved, it is guaranteed to be unique with respect to all other reserved atoms.

When a client is done with a temporary property name, it should call XtReleasePropertyAtom() to delete the property named by the atom and allow Xt to reuse the atom. This routine marks the specified property name as no longer in use. It also ensures that any property having that name on the specified widget's window is deleted. If the specified atom is not one returned by XtReservePropertyAtom(), the results of releasing the atom are undefined.

## 3.4    *Geometry Management*

X11R6 has introduced the XtChangeManagedSet() routine to optimize changes in geometry of managed children of a composite widget. The routine provides a way to unmanage and manage a set of children with a single function call (and one geometry negotiation), which can be more efficient than separate unmanage and manage calls (which cause multiple negotiations). Depending on the composite widget being used, calling XtChangeManagedSet() may result in a separate invocation of the change_managed() method for both the unmanage and manage processes, or just a single invocation. An application can also specify a procedure that modifies the geometry of several children while they are unmanaged, which is far more efficient than making the same changes while the widgets are managed.

There are two basic uses for XtChangeManagedSet(). The first is to unmanage one set of widgets and manage a different set in an efficient manner. In this case, an application specifies non-overlapping sets of widgets for unmanage_children and manage_children and do_change_proc is NULL.

The second use of XtChangeManagedSet() is to perform multiple geometry changes efficiently for a set of widgets. It is most efficient to change the size and position of widgets when they are unmanaged because the changes can be made without geometry negotiation. When the widgets are managed again, the geometry changes are effectively batched into a single round of geometry negotiation.

The two common uses for XtChangeManagedSet() are not mutually exclusive. For example, you could use this function to unmanage five children, change the size and position of three of them, and then manage those three children again along with one other that was previously unmanaged.

XtChangeManagedSet() takes six parameters: a list of widgets to unmanage and the number of such widgets, a procedure to invoke after the widgets have been unmanaged, optional client data for this procedure, and a list of widgets to manage and the number of such widgets. If num_unmanage_children and num_manage_children are both 0, the routine returns immediately. If all of the specified widgets do not have the same parent, or if that parent is not a subclass of composite, the routine issues a warning and returns.

To use the routine to make multiple geometry changes, an application specifies the same list of widgets for unmanage_children and manage_children and also specifies a do_change_proc procedure that makes the necessary geometry changes. To realize the advantage of this process, be sure that every child that is affected by the do_change_proc is included in the list of widgets to be unmanaged and managed.

The do_change_proc is of type XtDoChangeProc. This procedure is passed the to composite parent widget: the list of children that have just been unmanaged, the list of children that will be added to the managed set, and the optional client data. Example 3-7 shows a simple example of using XtChangeManagedSet() with a do_change_proc that arbitrarily changes the height of some widgets.

**Example 3-7:** Using XtChangeManagedSet to make multiple geometry changes

```
/* managed.c -- simple program to demonstrate multiple geometry changes */

#include <stdio.h>
#include <X11/Intrinsic.h>
#include <X11/StringDefs.h>
#include <X11/Shell.h>
```

```
#include <X11/Xaw/Command.h>
#include <X11/Xaw/Box.h>

Widget button[5];
static char *button_names[] =
    {"GO", "Button 1", "Button 2", "Button 3", "Button 4"};

/* make_geo_changes() -- change the height of all the children
 * that have been unmanaged in the call to XtChangeManagedSet.
 */
void make_geo_changes (parent, unmanage_children, num_unmanage_children,
                       manage_children, num_manage_children, client_data)
Widget parent;
WidgetList unmanage_children;
Cardinal *num_unmanage_children;
WidgetList manage_children;
Cardinal *num_manage_children;
XtPointer client_data;
{
    int i;

    for (i = 0; i < *num_unmanage_children; i++)
        XtVaSetValues (unmanage_children[i],
            XtNheight, (i + 1) * 50,
            NULL);
}

/* change_geometry() -- Unmanaged all but the first button, make
 * geometry changes, and manage the buttons again.
 */
void change_geometry (widget, client_data, call_data)
Widget widget;
XtPointer client_data;
XtPointer call_data;
{
    XtChangeManagedSet (&button[1], 4, make_geo_changes, NULL, &button[1], 4);
}

main (argc, argv)
int     argc;
char    **argv;
{
    Widget toplevel, box;
    XtAppContext app_context;
    int i;

    toplevel = XtVaOpenApplication (&app_context, "Managed", NULL, 0, &argc,
        argv, NULL, sessionShellWidgetClass, XtNallowShellResize, True, NULL);

    box = XtCreateManagedWidget ("box", boxWidgetClass, toplevel, NULL, 0);

    /* Create a bunch of buttons so we can demonstrate how to use
     * XtChangeManagedSet.
     */
    for (i = 0; i < XtNumber (button); i++)
        button[i] = XtCreateManagedWidget (button_names[i],
            commandWidgetClass, box, NULL, 0);
```

```
        /* Put a callback on the first button that makes the geometry
         * changes.
         */
        XtAddCallback (button[0], XtNcallback, change_geometry, NULL);

        XtRealizeWidget (toplevel);
        XtAppMainLoop (app_context);
    }
```

Exactly how XtChangeManagedSet() works depends on the composite widget that manages the children. As we'll explain shortly, there is a new field in the composite class extension record, allows_change_managed_set, that specifies if the widget supports bundled changes. If this field is set to False, calling XtChangeManagedSet() is equivalent to calling XtUnmanageChildren(), invoking the do_change_proc, and then calling XtManageChildren(). In this case, the only efficiency advantage is that the geometry changes to the children are made while they are unmanaged, so there is only one geometry negotiation. The change_managed() method of the composite widget is still called twice.

However, if allows_change_managed_set is True, the geometry changes are made more efficiently. In this situation, the widgets on the unmanage_children list are marked as unmanaged, and they are unmapped (if mapped_when_managed is True). If do_change_proc is non-NULL, the procedure is invoked. Then the widgets on the manage_children list are marked as managed. After all of the children have been marked and as long as the parent is realized, the change_managed() method is invoked a single time.

## 3.5   Resource Conversion

In Release 6, Xt registers resource converters for window gravity as well as three new resource types related to session management: XtRRestartStyle, XtRDirectoryString, and XtRCommandArgArray.

The converter for XtRGravity accepts string values that are the names of window and bit gravities, as well as their numerical equivalents. This converter works for the Shell widget resource XtNwinGravity. The actual values, defined by Xlib, are: ForgetGravity, UnmapGravity, NorthWestGravity, NorthGravity, NorthEastGravity, WestGravity, CenterGravity, EastGravity, SouthWestGravity, SouthGravity, SouthEastGravity, and StaticGravity. Case is not important in this conversion. For an explanation of window and bit gravity, see Chapter 4 of *Xlib Programming Manual.*

The converter for XtRCommandArgArray parses a string into an array of strings. This converter is used for the various command resources defined by the SessionShell widget class, such as XtNcloneCommand and XtNrestartCommand. White space characters separate elements of the command. The converter recognizes the backslash character (\) as an escape character to allow the following white space character to be part of an array element.

The `XtRDirectoryString` converter recognizes the string `XtCurrentDirectory` and returns the result of a call to the operating system to get the current directory. This converter is useful for the `XtNcurrentDirectory` resource of the `SessionShell`.

The converter for `XtRRestartStyle` accepts string values that correspond to the possible values of the `XtNrestartStyle` resource: `RestartIfRunning`, `RestartAnyway`, `RestartImmediately`, and `RestartNever`. These values are explained in Section 2.1.2.1.

## 3.6   Widget Internals

Some of the changes to Xt in Release 6 are of interest only to widget writers. One significant change is the addition of widget methods for instance allocation and deallocation. These methods allow widgets to be treated as C++ objects in a C++ environment. There is also a new mechanism that allows a composite widget to make bundled changes to its set of managed children (supporting the application-level features described in Section 3.4). Other changes merely provide clarification in the Xt specification about various widget processes, so that widget writers can rely on the exact order of the processes.

### 3.6.1   Instance Allocation and Deallocation

In Release 6, a widget class may provide optional instance allocation and deallocation methods by specifying procedures for the `allocate` and `deallocate` fields of the object class extension record. These routines are called by Xt to allocate and deallocate widget instance records, respectively. When these methods are defined, a widget can be treated as a C++ object, as well as a valid Xt object.

At widget allocation time, if the object class extension record has its `record_type` field set to `NULLQUARK` and `allocate` is not `NULL`, the specified `allocate()` method is invoked to allocate memory for the widget. If a widget class specifies an `allocate()` method, it should also specify a matching `deallocate()` method.

The `allocate()` and `deallocate()` methods are not chained. A widget class can inherit these methods from its superclass by specifying `XtInheritAllocate` and `XtInheritDeallocate` for the appropriate fields of the object class extension record. The widget class can also omit the object class extension record altogether, which causes Xt to assume superclass inheritance. If the `allocate` field is set to `NULL`, however, the method is not inherited and Xt simply allocates the necessary memory internally. Similarly, if `deallocate` is set to `NULL`, Xt simply frees the necessary memory internally.

To understand why you need to write `allocate()` and `deallocate()` methods to make a widget a valid C++ object, you first need to understand how Xt handles instance allocation. By default, Xt allocates a single block that is large enough for the widget's instance record and its constraint record if it has one. Then the constraint pointer in the instance record is set to the portion of the memory allocated for the constraint record.

However, C++ controls its own instance allocation and deallocation, so Xt's default functionality does not work. In C++, the instance record and the constraint record need to be allocated separately, so they can be destroyed separately. The `allocate()` method also allows the widget writer to allocate memory if that is necessary, and set up any initial values or virtual function tables.

### 3.6.1.1 The allocate method

The `allocate()` method is of type `XtAllocateProc`. It is passed a number of arguments related to the widget being created, including the widget class, the size of the constraint record to allocate, the amount of auxiliary memory to allocate, and lists of arguments and typed arguments specified in the call to create the widget. Widgets typically don't use the `args` and `typed_args` lists passed to this method, although it is conceivable that a widget class could optimize its allocation based on these resource values. Note, however, that these lists only specify resource values that are hard-coded by an application, not resource values set through the resource database.

The `allocate()` method also has two return parameters: `new_return` and `more_bytes_return`. The memory allocated for the widget instance is returned in `new_return`, while any auxiliary memory that is requested is returned in `more_bytes_return`.

The `allocate()` method must allocate at least `widget_class-> core_class.widget_size` bytes for the new widget and the memory must be double-word aligned. If an allocation error occurs, the method should return NULL in `new_return`. If `constraint_size` is 0, the `allocate()` method must initialize the `core.constraints` field in the newly allocated instance record to NULL. Otherwise, the method must allocate `constraint_size` bytes, double-word aligned, and initialize `core.constraints` to point to this memory. If `more_bytes` is non-zero, the method must also allocate the specified number of bytes, double-word aligned, and return this memory in `more_bytes_return`. Again, if an allocation error occurs, NULL should be returned. If no auxiliary memory is requested, this return value should not be changed.

If a class allocation procedure envelops the allocation procedure of a superclass, it must rely on the enveloped procedure to perform the instance and constraint allocation. Allocation procedures are discouraged from initializing fields in the widget record. If an `allocate()` procedure chooses to initialize fields, it should do so only in the instance part record of its own class. In other words, it should not modify the instance part of any superclass.

### 3.6.1.2    The deallocate method

The `deallocate()` method is of type `XtDeallocateProc`. This method takes two arguments: the widget being destroyed and a pointer to any auxiliary memory that was allocated for the widget. The `deallocate()` method is responsible for freeing the memory specified by `more_bytes` if it is not `NULL`. It must also free the constraint record specified by the widget's `core.constraints` field if it is not `NULL`, and free the widget instance itself.

The `deallocate()` method for a widget class should be paired with a matching `allocate()` method. If the `allocate()` method envelopes the method of a superclass, it is usually safe to just inherit the corresponding `deallocate()` method of the superclass.

## 3.6.2    Geometry Management

Section 3.4 described the Release 6 routine `XtChangeManagedSet()` that makes it possible to bundle geometry changes. For maximum efficiency, this routine relies on a new field in the composite class extension record, `allows_change_managed_set`. If the `change_managed()` method for a widget can accomodate additions and deletions to its managed set of children in a single invocation, it should set the `allows_change_managed_set` field in the composite extension record to `True`.

When `XtChangeManagedSet()` is called, it checks the composite class extension record to see if it can optimize its functionality. If `allows_change_managed_set` is `True`, the routine performs as we've already described. If the composite class extension record doesn't exist, or if `record_type` is not `NULLQUARK` and `version` is not greater than 1, the routine determines whether or not it can inherit the value of this field from the superclass. If the widget has specified `XtInheritChangeManaged` in its class record, the value of `allow_change_managed_set` is inherited from the superclass. The value inherited from the composite widget class is `False`.

## 3.6.3    Exposure Compression

Release 6 adds a new exposure event compression flag that can be used to further optimize exposure compression. This flag, `XtExposeNoRegion`, can be ORed with the value of the `compress_exposure` field to specify that the widget does not use the final region argument passed to the `expose()` method. When this flag is used, Xt does not have to compute the damaged region, which saves processing time. However, the rectangle in the event passed to the `expose()` method still contains bounding box information for the series of compressed exposure events, so the widget can use this information as before.

## 3.6.4   Locating Extension Records

Xt provides a new utility function for widget writers in Release 6. The `XtGetClassExtension()` routine can be used to locate a particular class extension record for a given widget class. Class extension records are stored as a linked list, so this routine is a convenience for widget writers.

`XtGetClassExtension()` takes parameters that indicate the object class, the offset of the extension field in the class record, the type of the extension record, a minimum version number, and a minimum record size. The routine searches the list of extension records at the specified offset in the specified object class. If `XtGetClassExtension()` finds a record with the specified type, a version greater than the specified version, and a record size greater than or equal to the specified size, it returns a pointer to the record. Otherwise, the routine returns `NULL`.

If the caller is not the object class owner, it must not modify or free the extension record returned by `XtGetClassExtension()`.

## 3.6.5   Widget Creation and Destruction

The textual descriptions of the processes of widget creation and destruction have been edited in the Release 6 specification to clarify the processes, since widget writers may need to rely on the specific order of the stages of widget creation and destruction.

According to the specification, `XtCreateWidget()` performs all the boilerplate operations of widget creation, doing the following in order:

- Checks to see if the `class_initialize()` procedure has been called for this class and for all superclasses and, if not, calls the necessary procedures in a superclass-to-subclass order.

- Issues a fatal error if the specified class is not `coreWidgetClass` or a subclass thereof, and the parent's class is a subclass of `compositeWidgetClass` and either no extension record in the parent's composite class part extension field exists with the `record_type` `NULLQUARK` or the `accepts_objects` field in the extension record is `False`.

- Invokes the procedure to allocate memory for the widget instance if the specified class contains an extension record in the object class part `extension` field with `record_type` `NULLQUARK` and the `allocate` field is not `NULL`. If the parent is a member of the class `constraintWidgetClass`, the procedure also allocates memory for the parent's constraints and stores the address of this memory into the constraints field. If no `allocate()` procedure is found, the Intrinsics allocates memory for the widget and, when applicable, for the constraints, and initializes the constraints field.

- Initializes the Core nonresource data fields self, parent, widget_class, being_destroyed, name, managed, window, visible, popup_list, and num_popups.

- Initializes the resource fields (for example, background_pixel) by using the CoreClassPart resource lists specified for this class and all superclasses.

- Initializes the resource fields of the constraints record by using the Constraint-ClassPart resource lists specified for the parent's class and all superclasses up to constraintWidgetClass if the parent is a member of the class constraint-WidgetClass.

- Calls the initialize() methods for the widget starting at the Object initialize() method on down to the widget's initialize() method.

- Calls the ConstraintClassPart initialize() methods, starting at constraint-WidgetClass on down to the parent's ConstraintClassPart initialize() method if the parent is a member of the class constraintWidgetClass.

- Puts the widget into its parent's children list by calling its parent's insert_child() method if the parent is a member of the class compositeWidgetClass.

The description of phase 2 of the widget destruction process has also been clarified. According to the specification, XtDestroyWidget() performs the following on each entry in the destroy list in the order specified:

- Calls XtUnmanageChild() on the widget, and then calls the widget's parent's delete_child() method if the widget is not a pop-up child and the widget's parent is a subclass of compositeWidgetClass, and if the parent is not being destroyed.

- Calls the destroy callback procedures registered on the widget and all normal and pop-up descendants in postorder (it calls child callbacks before parent callbacks).

The XtDestroyWidget() function then makes a second traversal (still in phase 2) of the widget and all normal and pop-up descendants to perform the following items on each widget in postorder:

- Calls the ConstraintClassPart destroy() method for the parent, then for the parent's superclass, until finally it calls the ConstraintClassPart destroy() method for constraintWidgetClass if the widget is not a pop-up child and the widget's parent is a subclass of constraintWidgetClass.

- Calls the CoreClassPart destroy() method declared in the widget class, then the destroy() method declared in its superclass, until finally it calls the destroy() method declared in the Object class record. Callback lists are deallocated.

- Calls the `deallocate()` procedure to deallocate the instance and if one exists, calls the constraint record if the widget class object class part contains an `Object-ClassExtension` record with the `record_type` NULLQUARK, and the `deallocate` field is not NULL. Otherwise, the Intrinsics deallocates the widget instance record and if one exists, the constraint record.

- Calls `XDestroyWindow()` if the specified widget is realized (that is, if it has an X window). The server recursively destroys all normal descendant windows. (Windows of realized pop-up Shell children, and their descendants, are destroyed by a shell class destroy procedure.)

The final wording change involves the process performed by `XtUnmanageChildren()`. According to the specification, this routine performs the following:

- Returns immediately if the common parent is being destroyed.

- Issues an error if the children do not all have the same parent or if the parent is not a subclass of `compositeWidgetClass`.

- Ignores the child if it is unmanaged for each unique child on the list; otherwise it performs the following:

  - Marks the child as unmanaged.
  - If the child is realized and the `mapped_when_managed` field is `True`, it is unmapped.

- Calls the `change_managed()` method of the widgets' parent if the parent is realized and if any children have become unmanaged.

## 3.7  Hooks for External Agents

In Release 6, an external agent that wants to track application activity can register callbacks on a per-display basis for notification about a large variety of operations in the X Toolkit. The addition of these hooks makes it possible for an external agent to communicate with and instrument an application for the purpose of accessibility, testing, or customization. For example, the hooks can be used to notify an external agent, such as an interactive resource editor or an aid for physically-challenged users, about X Toolkit events like widget creation.

An external agent and an application communicate using a shared protocol that is transparent to the application. The X Consortium's x-agent working group is working on the development of one such protocol for eventual review as a Consortium standard. Once this protocol is developed, the intent is to hide the implementation in the `VendorShell` widget, so that an application writer does not have to do anything to support external agents except link with a widget set that supports this functionality. Until this protocol is completed, however, there really is no practical use of the external agent functionality. The information provided here is simply meant to help you understand how an external agent would work.

## 3.7.1    The Hook Object

An external agent gets access to the hooks into an application through a hook registration object. Under the protocol being developed, the external agent would notify the application of its presence, which would cause an event handler in the `VendorShell` to call `XtHooksOfDisplay()` to get the Hook object for the display. This routine takes a display pointer and returns the Hook object, which is a private, implementation-dependent, subclass of `Object`. The Hook object has no parent. This object has callback resources that provide hooks for many important Xt operations, as well as two read-only resources that report all of the parentless shell widgets associated with the display.

The Hook object can be passed to a number of Xt routines. The Hook object can be passed as the *widget* argument to all of the Xt routines that deal with callbacks, such as `XtAddCallback()` and `XtRemoveCallback()`. The Hook object can also be passed to `XtGetValues()` to get the values of the `XtNshells` and `XtNnumShells` resources. These are read-only resources that specify a list of the parentless shell widgets of a display and the number of such widgets. The protocol being developed will provide a way for an external agent to request the values of these resources.

An external agent uses the protocol to indicate that it wants to be notified about certain Xt operations in an application. When the application receives this notification, the `VendorShell` causes the appropriate callbacks to be registered on the Hook object. These callbacks are internal to the `VendorShell`; the application does not need to provide them. When an Xt operation in the application causes one of the Hook callbacks to be invoked, the callback simply uses the protocol to notify the external agent about the operation. Figure 3-3 shows the interaction between an external agent and an Xt application.

The Hook object provides the following callback resources:

XtNcreateHook

> This callback list is invoked whenever a widget creation event occurs, which means that it is called by `XtCreateWidget()`, `XtCreateManagedWidget()`, `XtCreatePopupShell()`, `XtAppCreateShell()`, and their corresponding varargs versions.

XtNchangeHook

> This callback list is invoked whenever something about the state of the application changes. This means that the list is called by functions like `XtSetValues()`, `XtManageChild()`, and `XtAddCallback()`, to name just a few. See the Hook object reference page for the complete list of functions that call `XtNchangeHook`.

XtNconfigureHook

> This callback list is called any time the Intrinsics moves, resizes, or configures a widget. It is also called when `XtResizeWindow()` is called.

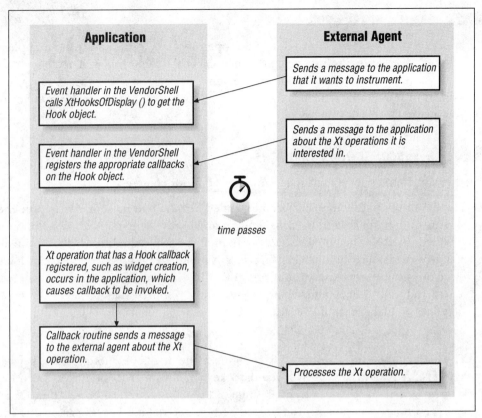

**Application**

Event handler in the VendorShell calls XtHooksOfDisplay () to get the Hook object.

Event handler in the VendorShell registers the appropriate callbacks on the Hook object.

*time passes*

Xt operation that has a Hook callback registered, such as widget creation, occurs in the application, which causes callback to be invoked.

Callback routine sends a message to the external agent about the Xt operation.

**External Agent**

Sends a message to the application that it wants to instrument.

Sends a message to the application about the Xt operations it is interested in.

Processes the Xt operation.

**Figure 3-3:**    How an external agent interacts with an Xt application

`XtNgeometryHook`

This callback list is invoked when geometry negotiations occur. It is called by `XtMakeGeometryRequest()` and `XtMakeResizeRequest()` both before and after geometry negotiation.

`XtNdestroyHook`

This callback list is called when a widget is destroyed.

Each of these callback lists passes a particular type of `call_data` to its callback routines. The `call_data` structure contains information that is relevant to the specific Xt event that occurred. Each of the `call_data` structures also contains a `type` field that identifies which Xt routine invoked the hook callback. See the Hook object reference page for information about the actual `call_data` structures.

### 3.7.2    Getting the Open Displays

An application may need to get a list of the open displays associated with an application context, so that it can then get the Hook object for each display. The XtGetDisplays() routine takes an application context and returns just such a list. The routine allocates storage for and returns a list of Display pointers, as well as the number of open displays. The list of displays should be freed using XtFree().

# 3.8    Miscellaneous Changes

The Release 6 version of Xt includes a number of minor changes:

- The file search path syntax has been extended in X11R6 to make it easy to prepend and append path elements to the default search path. The new %D substitution is replaced by the value of the implementation-specific default path that controls resource database construction. This substitution can be used to allow additional directories to be searched without preventing Xt from finding resources in the system directories. For example, a user installing resource files under a directory called *mydir* might set XFILESEARCHPATH to:

    ```
    %D:mydir/%T/%N%C:mydir/%T/%N
    ```

- The default key translator in R6 recognizes the NumLock modifier for keypad keysyms. A keypad keysym is a standard keysym with a "KP" prefix or a vendor-specific keysym in the hexadecimal range 0x11000000 to 0x1100FFFF. If NumLock is on and the second keysym is a keypad keysym, the default key translator uses the first keysym if Shift and/or ShiftLock is on or the second keysym if neither is on. Otherwise the translator ignores NumLock and applies normal protocol semantics.

- The Release 6 implementation of Xt no longer allows an application to pass NULL as the value in a name or value pair passed to XtGetValues(). Now the default behavior is to print an error message and exit. To restore the Release 5 behavior, Xt needs to be compiled with the GetValuesBC configuration option.

- Motif 1.2 defines the types XtTypedArg and XtTypedArgList in *VaSimpleP.h*. However, in Release 6, these types are defined in *IntrinsicP.h*. Making Motif 1.2 work with Release 6 requires making some changes to the Motif source. In *VaSimple.c*, make sure *IntrinsicP.h* is included before *VaSimpleP.h*. In *VaSimpleP.h*, enclosed the type declarations with #if (XT_REVISION < 6) and #endif.

- Xt (and Xlib) now support using the poll() system call instead of select() for collecting input from a set of file descriptors. Previous implementations of Xt have used just select() to get input from file descriptors. The advantage of poll() is that it provides asynchronous I/O multiplexing, while select() only provides synchronous behavior. This option must be set when Xt is compiled by using the HasPoll configuration option.

# Multithreading

*Ajay Vohra*

Subject to some limitations, X11R6 Xt allows all its interfaces to be accessed in multiple threads. In general, writing multithreaded Xt applications requires familiarity with:

- General concurrent programming principles

- System-specific threads interfaces

- New interfaces in X11R6 Xt for multithreaded Xt applications

This chapter introduces the first two concepts and covers Xt in detail. In Section 4.1, we explore the motivations for writing multithreaded Xt applications. Section 4.2 explains some basic concepts associated with multithreading. To illustrate the multithreading concepts with some specific code examples, we use Solaris[†] threads interfaces. Next, we describe the new interfaces in X11R6 Xt that are useful for writing multithreaded Xt applications. In Section 4.4, we look at some code examples of multithreaded Xt applications. Finally, in Section 4.5, we offer some guidelines for writing multithread-safe Xt widgets.

## 4.1    Why Multithreading?

Xt applications are based on a paradigm wherein the application operates in an infinite loop, checking for input and dispatching the input to the appropriate place. The input consists of X events arriving from the display server, input from alternate input sources, and timeout values. The code for the input processing loop looks something like the code in Example 4-1:[‡]

---

**Ajay Vohra** is a senior software engineer at Sun Microsystems and was involved in designing the Release 6 multithreading support.
† Solaris threads is an implementation of the UNIX International standard for threads.
‡ This code is slightly different in X11R6 Xt, as we shall see in Section 3.

**Example 4-1:** Input Processing Loop

```
while(TRUE)      {
        XEvent event;
        XtAppNextEvent(app, &event);
        XtDispatchEvent(&event);
}
```

The app refers to an application context in the Xt application. `XtAppNextEvent()` removes and returns the event from the head of app's X event queue. If the X event queue is empty, `XtAppNextEvent()` waits for an X event to arrive, meanwhile looking at alternate input sources and timeout values and calling any callback procedures triggered by them. After `XtAppNextEvent()` returns, `XtDispatchEvent()` dispatches the X event to the appropriate place. Dispatching the X event typically involves invoking some event handlers, action procedures, or callback procedures. For the purposes of our discussion, we will henceforth refer to event handlers, action procedures, callback procedures, input callback procedures, and timer callback procedures, collectively as "callbacks."

Typically, every Xt application does its useful work in its "callbacks." If the work done in a "callback" is time consuming (and indivisible),[†] the processing of the next event on the X event queue may be noticeably delayed, causing degradation in the responsiveness of the application. As we shall see in Section 4.4, multithreading can help avoid the delay in the processing of X events and thus alleviate the problem of poor responsiveness (or interactivity).

However, this is not the only motivation. Others include a more "natural" program structure for inherently concurrent Xt applications and better performance of Xt applications on multiple-processor machines (or on a configuration of multiple machines). In the following subsections, we look at some examples of applications that do time-consuming work in their "callbacks," and thus are susceptible to periods of poor responsiveness.

## 4.1.1    Electronic Mail Application

Most contemporary desktops provide an electronic mail application for their users. The purpose of an electronic mail application is to allow the user to compose mail messages, to send the composed mail messages to other users on the network, to receive mail messages from other users on the network, to store mail messages in file folders, and to retrieve mail messages from file folders. Like all desktop window system applications, an electronic mail application is made up of two distinct components:

- The graphical component visible on the desktop. The user directly interacts with this part.

---

† This aspect is relevant because such work cannot be done in work procedures.

- The underlying core component that implements the functionality for sending, receiving, storing, and retrieving mail messages.

One of the goals of an electronic mail application is to promptly inform the user about new incoming mail messages. One of the ways of finding out if there is any new mail is to periodically check for it. The code for an Xt timer callback procedure that periodically checks for new mail may look something like the code in Example 4-2:

**Example 4-2:** A Timer Callback Procedure for Updating a Mail box

```
void UpdateMailBox(XtPointer client_data, XtIntervalId *id)
{
        /* widget to display message titles */
        Widget scrolled_msgs = (Widget)client_data;
        unsigned long timeout_interval;

        XtAppContext app = XtWidgetToApplicationContext(scrolled_msgs);
        /* Check if there are new incoming messages: "useful" work*/
                        ...
        /* Load new incoming messages into the mail box: "useful" work*/
                        ...
        /* Update the scrolled_msgs widget to show the new
                messages: "useful" work*/
                        ...
        /* Get the value of the time out interval resource */
        XtVaGetValues(scrolled_msgs, XtNtimeOut,
                &timeout_interval, NULL);
        /* Add the timer again for next check and update */
        XtAppAddTimeOut(app, timeout_interval,
                UpdateMailBox, client_data);
}
```

In Example 4-2, we have not shown the code for most of the useful work done in the timer callback procedure, namely checking for mail messages, loading of new mail messages, and updating of the message widget, because we are not so much interested in what the code does as in the fact that whatever it does can sometimes take substantial amounts of time.

Imagine a scenario where the application's incoming mailbox resides on a remote machine, and the network to the remote machine is congested and is causing delays. It is instructive to trace the execution of the input processing loop (see Example 4-1) under such a scenario. Imagine the loop is in XtAppNextEvent(), and the timer for UpdateMailBox() has just expired. The expiration of the timer triggers the calling of UpdateMailBox(). Inside UpdateMailBox(), the input processing loop checks to see if there are any new incoming mail messages, but because of the congested network, it gets delayed at this point for some nontrivial amount of time. Meanwhile, the user clicks on some button and commands in the graphical user interface to provide the user with a new composition window. The user's command reaches the electronic mail application as an X event, but the application is unable to process any more X events for a while because it is delayed in UpdateMailBox(). As a result, the user sees no response to the commands and feels frustrated.

At this point, an alert reader might be thinking, "if only we could somehow do the work of checking for new mail, the loading of mailbox, andthe updating of message widget in a separate thread, we would be free to process incoming X events." Hold that thought; we will expand on it in Section 4.4. One last point before we move onto the next example. The two operations, checking for new mail and composing a message in a composition window, are inherently concurrent. So, it is only natural that one should think about executing them concurrently.

## 4.1.2    Performance Meter

A performance meter application illustrates another motivation for writing multi-threaded applications. A performance meter monitors the vital signs of a machine; the CPU usage, page faults, interrupts, context switches, disk usage, process swaps, overall system load, packets transmitted, and packet collisions on the network. Like the electronic mail application, a performance meter is made up of two distinct components: the graphical interface and the underlying infrastructure that does the "real" work.

One of the main goals of the performance meter is to periodically update its graphical interface with the performance data. In our example, the performance meter periodically fetches the performance data in a timer callback procedure and updates the performance meter appropriately. The code for such a timer callback procedure might look something like the code in Example 4-3:

**Example 4-3:** Timer Callback Procedure for Performance Meter Update

```
void Update(XtPointer client_data, XtIntervalId *timer)
{
        Data d = (Data)client_data; /* Data is a typedef that
                                  encapsulates application data */

        /* Get performance data: "useful" work */
                      ...
        /* Update the performance meter with the
              performance data: "useful" work*/
                      ...
        /* Add the timer for the next update */
        XtAppAddTimeOut(d->app, d->interval, Update, d);
                /* d->app is the application context, d->interval is the
                          update interval */
}
```

If the machine being monitored by the performance meter is a remote machine, the step of fetching the performance data is susceptible to network delays and can lead to a degradation in the responsiveness of the performance meter. Up to this point, things are very similar to the case of loading the mailbox in the electronic mail application (see Example 4-2.) However, there is one additional interesting point about the performance meter. If the performance meter is capable of monitoring more than one

*4. Multithreading*

machine at a time, a delay in the timer callback procedure of any one of the machines can impair the responsiveness of the whole application. Still a worse situation is a crash of one of the remote machines can "freeze" the whole application for a significant amount of time. From a user's point of view, this behavior is unacceptable. After all, conceptually, there is no reason why monitoring one machine should interfere with monitoring another machine.

On the other hand, if each machine is being monitored in a separate thread, delay in communicating with one machine will not affect the overall responsiveness of the application. In fact, if the application is running on a multiple processor machine, we could see an overall improvement in the application performance.

To summarize, we have discussed three motivations for writing multithreaded applications:

- Applications that do time-consuming work in their "callbacks" can suffer from poor GUI responsiveness. Multithreading can address this problem.

- Applications that are inherently concurrent have a more natural program structure when they are multithreaded.

- Multithreading inherently concurrent applications is an effective way of improving their performance, especially when such applications are run on multiple processors.

Before we can show how to write multithreaded applications, we need to understand some basic multithreading concepts. In the section called "Using Threads", we introduce the notion of a thread and explain the need for synchronization. In addition, we briefly describe the problem of deadlock and suggest one possible strategy to avoid deadlock. Readers familiar with threads programming may want to skim that section.

## 4.2    Using Threads

In general, there are two ways of specifying program concurrency: through two or more processes or through two or more threads. The former approach is known as multiprocessing and the latter approach is known as multithreading. There are two main reasons for choosing multithreading over multiprocessing:

- Multiprocessing requires expensive interprocess communication, while separate threads can directly share data.

- Compared to process creation and process context switches, thread creation and thread context switches are inexpensive operations.

So that you can understand the various concepts related to multithreading, the next section introduces the basic notion of a thread.

## 4.2.1    Threads

A thread is a unit of execution within a process. Typically, a thread has the following properties:

- A thread has its own program counter.

- A thread has its own stack.

- A thread has its own signal mask.

- All threads share the process address space.

- All threads share the process file descriptors.

The relative execution speed of a thread with respect to other threads is unpredictable. [†]

The interfaces required to manipulate threads are operating system dependent. Example 4-4 provides a sampling of Solaris threads interfaces. In particular, the example illustrates the use of following interfaces:

- `thr_create()` to create a new thread

- `thr_self()` to obtain a thread's own id

- `thr_join()` to wait for the termination of another thread

For details on Solaris threads interfaces, please refer to the Solaris threads reference manual.

When the program in Example 4-4 is executed, the *main()* function starts executing in a thread called the main thread. The main thread creates a new thread by calling `thr_create()`, passing `arg` and `start_routine()` as parameters to `thr_create()`. In general, `arg` points to some data passed from the parent thread to the new thread, and `start_routine()` acts as the initial point of execution for the new thread. In Example 4-4, `arg` points to the main thread's id. The main thread obtains its own id by calling `thr_self()` and stores the returned value in the memory pointed to by `arg`.

**Example 4-4:** Creating a Thread in the Solaris Environment

```
#include <thread.h>
typedef struct _Arg {
        thread_t parent_id; /* thread_t is a data type for thread ID. */
} Arg;
void *start_routine(void *arg)
{
        Arg *a = (Arg *)arg;
        fprintf(stdout, "My thread id is:%d\n", thr_self());
        fprintf(stdout, "My parent's thread id is:%d\n", a->parent_id);
        return (void *)NULL;
}
void main(int argc, char *argv[])
```

---

† This statement is true even when the application is running on a single-processor machine.

**Example 4-4:** Creating a Thread in the Solaris Environment (continued)

```
{
int ret = 0;
thread_t new_thread, departed;
void *status; /* exit status of departed thread */
Arg *arg = 0; /* arg passed to new thread */

if(!(arg = (Arg *)malloc(sizeof(Arg)))) {
        fprintf(stderr, "malloc failed\n");
        exit(0);
}
arg->parent_id = thr_self();
if((ret = thr_create((void *)NULL, (size_t)0,
        start_routine, (void *)arg, 0, &new_thread))) {
                fprintf(stderr, "thr_create failed:%d\n", ret);
                exit(0);
}
/* Wait for the termination of new_thread by calling thr_join() */
thr_join(new_thread, &departed, &status);
}
```

When the main thread exits, all other threads in the process exit, too. Therefore, the main thread uses `thr_join()` to wait for the termination of the new thread.

The new thread starts executing by printing out its own thread id. Next, it uses the passed `arg` to print out its parent's thread id. After the new thread exits, the main thread returns from `thr_join()`.

## 4.2.2    Synchronization Among Multiple Threads

Let us modify Example 4-4 to illustrate the need for synchronization among multiple threads. We modify the code to create ten threads, instead of one. After the main thread successfully creates ten threads, it waits for all the spawned threads to exit. As in Example 4-4, each of the spawned threads starts executing in `start_routine()`. However, unlike Example 4-4, the main thread can not use `thr_join()` to wait for the termination of spawned threads, because the main thread has to wait for the termination of ten threads, and `thr_join()` can be used to wait for one thread at most. The solution is to maintain a global count of running threads. The global count is incremented each time a new thread is created and is decremented each time a spawned thread exits. When the global count reaches zero, the main thread exits. The global count is maintained in the variable `threads_running`. Unfortunately, `threads_running` is directly shared among all threads. Therefore, in order to maintain the integrity of `threads_running`, we need to provide mutually exclusive access to `threads_running`. Why do we need mutually exclusive access to shared data? For the answer to this question, read on.

**Example 4-5:** Showing the Need for Synchronization

```
#include <thread.h>
#include <synch.h>
#define NTHREADS 10
```

**Example 4-5:** Showing the Need for Synchronization (continued)

```
static int threads_running = 0;
static mutex_t mutex;
static cond_t cond;
typedef struct _Arg {
        thread_t parent_id;
} Arg;
void *start_routine(void *arg)
{
        Arg *a = (Arg *)arg;

        fprintf(stdout, "My thread id is:%d\n", thr_self());
        fprintf(stdout, "My parent's thread id is:%d\n", a->parent_id)
        mutex_lock(&mutex);
        threads_running--;
        cond_signal(&cond);
        mutex_unlock(&mutex);
}
void main(int argc, char *argv[])
{
int ret = 0;
void *status; /* exit status of departed thread */
Arg*arg = 0;          /* arg passed to new thread */

if(!(arg = (Arg *)malloc(sizeof(Arg)))) {
        fprintf(stderr, "malloc failed\n");
        exit(0);
}
arg->parent_id = thr_self();
for(i = 0; i < NTHREADS; i++) {
        if((ret = thr_create((void *)NULL, (size_t)0,
                start_routine, (void *)arg, 0, NULL))) {
                        fprintf(stderr, "thr_create failed:%d\n", ret);
                        exit(0);
        }
mutex_lock(&mutex);
threads_running++;
mutex_unlock(&mutex);
}
mutex_lock(&mutex);
while(threads_running)
        cond_wait(&cond, &mutex);
mutex_unlock(&mutex);
}
```

On each machine architecture, many operations are not executed atomically.[†] For example, on the Sparc architecture, the following C code:

```
threads_running++;
```

would be broken down into the following (possibly) atomic steps:

---

[†] The state of a program is defined by the value of all its variables, including the implicitly defined variables like the program registers. Each program statement transforms the state of a program. An operation is considered atomic if it makes an indivisible state transformation in the program.

1. Load the value of threads_running into a register. [†]

2. Increment the register.

3. Store the value of the register in the variable `threads_running`.

Let us assume, at some point, `threads_running` has the value 5. Let us further assume that at the point in question, the main thread executes the statement:

```
/* Main Thread: */
        threads_running++;
```

and one of the spawned thread executes the statement:

```
/* One Of The spawned Threads: */
        threads_running--;
```

If there is no arrangement for mutually exclusive access to the variable `threads_running`, it could have a final value of 5, 6, or 4. The reader may quickly figure out how value 5 is possible, but values 6 and 4 may appear implausible. Therefore, we elaborate on how values 4 and 6 are possible. Consider the scenario in which the main thread loads the value 5 into a register and increments it. While the main thread is incrementing the value 5 in its register, the spawned thread could also load the value 5 into its register and decrement it. Now, depending upon the order of storage (from the registers back into the variable) of the main thread and the spawned thread, the final value could be 4 or 6. Therefore, in order to maintain the semantics and integrity of shared data, we need to ensure mutually exclusive access to all shared data that is being written by more than one thread or is being written and read by two separate threads.

In Solaris threads, the recommended way of providing mutual exclusion is to use a system-defined primitive for this purpose. An example of such a primitive is known as a mutex. In Solaris, the data type for a handle to a mutex is defined as `mutex_t`. A variable of type `mutex_t` can be locked and unlocked through `mutex_lock()` and `mutex_unlock()`. The programmer establishes a semantic association between a mutex and a shared resource.[‡] Whenever the shared resource needs to be accessed atomically, the programmer locks the associated mutex. In our example, the variable mutex is used to provide mutually exclusive access to the shared resource `threads_running`.

Besides mutual exclusion, threads require another type of synchronization; condition synchronization. Condition synchronization is the need to delay the progress of a thread until some Boolean condition is satisfied. An example of condition synchronization is the waiting of the main thread for all the spawned threads to exit. For example,

---

† Depending on the architecture and the data type, the loading and storing of a variable may not be atomic.
‡ A shared resource can be a shared variable, a shared file, or any other system resource that is being directly shared among multiple threads.

in Example 4-5, the main thread is not allowed to exit until the following Boolean condition is satisfied:

```
threads_running == 0
```

In Solaris threads, condition synchronization is achieved through a combination of a Boolean condition, a *condition variable* and a mutex. Like a mutex, a condition variable is a system-defined synchronization primitive used to establish a semantic relationship between a Boolean condition[†] and a mutex. In Solaris, the data type for a handle to a condition variable is defined as cond_t. The combination of a Boolean condition, a condition variable, and a mutex implements condition synchronization is:

1. The programmer establishes a mutex, a condition variable, and a Boolean condition.

2. A given thread, say thread A, locks the associated mutex.

3. Thread A inspects the Boolean condition. If the Boolean condition is true, thread A proceeds. If the Boolean condition is false, thread A calls cond_wait().

4. In cond_wait(), thread A unlocks the associated mutex and blocks until some other thread, say thread B, executes a cond_signal() on the associated condition variable. When thread B executes a cond_signal(), thread A returns from cond_wait().

5. When thread A returns from cond_wait(), it has the associated mutex locked. Next, thread A goes back to Step 3.

In Example 4-5, the following code in main():

```
mutex_lock(&mutex);
while(threads_running)
        cond_wait(&cond, &mutex);
mutex_unlock(&mutex);
```

and the following code in start_routine():

```
mutex_lock(&mutex);
threads_running--;
cond_signal(&cond);
mutex_unlock(&mutex);
```

collectively implements condition synchronization. If the Boolean condition

```
threads_running == 0
```

is false, the main thread executes a cond_wait() on the condition variable *cond*. In cond_wait(), the main thread unlocks mutex and blocks. When a spawned thread calls cond_signal(), the main thread returns from cond_wait(). On return from

---

† A Boolean condition is a predicate involving program variables. The term condition variable is sometimes used to refer to a program variable that is part of a boolean condition. This overloading of the term condition variable is unfortunate.

`cond_wait()`, the main thread has the mutex locked and it proceeds to examine the following Boolean condition atomically:

```
threads_running == 0
```

If the Boolean condition is false, it calls `cond_wait()` and repeats the whole process.

### 4.2.3    Deadlock Among Multiple Threads

Whenever an application uses more than one synchronization primitive, it needs to be aware of the possibility of deadlock. Deadlock between two threads occurs when each thread is waiting for another to do some action. Imagine the situation in Example 4-6.

**Example 4-6:** Deadlock Between Thread A and Thread B

```
/* Code in Thread A */
mutex_lock(&mutex1);
mutex_lock(&mutex2);
/* some critical code */
mutex_unlock(&mutex2);
mutex_unlock(&mutex1);

/* Code in Thread B */
mutex_lock(&mutex2);
mutex_lock(&mutex1);
/* some critical code */
mutex_unlock(&mutex1);
mutex_unlock(&mutex2);
```

If thread A locks mutex1 and thread B locks mutex2, concurrently, we have a deadlock. This is an example of direct deadlock. However, there is also such a thing as indirect deadlock. When there is a cycle in the "wait for" graph of multiple threads, we have an indirect deadlock. For example, thread A could be waiting for thread B to do something, thread B could be waiting for thread C to do something and, to close the cycle, thread C could be waiting for thread A to do something.

Most of the time, deadlock can be avoided by using the simple strategy of acquiring multiple mutex locks in the same order in all threads. More sophisticated strategies for avoiding deadlock are beyond the scope of this discussion. This concludes our overview of basic multithreading concepts. In Section 4.3, we give an overview of the X11R6 Xt interfaces for writing multithreaded Xt applications.

## 4.3    Xt Interfaces for Multithreading

The X11R6 version of Xt provides interfaces to support multithreaded application programming. These interfaces are required only if the multithreaded application calls Xt interfaces in multiple threads. It is possible to write multithreaded Xt applications in which Xt interfaces are invoked only from a single thread. In such applications, the following interfaces may not be required.

In addition to these Xt interfaces, X11R6 declares functions and data types providing a partial portable interface to threads primitives, in the file *<X11/Xthreads.h>*. Since threads interfaces are operating system dependent, including this file instead of the system-specific file increases portability. In our example code for a multithreaded performance meter, in Section 4.4, we have tried to use these data types and functions as far as possible. However, to better suit our needs, we have redefined some function declarations and added new defines for some missing function declarations. For example, we have redefined `xthread_fork` to:

```
#undef xthread_fork
#define\
xthread_fork(func,closure,new_thread)\
thr_create(NULL,0,func,closure,THR_NEW_LWP,new_thread)
```

and we have defined a new function declaration:

```
#define xthread_join(thread) thr_join(thread, NULL, NULL)
```

These definitions currently use Solaris threads. To support other operating systems, only these definitions would change, not application code that uses the Xthread interfaces.

## 4.3.1    Initializing Xt for Use in Multiple Threads

An Xt application that creates multiple application threads must call `XtToolkit-ThreadInitialize()`, which initializes Xt for use in multiple threads. `XtToolkit-ThreadInitialize()` returns True if the given Xt supports multithreading, otherwise it returns False. A programmer can use the return value to write portable code, as described in Section 4.4.4.

`XtToolkitThreadInitialize()` may be called before or after `XtToolkitInitialize()`, and may be called more than once. But, it must not be called concurrently from multiple threads. An application must call `XtToolkitThreadInitialize()` before calling `XtAppInitialize()`, `XtSetLanguageProc()`, `XtOpenApplication()`, or `XtCreateApplicationContext()`.

## 4.3.2    Locking X Toolkit Data Structures

To lock and unlock an application context and all widgets and display connections in the application context, an application must use `XtAppLock()` and `XtAppUnlock()`, respectively.

All Xt functions[†] that take an application context, widget, or display connection as a parameter implicitly lock their associated application context for the duration of the function call. Therefore, with a few exceptions, an application does not need to call `XtAppLock()` or `XtAppUnlock()`. The first exception is the situation in which an application needs to make a series of Xt function calls atomically. In such a situation,

---

† After a successful call to `XtToolkitThreadInitialize()`.

an application can enclose the series of Xt calls within a matching pair of XtAppLock() and XtAppUnlock(). For example, if an application wants to check and update the height of a widget atomically, it might do it as follows:

**Example 4-7:** Using XtAppLock and XtAppUnlock

```
XtAppContext app;
Dimension ht = 0;
Widget w;
...
XtAppLock(app);
XtVaGetValues(w, XtNheight, &ht, NULL);
if((int)ht < 10) {
        ht += 10;
        XtVaSetValues(w, XtNheight, ht, NULL);
}
XtAppUnlock(app);
```

Another exception is the situation in which an application wants to directly invoke an Xt-defined resource converter. For example, if an application calls the String to Pixel converter, XtCvtStringToPixel(), it must do so within a matched pair of XtAppLock() and XtAppUnlock().

To provide mutually exclusive access to global data structures within Xt, widget writers can use XtProcessLock() and XtProcessUnlock(). The use of XtProcessLock() and XtProcessUnlock() is described in Section 4.5.

Both XtAppLock() and XtProcessLock() can be called recursively. To unlock to the top-level, XtAppUnlock() and XtProcessUnlock() must be called the same number of times as XtAppLock() and XtProcessLock(), respectively. To lock an application context and Xt's global data at the same time, first call XtAppLock() and then XtProcessLock(). To unlock, first call XtProcessUnlock() and then XtAppLock(). The order is important to avoid deadlock.

## 4.3.3    New XtAppMainLoop

In the X11R5 version of Xt, XtAppMainLoop() is an infinite loop that calls XtAppNextEvent() and then XtDispatchEvent(). In a multithread-safe Xt, an infinite XtAppMainLoop() would prevent an event processing thread from exiting its XtAppMainLoop() without simultaneously exiting its thread. This situation may lead to the following problems:

- Memory leaks

- Dangling threads

- Complicated synchronization between the input processing thread and other threads

The manner in which the above problems might arise can be best explained by an example such as the performance meter example described in Section 4.1.2. The performance meter has two threads for each machine it monitors: an event-processing thread and a data update thread. Let us suppose the threads processing the user input are executing a Release 5 style `XtAppMainLoop()`, and the user clicks on the exit button of one of the logical applications. How does the logical application safely destroy its application context? If the logical application is called `XtDestroyApplication-Context()` in the exit callback, it could lead to a memory segmentation fault in the associated `XtAppMainLoop()`[†]. The application could call `thr_exit()`[‡] before returning from the exit callback and thus prevent the core dump in `XtAppMainLoop()`. But this process would require complicated synchronization between the update thread and the input processing thread, and even then it would not work if the input processing thread was the main thread. If the application didn't destroy the application context at all, it would lead to a memory leak, and in addition, the thread running the `XtAppMainLoop()` would be left dangling.

In order to elegantly address the problems described above, the X11R6 version of `XtAppMainLoop()` is a conditional loop that calls `XtAppNextEvent()` and then `XtDispatchEvent()`. Then X11R6 checks at the bottom of the event loop if the application is finished with the application context, by checking a new application context exit flag. If the exit flag is set to True, `XtAppMainLoop()` exits the event-processing loop. Example 4-8 shows one implementation for the new `XtAppMainLoop()`.

**Example 4-8:** New XtAppMainLoop() in X11R6 Xt.

```
XtAppContext app;
do {
        XEvent event;
        XtAppNextEvent(app, &event);
        XtDispatchEvent(&event);
} while(XtAppGetExitFlag(app) == FALSE);
```

The application context's exit flag can be set to True by calling `XtAppSetExitFlag()`, and its value can be obtained through `XtAppGetExitFlag()`. The new `XtAppMain-Loop()` offers an effective way of destroying an application context, without having to exit from the event processing thread. Section 5.3.4 describes the details of destroying an application context in multithreaded Xt applications.

## 4.3.4    Destroying an Application Context

In multithreaded Xt applications, the recommended way of destroying an application context is the following:

---

† This progression occurs because once the current event dispatch is complete, the application context would have been destroyed and the subsequent `XtAppNextEvent()` in `XtAppMain-Loop()` would be accessing just freed memory associated with the recently destroyed application context.
‡ `thr_exit()` terminates the calling thread.

*4. Multithreading*

- After the event processing thread returns from `XtAppMainLoop()`, and after it has been determined that no other thread is referring to the associated application context, call `XtDestroyApplicationContext()`. This method is illustrated in Example 4-20.

- Use `XtAppGetExitFlag()` to synchronize between an event-processing thread and other threads. This method is illustrated in Example 4-22.

- Call `XtAppSetExitFlag()` in the exit callback. This action causes the associated `XtAppMainLoop()` to exit but does not terminate the event-processing thread. This method is illustrated in Example 4-24.

### 4.3.5 Event Management in Multiple Threads

When multiple threads call into event management functions concurrently, they return from these functions in last-in first-out order. Another way of looking at this is to imagine that if multiple threads get blocked for event in any of the event management functions, they are pushed on a per-application-context stack of blocked threads. Whenever there are some events to process, a thread is popped off the stack and allowed to process the events.

For example, let's assume thread A, the event processing thread, is blocked for event in `XtAppMainLoop()` so that it is on the per-application-context stack of blocked threads. Assume that subsequently one of the other[†] threads, thread B, detects some error condition and decides to popup a message box and temporarily take over event processing from thread A. The fact that blocked threads get stacked allows thread B to easily take over event processing from thread A. Thread B accomplishes this by executing a form of event processing loop within a matched pair of `XtAppLock()` and `XtAppUnlock()`, as shown in Example 4-9. Because thread B calls into `XtAppNextEvent()` after thread A does, thread B gets stacked above thread A. Subsequently, whenever events arrive, thread B is popped off the stack and allowed to process the events.

**Example 4-9:** Event Management in Multiple Threads

```
/* This code is in a thread other than the event processing thread */
XtAppContext app;
Widget error_dialog;
XEvent event;

XtAppLock(app); /* Lock the application context */
XtPopup(error_dialog, XtGrabExclusive); /* popup error dialog */
do {/* Take over input processing */
        XtAppNextEvent(app, &event);
        if(/* some boolean condition involving event */)
                XtDispatchEvent(&event);
} while(/* some boolean condition */)
XtAppUnlock(app);
```

---

† "Other" thread denotes any thread that is not an event processing thread.

## 4.3.6    Limitations on Some Xt Functions

The following Xt functions, when called from a thread other than an event-processing thread, may not have the intended effect on threads that are blocked in an event management function (i.e., threads lying on the per-application-context of blocked threads):

- `XtOpenDisplay()` and `XtCloseDisplay()`

- `XtAppAddTimeOut()` and `XtRemoveTimeOut()`

- `XtAppAddInput()` and `XtRemoveInput()`

- `XtNoticeSignal()`

For example, while thread A is blocked in `XtAppNextEvent()`, thread B may call `XtOpenDisplay()` and successfully open a new display connection. But, thread A may[†] not start detecting events on the new display connection until thread A returns from `XtAppNextEvent()`.

## 4.3.7    Avoiding Deadlock

When an event-processing thread dispatches an X event, it may result in the calling of a "callback." When the event-processing thread enters the "callback," it is holding the application context lock. Application programmers need to be aware of this situation to prevent deadlock. If the application uses its own locks, it needs to lock and unlock all application-defined locks in a consistent order, after Xt locks. For example, if thread A executes the code in Example 4-10:

**Example 4-10:** Code Executed in Thread A

```
xmutex_rec g_lock;
void Callback(Widget w, XtPointer call_data, XtPointer client_data)
{
        /* Thread A is already holding the app lock at this point */
        xmutex_lock(&g_lock);
            ...
        xmutex_unlock(&g_lock);
}
```

and if thread B executes the code in Example 4-11, a direct deadlock will result, because the effective order of the locks is opposite the order in Example 4-10, so each will be waiting for the other.

**Example 4-11:** Code Executed in Thread B (Deadlocks)

```
xmutex_lock(&g_lock); /* acquire the g_lock */
XtAppLock(app); /* acquire the app lock */
...
```

---

† Under some conditions, thread A may start detecting the events before it returns from `XtAppNextEvent()`. But such conditions must not be relied upon.

**Example 4-11:** Code Executed in Thread B (Deadlocks) (continued)

```
XtVaSetValues(w, XtNheight, 10, NULL);
XtAppUnlock(app);
xmutex_unlock(&g_lock);
```

The right thing to do is to maintain a consistent order of locking between thread A and thread B[†] , by executing the following code in Example 4-12:

**Example 4-12:** Code Executed in Thread B to Avoid Deadlock

```
XtAppLock(app); /* First acquire the app lock */
xmutex_lock(&g_lock); /* Then acquire the g_lock */
...
XtVaSetValues(w, XtNheight, 10, NULL);
xmutex_unlock(&g_lock);
XtAppUnlock(app);
```

## 4.3.8    Resource Converters

Applications and widgets invoking resource converters need to provide sufficient storage space for return values. If the applications or widgets neglect to do so, Xt will return pointers to local data, and in a multithreaded application this process can lead to corruption of data. For example, in a single-threaded Xt application, one can invoke the String to Pixel resource converter as shown in Example 4-13.

**Example 4-13:** Resource Converters

```
XrmValue src;
Pixel pixel; /* space for return value */
Widget w;

src.size = strlen("olivegreen");
src.addr = "olivegreen";
dst.size = sizeof(Pixel);
dst.addr = NULL;

if(!XtConvertAndStore(w, XtRString, &src, XtRPixel, &dst)) {
        /* could not convert */
}
```

In Example 4-13, the application programmer passes a NULL pointer in dst.addr, and Xt returns a reference to some local static memory space in dst.addr. If this was done in a multithreaded application, two separate threads could get back a reference to the same memory location, and the Pixel value read by the threads may depend upon which thread updated the shared memory space last. This phenomenon is known as a *race condition*: the final value in a memory space depends upon a race between two or more threads. Therefore, in multithreaded Xt applications, the proper way to invoke the String to Pixel converter is not to pass NULL in dst.addr. Instead, pass the address of memory you have allocated in this thread, as shown in Example 4-14.

---

† That is, first acquire the App Lock, then the application defined lock.

**Example 4-14:** Resource Converters

```
XrmValue src, dst;
Pixel pixel; /* space for return value */
Widget w;

src.size = strlen("olivegreen");
src.addr = "olivegreen";
dst.size = sizeof(Pixel);
dst.addr = &pixel; /* Do not pass NULL in multithreaded apps */

if(!XtConvertAndStore(w, XtRString, &src, XtRPixel, &dst)) {
        /* could not convert */
}
```

Armed with the knowledge of the Xt interfaces and general multithreading concepts, we are ready to tackle the task of developing a multithreaded Xt application. In Section 4.4 we develop a complete multithreaded performance meter. We use code excerpts from the performance meter to illustrate the important concepts associated with writing multithreaded Xt applications. The remaining code that is not related to multithreading is available by FTP as described in the Preface.

# 4.4    *Complete Multithreaded Application*

Our performance meter monitors ten different statistics: CPU usage, page faults, interrupts, context switches, collisions of transmitted packets, packets transmitted, process swaps, disk usage, overall system load, and errors. Four of these statistics are shown in Figure 4-1. The current performance information is displayed in a dial, and a running history is displayed in the form of a moving histogram. Since all the statistics, except for CPU usage, have an unbounded maximum value, the scale is updated whenever appropriate.

The performance meter application has two distinct parts: the graphical user interface and the underlying mechanism that obtains performance data. The performance data is obtained by making an RPC (Remote Procedure Call) that invokes a particular program on the machine being monitored. The RPC, if successful, returns the performance data. The graphical interface is constructed using the Motif widget set and Xt interfaces. Most of the graphical interface information is contained in a UIL[†] (User Interface Language) file. This information is compiled by the UIL compiler into a form that is read in by the Motif resource manager (Mrm) at run time.

As mentioned in Section 4.1.2, the RPC call that fetches the performance data is susceptible to network delays. Such delays, in turn, can block all input processing and render a single-threaded application temporarily unresponsive. We remarked earlier in Section 4.1.2 that the activity of monitoring different machines is inherently concur-

---

† Please refer to *Motif Programming Manual* and *Motif Reference Manual* both published by O'Reilly & Associates, Inc.

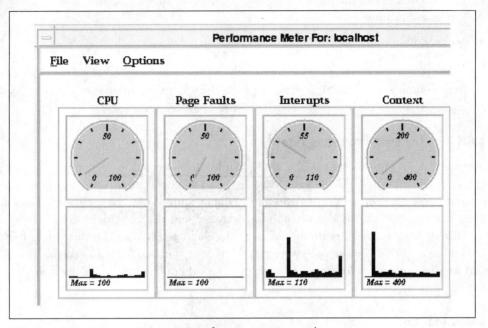

**Figure 4-1:** Performance meter application

rent and can thus be done in different threads. Therefore, our overall strategy in writing a multithreaded performance meter is to have two levels of concurrency:

- Each machine being monitored is a distinct logical application, with its own application context, within the performance meter application. Also, each of these logical applications can be displayed on a separate X server.

- Each logical application has two threads dedicated to it: one to process events and the other to make RPC calls to fetch performance data and then update the application with the latest data.

In Section 4.1 we talked about spawning threads in "callbacks." In the case of the performance meter, it makes more sense to spawn the thread that makes the RPC calls in the main() function. The reason for this is simple: fetching performance data is an asynchronous activity that must go on in parallel with the input processing loop. In single-threaded applications, we have no choice but to use Xt timers to simulate the "parallelism." In multithreaded applications, we can do better. We can create concurrent top-level threads that execute in "parallel" with the input processing thread.

The complete code for the multithreaded performance meter application[†] is portable to operating systems that do not support multithreading and is divided into four files:

---

† The name of the multithreaded performance meter application is *pm*.

- *perfm.h* contains all the data structures required to encapsulate the state of a single logical application.

- *perfm.c* contains the code related to RPC calls.

- *perfm.uil* defines the graphical interface of the performance meter.

- *pm.c* contains the functions that connect the graphical interface with the "callbacks." It also contains all the code excerpts shown in Section 4.4.

### 4.4.1  The Input Processing Thread

The `main()` function is shown in code Examples 4-15 through 4-20, interspersed with commentary. The first thing to do in `main()` is to allocate some memory for a data structure `perfData` that encapsulates all the data required by each logical application. `Data` is a `typedef` that is a pointer to `perfData`. Next, the `lock` field in `perfData` is initialized. `lock` provides mutually exclusive access to `perfData`. The next thing to do is to make copies of the incoming `args` because they get modified in certain Xt calls, and we need to pass a fresh copy to each new logical application that is invoked within the performance meter.

**Example 4-15:** Copy the Incoming args

```
static Boolean mt_x= FALSE; /* are threads supported by OS*/
static xmutex_rec mutex_threads_running;
static xcondition_rec cond_threads_running;
static int threads_running = 0;

main(int argc, char *argv[])
{
        int         i = 0;
        int         err_code = 0;
        Data d;
        void (*disp)(int);

        d = (Data)XtCalloc(1, sizeof(struct perfData));
        xmutex_init(&d->lock);
        /* Make a copy of the incoming args */
        d->argv = (String *)XtCalloc(argc, sizeof(String));
        for (i = 0; i < argc; i++)
                d->argv[i] = XtNewString(argv[i]);
        d->argc = argc;
```

The next step is to initialize Xlib and Xt for use in multiple threads. Some operating systems provide no multithreading support at all. Thus, one of the goals in writing portable multithreaded Xt programs is to write programs that can achieve the program objective (albeit with reduced performance) whether or not multithreading is available. This step requires predicating some parts of the algorithm on the availability of multithreading. For example, in the case of the performance meter, we can define a global Boolean variable, `mt_x`, in which we can store the return values from

XInitThreads() and XtToolkitThreadInitialize(). mt_x then can be used to predicate critical parts of the algorithm. Only applications that directly use Xlib interfaces in multiple threads, like this one, need to call XInitThreads(). This step is followed by the initialization of Xt, the initialization of the Motif Resource Manager (Mrm), and the registering of mrm_names with Mrm.

**Example 4-16:** Initialize the Toolkit

```
mt_x = XInitThreads(); /* Initialize Xlib for threads */
mt_x = XtToolkitThreadInitialize(); /* Initialize Xt for mt*/
XtToolkitInitialize(); /* Initialize Xt */
MrmInitialize(); /* Initialize Mrm */
MrmRegisterNames(mrm_names, (MrmCount)XtNumber(mrm_names));
```

Next, we do some more initialization and then invoke setup(). setup initializes the RPC connection to the machine being monitored. If such a connection is successful, we create the graphical user interface by calling CreateGUI(). Once the GUI is created, we realize the application shell and create some GCs for drawing dials and histograms.

Now we create the update thread. We first allocate space for a thread ID of type xthread_t. We then pass to xthread_fork() a pointer to Data d and a pointer to Update(). Update() acts as the start program counter for the new thread. Data d is the client data passed to the new thread. If the new thread is created successfully, xthread_fork() points d->update_t to the new thread ID. We start processing input by calling XtAppMainLoop().

**Example 4-17:** Spawn the Update Thread

```
d->interval = 1000; /* interval between RPC calls */
d->select_flag = MANAGE_ALL_FLAG; /* show all categories */
d->hostname = XtNewString("localhost"); /* default machine */
d->display = NULL;
for (i = 0; i < MAXMETERS; i++)
    d->cmax[i] = 100; /* initialize maxmimum values */
d->vers = RSTATVERS_VAR;
if (setup(d) != 0) {/* RPC connection not intialized */
    fprintf(stderr, "No response from %s\n", d->hostname);
    XtFree((char *)d);
} else {
    if(mt_x == TRUE) {
        CreateGUI(d); /* Create the GUI */
        XtRealizeWidget(d->appshell);
        CreateGC(d);
        d->update_t = (xthread_t * )
            XtCalloc(1,sizeof(xthread_t));
        if ((err_code = xthread_fork(Update, d, d->update_t))) {
            fprintf(stderr, xthread_fork: %d\n", err_code);
            exit(err_code);
            }
        XtAppMainLoop(d->app); /* Start processing input */
    } else
        XtAppAddTimeOut(d->app, d->interval, UpdateTimer, d);
```

**Example 4-17:** Spawn the Update Thread  (continued)

```
        }
```

The `UpdateTimer()` is an Xt timer that calls the `Update()` function. The code for `UpdateTimer()` is shown in Example 4-18.

**Example 4-18:** Fall Back on Xt Timer for Operating Systems with No Multithreading

```
static void
UpdateTimer(XtPointer client_data, XtIntervalId *timer)
{
        Data d = (Data)client_data;

        Update((void *)client_data);
        XtAppAddTimeOut(d->app, d->interval, UpdateTimer, client_data);
}
```

Before `UpdateTimer()` returns, it uses `XtAppAddTimeOut()` to add itself to the list of timers, with `d->interval` as the time-out value. Once we exit the `XtAppMainLoop()`, we synchronize with the update thread to make sure we do not destroy any data that the update thread may be referring to. We do so by checking if the update thread is still running, and if it is, then we call `xthr_join()` and wait for the update thread to exit.

**Example 4-19:** Synchronization with the Update Thread

```
        if(mt_x) {
                xmutex_lock(&d->lock);
                if(d->update_thr_running) {
                        xmutex_unlock(&d->lock);
                        xthr_join(*d->update_t);
                } else
                        xmutex_unlock(&d->lock);
        }
```

Now we are in a safe position to destroy the application shell and the associated application context. Finally, we wait for all other threads in the application to exit. We do so through condition synchronization on the Boolean condition that the "number of other threads running is zero."

**Example 4-20:** Synchronization of the Main Thread with All Other Threads

```
        XtDestroyWidget(d->appshell);
        XtDestroyApplicationContext(d->app);

        XtFree((char *)d->update_t);
        XtFree((char *)d);

        if(mt_x) {
                xmutex_lock(&mutex_threads_running);
                while (threads_running > 0)
                        xcondition_wait(&cond_threads_running,
                        &mutex_threads_running);
```

```
                xmutex_unlock(&mutex_threads_running);
        }
}
```

## 4.4.2    The Update Thread

The Update() function is executed by the update thread. The details of Update() are described with code Examples 4-21 through 4-23. The first thing Update() does is to increment the global thread count called threads_running. Next it initializes the Boolean variable d->update_thr_running to True.

**Example 4-21:** Do Synchronization Steps

```
static void
*Update(void *client_data)
{
        Data d = (Data) client_data;
        int interval;
        int        *res = NULL;
        int        i,j;
        int        ret = 0;
        Display *dpy = d->dpy;
        int update_count = 0;

        if(mt_x) {
                xmutex_lock(&mutex_threads_running);
                threads_running++;
                xmutex_unlock(&mutex_threads_running);

                mutex_lock(&d->lock);
                d->update_thr_running = TRUE;
                xmutex_unlock(&d->lock);
        }
}
```

Example 4-22 shows the most important part of the Update() function: the update loop. It begins with a check (through XtAppGetExitFlag()>) to see if the associated application context's exit flag is True. If so, we break out of the update loop. If not, we proceed by calling getdata_var(), the RPC call to fetch performance data. If this call is successful, we proceed to update the dials and histograms displaying performance data, otherwise we sleep for a minute to avoid thrashing. As we mentioned before, since all categories except CPU usage have an unbounded maximum, we change the scale whenever appropriate: revising the maximum value upward when it increases, and downward, if required, after every *MAXUPDATE* number of updates.

Notice the call to XFlush() at the bottom of the update loop. This is required because the functions UpdateDial(), DrawDial(), and DrawHist() generate X protocol requests. In single-threaded applications, such X requests are generated from "callbacks" that are invoked during the dispatching of an X event. At the end of each X event dispatch, the input processing loop flushes the X requests queue if there are no more X events to dispatch. But Update() is running outside of the input loop, hence we flush the X request queue ourselves.

**Example 4-22:** The Update Loop

```
do {
    if(XtAppGetExitFlag(d->app))
        break;
    if ((res = getdata_var(d)) != NULL) {
        for (i = 0; i < MAXMETERS; i++) {
            if(update_count == MAXUPDATE) {
                UpdateMaximum(d);
                update_count = 0;
            }
            d->hist[d->last][i] = res[i];
            if (res[i] > d->cmax[i]) {
                d->cmax[i] = RoundOfMax(res[i]);
                RedrawHist(d,i);
                DrawDial(d,i);
                UpdateDial(d,i);
            } else {
                UpdateDial(d,i);
                DrawHist(d, i);
            }
        }
        d->last = (d->last+1)%SAMPLES;
        XFlush(dpy);
        update_count++;
    } else {
        sleep(60); /* don't thrash */
        continue;
    }
} while(mt_x);
```

If mt_x is true, the do-while loop shown above is effectively an infinite while loop.[†] If mt_x is false, the do loop above gets executed exactly once. Some other points that need to be kept in mind to make the performance meter portable are: If case mt_x is false, we need to have a single XtAppMainLoop() in the program, and although it is not essential, it simplifies things to have a single application context, as well. There-fore, in NewApp(), we create all new logical applications in the existing application context. In CreateAppShell()[‡] we need to create a new application context only for the first logical application.

Once we break out of the update loop, we synchronize with the corresponding input processing thread. We do so by setting d->update_thr_running to False. Next we decrement the global thread count and exit out of the Update() function. Concur-rently, if the associated input processing thread is waiting in xthr_join() for the update thread to exit, the input processing thread returns from xthr_join().

---

† This is because mt_x is never modified after the call to XtToolkitThreadInitialize().
‡ CreateAppShell() creates a new application shell.

**Example 4-23:** More Synchronization

```
                    if(mt_x) {
                            xmutex_lock(&d->lock);
                            interval = d->interval;
                            xmutex_unlock(&d->lock);
                    }

                    /* poll for d->interval between RPC calls */
                    if ((ret = poll((struct pollfd *)NULL,
                            (unsigned long)0, (int)interval)) == -1)
                            fprintf(stderr, "error during polling\n");
            }
            if(mt_x) {
                    xmutex_lock(&d->lock);
                    d->update_thr_running = FALSE;
                    xmutex_unlock(&d->lock);

                    xmutex_lock(&mutex_threads_running);
                    threads_running--;
                    xcondition_signal(&cond_threads_running);
                    xmutex_unlock(&mutex_threads_running);
            }
    }
```

At the beginning of Section 4.4, we mentioned that the performance meter has two levels of concurrency: between the event thread and the update thread, and among multiple sets of such threads. Each event-processing thread is capable of starting a new logical application and monitoring a distinct machine. The user can do so by pulling down the File cascade menu from the menu bar (Figure 4-1) and selecting the New item (not shown in Figure 4-1) in the File cascade which invokes the PopupDialogCB() callback. This callback pops up a dialog that asks the user about the name of the machine to monitor, the name of the display, and the time interval between successive RPC calls. Once the user presses the OK button on the popped up dialog box, the dialog box is dismissed, and the OkCB()> callback is invoked. This callback spawns a new thread to start a new logical application. The new logical application starts executing the function NewApp(). Of course, in NewApp(), we spawn off another thread to execute the corresponding update loop.

### 4.4.3    The Exit Callback

The user can use the Exit button in the File cascade menu to exit from each logical application. The code for the exit callback is shown in Example 4-24. After this callback returns, and the current event dispatch is complete, the associated XtAppMainLoop() exits.

**Example 4-24:** Exit Callback of Each Logical Application

```
    static void
    ExitCB(Widget w, XtPointer client_data, XtPointer call_data)
    {
            Data d = (Data)client_data;
```

**Example 4-24:** Exit Callback of Each Logical Application (continued)

```
        XtAppSetExitFlag(d->app); /* Set exit flag to True */
    }
```

This section completes our discussion of writing multithreaded applications. In this section, we have implicitly assumed that all the Motif library interfaces used by the performance meter application can be safely accessed in multiple threads, which is not the case in Release 1.2 or 2.0. This problem leads us to the question of developing a multithread safe widget set. In Section 4.5, we provide some guidelines for developing multithreaded safe widgets.

# 4.5  *Multithread Safe Widgets*

Briefly, multithread safe widgets are widgets that can be instantiated, accessed, and manipulated in a multithreaded environment. Each widget has two structures associated with it: the widget class structure and the widget instance structure. A widget class structure is accessed by all widget instances. A widget instance structure is accessed only by a specific object. With that background, we proceed to offer some guidelines for writing multithreaded safe widgets. As the reader will notice, most of these guidelines are fairly intuitive.

## 4.5.1  Avoid Global And Static Data

The first advice is to avoid defining global variables inside widget code. When such variables are unavoidable, use XtProcessLock() and XtProcessUnlock() to serialize access to such variables. Also, avoid using static variables inside functions that retain state across function calls. When such variables are unavoidable, use thread-specific data storage mechanisms to store and retrieve such thread-specific data.

Example 4-25 illustrates the thread-specific data storage mechanism in Solaris. First, we use thr_keycreate() to create a key that is used to identify thread-specific data. The key must be created atomically. Therefore, the call to thr_keycreate() is within a matching pair of mutex_lock() and mutex_unlock(). In general, the second argument to thr_keycreate() is a pointer to a memory destructor function; in our case the function is free(). For a given thread, if there is a non-NULL destructor function associated with the key, and if there is a non-NULL value associated with the key, then the destructor function is called with the current value when the thread exits. Next, we call thr_getspecific() to retrieve the current value associated with the key. If there is no current value, thr_getspecific() stores NULL in ptr. Finally, we use thr_setspecific() to store the current value with the key.

**Example 4-25:** Storing and Retrieving Thread Specific Data

```
foo_function()
{
        static mutex_t keylock;
        static thread_key_t key;
```

**Example 4-25:** Storing and Retrieving Thread Specific Data (continued)

```
            static Boolean first_time = TRUE;
            void *ptr = NULL; /* Current value */

            /* Create key atomically */
            if(first_time == TRUE) {
                    (void) mutex_lock(&keylock);
                    if(first_time == TRUE) {
                            thr_keycreate(&key, free);
                            first_time = FALSE;
                    }
                    (void)mutex_unlock(&keylock);
            }

            (void) thr_getspecific(key, ptr); /* Get current value */
            if(ptr == NULL) {
                    ptr = malloc(SIZE);
                    (void) thr_setspecific(key, ptr); /* Store current value */
            }
    }
```

## 4.5.2  Accessing Class Methods

Whenever widgets directly access any class methods, they should enclose such access between an XtProcessLock() and XtProcessUnlock(). For example, some widgets like to envelope their superclass's method (do some extra work in their method and then call their superclass's method). The recommended way to do that in a multi-thread-safe widget is shown in Example 4-26.

**Example 4-26:** Enveloping in Multithreaded Safe Widgets

```
    void Redisplay(Widget w, XEvent event, Region regio)
    {
            XtClass super_class;
            XtExposeProc         expose;

            /* do some extra work */
            XtProcessLock();
            super_class = (fooWidgetClassRec.core_class.superclass);
            expose = super_class->core_class.expose;
            XtProcessUnlock();
            (*expose)(w, event, region);
    }
```

Note, we do not enclose the invoking of the class method within XtProcessLock() and XtProcessUnlock(). We provide process locking only while accessing the class data structure.

### 4.5.3   Protecting Access To Widget Public Functions

All public interfaces defined by a widget should be enclosed within a matched pair of
`XtAppLock()` and `XtAppUnlock()`. This situation ensures mutually exclusive access to
the widget set and Xt, on a per-application-context basis. For example, a public interface function for creating a widget instance can be written as shown in Example 4-27.

**Example 4-27:** Protecting Public Interfaces

```
Widget CreateWidgetFoo(Widget parent, String name,
        ArgList args, Cardinal num_args)
{
Widget widget;
XtAppContext app = XtWidgetToApplicationContext(parent);

XtAppLock(app);
/* create the widget */
widget = XtCreateManagedWidget(name, fooWidgetClass, parent,
                        args, num_args);
XtAppUnlock(app);
return widget;
}
```

### 4.5.4   Exclusive Input Processing in Widget Code

The widget writer needs to understand the implications of event management in multiple threads (see also Section 4.3.5.) Because calls to event management functions in
multiple threads return in last-in first-out order, a widget writer can not always rely on
Xt's event management functions to do exclusive event processing. For example,
assume a widget, W, needs to implement a *drag-and-drop* protocol. Typically, a user
begins a drag operation by pointing at an object on the desktop while holding down
the drag button. The drag operation continues as the user moves the pointer across
the desktop. The drag operation concludes in a drop as the user releases the drag button over the destination. As the dragged object moves over various sites on the desktop, the drag cursor and the site below the drag cursor may animate to provide
relevant feedback to the user. During the drag-and-drop operation, the source widget
takes control of the input processing, using code similar to that shown in Example 4-28
in thread A:

**Example 4-28:** Widget Code Implementing Drag-and-Drop Input Processing

```
XEvent event;
while(/* drag and drop not over */){
        XtAppNextEvent(app, &event);
        if(/* some boolean condition involving event */){
                /* process event in the appropriate manner */
        } else
                XtDispatchEvent(&event);
}
```

Let us further assume that at some point thread A blocks in `XtAppNextEvent()`. Since, in a multithreaded Xt application, the widget code has no control over the overall order of calls into Xt's event management functions, it is possible for another thread, thread B, to call into `XtAppNextEvent()` while thread A is blocked in `XtAppNextEvent()`. When the next event arrives, thread B may steal the event from thread A. This steal may or may not be relevant to the correct functioning of the drag-and-drop code in widget W. All the same, widget W needs to be aware of this possibility.

The widget writer can avoid the above problem by using Xt's event management functions in such a way that they do not block inside Xt, as shown in Example 4-29.

**Example 4-29:** Exclusive Input Processing for Drag-and-Drop

```
XEvent event;
XtInputMask mask;
XtAppContext app = XtWidgetToApplicationContext(w);
while (/* drag and drop not over */){
        while(!(mask = XtAppPending(app)))
                ; /* busy waiting */
        if(mask & XtIMXEvent) {
                XtAppPeekEvent(app, &event);
                if(/* some boolean condition involving event */){
                        /* process event */
                        continue;
                }
        }
        XtAppProcessEvent(app, mask);
}
```

In Example 4-29, we use `XtAppPending()` to wait for input. `XtAppPending()` does not block for input inside Xt. It returns zero if no input is available, otherwise it returns a mask that has some combination of the flags for an X event, an Xt timer, or an Xt alternate input source OR'ed together to indicate the kind of source that is ready to supply input. However, because `XtAppPending()` is called inside a `while` loop, we have a situation that is commonly referred to as *busy waiting*. Busy waiting wastes CPU cycles and is not always acceptable. Therefore, the widget writer needs to weigh all the pros and cons and arrive at a decision.

In order to get around the problem described in Example 4-29, it is also possible to use Xlib event processing functions. However, use of Xlib functions has the disadvantage that all event processing is on a per-display basis. Since an application context may have multiple display connections, using Xlib functions may require some creative programming so that all display connections may have their events processed while drag-and-drop is in progress.

Note, in Example 4-28 and Example 4-29, that we do not lock the application context explicitly because the code is inside a widget. Since all entry points into a widget require an application context lock, we don't need to explicitly lock the application context inside a widget, except in a widget's public functions, as noted in Section 4.5.3.

# CHAPTER 5

# New Font Technology

*Nathan Meyers*

For years, interest in advanced font-rendering capabilities centered around the creation of an X Typographic Extension—a bundle of capabilities that would address X's many text imaging weaknesses. Among the desired capabilities: subpixel character placement, kerning, resolution-independent character metrics, anti-aliasing, render-time transformation of characters, and more. The X Typographic Extension suffered the usual fate of innovations that try to do too much: it ended up mired in a bog of conflicting requirements. Despite occasional attempts to resurrect the Extension, it is considered dead. The growing popularity of Display PostScript® for solving advanced text-imaging problems virtually seals the fate of the X Typographic Extension.

There are, however, clients whose needs fall into the void between basic text rendering and full typographic capability. The first attempt to provide advanced text capabilities through the X Logical Font Description convention (XLFD) was the Hewlett-Packard XLFD Enhancements, introduced with its X11R4 product offering. Using modifications to the XLFD name the HPXLFD Enhancements provided many capabilities: anamorphic scaling, obliquing, rotation, and mirroring. The HP XLFD Enhancements were the starting point for the discussion that ultimately led to the design of the R6 Matrix XLFD Enhancement. Interested readers are referred to a 1992 article by Deininger and Meyers[†] for more information about the HP XLFD Enhancements.

X11R5 introduced the networked font server and scalable fonts. Font technology has continued to evolve with X11R6, attempting to meet more sophisticated rendering needs, and better utilizing the distributed architecture of the X font server/client relationship.

---

**Nathan Meyers** (*nathanm@cv.hp.com*) is a Member of Technical Staff at Hewlett-Packard Company, and lead engineer for HP's X Font Technology. He authored the sample implementation of the enhancements described in this article.
† Axel Deininger and Nathan Meyers, "Using the New Font Capabilities of HP-Donated Font Server Enhancements," *The X Resource*, Issue 3, Summer 1992, pp. 97-119.

This chapter discusses four major changes introduced with X11R6:

- **Matrix XLFD Enhancement**: Through enhancements to the existing font naming mechanism, you can now specify transformations of existing bitmapped and scalable fonts. Using the powerful expressive capabilities of affine† transformation matrices, applications can create simple variations on fonts (wide, narrow, obliqued) or generate special effects (rotation and mirroring) for specific text rendering needs. A related feature, charset subsetting, allows a client to request loading of only the characters needed instead of a whole font.

- **Glyph Caching**: Glyph caching — deferred loading of character glyphs—allows X to reduce memory and computation requirements associated with generation of fonts. By deferring creation of characters that might not be needed, glyph caching can achieve significant savings, particularly for large, sparsely-used Asian fonts. X11R6 implements glyph caching in the X server's interface to the font server, reducing the X server's font memory requirements and enabling glyph caching to be implemented in individual font rasterizers. Glyph caching is not implemented in the sample implementation font rasterizers.

- **Authorization Protocol**: X11R6 contains a sample authorization protocol that can be used for access to fonts from a networked font server. The protocol allows a font server to identify the end consumer of a font and can serve as an enabling technology for font licensing.

- **Scalable Aliases**: Capabilities of font name aliases have been increased. Aliases can now be defined for scalable font names, and the aliasing mechanism can be used in conjunction with the Matrix XLFD Enhancement to create font variations.

## 5.1    The Matrix XLFD Enhancement

New semantics for the pointsize and pixelsize fields in the XLFD name allow the specification of a matrix instead of a scalar in either or both of these fields. As described in the original proposal:

> An XLFD name presented to the server can have the POINT_SIZE or PIXEL_SIZE field begin with the character "[". If the first character of the field is "[", the character must be followed with ASCII representations of four floating-point numbers and a trailing "]", with white space separating the numbers and optional white space separating the numbers from the "[" and "]" characters. Numbers use standard floating-point syntax but use the character "~"(tilde) to represent a minus sign in the mantissa or exponent. Numbers can optionally use the character "+" to represent the plus sign in the mantissa or exponent.

---

† An "affine" transformation is one in which finite quantities remain finite (and infinite quantities remain infinite).

The string *[a b c d]* represents a graphical transformation of the glyphs in the font by the matrix

$$\begin{bmatrix} a & b & 0 \\ c & d & 0 \\ 0 & 0 & 1 \end{bmatrix}.$$

All transformations occur around the origin of the glyph (the lower left corner). The relationship between the current scalar values and the matrix transformation values is that the scalar value N in the POINT_SIZE field produces the same glyphs as the matrix *[N/10 0 0 N/10]* in that field, and the scalar value N in the PIXEL_SIZE field produces the same glyphs as the matrix *[N\*RESOLUTION_X/RESOLUTION_Y 0 0 N]* in that field.

If matrices are specified for both the POINT_SIZE and PIXEL_SIZE, they must bear the following relationship to each other within an implementation-specific tolerance:

PIXEL_SIZE_MATRIX = POINT_SIZE_MATRIX • [S$x$ 0 0 S$y$]

where

S$x$ = RESOLUTION_X / 72.27
S$y$ = RESOLUTION_Y / 72.27

If either the POINT_SIZE or PIXEL_SIZE field is unspecified (either "0" or wild-carded), the preceding formulas can be used to compute one from the other.[†]

A typical 12-point font name, specified with a transformation matrix, would look like this:

```
-adobe-utopia-medium-r-normal--0-[12 0 0 12]-100-100-p-0-iso8859-1
```

The numbers in the matrix are floating-point, and the value of the *FONT* property returned with a font contains matrices in both the POINT_SIZE and PIXEL_SIZE fields, consistent with each other and with the resolution fields as described above.

The following subsections discuss how the transformation matrix can be used to achieve font variations and effects.

## 5.1.1 Obtaining Simple Font Variations Through the Transformation Matrix

While some capabilities, such as font rotation, require advanced functionality in an X client to be useful, the Matrix XLFD Enhancement offers one capability of immediate use: the ability to generate font variations. Two transformations in particular—scaling and horizontal shearing—can generate useful variations on existing fonts.

---

† Paul Asente, "A Matrix Transformation XLFD Extension" (X Consortium Fontwork mailing list)

New Font Technology

### 5.1.1.1    Anamorphic Scaling

The ability to separately specify the X and Y components of the scaling matrix allows for separate specification of a font's pointsize (vertical size) and setsize (horizontal size). By definition, a normally proportioned font is one whose setsize equals its pointsize. Figure 5-1 shows the variations possible with anamorphic scaling.

-adobe-utopia-medium-r-normal—0-[6 0 0 8]-200-200-p-0-iso8859-1

-adobe-utopia-medium-r-normal--0-[8 0 0 8]-200-200-p-0-iso8859-1

-adobe–utopia–medium–r–normal--0-[12 0 0 8]–200–200–p–0–iso8859–1

**Figure 5-1:**    Three variations on the same scalable font: pointsize=8, setsize=6, 8, and 12

### 5.1.1.2    Horizontal Shearing

Horizontal shearing, or obliquing, generates slanted versions of existing fonts. The transformation for horizontal shearing is:

$$\begin{bmatrix} 1 & 0 \\ -\tan(\phi) & 1 \end{bmatrix},$$

where $\varphi$ is the slant angle counterclockwise from vertical. Figure 5-2 illustrates the effects of multiplying a 10-point scaling matrix by various horizontal shearing matrices:

$$\begin{bmatrix} 10 & 0 \\ 0 & 10 \end{bmatrix} \bullet \begin{bmatrix} 1 & 0 \\ -\tan(\phi) & 1 \end{bmatrix}.$$

-adobe–utopia–medium–r–normal--0-[10 0 3.64 10]–200–200–p–0–iso8859–1

-adobe–utopia–medium–r–normal--0-[10 0 ~2.68 10]–200–200–p–0–iso8859–1

**Figure 5-2:**    A 10-point font obliqued by -20 and +15 degrees CCW

## 5.1.2    Obtaining Special Effects Through the Transformation Matrix

Affine transformation matrices allow considerable power in specifying font transformations. Figure 5-3 illustrates the use of the variations discussed above, plus rotation and mirroring (all obtained from the same Adobe Utopia scalable font).

**Figure 5-3:** Some of the effects achievable with affine transformation matrices.

The transformations that are required to achieve rotation and mirroring are shown in Figure 5-4.

| Horizontal Mirroring | Vertical Mirroring | Rotation |
|:---:|:---:|:---:|
| $\begin{bmatrix} -1 & 0 \\ 0 & 1 \end{bmatrix}$ | $\begin{bmatrix} 1 & 0 \\ 0 & -1 \end{bmatrix}$ | $\begin{bmatrix} \cos(\theta) & \sin(\theta) \\ -\sin(\theta) & \cos(\theta) \end{bmatrix}$ |

**Figure 5-4:** Matrix transformations for mirroring and rotation; $\theta$ represents CCW rotation

While generating rotated and mirrored fonts is straightforward, using them is more challenging: a mirrored or rotated font cannot simply be dropped into an existing application and expected to generate useful output. Because X provides no functionality for drawing rotated text, the client is responsible for placement of each individual character when rendering text on a non-horizontal baseline. The remainder of this section discusses how clients must combine the transformation matrix, *a priori* knowledge of the intent of the transformation, and information returned in the font structures to properly place text.

### 5.1.2.1    Intent of the Transformation

While a transformation matrix describes the mathematical manipulations to be performed on a font, it conveys no information about where text is to be rendered. For example, the matrix

$$\begin{bmatrix} 10 & 4 \\ 0 & 10 \end{bmatrix}$$

might be describing a 10-point font with 21.8(degree) of vertical shearing, or it might describe an anamorphically scaled 10-point font with -21.8(degree) of horizontal shearing that has been rotated 21.8(degree). Indeed, any transformation matrix can represent an infinite number of histories. Figure 5-5 shows these two possible placements of a font generated with the above transformation matrix placement:

- as a vertically sheared unrotated font and placement
- as a horizontally sheared rotated font

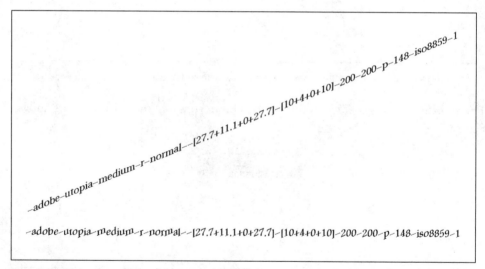

**Figure 5-5:**    Two placements of the same font with the same [10 4 0 10] transformation matrix

So the client must place the characters based on its knowledge of the intent with which the transformation was generated. It is thus not possible to prescribe a canonical method for rendering non-horizontal text.

However, a simplification is possible—a usage model that will allow us to prescribe methods for rendering rotated text. Many applications needing rotated text are not typographically demanding or interested in unusual effects; they simply need to write normal text at an angle: for example, to label non-horizontal axes of a plot. For these applications, the process of building a font matrix can be modeled as the sequence: scale, oblique, rotate. That is, the transformation matrix is generated by applying those transformations in the order:

$$\begin{bmatrix} setsize & 0 \\ 0 & pointsize \end{bmatrix} \bullet \begin{bmatrix} 1 & 0 \\ -\tan(\emptyset) & 1 \end{bmatrix} \bullet \begin{bmatrix} \cos(\emptyset) & \sin(\emptyset) \\ -\sin(\emptyset) & \cos(\emptyset) \end{bmatrix}.$$

For applications following this model, we can unambiguously determine the rotation angle and other relevant parameters entirely from the matrix (Figure 5-5, above, was rendered by interpreting the matrix according to the model). The sections below describe how to render text on a non-horizontal baseline using information from a transformation matrix generated under the model.

### 5.1.2.2    Font and Character Metrics for Transformed Fonts

The fundamental problem to be solved when rendering a line of text is that of applying the *escapement*—the spacing that separates one character from the next. Escapement is a vector: the character origin can move in both the horizontal and vertical direction after each character is drawn. The X protocol was designed to handle only horizontal rendering, and so treats the escapement as a scalar to be applied in the horizontal direction (the XCharStruct *width* field). There is no room provided in the protocol to return a two-component escapement vector.

The Matrix XLFD Enhancement solves this problem in an elegant way, by using a previously unused field in the per-character XCharStruct metrics. The *attributes* field, whose purpose had never before been defined, now contains the character escapement that would have resulted had the font been scaled by a *pixelsize* matrix of *[1000 0 0 1000]*. This *1000-pixel escapement*, in conjunction with information in the pixelsize transformation matrix, provides enough resolution for very accurate placement of glyphs—with no change to the protocol. Using the pixelsize matrix, the escapement vector for any given character in X's coordinate system can be computed as

$$\begin{bmatrix} \dfrac{1000\text{-pixel escapement}}{1000} & 0 \end{bmatrix} \bullet \begin{bmatrix} pixelsize\ matrix \end{bmatrix} \bullet \begin{bmatrix} 1 & 0 \\ 0 & -1 \end{bmatrix}.$$

For example, if the client opens the font

```
-adobe-utopia-medium-r-normal--0-[8+4~4+8]-110-110-p-0-iso8859-1
```

it can examine the resulting FONT property:

```
-adobe-utopia-medium-r-normal--[12.2+6.09~6.09+12.2]-[8+4~4+8]-110-110-p-
    64-iso8859-1
```

and parse out the pixelsize matrix for use in the escapement computations. If the *attributes* field for the letter "A" reports a value of 635, the escapement vector for "A" in X's coordinate system is

$$\begin{bmatrix} \dfrac{635}{1000} & 0 \end{bmatrix} \cdot \begin{bmatrix} 12.2 & 6.09 \\ -6.09 & 12.2 \end{bmatrix} \cdot \begin{bmatrix} 1 & 0 \\ 0 & -1 \end{bmatrix} = \begin{bmatrix} 7.75 & -3.87 \end{bmatrix}$$

Figure 5-6, later in this chapter, contains a code fragment illustrating rendering of a line of non-horizontal text, one character at a time, using the above computation.

Having discussed the XCharStruct *attributes* field, we briefly examine how the existing XCharStruct fields and the other components of the XFontStruct are affected by the Matrix XLFD Enhancement.

XCharStruct *ascent, descent, lbearing,* and *rbearing*

> These fields describe the pixel extent of each glyph horizontally and vertically relative to the origin. They do not—cannot—apply in a transformed coordinate space; doing so would render them useless to the X server's glyph rendering logic.

XCharStruct *width*

> This field contains the horizontal component of the escapement: the rounded X value from the escapement computation (above). For fonts with no rotation component, this value corresponds to the existing *width* definition, so existing text rendering calls will function correctly for mirrored or obliqued fonts (horizontally mirrored fonts are, as expected, rendered in the reverse direction from normal). For fonts with a rotation component, the *width* values do not contain enough information for character placement, and the *attributes* values must be used.

XFontStruct *ascent* and *descent*

> These fields contain the vertical component, after transformation by the matrix, of the font overall ascent and descent. For fonts with no rotation or vertical mirroring, these correspond to the existing definitions. These metrics are useful for any mirrored or obliqued font, but inadequate for fonts with a rotation component. For rotated fonts, meaningful values must be computed from the *RAW_ASCENT* and *RAW_DESCENT* properties (see Section 5.1.2.3).

### 5.1.2.3   Font Properties for Transformed Fonts

The Matrix XLFD Enhancement modifies the definitions of properties as follows:

> All font properties that represent horizontal widths or displacements have as their value the horizontal X component of the transformed width or displacement. All font properties that represent vertical heights or displacements have as their value the Y component of the transformed height or displacement. Each such property will be

accompanied by a new Z property, named as the original except prefixed with *RAW_*, that gives the value of the width, height, or displacement in 1000 pixel metrics.[†]

In other words, for a font with the pointsize [pixelsize] transformation matrix,

$$\begin{bmatrix} a & b \\ c & d \end{bmatrix},$$

the vertical properties (POINT_SIZE, CAP_HEIGHT, etc.) will have the same values as those for a normal (i.e., without a transformation matrix specified) $d$-point[pixel] font, and the horizontal properties (NORM_SPACE, AVERAGE_WIDTH, etc.) will have the same values as those for a normal $a$-point[pixel] font. If $a$ or $d$ is negative, the corresponding properties have negative values.[‡]

For normal fonts, these new definitions of the existing properties match existing definitions. And they continue to be useful for fonts with obliquing and mirroring. But they are generally not useful for fonts with a rotation component ($b \neq 0$, in our usage model). More information is needed for this case, which is provided by the *RAW_* properties.

The Matrix XLFD Enhancement defines new properties, corresponding to all existing numeric vertical and horizontal properties, but prefixed with "RAW_." These properties describe the metrics for an untransformed 1000-pixel version (*[1000 0 0 1000]*) of the font, for example: RAW_PIXEL_SIZE, RAW_UNDERLINE_POSITION, RAW_MAX_SPACE, etc. These 1000-pixel metrics, like the *attributes* fields discussed above, provide high-resolution values that can be scaled for use with transformed fonts.

Two additional properties are defined: RAW_ASCENT and RAW_DESCENT. These properties provide the 1000-pixel versions of the overall font ascent and descent values, corresponding to *ascent* and *descent* from the XFontStruct.

## 5.1.2.4    *Applying Font Properties to Transformed Fonts*

For fonts with a rotation component, the RAW_ properties provide the information needed to apply the corresponding metrics to the transformed text. For properties representing horizontal displacements or offsets RAW_MIN_SPACE, RAW_QUAD_WIDTH, etc.), the transformation is the same as that used for the escapements (above):

---

† Paul Asente, "A Matrix Transformation XLFD Extension" (X Consortium Fontwork mailing list).
‡ To support the possibility of negative values, all numeric horizontal and vertical properties are now INT32's. Clients using normal fonts will not suddenly see negative POINT_SIZE properties or other such surprises, but the change allows any property to assume a negative value if the corresponding component of the transformation matrix is negative.

$$\left[ \begin{array}{cc} \dfrac{RAW\ PROPERTY}{1000} & 0 \end{array} \right] \bullet \left[ \begin{array}{c} pixelsize\ matrix \end{array} \right] \bullet \left[ \begin{array}{cc} 1 & 0 \\ 0 & \text{-}1 \end{array} \right].$$

The result, as with the escapement computation, is a vector in X's coordinate system that applies in the direction of writing.

The transformation of properties representing vertical displacements or offsets (RAW_ASCENT, *RAW_DESCENT*, etc.) is somewhat trickier: the matrix must be modified to remove any obliquing component (as understood in the context of our usage model) that would skew the resulting vectors. Describing the pixelsize matrix as

$$P = \left[ \begin{array}{cc} a & b \\ c & d \end{array} \right],$$

define a new matrix

$$P' = \left[ \begin{array}{cc} a & b \\ \dfrac{b^2 c - abd}{a^2 + b^2} & \dfrac{a^2 d - abc}{a^2 + b^2} \end{array} \right].$$

P is, in the context of our usage model, the pixelsize matrix with the obliquing component removed, now ready for use with the raw font properties. To transform the raw font properties representing vertical offsets or displacements, apply the new matrix thus:

$$\left[ \begin{array}{cc} 0 & \dfrac{RAW\ PROPERTY}{1000} \end{array} \right] \bullet P' \bullet \left[ \begin{array}{cc} \text{-}1 & 0 \\ 0 & 1 \end{array} \right].$$

The result is a vector, in X's coordinate system, perpendicular to the direction of writing. This vector is used analogously to the core X properties: added to the current position if the corresponding property is normally added (e.g., *UNDERLINE_POSITION*), subtracted from the current position if the corresponding property is normally subtracted (e.g., *STRIKEOUT_ASCENT*). Use of this transformation is illustrated in Example 5-1, which shows a code fragment illustrating the use of the 1000-pixel metrics with the pixelsize transformation matrix for placement of non-horizontal text. The attributes field is used with the pixelsize matrix for escapement computations, and the value of the RAW_UNDERLINE_POSITION property is used with the P¢ matrix to place an underline.

**Example 5-1:** Placing non-horizontal text

```
char *stringptr;              /* Null-terminated string to write */
int xorigin, yorigin;         /* Location of string origin */
double pixmatrix[4];          /* The pixel matrix, parsed from font name */
XFontStruct *fontinfo;        /* The fontstruct for this font */
int raw_underline_position;   /* Offset from baseline of 1000-pixel font to
                                 underline; from RAW_UNDERLINE_POSITION
                                 property or otherwise computed */
double offset, underline_offset_x, underline_offset_y;      /* stuff */

  /* Output the text */

#define IROUND(x) (int)((x) > 0 ? (x) + .5 : (x) - .5)

  offset = 0.0;
  while (*stringptr)
  {
    /* Computation of charno and char_metric_offset specific to 8-bit
       text. */
    int charno = *(unsigned char *)stringptr;
    int char_metric_offset = charno - fontinfo->min_char_or_byte2;

    XDrawString(display, drawable, gc,
                IROUND((double)xorigin + offset * pixmatrix[0] / 1000.0),
                IROUND((double)yorigin - offset * pixmatrix[1] / 1000.0),
                stringptr, 1);
    stringptr++;

    offset += (double)(fontinfo->per_char ?
                       fontinfo->per_char[char_metric_offset].attributes :
                       fontinfo->min_bounds.attributes);
  }

  /* Output an underline */

#define A (pixmatrix[0])
#define B (pixmatrix[1])
#define C (pixmatrix[2])
#define D (pixmatrix[3])

  underline_offset_x = -(double)raw_underline_position *
                       (B*B*C - A*B*D)/(A*A + B*B);

  underline_offset_y = (double)raw_underline_position *
                       (A*A*D - A*B*C)/(A*A + B*B);

  XDrawLine(display, drawable, gc,
            IROUND((double)xorigin + underline_offset_x / 1000.0),
            IROUND((double)yorigin + underline_offset_y / 1000.0),
            IROUND((double)xorigin +
                   (underline_offset_x + offset * pixmatrix[0]) / 1000.0),
            IROUND((double)yorigin +
                   (underline_offset_y - offset * pixmatrix[1]) / 1000.0));
```

New Font
Technology

### 5.1.2.5    What Values and Properties Can Clients Expect?

Given the possibility that a client may encounter font sources that support the Matrix XLFD Enhancement and some that do not, it counts on the following to be true only if a font is successfully opened with a matrix in the pointsize and/or pixelsize field:

- The XCharStruct fields *width* and *attributes* are defined according to their new definitions (as described above).

- The XFontStruct fields *ascent* and *descent* are defined according to their new definitions (as described above).

- The *RAW_ASCENT* and *RAW_DESCENT* properties are provided.

- For every numeric property provided representing an X or Y displacement or offset (such as *POINT_SIZE, UNDERLINE_POSITION*, etc.), a corresponding *RAW_* property is provided.

Conversely, if a font is opened without a matrix in the pointsize or pixelsize fields, there is no guarantee that the above will be true: clients cannot rely on finding useful *attributes* fields or RAW_ properties in a font opened with scalar values in the pointsize and pixelsize fields.

There is an unfortunate exception to the above guarantees: pre-R6 font servers zeroed out the *attributes* fields. If a font is obtained through a chained pre-R6 font server, the *attributes* fields are lost.

### 5.1.2.6    Support Utilities

As of this writing, there is an unfilled need for client-side support utilities to enable easy use of the XLFD transformation matrix. Among the requirements:

- Assembling an XLFD name from a raw name and a transformation matrix

- Parsing a matrix out of an XLFD name

- Generation of matrices for common transformations

- DrawString and DrawImageString implementations for 8-bit and 16-bit fonts and for font sets

## 5.1.3    Charset Subsetting

The Matrix XLFD Enhancement has a weakness: it must be applied when a font is opened; it cannot be applied at render time. When clients generate special effects that require a different transformation for virtually every character (such as in Figure 5-3), must be opened a different font for every character.

Opening dozens of fonts is slow and particularly burdensome when very few of the characters being generated are needed. While glyph caching (discussed later in this chapter) offers the eventual hope that X and font servers will not waste time building unneeded characters, that hope is still distant and unlikely to be fully realized.

So X11R6 includes another capability in support of the Matrix XLFD Enhancement: the ability to hint—through the font name—which characters are of interest. The charset subset specification, appended at the end of the XLFD name, is of the form:

```
[value value_value]
```

A value is a hex, a decimal, or decimal number; two values separated by a "_" specify a range. Values and ranges are separated by spaces. So, for example, the name

```
-adobe-utopia-medium-r-normal--0-120-0-0-p-0-iso8859-1[65_67 0xe0_255 32]
```

indicates that the client is interested in the characters 65-67, 224-255, and 32. The font source can use this hint to save computation by generating a font containing only these characters (or any superset of these characters).

In Release 6, charset subsetting is supported by the Speedo and Type1 rasterizers, and by the bitmap scaler. That means that if you ask for a font that comes from a bitmap, charset subsetting is observed if the bitmap is scaled by the bitmap scaling engine, but ignored if the font is used verbatim from the bitmap file.

## 5.1.4    Advertising of Capabilities

To use the Matrix XLFD Enhancement on a font, a client must be able to determine which fonts can support it. This need to query capability is now supported by ListFonts: if a capability is included in the name specification passed to ListFonts, only fonts whose rasterizers support that capability will be returned. For example, passing the name:

```
-*-*-*-*-*-*-*-[1 0 0 1]-*-*-*-*-*-*
```

to ListFonts (the particular choice of numbers in the matrix is immaterial) returns all font names that can support the Matrix XLFD Enhancement.

Support for charset subsetting is similarly advertised through ListFonts; including a charset subset specification in the name returns only font names that support charset subsetting.

# 5.2    Scalable Aliases

The font name aliasing mechanism has been enhanced to support scalable names. If an alias in fonts.alias consists of a scalable font name in both the alias and real names, then the alias applies to all sizes of the font, and enhancements specified in the alias name are applied to the real name.

For example, an alias entry of:

```
-foo-bar-medium-r-normal--0-0-0-0-c-0-iso8859-1 \
-misc-fixed-medium-r-normal--0-0-0-0-c-0-iso8859-1
```

New Font
Technology

maps any request for the "*-foo-bar...*" font to an equivalent request for the "*-misc-fixed...*" font. An attempt to open font

```
-foo-bar-medium-r-normal--0-[24 0 0 12]-110-110-c-0-iso8859-1[65_67]
```

results in opening

```
-misc-fixed-medium-r-normal--0-[24 0 0 12]-110-110-c-0-iso8859-1[65_67] .
```

### 5.2.1    Scalable Aliases and the Matrix XLFD Enhancement

Scalable alias entries can incorporate matrices to generate font variations. A matrix specified in either the pixelsize or pointsize (but not both) field of the destination name is multiplied by the source pointsize and pixelsize matrices when generating the destination. Multiplication order is: [*destination matrix*] = [*alias matrix*] • [*source matrix*].

For example, an alias entry of:

```
-misc-fixed-medium-o-normal--0-0-0-0-c-0-iso8859-1 \
"-misc-fixed-medium-r-normal--0-[1 0 .3 1]-0-0-c-0-iso8859-1"
```

defines an obliqued version of the font; requesting

```
-misc-fixed-medium-o-normal--0-120-110-110-c-0-iso8859-1
```

(or its XLFD matrix equivalent) results in opening the obliqued font:

```
-misc-fixed-medium-r-normal--0-[12 0 3.6 12]-110-110-c-0-iso8859-1 .
```

Similar entries could be devised to achieve wide, narrow, and other variations:

```
-misc-fixed-medium-r-wide--0-0-0-0-c-0-iso8859-1 \
"-misc-fixed-medium-r-normal--0-[1.5 0 0 1]-0-0-c-0-iso8859-1"
-misc-fixed-medium-r-narrow--0-0-0-0-c-0-iso8859-1 \
"-misc-fixed-medium-r-normal--0-[.75 0 0 1]-0-0-c-0-iso8859-1" .
```

## 5.3    Glyph Caching

In the X11R5 sample implementation, obtaining a font from a font server causes a sequence of transactions between the X client, the X server, the font server, and the rasterizers within the font server, as shown in Figure 5-6.

What is wrong with this picture? Before the client has issued a single text-rendering request using this font, two complete copies of the font and its glyphs already exist: in the font server and in the X server. The rasterizer consumed the cycles to build the glyphs and the memory to store them, and the X server took the network bandwidth and memory to obtain and store its own complete copy of the font.

Ideally, this should not happen. In the interest of memory usage and performance, only glyphs that are needed should be built. This is critical for Asian fonts: ideographic fonts such as Japanese Kanji have thousands of glyphs, but are very sparsely used.

*Glyph caching* is a term for the practice of managing memory caches containing glyphs that have been selectively realized. One aspect of glyph caching, *deferred loading*, has been implemented in *libfont*'s interface to the font server.

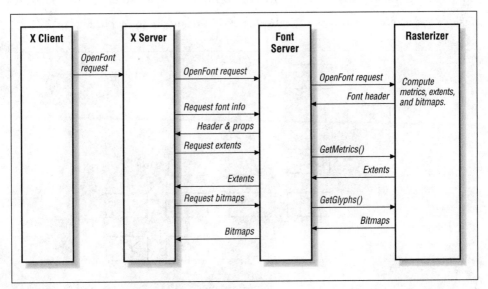

**Figure 5-6:** Transactions between the various font system components when a font is opened

When deferred loading is enabled, the last transaction shown in Figure 5-6—obtaining the bitmaps—is deferred. Instead, bitmaps are obtained a few at a time as they are referenced in text rendering requests. All other transactions still occur at font-open time; deferring them would be pointless, since virtually all X clients request the font header, properties, and extents immediately after opening a font.

## 5.3.1   Turning on Glyph Caching

Default behavior of the X and font servers is not to perform deferred loading. Deferred loading can be enabled in the X server with the command-line option:

```
-deferglyphs 16
```

Specifying "16" causes the X server to defer loading for 16-bit fonts; "all" defers loading for all fonts; "none" means no deferred loading.

Deferred loading is controlled in the font server through its *config file*. The command:

```
deferglyphs=16
```

functions similarly to the X server's *-deferglyphs* option. The option affects the font server's behavior when it obtains fonts from an upstream font server.

New Font
Technology

## 5.4    Sample Authorization Protocol

X11R6 includes a sample font authorization protocol: *hp-hostname-1*, a non-authenticating protocol used to identify the hostname of the end consumer of a font.

Consider the arbitrary network of X display and font servers shown in Figure 5-7.

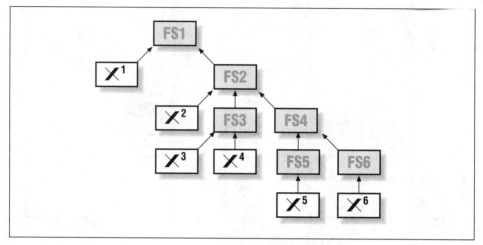

**Figure 5-7:**   A network of X display and font servers; arrows indicate client → server relationship

The font server FS1 in Figure 5-7 can receive requests from six X servers, passing through as many as three chained font servers. For OpenFont, `ListFonts`, and `List-FontsWithInfo` requests from any X server, the *hp-hostname-1* protocol (see Table 5-1) identifies which X server has issued the request.

**Table 5-1:** Semantics of the hp-hostname-1 Authorization Protocol

| Name | "hp-hostname-1" (null-terminated) |
| --- | --- |
| X Server Semantics | data = full TCP hostname (null-terminated) |
| Font Server Semantics | data = data field of client on whose behalf request is issued |
| Challenges | none expected or handled |

When, for example, server X5 issues an OpenFont request, it sends an authorization protocol packet with the name field "hp-hostname-1" and the data field containing its TCP hostname. All chained font servers—FS5, FS4, and FS2—pass this information upstream, allowing FS1 to ascertain the hostname of the X server requesting the font by examining the client structure. This information can be used by the font server to implement host-based font licensing.

For X servers or font servers not supporting the protocol, upstream font servers see either an empty data string or no authorization protocol in the client structure. For

*5. New Font Technology*

example, if FS3 does not support *hp-hostname-1*, FS1 and FS2 see no *hp-hostname-1* data for requests from X3 or X4.

The protocol is non-authenticating, and therefore not secure. For licensing applications for which this is unsatisfactory, the sample implementation of the *hp-hostname-1* protocol can serve as a template for a more robust mechanism.

### 5.4.1    Related Work

Some related work was carried out in the X11R6 font server code.

A related protocol, *hp-printername-1*, is supported by the sample font server to enable licensing for printers. As with *hp-hostname-1*, the font server logic passes *hp-printername-1* data to upstream font servers. The contents of the data field have not yet been defined.

Implementation of *hp-hostname-1* was accompanied by some fixes and enhancements to the font-caching logic. If a font obtained from a rasterizer or an upstream font server is cachable, any font server or X server willingly shares that font with other clients. If the font is not cachable, a request to open the font is always referred back to the font source.

Referring to Figure 5-7, if a font obtained by X5 from FS1 is not cachable, and X6 requests the same font, FS4, FS2, and FS1 will not automatically share the font. FS1 will receive the request and pass it to the rasterizer that created the font. That rasterizer, after exercising its licensing logic, must provide the font.

## 5.5    Conclusion

X11 font technology is still very much in evolution. This chapter has described the four major font technology enhancements offered in X11R6: the Matrix XLFD Enhancement, smarter glyph caching, font authorization, and scalable aliases.

## 5.6    Acknowledgments

The design of the Matrix XLFD Enhancement is due primarily to Paul Asente (Adobe Systems Inc.) Paul's design evolved through lively discussion in the fontwork mailing list with other fanatically interested parties, including Jim Graham (Sun Microsystems), Axel Deininger (Hewlett-Packard Company), Bob Scheifler, Stephen Gildea, and Dave Wiggins (all of the X Consortium staff), and the author.

Glyph caching was designed to meet the performance needs of Hewlett-Packard's Japanese System Environment, where it received extensive exposure and testing thanks to the efforts of Takumi Ohtani, Hiroyuki Date, Daisaburo Muraoka, and Hideyuki Hayashi.

**New Font Technology**

Scalable aliases were developed independently by Hewlett-Packard Company and Sun Microsystems. The idea of adding matrix transformation capabilities to scalable aliases came from Jim Graham of Sun Microsystems.

CHAPTER **6**

# Internationalization

*Hideki Hiura*

Internationalization (abbreviated i18n, since there are 18 letters between the 'i' and 'n') of the X Window System, which was originally introduced in Release 5, has been significantly improved in X11R6. The X11R6 i18n architecture is based on the locale model used in ANSI C and POSIX (like X11R5), with most of the i18n capability provided by Xlib. X11R5 introduced a fundamental framework for internationalized input and output. It enables basic localization for left-to-right, non-context sensitive, 8-bit or multi-byte codeset languages and cultural conventions. Release 5 did not deal with all possible languages and cultural conventions, and Release 6 doesn't either. However, Release 6 does contain substantial new Xlib interfaces to support i18n enhancements, enabling additional language support and more practical localization.

The additional support is mainly in the area of text display. In order to support multibyte encodings, the concept of a FontSet was introduced in X11R5. In Release 6, Xlib enhances this concept to a more generalized notion of output methods (abbreviated XOM) and output contexts (abbreviated XOC). Just as input methods and input contexts support complex text input, output methods and output contexts support complex and more intelligent text display, dealing not only with multiple fonts but also with context dependencies. The result is a general framework to enable bi-directional, context-sensitive text display.

The substantial feedback from people who worked on localization of X11R5 implementations is incorporated into Release 6, in order to support the practical localization of the languages and cultural conventions which were already enabled by X11R5. The enhancements in this area are mainly in the area of input methods. Key features in this category are non-XEvent based input (or text retrieval) for re-conversion and context sensitive composition called String Conversion, several interfaces to improve efficiency, a facility for temporal escape and return from pre-editing, and the enhanced input

---

**Hideki Hiura** is a software engineer at Sun Microsystems and was involved in designing and developing the internationalization features of Release 6.

method server error and restart handling called *IMInstantiateCallback* and *DestroyCall-back*. By using *IMInstantiateCallback* with the *DestroyCallback* facility, a client can continue communicating with an input method server even if the user changes input method servers while a client is running. In other words, just as a user can change window managers without impacting clients, a user can now change input method servers on the fly.

The Xt interfaces have not changed to support i18n. Xt itself does not need to utilize output methods and contexts; the Xlib i18n functionality which is newly introduced in X11R6, because Xt does not draw text Release 6 Xaw (and recent versions of motif) do use the new Release 6 Xlib interfaces..

X11R5, as shipped from the X Consortium, contains two separate, mutually exclusive implementations of the input method i18n facilities. Each implementation defines its own protocol for communication between Xlib and input methods (which are implemented as separate processes). These two implementations are called "Ximp" and "Xsi." Ximp comes with six contributed input method servers; Xsi comes with one. The input method protocols used by Ximp and by Xsi input method servers are not compatible. Xlib built for Xsi cannot connect to Ximp input method servers, and vice versa.

X11R6 provides a single implementation of input method i18n facilities and a single X Consortium standard XIM protocol. However, the new XIM protocol is not compatible with either X11R5 XIM protocol.

In order to maintain backward compatibility and to make transition easier, you may configure Xlib to include the X11R5 Ximp XIM protocol facility.

This chapter assumes you have a basic knowledge of Release 5 i18n. If you don't, we suggest you read one of the chapters on i18n in *Xlib Programming Manual*, or the *Programmer's Supplement for Release 5*, both published by O'Reilly & Associates, Inc.

## 6.1    *Setting Up an i18n Programming Environment*

X11R6 consists of multiple components for i18n and localization support. Since some of them are interdependent, you may need to set up an i18n programming and execution environment first, before you can build and run internationalized programs.

The fundamental requirement for i18n programming and execution environment is the ANSI-C i18n features, and the localization features of the target locale on the system. Many systems support ANSI-C i18n, but often do not ship the localization modules, such as database files, locale definition files, and locale-specific dynamically loadable modules, as part of the base system. The localization modules are usually shipped as separate packages.

If your system does not have those localization modules, and even if your system does not support ANSI-C i18n, you may still be able to utilize the X11R6 i18n features with alternatives provided by Xlib.

i18n consists of multiple components; however, not all of them are provided as a part of the core distribution of X11R6. To build a complete i18n environment, it is mandatory to deal with many pieces of contributed (not X Consortium-supported) software. Because of the nature of the contributed software, it will often be difficult to build, install, and set up. This section covers the whole i18n environment, including the contributed software.

The section below describes building language engines and input method servers, and it discusses the limits of the local (Xlib) input method.

## 6.1.1    Building Language Engines

Some of the Input Method Servers that perform complex input pre-editing will connect to a third process that performs the language-specific composition, dictionary lookup, and conversion. The X11R6 distribution includes two language engines for Japanese. One is the *Canna32* system from NEC, and the other is the *sj3* system from SONY. Lately, the Canna system is the more trendy language engine. It has been actively maintained, tuned, and tested on many platforms. The *sj3* system is famous for its high conversion hit-rate and compactness. It is a matter of taste whether to chose Canna or *sj3*.

You need to build one or more language engines before you can build an input method server.

### 6.1.1.1    Building the Canna32 Language Engine

Canna is a Japanese language engine using a client-server architecture for kana-to-kanji (i.e., phonetic character to ideographic character) conversion.

To build the Canna32 language engine, go to the *contrib/programs/Canna32* directory, and edit the configuration file *Canna.conf* for your system configuration. (The instructions in this file are written in Japanese as C comments. For English instructions, refer to section 1.1 of the file *INSTALL*.) On most platforms, you should be able to build Canna as follows:

```
% xmkmf
% make Makefile
% make canna
% su
# make install
# make install.man
```

For a detailed explanation of the build procedures, please refer to the file *INSTALL*.

### 6.1.1.2 Building the sj3 Language Engine

*sj3* is another Japanese language engine using a client-server architecture for kana-to-kanji (i.e., phonetic character to ideographic character) conversion.

To build and install the *sj3* language engine, go to the *contrib/programs/sj3* directory and enter the following commands.

```
% xmkmf
% make Makefiles
% su
# make install
# make install.man
```

## 6.1.2 Building Input Method Servers

An internationalized X application gets user text input by communicating with an input method. At application startup, an application is localized by opening the particular input method appropriate for the locale. The input method can be either a local input method, which is implemented directly in Xlib, or a remote input method, which is implemented as a separate process known as the "input method (IM) server." In languages that require complex input pre-editing, opening an input method often causes Xlib to establish a connection to the IM Server. The IM server can provide input method service to multiple X clients that use the same locale. Sometimes an IM server will connect to a third process known as a "language engine," which typically performs dictionary lookup and translation from pre-edit text (which is often phonetic) to composed text (which is often ideographic).

The X11R5 distribution included seven IM servers, but not all of them are available in X11R6. The X11R6 distribution includes three IM Servers which are basically ported from X11R5 and enhanced for X11R6. The X11R6 distribution includes one IM server developer's kit, which is the C language binding of the XIM protocol for developing input method servers; similarily, Xlib provides a C language binding for the X Window System protocol.

In order to build and run the IM servers that come with the X11R6 distrution, you will need to build the language engine. The X11R6 distribution also includes two language engines in *contrib/programs*, *canna32*, and *sj3*. The contributed IM servers are *kinput2*, *sjxa*, and *xfeoak*, also in *contrib/programs*. The contributed IM server developer's kit is called "IMdkit", in the *contrib/lib* directory. Table 6-1 shows the contributed IM servers and their support of the input method protocols and the language engines.

**Table 6-1:** Contributed IM Servers

| IM Server | Supported Input Method Protocol | Supported Language Engine |
|-----------|--------------------------------|---------------------------|
| kinput2 | X11R6 XIM protocol<br>X11R5 XIMP<br>kinput2 protocol<br>kinput protocol<br>jinput(Matsushita)<br>xlc(Sony) protocol | Canna32 canna server<br>sj3 sj3serv<br>wnn jserver |
| sjxa | X11R6 XIM protocol<br>X11R5 XIMP<br>kinput protocol<br>xlc(Sony) protocol<br>sjx(Sony) protocol | sj3 sj3serv |
| xfeoak | X11R6 XIM protocol<br>X11R5 XIMP | sj3 sj3serv<br>oak(Fujitsu) |
| IMdkit | X11R6 XIM protocol<br>X11R5 XIMP | N/A |

Table 6-2 provides more information about the contributed language engines.

**Table 6-2:** Contributed Language Engines

| Package Name | Language Engine Name | Supported Language | Dictionary |
|--------------|---------------------|--------------------|--------------|
| Canna32 | cannaserver | Japanese | pubdic+ |
| sj3 | sj3serv | Japanese | sj3 dictionary, pubdic+ |

### 6.1.2.1    Building the Kinput2 IM Server

The kinput2 IM server is long-established as one of the most popular freely distributed IM servers. Because of its extensible architecture, many commercial IM servers are based on the kinput2 IM server.

Figure 4-1 shows the kinput2 window being used for Root-window-style pre-editing.

You need to build one or more of the language engines above before building the kinput2 IM Server. You can choose which engine to use at compilation time of the kinput2. If you build more than one, you can choose a language engine by a command line option when you invoke kinput2. You can configure kinput2 by modifying the file *kinput2.conf.* The default setting of this file, which includes the Wnn language engine

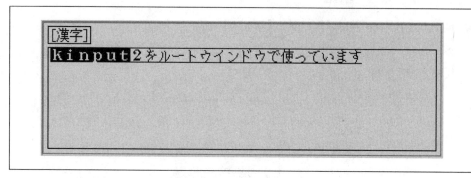

**Figure 6-1:** kinput2 window

(which is not a part of the X11R6 distribution, but is in the Release 5 distribution), appears as follows:

```
#define UseWnn       /* define if you are going to use Wnn */
#define UseCanna     /* define if you are going to use Canna */
#define UseSj3       /* define if you are going to use Sj3 */
```

To build the kinput2 IM Server with only the X11R6 distribution, the Wnn language engine entry must be commented out as follows:

```
/*#define UseWnn      define if you are going to use Wnn */
#define UseCanna     /* define if you are going to use Canna */
#define UseSj3       /* define if you are going to use Sj3 */
```

Also, there is a problem with the default configuration of Canna. You should modify the configuration by uncommenting the first set of definitions and commenting out the second set. Change the following:

```
/*
 * If you have already installed Canna header files and libraries..
 */
XCOMM use installed headers/libraries
XCOMM CANNAINSTDIR = /usr/local/canna
XCOMM CANNASRC = $(CANNAINSTDIR)/include
XCOMM CANNALIB = -lcanna16
/*
 * If you have compiled Canna that came with X11R6 (contrib/programs/Canna),
 * but not installed yet..
 */
XCOMM use headers/libraries in the source tree
CANNASRC = $(CONTRIBSRC)/programs/Canna
CANNALIB = -L$(CANNASRC)/lib/canna16 -lcanna16
```

to:

```
/*
 * If you have already installed Canna header files and libraries..
 */
XCOMM use installed headers/libraries
CANNAINSTDIR = /usr/local/canna
```

```
CANNASRC = $(CANNAINSTDIR)/include
CANNALIB = -lcanna16
/*
 * If you have compiled Canna that came with X11R6 (contrib/programs/Canna),
 * but not installed yet..
 */
XCOMM use headers/libraries in the source tree
XCOMM CANNASRC = $(CONTRIBSRC)/programs/Canna
XCOMM CANNALIB = -L$(CANNASRC)/lib/canna16 -lcanna16
```

In order to build the Canna language engine with this configuration, the Canna system must be installed in advance.

On most platforms, you should be able to build *kinput2* as follows:

```
% xmkmf -a
% make
% su
# make install
```

### 6.1.2.2   Building the sjxa IM Server

The *sjxa* IM Server is derived from the *sjxm* IM Server, which is SONY's Motif-based commercial IM Server. The *sjxa* IM Server uses the Athena widget instead of Motif. The sophisticated user interface of the *sjxa* IM Server is the most suited for GUI-oriented operation among the free IM Servers.

Figure 6-2 shows the *sjxa* window, which is used for the Root-window-style pre-editing.

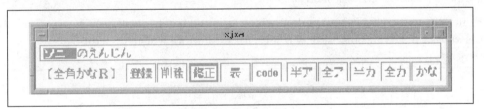

**Figure 6-2:**   sjxa window

The *sjxa* IM Server requires the *sj3serv* language engine which may be found in *contrib/program/sj3*. You need to build the *sj3* system before building *sjxa*. You may want to install the *sj3* system in advance. Otherwise, you have to specify the location of the libsj3lib.a library in the *Imakefile* before building the *sjxa* IM server.

One of the strengths of the *sjxa* IM server is the support for multiple Input Method protocols. The *sjxa* server supports not only the X11R6 XIM protocol standard, but also X11R5 Ximp 3.5 and 4.0 XIM protocol, the XLC protocol (which is an upward compatible protocol with kinput protocol), and the SJX protocol, a SONY proprietary IM protocol. You can configure *sjxa* by modifying the file "CONFIG." The default setting, except on the SONY machine, is as follows:

```
#define UseInstalledSj3Lib      NO
/*#define Sj3LibDir             $(TOP)/xim/engine/sj3/sj3lib*/
#define HasSjisLocale           NO
#define HasJlsFunction          NO
#define UseXIMCP                YES
#define UseXIMP                 YES
#define UseXLC                  NO
#define UseSJX                  NO
#define JapaneseManLocale       eucJP
#define JapaneseManDir          /usr/share/man/ja_JP.EUC/man1
#define ManDir                  /usr/share/man/C/man1
```

If you have libsj3lib.a installed, you should change the first two lines to:

```
#define UseInstalledSj3Lib      YES
/*#define Sj3LibDir             $(TOP)/xim/engine/sj3/sj3lib*/
```

Otherwise, you should change the first two lines to:

```
#define UseInstalledSj3Lib      NO
#define Sj3LibDir               $(TOP)/../contrib/programs/sj3/sj3lib
```

On most platforms, you should be able to build the Canna system as follows:

```
% xmkmf -a
% make
% su
# make install
# make install.man
```

### 6.1.2.3   Building the xfeoak IM Server

Figure 6-3 shows the *xfeoak* window, which is immediately displayed when you invoke the *xfeoak* IM Server. This window is used for Root-window-style pre-editing.

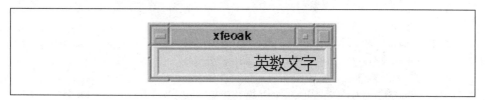

**Figure 6-3:**   xfeoak window

The *xfeoak* IM Server requires the *sj3serv* language engine, which may be found in the directory *contrib/program/sj3*. You need to build the *sj3* system before building *xfeoak*. You need to either install the *sj3* system, or specify the location of the *libsj3lib.a* library in the Imakefile before building the *xfeoak* IM server.

The default configuration of *xfeoak* in the Imakefile does not include the *sj3* language engine. You should modify the Imakefile to add the following line in the beginning:

```
#define SJ3_DICTIONARY
```

Then you should be able to build *xfeoak* simply as follows:

```
% xmkmf -a
% make

% su
# make install
```

#### 6.1.2.4    Building the IM Server Developers' Kit

The IM Server Developers' kit (*IMdkit* for short) is a C language binding of the XIM protocol, just as Xlib provides a C language binding of the X Window System protocol. IMdkit provides a low-level interface to the XIM protocol. It encapsulates the details of the XIM protocol—multiple transport layers, different byte orders, and multiple XIM protocols.

The IMdkit is not necessary for building the *kinput2, sjxa,* and *xfeoak* IM Servers, because all of these IM servers are using their own implementation of the XIM protocol handlers. The IMdkit is designed for IM Server developers who need to write the XIM protocol handlers for their own new IM Servers.

IMdkit supports X11R6 XIM protocol and X11R6 Ximp protocol. The default configuration switch is:

```
#define BuildXi18n YES
#define BuildXimp YES
```

On most platforms, you should be able to build the IMdkit as follows:

```
% xmkmf -a <path to the top dir> <path from current dir>
% make
% su
# make install
```

### 6.1.3    Local Input Method

The input method you use can be either a local input method, which is implemented directly in Xlib, or a remote input method, which is implemented as a separate process known as the input method (IM) server. X11R6 provides the local input method capability as well as the remote input method capability. In X11R6, the locale input method built into Xlib performs only simple compositions, although technically it is possible to provide full input method functionality as the local input method. In the X11R6 local input method, the composition sequence and the key bindings are user definable, but the pre-editing feedback style and the status feedback style are limited to XIMPreedit-None and XIMStatusNone. Therefore, no feedback is provided when the user specifies the local input method as her input method through the XMODIFIERS environment variable or XSetLocaleModifiers function. The X11R6 local input method uses the composition sequence definition file *Compose* for defining the composition sequence and the key bindings. The X11R6 distribution includes a sample composition sequence definition file for *iso8859-1* locales.

## 6.2 Multi-Script Terminal Emulators

X11R6 includes several terminal emulators that support multi-script and input methods. It is useful to have a terminal emulator that supports the scripts of the target language when you localize an application (and to test the language engines and IM
Servers you just built). This section explains the multi-script capable terminal emulators that come with the X11R6 distribution.

### 6.2.1 mterm

*mterm* is an enhancement of xterm to support the multiple codesets based on iso2022,
which is an international standard encoding using the shiftlock key to change between
multiple character sets. Although *mterm* does not come with any documents other than
the README file written in Japanese, *mterm* is not designed to be a Japanese-specific terminal emulator. *mterm* actually supports the charsets listed in Table 6-3.

**Table 6-3:** mterm Supported Charsets

| Charset | ISO IRV |
|---------|---------|
| 94 charset | United Kingdom |
| | ASCII |
| | Swedish/Finish |
| | Norwegian/Danish |
| | German |
| | JIS Roman |
| | JIS Kana |
| | French |
| | Italian |
| | Spanish |
| | Special Graphics |
| 96 charset | Latin1/ISO8859-1 |
| | Latin2/ISO8859-2 |
| | Latin3/ISO8859-3 |
| | Latin4/ISO8859-4 |
| | Cyrillic/ISO8859-5 |
| | Arabic/ISO8859-6 |
| | Greek/ISO8859-7 |
| | Hebrew/ISO8859-8 |
| | Latin5/ISO8859-9 |

**Table 6-3:** mterm Supported Charsets (continued)

| Charset | ISO IRV |
|---|---|
| multibyte charset | Kanji JIS-X0208 |
| | Hanzi GB-2312 |
| | Hangul/Hanja KSC5601 |

A user can specify the codeset to be used for input either from the menu or with the -ic command line option, or with the resource "inputCode." Table 6-4 lists the supported codesets and the corresponding resource names.

**Table 6-4:** mterm Supported Input Codesets

| Codeset | Resource/Option Value |
|---|---|
| Latin1/ISO8859-1 | latin1 |
| Latin2/ISO8859-2 | latin2 |
| Latin3/ISO8859-3 | latin3 |
| Latin4/ISO8859-4 | latin4 |
| Cyrillic/ISO8859-5 | cyrillic |
| Arabic/ISO8859-6 | arabic |
| Greek/ISO8859-7 | greek |
| Hebrew/ISO8859-8 | hebrew |
| Latin5/ISO8859-9 | latin5 |
| Japanese JIS | jis |
| Japanese MS-Kanji | sjis |
| Japanese EUC | jeuc |
| Korean EUC | keuc |
| Chinese EUC | ceuc |

### 6.2.1.1    Building mterm

To build and install *mterm*, go to the directory *contrib/programs/mterm*, and enter the following commmands:

```
% xmkmf -a
% make
% su
# make install
```

On most systems, line 157 of file *input.c* cannot be compiled. Here is the context:

```
#ifdef I18N
#ifdef USE_XIM
        if (screen->ic) {
                char inbuf[STRBUFSIZE];
                Status xim_status;
                char *p[2] = { inbuf, NULL}; /* <---line 157 HERE */
                XTextProperty prop;
```

If you have this problem, modify the code as follows:

```
#ifdef I18N
#ifdef USE_XIM
        if (screen->ic) {
                char inbuf[STRBUFSIZE];
                Status xim_status;
                char *p[2] ;
                XTextProperty prop;
                p[0] = inbuf;
                p[1] = NULL ;
```

### 6.2.1.2    Running mterm

*mterm* does not use XOM (Release 6 output methods) or `XFontSet` for displaying text. Instead it directly handles codesets and corresponding fonts given as an option or resource setting. Therefore, *mterm* does not require the platform to support the locale consisting of the codesets specified. It requires only the fonts, unless you use an XIM.

Because *mterm* is not bound to a locale, it requires the user to specify the font either as a command-line argument or as a resource. The command-line arguments for specifying the codeset are as follows:

| Option | Description |
|---|---|
| -ic type | Input code |
| -gl number | Plane number to be mapped to GL (graphic character set left) |
| -gr number | Plane number to be mapped to GR (graphic character set right |
| -gs string | Four characters representing the code to be used for places G0 to G3. The multi-byte charset requires $ prefix, and the 96 charset requires - prefix. For example, "B$BIB" is for Japanese EUC. |
| -ps string | XIM input style. Possible values are "OverTheSpot", "OffTheSpot", or "Root." |

The resources for codeset and i18n are as follows:

| Resource | Description |
|---|---|
| *international | Enable XIM if it is true |
| *inputCode | Initial codeset |
| *gLeft | Plane number to be mapped to GL |
| *gRight | Plane number to be mapped to GR |
| *gSet | Four characters representing the code to be used for places G0 to G3. The multibyte charset require $ prefix, and the 96 charset requires - prefix. For example, "B$BIB" is for Japanese EUC. |
| *preeditStyle | XIM input style. Possible values are OverTheSpot, OffTheSpot, or Root. |

## 6.2.2    hterm

*hterm* is an i18n enhancement to the X11R5 xterm to support XFontSet and XIM. Unlike *mterm*, *hterm* uses XFontSet for its internationalized text rendering.

Because *hterm* is based on an older revision of xterm, it inherits problems that have since been fixed in later versions of xterm. For example, *hterm* cannot be compiled as is on Solaris2.x. To compile *hterm* on Solaris2.x, lines such as the following in the file *main.c*:

```
#ifdef sun
#ifdef TIOCSSIZE
```

should be modified as shown below.

```
#if defined(sun) && !defined(SVR4)
#ifdef TIOCSSIZE
```

*hterm* does not call XSetLocaleModifiers. Therefore, the input method name cannot be specified with the XMODIFIERS environment variable.

The command line arguments for i18n are as follows:

-fs *string*
   Font name list of fontset

-is *string*
   Input style of XIM. Possible values are "over", "off", or "root."

The resources for i18n are as follows:

*fontSet
   Font name list of fontset.

*inputStyle
   Input style of XIM. Possible values are over, off, or root.

### 6.2.3    kterm

*kterm* is a direct localization enhancement of xterm for Japanese without using any of the X11 il8n features. Though *kterm* does not use XIM, it can talk to the kinput2 IM Server via its private input method protocol.

For more detail, please refer to the *README.kt* file and *kterm.man* in the directory *contrib/programs/kterm-6.1.0.*

### 6.2.4    cxterm

*cxterm* is a direct localization enhancement of xterm for Chinese without using any of the X11 il8n features. Because *cxterm* does not use XIM, it includes a set of built-in Chinese language engines.

The *cxterm* package also includes a small set of Chinese language processing programs to be used in *cxterm,* such as a Chinese vi editor, a file viewer called *cless,* a Chinese text to Postscript converter, an on-screen code conversion program called *hztty,* some Chinese encoding conversion programs, and the HBF font library (HBF is described in the *X Resource, Issue 10* published by O'Reilly & Associates, Inc.).

For more detail, please refer to the file *README* in the directory *contrib/programs/cxterm.*

## 6.3    X Locale Database

The locale-sensitive functions in Xlib refer to the *X locale database.* The constituent elements of an X locale database are:

*locale.alias*
> This file contains the mapping from the platform-specific locale name to the X internal locale name.

*locale.dir*
> This file contains the directory of the locale definition file(XLC_LOCALE) corresponding to each X internal locale name.

*compose.dir*
> This file contains the locale-specific directory location of the corresponding X internal locale name, where the Compose file is located.

*locale dir*

>  The directories are used to group a set of locales which share the same codeset.

*locale dir/Compose*

>  This file contains the compose sequence rule of the locale for the *local IM*.

*locale dir/XLC_LOCALE*

>  This file contains a locale definition.

*tbl_data/charset table*

>  This file contains the charset conversion table for each charset.

The X11R6 sample implementation uses directory hierarchy to group the similar locales in addition to the files explained in this section. The location of the X locale database can be specified by the XLOCALEDIR environment variable. If XLOCALEDIR is left unspecified, its value is:

```
$(ProjectRoot)/lib/X11/locale
```

The X11R6 distribution includes the following database files and the directories.

```
% ls -FC /usr/X11R6/lib/X11/locale
C/              iso8859-3/      iso8859-8/      ko/             zh/
compose.dir     iso8859-4/      iso8859-9/      locale.alias    zh_TW/
en_US.utf/      iso8859-5/      ja/             locale.dir
iso8859-1/      iso8859-6/      ja.JIS/         tbl_data/
iso8859-2/      iso8859-7/      ja.SJIS/        th_TH.TACTIS/
% ls -FC /usr/X11R6/lib/X11/locale/iso8859-1
Compose         XLC_LOCALE
```

The following sections discuss each file in an X locale database in more detail.

## 6.3.1    locale.alias

X11R6 Xlib refers to multiple database files to determine the internal locale and the behavior. The *locale.alias* file is referenced first to map the platform-specific locale name to the X internal locale name. Xlib uses the X internal locale name to lookup further information. The syntax of the *locale.alias* file is:

*platform-specific locale name    X internal locale name*

For example, to map the platform-specific locale name *ja* to the X internal locale name *ja_JP.SJIS*, add (or modify, if it already exists) the following line in the *locale.alias* file:

```
ja              ja_JP.SJIS
```

The default platform-specific locale names supported in X11R6 are shown in Table 6-5.

**Table 6-5:** Default platform-specific locale names supported in X11R6

| Aliases | Locale Names |
| --- | --- |
| ar, ar_AA, arabic.iso | ar_AA.ISO8859-6 |
| bg, bg_BG, bulgarian | bg_BG.ISO8859-5 |
| cs, cs_CS, czech | cs_CS.ISO8859-2 |
| cz, cz_CZ | cz_CZ.ISO8859-2 |
| da, da_DK, da_DK.88591, da_DK.88591.en, danish.iso88591 | da_DK.ISO8859-1 |
| de, de_DE, de_DE.88591, de_DE.88591.en | de_DE.ISO8859-1 |
| GER_DE.8859, GER_DE.8859.in | de_DE.ISO8859-1 |
| de_AT | de_AT.ISO8859-1 |
| de_CH, german.iso88591 | de_CH.ISO8859-1 |
| el, el_GR, greek.iso88597 | el_GR.ISO8859-7 |
| english.iso88591 | en_EN.ISO8859-1 |
| en, american.iso88591, iso8859-1, ISO8859-1 | en_US.ISO8859-1 |
| en_GB, en_GB.88591, en_GB.8859.en, ENG_GB.8859, ENG_GB.8859.in | en_GB.ISO8859-1 |
| en_AU | en_AU.ISO8859-1 |
| en_CA | en_CA.ISO8859-1 |
| en_US, en_US.88591, en_US.88591.en | en_US.ISO8859-1 |
| es, es_ES, es_ES.88591, es_ES.88591.en, spanish.iso88591 | es_ES.ISO8859-1 |
| fi, fi_FI, fi_FI.88591, fi_FI.88591.en, finnish.iso88591 | fi_FI.ISO8859-1 |
| fr | fr_FR.ISO8859-1 |
| fr_BE, fr_BE.88591, fr_BE.88591.en | fr_BE.ISO8859-1 |
| fr_CA, fr_CA.88591, fr_CA.88591.en, c-french.iso88591 | fr_CA.ISO8859-1 |
| fr_CH, fr_CH.88591, fr_CH.88591.en, french.iso88591 | fr_CH.ISO8859-1 |
| fr_FR, fr_FR.88591, fr_FR.88591.en, FRE_FR.8859, FRE_FR.8859.in | fr_FR.ISO8859-1 |
| hr, hr_HR, croatian | hr_HR.ISO8859-2 |

**Table 6-5:** Default platform-specific locale names supported in X11R6 (continued)

| Aliases | Locale Names |
|---|---|
| hu, hu_HU, hungarian | hu_HU.ISO8859-2 |
| is, is_IS, icelandic.iso88591 | is_IS.ISO8859-1 |
| it, it_IT, it_IT.88591, it_IT.88591.en, italian.iso88591 | it_IT.ISO8859-1 |
| it_CH | it_CH.ISO8859-1 |
| iw, iw_IL, hebrew.iso88598 | iw_IL.ISO8859-8 |
| ja, ja_JP, ja_JP.ujis, ja_JP.eucJP, JP_JP, ja_JP.AJEC, ja_JP.EUC, japanese/euc, japan, Japanese-EUC, japanese | ja_JP.eucJP |
| ja_JP.ISO-2022-JP, ja_JP.JIS, ja_JP.jis7 | ja_JP.JIS7 |
| ja_JP.mscode, ja_JP.SJIS | ja_JP.SJIS |
| ko, ko_KR, ko_KR.EUC, ko_KR.euc, korean | ko_KR.eucKR |
| mk, mk_MK | mk_MK.ISO8859-5 |
| nl | nl_NL.ISO8859-1 |
| nl_BE, nl_BE.88591, nl_BE.88591.en, dutch.iso88591 | nl_BE.ISO8859-1 |
| nl_NL, nl_NL.88591, nl_NL.88591.en | nl_NL.ISO8859-1 |
| no, no_NO, no_NO.88591, no_NO.88591.en, norwegian.iso88591 | no_NO.ISO8859-1 |
| pl, pl_PL, polish | pl_PL.ISO8859-2 |
| pt, pt_PT, pt_PT.88591, pt_PT.88591.en, portuguese.iso88591 | pt_PT.ISO8859-1 |
| ro, ro_RO, rumanian | ro_RO.ISO8859-2 |
| ru, ru_RU | ru_RU.ISO8859-5 |
| ru_SU, russian | ru_SU.ISO8859-5 |
| sh, sh_YU, sh_SP, serbocroatian | sh_YU.ISO8859-2 |
| sk, sk_SK, slovak | sk_SK.ISO8859-2 |
| sl, sl_CS, slovene | sl_CS.ISO8859-2 |
| sl_SI | sl_SI.ISO8859-2 |
| sp, sp_YU | sp_YU.ISO8859-5 |
| sr_SP | sr_SP.ISO8859-2 |

**Table 6-5:** Default platform-specific locale names supported in X11R6 (continued)

| Aliases | Locale Names |
|---|---|
| sv, sv_SE, sv_SE.88591, sv_SE.88591.en, swedish.iso88591 | sv_SE.ISO8859-1 |
| th_TH | th_TH.TACTICS |
| tr, tr_TR, turkish.iso88599 | tr_TR.ISO8859-9 |
| zh, zh_CN, zh_CN.EUC, chinese-s | zh_CN.eucCN |
| zh_TW, zh_TW.EUC, chinese-t | zh_TW.eucTW |

## 6.3.2    locale.dir

The *locale.dir* file is referenced after the locale.alias file to determine the locale definition file corresponding to the X internal locale name. The syntax of the *locale.dir* file is:

*locale definition file path name    X internal locale name*

Example 6-1 shows the default *locale.dir* file provided in X11R6.

**Example 6-1:** Default entries locale.dir file in X11R6

```
C/XLC_LOCALE            C
iso8859-6/XLC_LOCALE    ar_AA.ISO8859-6
iso8859-5/XLC_LOCALE    bg_BG.ISO8859-5
iso8859-2/XLC_LOCALE    cs_CS.ISO8859-2
iso8859-1/XLC_LOCALE    da_DK.ISO8859-1
iso8859-1/XLC_LOCALE    de_DE.ISO8859-1
iso8859-1/XLC_LOCALE    de_AT.ISO8859-1
iso8859-1/XLC_LOCALE    de_CH.ISO8859-1
iso8859-7/XLC_LOCALE    el_GR.ISO8859-7
iso8859-1/XLC_LOCALE    en_US.ISO8859-1
iso8859-1/XLC_LOCALE    en_GB.ISO8859-1
iso8859-1/XLC_LOCALE    en_AU.ISO8859-1
iso8859-1/XLC_LOCALE    en_CA.ISO8859-1
iso8859-1/XLC_LOCALE    es_ES.ISO8859-1
iso8859-1/XLC_LOCALE    fi_FI.ISO8859-1
iso8859-1/XLC_LOCALE    fr_FR.ISO8859-1
iso8859-1/XLC_LOCALE    fr_BE.ISO8859-1
iso8859-1/XLC_LOCALE    fr_CA.ISO8859-1
iso8859-1/XLC_LOCALE    fr_CH.ISO8859-1
iso8859-2/XLC_LOCALE    hr_HR.ISO8859-2
iso8859-2/XLC_LOCALE    hu_HU.ISO8859-2
iso8859-1/XLC_LOCALE    is_IS.ISO8859-1
iso8859-1/XLC_LOCALE    it_IT.ISO8859-1
iso8859-1/XLC_LOCALE    it_CH.ISO8859-1
iso8859-8/XLC_LOCALE    iw_IL.ISO8859-8
ja/XLC_LOCALE           ja_JP.eucJP
ja.SJIS/XLC_LOCALE      ja_JP.SJIS
ja.JIS/XLC_LOCALE       ja_JP.JIS7
ko/XLC_LOCALE           ko_KR.eucKR
ISO8859-5/XLC_LOCALE    mk_MK.ISO8859-5
iso8859-1/XLC_LOCALE    nl_NL.ISO8859-1
iso8859-1/XLC_LOCALE    nl_BE.ISO8859-1
```

**Example 6-1:** Default entries locale.dir file in X11R6 (continued)

```
iso8859-1/XLC_LOCALE    no_NO.ISO8859-1
iso8859-2/XLC_LOCALE    pl_PL.ISO8859-2
iso8859-1/XLC_LOCALE    pt_PT.ISO8859-1
iso8859-2/XLC_LOCALE    ro_RO.ISO8859-2
iso8859-5/XLC_LOCALE    ru_SU.ISO8859-5
iso8859-2/XLC_LOCALE    sh_YU.ISO8859-2
iso8859-2/XLC_LOCALE    sk_SK.ISO8859-2
iso8859-2/XLC_LOCALE    sl_CS.ISO8859-2
iso8859-5/XLC_LOCALE    sp_YU.ISO8859-5
iso8859-1/XLC_LOCALE    sv_SE.ISO8859-1
iso8859-1/XLC_LOCALE    sv_SE.ISO8859-1
th_TH/XLC_LOCALE        th_TH.TACTIS
iso8859-9/XLC_LOCALE    tr_TR.ISO8859-9
zh/XLC_LOCALE           zh_CN.eucCN
zh_TW/XLC_LOCALE        zh_TW.eucTW
en_US.utf/XLC_LOCALE    en_US.utf
```

### 6.3.3    compose.dir

The *compose.dir* file is analogous to *locale.dir*. It specifies the location of the composition rule-set file of the locale. The syntax of the *compose.dir* file is:

*composition rule-set file path name    X internal locale name*

Example 6-2 shows the default *compose.dir* file provided in X11R6.

**Example 6-2:** Default entries of locale.dir file in X11R6

```
iso8859-1/Compose       C
iso8859-1/Compose       da_DK.ISO8859-1
iso8859-1/Compose       de_DE.ISO8859-1
iso8859-1/Compose       de_AT.ISO8859-1
iso8859-1/Compose       de_CH.ISO8859-1
iso8859-1/Compose       en_US.ISO8859-1
iso8859-1/Compose       en_GB.ISO8859-1
iso8859-1/Compose       en_AU.ISO8859-1
iso8859-1/Compose       en_CA.ISO8859-1
iso8859-1/Compose       es_ES.ISO8859-1
iso8859-1/Compose       fi_FI.ISO8859-1
iso8859-1/Compose       fr_FR.ISO8859-1
iso8859-1/Compose       fr_BE.ISO8859-1
iso8859-1/Compose       fr_CA.ISO8859-1
iso8859-1/Compose       fr_CH.ISO8859-1
iso8859-1/Compose       is_IS.ISO8859-1
iso8859-1/Compose       it_IT.ISO8859-1
iso8859-1/Compose       it_CH.ISO8859-1
iso8859-1/Compose       nl_NL.ISO8859-1
iso8859-1/Compose       nl_BE.ISO8859-1
iso8859-1/Compose       no_NO.ISO8859-1
iso8859-1/Compose       pt_PT.ISO8859-1
iso8859-1/Compose       sv_SE.ISO8859-1
iso8859-1/Compose       sv_SE.ISO8859-1
```

## 6.3.4     XLC_LOCALE

An XLC_LOCALE directory, which is also known as an X Locale Database, contains the locale definition information for Xlib. It contains files, one for each locale. Each locale file contains one or more category definitions. In X11R6, the category XLC_FONTSET defines the XFontSet related information, and the category XLC_XLOCALE defines the character classification and encoding conversion information. Each category definition consists of one or more class definitions. Each class definition has a class name/class value pair, or has several subclasses which are enclosed by the left brace ({) and the right brace (}).

Table 6-6 shows the syntax definition of an X Locale Database file.

**Table 6-6:** Syntax definition of X Locale Database file

| | |
|---|---|
| CategoryDefinition | CategoryHeader CategorySpec CategoryTrailer |
| CategoryHeader | CategoryName NL |
| CategorySpec | { ClassSpec } |
| CategoryTrailer | "END" Delimiter CategoryName NL |
| CategoryName | String |
| ClassSpec | ClassName Delimiter ClassValue NL |
| ClassName | String |
| ClassValue | ValueList | "{" NL { ClassSpec } "}" |
| ValueList | Value | Value ";" ValueList |
| Value | ValuePiece | ValuePiece Value |
| ValuePiece | String | QuotedString | NumericString |
| String | Char { Char } |
| QuotedString | """ QuotedChar { QuotedChar } """ |
| NumericString | "\o" OctDigit { OctDigit } |
| | | "\d" DecDigit { DecDigit } |
| | | "\x" HexDigit { HexDigit } |
| Char | XPCS except NL, Space or unescaped reserved symbols |
| QuotedChar | XPCS except unescaped """ |
| OctDigit | character in the range of "0" - "7" |
| DecDigit | character in the range of "0" - "9" |
| HexDigit | character in the range of "0" - "9," "a" - "f," "A" - "F" |
| Delimiter | Space { Space } |
| Space | space | horizontal tab |
| NL | newline |

The category XLC_FONTSET contains the CHARSET_REGISTRY-CHARSET_ENCODING name and character mapping side (GL, GR, etc.) information as class *fsN* (where *N*=0,1,2 ... ). The fs*N* class has two subclasses: *charset*, which specifies encoding information to be used internally in Xlib for this fontset, and *font*, which specifies a codeset of the font to be used internally in Xlib for this fontset.

XLC_XLOCALE contains character classification, codeset conversion, and other character attributes. Table 6-7 shows class definitions in the XLC_LOCALE category.

**Table 6-7:** Class definitions in the XLC_LOCALE category

| Class | Super class | Description |
|---|---|---|
| encoding_name | | A codeset name of current locale. |
| mb_cur_max | | A maximum allowable number of bytes in a multi-byte character. |
| | | MB_CUR_MAX of "ISO/IEC 9899:1990 C Language Standard" |
| state_depend_encoding | | Whether encoding is state dependent or not. The value is true or false? |
| wc_encoding_mask | | A bit-mask of wide-character. Each wide character is applied bit-and operation with this bit-mask. |
| wc_shift_bits | | A number of bits to be shifted when conversion from a multi-byte character to a wide character, and vice-versa. |
| csN | | Nth charset (N=0,1,2, ... ). *csN* consists of five sub classes, '*side*', '*length*', '*mb_encoding*' '*wc_encoding*' and '*ct_encoding*'. |
| side | csN | Mapping side (GL, GR, etc). |
| length | csN | Length of a character. |
| mb_encoding | csN | For parsing *mb* string. |
| wc_encoding | csN | For parsing *wc* string. |
| ct_encoding | csN | List of encoding name for *ct*. |

Example 6-3 shows the sample locale definition file for the iso8859-1 locale.

**Example 6-3:** Sample Locale Definition for the iso8859-1 Locale

```
XLC_FONTSET
#       fs0 class
fs0     {
        charset         ISO8859-1:GL
        font            ISO8859-1:GL
}
```

**Example 6-3:** Sample Locale Definition for the iso8859-1 Locale  (continued)

```
#       fs1 class
fs1     {
        charset         ISO8859-1:GR
        font            ISO8859-1:GR
}
END XLC_FONTSET

XLC_XLOCALE
encoding_name           ISO8859-1
mb_cur_max              1
state_depend_encoding   False
wc_encoding_mask        \x00008080
wc_shift_bits           8
cs0     {
        side            GL:Default
        length          1
        wc_encoding     \x00000000
        ct_encoding     ISO8859-1:GL
}
cs1     {
        side            GR:Default
        length          1
        wc_encoding     \x00008080
        ct_encoding     ISO8859-1:GR
}
END XLC_XLOCALE
```

## 6.3.5    Compose

The *Compose* file defines the composition sequence for the local IM built into Xlib, which performs simple pre-editing, such as European language composition.

Table 6-8 shows the syntax definition of the *Compose* file.

**Table 6-8:** Syntax definition of Compose file

| | |
|---|---|
| FILE | { [PRODUCTION] [COMMENT] "\n"} |
| PRODUCTION | LHS ":" RHS |
| COMMENT | "#" {any character except null or newline} |
| LHS | EVENT { EVENT } |
| EVENT | [MODIFIER_LIST] "<" keysym ">" |
| MODIFIER_LIST | ("!" {MODIFIER} ) I "None" |
| MODIFIER | ["~"] modifier_name |
| RHS | ( STRING I keysym I STRING keysym ) |
| STRING | "" { CHAR } "" |
| CHAR | GRAPHIC_CHAR I ESCAPED_CHAR |
| GRAPHIC_CHAR | Locale (codeset) dependent code |
| ESCAPED_CHAR | ('\' I '\"' I OCTAL I HEX ) |

**Table 6-8:** Syntax definition of Compose file (continued)

| | |
|---|---|
| OCTAL | '\' OCTAL_CHAR [OCTAL_CHAR [OCTAL_CHAR]] |
| OCTAL_CHAR | (0|1|2|3|4|5|6|7) |
| HEX | '\' (x|X) HEX_CHAR [HEX_CHAR] |
| HEX_CHAR | (0|1|2|3|4|5|6|7|8|9|A|B|C|D|E|F|a|b|c|d|e|f) |

Example 6-4 shows part of the default composition sequence definition file for the iso8859-1 locale.

**Example 6-4:** Sample Composition Sequence Definition for the iso8859-1 Locale

```
#
# Sample composition sequence definition
#
<Multi_key> <plus> <plus>             : "#"    # Number Sign
<Multi_key> <apostrophe> <space>      : "'"    # Apostrophe
<Multi_key> <A> <A>                   : "@"    # Commercial at
<Multi_key> <parenleft> <parenleft>   : "["    # Opening Bracket
<Multi_key> <slash> <slash>           : "\"    # Backslash
<Multi_key> <slash> <less>            : "\"    # Backslash
<Multi_key> <parenright> <parenright> : "]"    # Closing bracket
<Multi_key> <asciicircum> <space>     : "^"    # Circumflex accent
<Multi_key> <greater> <space>         : "^"    # Circumflex accent
<Multi_key> <grave> <space>           : "`"    # Grave accent
<Multi_key> <parenleft> <minus>       : "{"    # Opening brace
<Multi_key> <slash> <asciicircum>     : "|"    # Vertical line
<Multi_key> <V> <L>                   : "|"    # Vertical line
<Multi_key> <v> <l>                   : "|"    # Vertical line
<Multi_key> <parenright> <minus>      : "}"    # Closing brace
<Multi_key> <asciitilde> <space>      : "~"    # Tilde
<Multi_key> <minus> <space>           : "~"    # Tilde
<Multi_key> <exclam> <exclam>         : "`"    # Inverted !
<Multi_key> <c> <slash>               : "¢"    # Cent sign
<Multi_key> <c> <bar>                 : "¢"    # Cent sign
<Multi_key> <l> <minus>               : "£"    # Pound sign
<Multi_key> <l> <equal>               : "£"    # Pound sign
<Multi_key> <y> <minus>               : "¥"    # Yen sign
<Multi_key> <y> <equal>               : "¥"    # Yen sign
<Multi_key> <s> <o>                   : "§"    # Section sign
<Multi_key> <s> <exclam>              : "§"    # Section sign
<Multi_key> <x> <o>                   : "¤"    # Currency sign
<Multi_key> <c> <o>                   : "©"    # Copyright
<Multi_key> <a> <underscore>          : "ª"    # Feminine ordinal indicator
<Multi_key> <o> <underscore>          : "º"    # Masculine ordinal indicator
<Multi_key> <less> <less>             : "«"    # Angle quotation mark left
<Multi_key> <greater> <greater>       : "»"    # Angle quotation mark right
<Multi_key> <0> <asciicircum>         : "°"    # Degree ign
<Multi_key> <0> <asterisk>            : "°"    # Degree sign
<Multi_key> <plus> <minus>            : "−"    # Plus/minus sign
<Multi_key> <slash> <u>               : "µ"    # Micro Sign
<Multi_key> <1> <asciicircum>         : "1"    # Superscript 1
<Multi_key> <s> <1>                   : "1"    # Superscript 1
<Multi_key> <2> <asciicircum>         : "2"    # Superscript 2
<Multi_key> <s> <2>                   : "2"    # Superscript 2
```

**Example 6-4:** Sample Composition Sequence Definition for the iso8859-1 Locale (continued)

```
<Multi_key> <3> <asciicircum>             : "³"      # Superscript 3
<Multi_key> <s> <3>                       : "³"      # Superscript 3
<Multi_key> <p> <exclam>                  : "¶"      # Paragraph sign
<Multi_key> <period> <asciicircum>        : "·"      # Middle dot
<Multi_key> <period> <period>             : "·"      # Middle dot
<Multi_key> <1> <4>                       : "¹/₄"    # Fraction one quarter
<Multi_key> <1> <2>                       : "¹/₂"    # Fraction one half
<Multi_key> <3> <4>                       : "³/₄"    # Fraction three quarter
<Multi_key> <question> <question>         : "¿"      # Inverted ?
<Multi_key> <space> <space>               : " "      # No break space
<Multi_key> <bar> <bar>                   : "|"      # Broken bar vertical
<Multi_key> <exclam> <asciicircum>        : "|"      # Broken bar vertical
                              .
                              .
                              .

# Accented Alphabet
<Multi_key> <A> <grave>                   : "À"      # A grave
<Multi_key> <A> <acute>                   : "Á"      # A acute
<Multi_key> <A> <asciicircum>             : "Â"      # A circumflex
<Multi_key> <A> <greater>                 : "Â"      # A circumflex
<Multi_key> <A> <asciitilde>              : "Ã"      # A tilde
<Multi_key> <A> <minus>                   : "Ã"      # A tilde
<Multi_key> <A> <quotedbl>                : "Ä"      # A umlaut
<Multi_key> <A> <asterisk>                : "Å"      # A ring
<Multi_key> <A> <E>                       : "Æ"      # A e Diphthong
                              .
                              .
                              .
```

# 6.4    Athena Widgets

The addition of i18n capabilities into Xaw is one of the major visible enhancements in X11R6. However, the X11R6 Athena Widget set remains at the X11R5 i18n functionality level, in that they don't use output methods or input contexts.

The widgets that are internationalized are the *AsciiText* widget, *Command* widget, *Label* widget, *List* widget, *Simple* widget, *smeBSB* object, and *Text widget.* By default, the i18n features are disabled in the internationalized widgets. To control the i18n features, new resources are introduced.

The following table shows the name, class, type and default value of each resource that is introduced in the X11R6 Athena Widgets for i18n. There is also a column containing notes describing special restrictions placed upon individual resources.

| Name | Class | Type | Default Value |
|---|---|---|---|
| international | International | Boolean | False |
| fontSet | FontSet | XFontSet | XtDefaultFontSet |
| inputMethod | InputMethod | String | NULL |

| Name | Class | Type | Default Value |
|------|-------|------|---------------|
| preeditType | PreeditType | String | NULL |
| openIM | OpenIM | Boolean | NULL |
| sharedIc | SharedIc | Boolean | False |

international

This is a boolean flag that can only be set at widget creation time. A value of
False signals the widget to not use i18n. A value of True directs the widget to act
in an internationalized manner, such as utilizing font sets for displaying text, etc.
This resource cannot be modified with XtSetValues().

fontSet

The text font set to use when displaying text, when the international resource is
True.

inputMethod

Undocumented resource that specifies the input method name. If this value is left
unspecified, the value of the XMODIFIERS environment variable "@im=*input-
method-name*" will be ignored because Xaw directly specifies "@im=none" through
XSetLocaleModifiers().[†] Xlib recognizes the value "@im=none" to indicate that
the local input method should be used, and a simple composition engine inside
Xlib is enabled.

openIM

Undocumented resource that determines whether or not to open an input
method. In this revision, it has no effect.

sharedIc

Undocumented resource that determines whether or not to share an input context among widgets. A value of True directs the widget to share an input context.

Example 6-5 shows sample resource settings for the internationalized *xedit* program.

**Example 6-5:** Sample Resource Settings for xedit

```
Xedit*international: true
Xedit*fontset: -*-fixed-medium-r-normal--16-*
Xedit*quit.label: 終了
Xedit*save.label: 保存
Xedit*load.label: ロード
Xedit*inputMethod: kinput2
Xedit*preeditType: OverTheSpot
```

---

[†] In general, specifying "@im=none" using XSetLocaleModifiers() is not encouraged
unless it is absolutely necessary for the application, because it overrides the user's setting and
eliminates the ability to use a remote input method for complex text composition.

Figure 6-4 shows the internationalized *xedit* program running on the Japanese locale with the resource settings shown in Example 6-5. The internationalized xedit loads the file named in Japanese from the */tmp* directory.

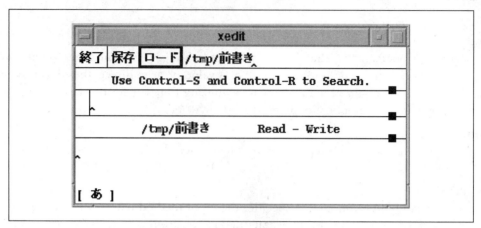

**Figure 6-4:** Internationalized xedit program—specifying file name

Figure 6-5 shows *xedit* with pre-editing turned on and text being composed in the Japanese locale. The phrase in reverse-video indicates that the pre-editing is in session, and the input method dialog displays the homonym choices to be looked up for that phrase.

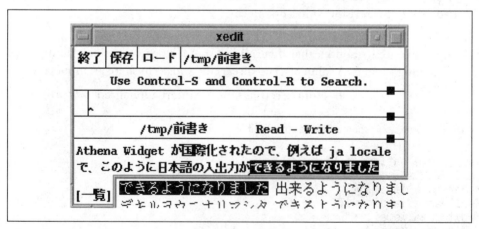

**Figure 6-5:** Internationalized xedit program—looking up the homonym choices

## 6.5 Locale Announcement

The X11R6 i18n architecture is based on the locale model used in ANSI C and POSIX. The user should specify the locale with either the LANG or LC_CTYPE environment variable before running an internationalized X application. For example:

```
% setenv LANG fr
```

If your system does not conform to POSIX, it may not have the setlocale() function. In that case, you have to build X11R6 by defining the X_LOCALE compilation flag in StandardDefines, an intimate config variable. StandardDefines may already be defined by the .cf file; if not, you should set it in your *site.def* file. The X_LOCALE flag enables the setlocale() implementation inside Xlib. If your system does not support setlocale(), it typically does not support POSIX wide character functions either, so you may also need to define X_WCHAR in StandardDefines. X_WCHAR should only be defined if stddefih doesn't define *wchar_t*.[†]

```
#define StandardDefines   -DX_WCHAR -DX_LOCALE
```

X11R6 recognizes a locale modifier *im*, which specifies the input method to be used for internationalized text input for the locale. The value of the *im* modifier is either none or the name of the Input Method server. If the value is none Xlib uses the local input method supplied by Xlib, which typically performs simple text composition. Otherwise, Xlib uses the XIM protocol to communicate with the remote input method (that is, the X Input Method server), which typically performs complex text composition. For example, to specify the "kinput2" Input Method server, set the XMODIFIERS environment variable, as follows:[‡]

```
% setenv XMODIFIERS @im=kinput2
```

## 6.6 Getting Started—Internationalized X Programming

The interface for setting the locale within an application has not been changed since the X11R5 release.

X applications should include <X11/Xlocale.h> instead of <locale.h>. The <X11/Xlocale.h> header is sensitive to the X_LOCALE definition, and embeds the API difference between the setlocale() supplied by the system and the setlocale() supplied by Xlib. If X_LOCALE is not defined, <X11/Xlocale.h> simply includes the standard header <locale.h>.

---

† There may be a non-standard flag XML left behind in some .cf files. However, unlike in X11R5, XML no longer enables an optional non-standard feature of Xlib. If your application uses the feature which is enabled by XML, you should modify your application to work with X11R6.
‡ The XMODIFIERS environment variable may not take effect if an application directly specifies the value of *im* modifier through XSetLocaleModifiers(), because the value specified through XSetLocaleModifiers() takes precedence over the value of the XMODIFIERS environment variable.

Next, an X application should call `setlocale()` as defined by POSIX in order to enable the locale-sensitive functions; the functions will adopt the locale or the current locale set the user specifies with either the LANG or LC_CTYPE environment variable.

Immediately after calling `setlocale()`, an application should call `XSupportsLocale()`, which returns `True` if the Xlib implementation supports the current locale. If this function returns `False`, an application can take either of the following approaches:

- Print the message `Locale not supported. Falling back to C locale`, set the locale to "C" by calling `setlocale()` again, and call `XSupportsLocale()` again. If the second call also fails, print `C Locale not supported.` and exit.

- Print the message `Locale not supported` and exit.

Even when `XSupportsLocale()` returns True, the program may encounter other errors due to lack of locale support in XOM or XIM. For example, `XSupportsLocale()` does not detect missing mandatory fonts for the specified locale.

When the locale is supported by X, an application should call `XSetLocaleModifiers()`.

`XSetLocaleModifiers()` allows the programmer to specify a list of modifiers (usually none) that will be concatenated with a list of user-specified modifiers to form an operating system environment variable (XMODIFIERS in POSIX). The string passed to `XSetLocaleModifiers()` and set in the XMODIFIERS environment variable is a null-terminated series of "@category=value" entries. The category must be encoded in the POSIX portable filename character set. The value is encoded in the character set of the current locale.

`XSetLocaleModifiers()` returns NULL if the specified modifiers are invalid. Otherwise, it returns the modifier string associated with the current locale before the modification. The string returned by `XSetLocaleModifiers()` is such that a subsequent call with the string will restore the modifiers to the previous setting.

Example 6-6 shows the code that calls `setlocale()` and the other two functions described here to correctly establish a locale.

**Example 6-6:** Locale Setting

```
#include <stdio.h>
#include <X11/Xlib.h>
/*
 * In order to embed the difference between Xsetlocale and
 * system's setlocale, include <X11/Xlocale.h> instead of
 * <locale.h>. <X11/Xlocale.h> include <locale.h> if the
 * X_LOCALE compilation flag is not defined.
 */
#include <X11/Xlocale.h>

char *program_name ;
```

**Example 6-6:** Locale Setting (continued)

```
main(argc, argv)
int argc;
char *argv[];
{
    program_name = argv[0];
    DISPLAY *display ;
    if (setlocale(LC_ALL, "") == NULL) {
        (void) fprintf(stderr, "%s: cannot set locale.\n",program_name);
        exit(1);
    }
    if ((display = XOpenDisplay(NULL)) == NULL) {
        (void) fprintf(stderr, "%s: cannot open Display.\n"
        exit(1);
    }
    if (!XSupportsLocale()) {
        (void) fprintf(stderr, "%s: X does not support locale \"%s\".\n",
                    program_name, setlocale(LC_ALL, NULL));
        exit(1);
    }
    if (XSetLocaleModifiers("") == NULL) {
        (void) fprintf(stderr,
            "%s: Warning: cannot set locale modifiers.\n", program_name);

        /*
         * Try setting the local IM as fallback
         */
        if (XSetLocaleModifiers("@im=none") == NULL) {
            (void) fprintf(stderr,
                "%s: Warning: cannot set fallback locale modifiers.\n",
                    program_name);
        }
    }
}
```

## 6.7   Internationalized Text Output

In internationalized X programming, you cannot assume that a character codepoint
(the number of the character code) is equal to the index of the character's glyph in a
particular font.

Before X11R5, there was no clear distinction between the character codepoint and the
character glyph index. Therefore, programs assumed that the two were the same. [†]

X11R5 introduced the new font handling abstraction, XFontSet. An XFontSet hides
the locale-specific fonts and their character set details from the program. In a sense,
the XFontSet appears to be a single composite font. An XFontSet is bound to the
locale in which it is created, and contains all the fonts needed to display text in that

---

† The *xfontsel* program, which can be found in *contrib/program* directory, is a good example of a
pre-X11R5 program. The *xfontsel* program specifies the font and its glyph index to display the
specified font by assuming the encoding of a character was identical to the index of the character's glyph in the font. Because the Athena Widget set is now internationalized, the *xfontsel* program no longer works well if the i18n feature of the Athena Widget set is turned on.

locale, and all the independent charsets used in the encoding of that locale. The internationalized functions, which take an XFontSet and a string to be processed, treat the string as a sequence of character codepoints which are independent of font index in any particular font. The translation of a character codepoint to a font index in a particular font is done implicitly within the internationalized functions.

X11R6 introduces new generalized output abstractions symmetric to the XIM and the XIC—the *X Output Method* (XOM) and the *X Output Context* (XOC). These new abstractions are in addition to XFontSet. This allows support for more complex output handling, such as direction-sensitive languages.

Opening an XOM is conceptually very similar to opening an XIM, and creating an XOC is conceptually very similar to creating an XIC. The XFontSet interface is now re-implemented as an emulation library that uses XOM and XOC. XOC is a broader, more generalized abstraction than XFontSet, designed as an upward compatible type with XFontSet in order to maintain backward compatibility to the X11R5 interfaces. In addition, the XCreateFontSet() function now returns an XOC object as an XFontSet object. Therefore, all internationalized interfaces which take XFontSet can also take XOC.

The next two sections describe how to open and use an OM and an OC.

## 6.7.1    Opening an Output Method

An output method is created with a call to XOpenOM(). This function checks the current setting of the locale and locale modifiers.

XOpenOM() returns an opaque handle of type XOM. Opening an output method is conceptually similar to opening a display, and the XOM returned is analogous to the Display * returned by XOpenDisplay(). An output method is bound to the particular locale that was in effect when it was created, even if this locale is subsequently changed. Example 6-7 shows a procedure that handles XOpenOM() and related OM functions.

**Example 6-7:** Opening an Output Method

```
/*
 * opening an output method
 */
#include <stdio.h>
#include <X11/Xlib.h>
#include <X11/Xresource.h>
#include <X11/Xlocale.h>
extern char* program_name ;
extern char* class_name ;
/*
 * Whether Xlib performs direction-dependent drawing or not.
 * Assume Xlib does not perform as default.
 * We'll query it after opening OM.
 */
```

**Example 6-7:** Opening an Output Method (continued)

```
Bool is_implicit_ddd = False;
/*
 * Whether Xlib performs context-dependent drawing or not.
 * Assume Xlib does not perform as default.
 * We'll query it after opening OM.
 */
Bool is_implicit_cdd = False;
/*
 * Default Orientation.
 */
XOMOrientation *orientation ;
XOM
open_om(display, ProgramName, ClassName)
    Display *display;
    char *ProgramName;
    char *ClassName;
{
    XOM om ;
    XrmDatabaserdb = XrmGetDatabase(display);

    if((om = XOpenOM(display, rdb, ProgramName, ClassName)) == NULL){
        (void)fprintf(stderr, "%s: Cannot open Output Method\n",
                    program_name);
        return (XOM)NULL ;
    }
    if(XGetOMValues(om, XNOrientation, &orientation, NULL)){
        /*
         * Assume Left to Right, Top to Bottom as fallback.
         */
        orientation = (XOMOrientation *)Xmalloc(sizeof(XOMOrientation));
#ifdef BUGFIX
        /*
         * In the original Release 6 release, there are bugs in Xlib.h.
         * The specification defines num_orientation and orientation
         * as members of XOMOrientation, but Xlib.h defines them
         * as num_orient and orient. Patches are available on ftp.x.org.
         */
        orientation->num_orientation = 1 ;
        orientation->orientation = (XOrientation *)Xmalloc(sizeof
            (XOrientation));
        *orientation->orientation = XOMOrientation_LTR_TTB ;
#else
        orientation->num_orient = 1 ;
        orientation->orient = (XOrientation *)Xmalloc(sizeof(XOrientation));
        *orientation->orient = XOMOrientation_LTR_TTB ;
#endif
    }
    XGetOMValues(om, XNDirectionalDependentDrawing, &is_implicit_ddd, NULL);
    XGetOMValues(om, XNContextualDrawing, &is_implicit_cdd, NULL);

    return om ;
}
```

## 6.7.2     **Output Context**

Just as the input method can manage multiple input contexts for a single client, an output method can maintain multiple output contexts for an application. The function XCreateOC() creates a new output context in an output method. The function returns an opaque handle of type XOC. Like the XIC type, XOC has a number of attributes which you can get and set. These attributes control the output behavior, such as writing direction, under that context.

Example 6-8 shows a procedure that handles XCreateOC() and related OC functions.

**Example 6-8:** Creating an Output Context

```
/*
 * creating an output context
 */
#include <stdio.h>
#include <X11/Xlib.h>
#include <X11/Xresource.h>
#include <X11/Xlocale.h>
char* program_name ;
#define DEFAULT_BASE_FONT "-misc-fixed-*-*-*-*-*-130-75-75-*-*-*-*"
XOC
create_oc(om, ProgramName, ClassName)
    XOM om ;
    char *ProgramName;
    char *ClassName;
{
    int i ;
    char    *base_font_name = DEFAULT_BASE_FONT ;
    XOC oc;
    XOMCharSetList *list;

    if ((oc = XCreateOC(om, XNBaseFontName, base_font_name, NULL)) == NULL){
        (void)fprintf(stderr, "%s: Cannot create Output Context\n",
                    program_name);
        return (XOC)NULL ;
    }

    /*
     * Check whether the requred charsets are missing or not.
     */
    if(!XGetOCValues(oc, XNMissingCharSet, &list, NULL)){
        if(list->charset_count > 0){
            /*
             * Having missing-charsets means that some characters
             * may not be displayed correctly (substituted by
             * default character), we should print warning message.
             */
            (void)fprintf(stderr,
                "%s: Warning: the following charsets are missing\n",
                program_name);
            for(i=0; i < list->charset_count ; i++){
                (void)fprintf(stderr,
                        "%s:        %s\n", program_name, list->charset_list[i]);
            }
```

**Example 6-8:** Creating an Output Context  (continued)

```
            }
       }
       return oc;
   }
```

# 6.8    I18n Text Input

The sections below present concepts, datatypes, and functions which are newly introduced or revised in X11R6 to support input methods.

## 6.8.1    Input Method Architecture

An internationalized X application gets user text input by communicating with an input method. The input method architecture may be either a local input method (library model), or a remote input method (client/server model). A local input method is typically used for simple text composition, such as for European languages. A remote input method is typically used for the complex composition, such as input methods for Asian ideographic languages. The X11R6 XIM architecture was designed to support both the local and the remote input method.

Figure 6-6 diagrams several possible connections between a client and its input method. X clients *B* and *C* use remote IMs for complex pre-editing and connect to a single IM server. X client *A* uses the local IM built into Xlib for simple pre-editing. The IM Server connects with a language engine which performs language-specific conversion and dictionary lookup.

The X11R6 XIM architecture was designed to support two event handling models (known as *front-end* and *back-end*) and two event flow control methods (known as *static event flow control* and *dynamic event flow control*. So there are four permutations of how an input method server can communicate with a client in the interest of the performance of input method communication.

A *front-end input method* intercepts events from the X server before they reach the application. A *back-end method* filters events from the application, before the application has processed them. A *static event flow control* lets the input method server handle events regardless of the pre-editing status. An application always processes the events which an input method has skimmed and has not consumed. A *dynamic event flow control* lets Xlib bypass an input method server whenever possible.

Figure 6-7 illustrates *dynamic event flow* with *back-end event handling*. Events always go to the client first, regardless of the pre-editing status. The Xlib filters the events from the application and decides whether to forward the events to the IM Server, or to return them to the application.

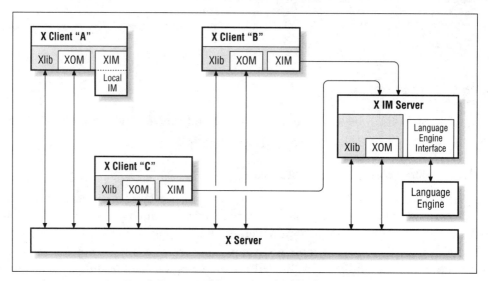

**Figure 6-6:** Possible input method architectures

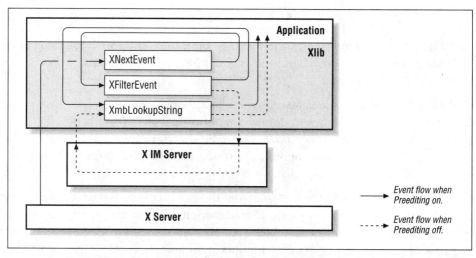

**Figure 6-7:** Dynamic event flow with back-end event handling model

Figure 6-8 shows *static event flow with back-end event handling model*. Events always go to the client first, regardless of pre-editing status. Xlib also unconditionally filters events from the application and forwards them to the IM Server. The IM Server keeps pre-editing status, and decides whether to perform pre-editing or to send back the events.

Figure 6-9 illustrates *dynamic event flow with front-end event handling model*. Xlib and the IM Server collaborate to dispatch the events depending on the pre-editing status. Xlib directly receives the events from X Server whenever the IM Server does not need the events, and the IM Server directly receives the events it needs from X Server.

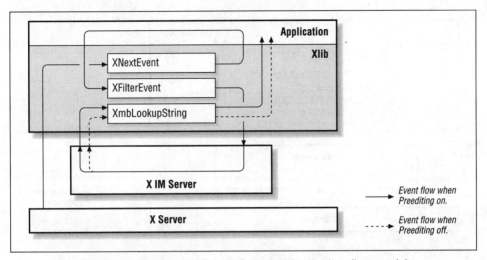

**Figure 6-8:** Static event flow with backend event handling model

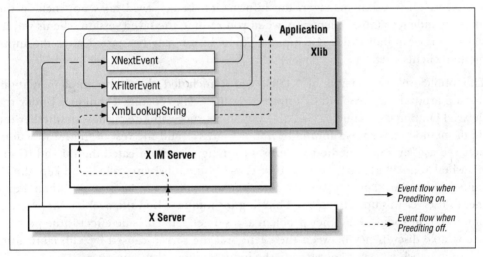

**Figure 6-9:** Dynamic event flow with front-end event handling model

Figure 6-10 shows *static event flow with front-end event handling model.* Events always go to the IM Server first, regardless of the pre-editing status. The IM Server keeps the pre-editing status, and decides whether to perform pre-editing or to forward the events.

## 6.8.2    Preparing for Dynamic IM Connection

X11R6 introduces the `IMInstantiateCallback` to support a dynamic IM connection facility. An input method server is both a client of the X server and a server of an input method client (the application). Therefore, an input method client can start before an input method server is up and available. For example, when you save the current

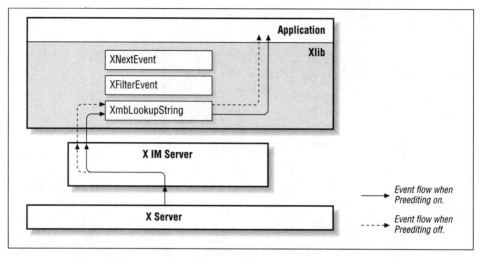

**Figure 6-10:** Static event flow with front-end event handling model

session via the session manager, the information being saved does not include the interdependency among clients; so, when you resume the saved session, clients will be started in a random order. An input method server may be started after the input method clients start.

The public release version of X11R5, which included the Ximp implementation, worked around this problem by introducing the *delayed-binding* technique. Under the delayed-binding technique, XOpenIM() was always successful, regardless of whether the input method server was running or not. XOpenIM() and the rest of the IM functions behaved as if an input method server was running. They fabricated the IM and IC values when XGetIMValues() or XGetICValues() functions were called, and kept the IC values when the XSetICValues() function was called for later usage when input method server was up. The delayed-binding technique solved the problem in practice; however, it introduced another problem as a side effect. The side effect is the possible irreparable discrepancy between the client and the server, caused by Xlib fabricating information which is not known until the input method comes up.

When an input method server is not running, a client could successfully set XIMPreeditPosition into XNInputStyle via XSetICValues, if the preceding call of XGetIMValues for XNQueryInputStyle indicates XIMPreeditPosition is supported. But, the input method server started later may not support XIMPreeditPosition.

In X11R6, IMInstantiateCallback is introduced to fix the side effect problem introduced in X11R5. IMInstantiateCallback solves the problem by introducing a *dynamic Input Method connection* facility. A client can register an IMInstantiateCallback function and Xlib will call it when an input method server is up. If an input method server is already up and running, the client's callback is called immediately.

Therefore, a client can dynamically open and create IMs and ICs inside `IMInstantiateCallback`. Example 6-9 shows a procedure that registers an `IMInstantiateCallback`.

**Example 6-9:** Preparing Dynamic IM Server Connection

```
#include <X11/Xlib.h>
#include <X11/Xresource.h>
#include <X11/Xlocale.h>
void app_im_init() ;
char *program_name;
char *class_name;
main(argc, argv)
int argc;
char *argv[];
{
    DISPLAY *display ;

    if (setlocale(LC_ALL, "") == NULL) {
        (void) fprintf(stderr, "%s: cannot set locale.\n",program_name);
        exit(1);
    }
    if ((display = XOpenDisplay(NULL)) == NULL) {
        (void) fprintf(stderr, "%s: cannot open Display.\n", program_name);
        exit(1);
    }
            .
            .
            .

    /*
     * initializeXIM function registers XIM instantiate callback if
     * IM Server is not running, otherwise call application's IM
     * initialize routine
     */
    initializeXIM(display, program_name, class_name, app_im_init);
            .
            .
            .

}
/*
 * Callback to instantiate an input method on demand.
 * invoke input method related application initialization routine.
 */
static void
im_instantiate_callback(display, client_data, call_data)
    Display *display;
    XPointer client_data;
    XPointer call_data;
{
    XIMProc app_im_init = (XIMProc)client_data ;

    (*app_im_init)(display); /* invoke application's im initialize
            routine */
}
/*
 * Register im instantiate callback.
```

**Example 6-9:** Preparing Dynamic IM Server Connection  (continued)

```
  * If IM Server is already runnning, im_instantiate_callback
  * is immediately invoked from here.
  */
void
initializeXIM(display, program_name, class_name, app_im_init)
    Display *display;
    char *program_name;
    char * class_name;
    XIMProc app_im_init ; /* Client data */
{
    XrmDatabaserdb = XrmGetDatabase(display);
    XRegisterIMInstantiateCallback(display, rdb,
                           program_name, class_name,
                           im_instantiate_callback,
                           (XPointer*)app_im_init);
}
```

The function *app_im_init* is described in the next section.

## 6.8.3    Opening an IM and Preparing for IM Disconnection

When a client receives notification of an input method's existence (the IMInstanti-ateCallback is called), a client can open a connection with the IM using a call to XOpenIM(). The locale determines the default input method that XOpenIM() connects to. The locale is bound to the input method when the IM is opened, and the locale will be used by all subsequent operations on the input method, including all input contexts of that input method.

In order to take full advantage of the dynamic input method connection facility, a client is encouraged to register a complementary function DestroyCallback to the input method. If DestroyCallback is registered, the client will be notified when an input method server is down. By using IMInstantiateCallback and DestroyCall-back, a client can continue communicating with an input method server even if the user changes input method servers while a client is running. In other words, just as a user can change window managers without impacting clients, a user can change input method servers on the fly.

Example 6-10 shows a procedure to be called from the IMInstantiateCallback that opens an input method and registers a *DestroyCallback* into the input method.

**Example 6-10:** Opening IM and Preparing IM Disconnection

```
#include <stdio.h>
#include <X11/Xlib.h>
#include <X11/Xresource.h>
#include <X11/Xlocale.h>
/*
 * Destroy callback. It gets invoked when an input method server
 * is gone.
 */
extern char* program_name ;
```

**Example 6-10:** Opening IM and Preparing IM Disconnection (continued)

```
extern char* class_name ;
extern XIM im;
extern XIC ic;
extern XIMValuesList im_values_list ;
extern XIMValuesList ic_values_list ;
static void
destroy_callback(ic, client_data, call_data )
    XIC         ic;
    XPointer    client_data;
    XPointer    *call_data;
{
    im = NULL;
    ic = NULL;
}
/*
 * Application specific XIM initialization
 */
void app_im_init(display)
    Display *display;
{
    XIMCallback destroy;
    XrmDatabaserdb = XrmGetDatabase(display);

    if(!(im = XOpenIM(display, rdb, program_name, class_name))){
        return;
    }
    /*
     * Retrieve supported XIM values list and XIC values list
     * for later usage.
     */
    if(XGetIMValues(im, XNQueryIMValuesList, &im_values_list, NULL)){
        fprintf(stderr, "%s: Warning: XNQueryIMValuesList failed\n",
                program_name);
    }

    /*
     * Check whether XNDestroyCallback is supported or not by using the
     * just retrieved im values list
     */
    if(is_supported(XNDestroyCallback, &im_values_list){
        destroy.callback = destroy_callback;
        destroy.client_data = NULL;
        XSetIMValues(im, XNDestroyCallback, &destroy, NULL );
    }
        .
        .
        .

}
```

## 6.8.4    Creating an Input Context

Just as the X server can display multiple windows for a single client, an input method can maintain multiple *input contexts* for an application. Once we have an IM connection (after the IMInstantiateCallback has been called), we can create an input context (IC). Example 6-11 shows the code to create an Input Context.

**Example 6-11:** Creating an IC

```
/*
 * Create an IC with best input style in given environment.
 */
XIC
create_ic(im, client_window, rdb, res_name, res_class)
XIM im;
Window client_window ;
XrmDatabase rdb;
char        *res_name ;
char        *res_class ;
{
    XIMStyles supported_list ;
    XIC ic ;
    static XIMStyle style = 0;
    /*
     * This list defines the input styles supported by the
     * application, and its priority order of input styles.
     * In general, it would be preferable if an application is neutral in
     * input style preference, because the input style preference order
     * itself is locale specific.
     */
    static XIMStyle supported_styles[] = {
        /*
         * Because the Callbacks styles require huge
         * support providing Callbacks routines in an application,
         * not many clients support the callback styles.
         * The #ifdef CALLBACK_SUPPORT indicates whether or not
         * an application supports the callback styles.
         */
#ifdef CALLBACK_SUPPORT
        XIMPreeditCallbacks|XIMStatusArea,
        XIMPreeditCallbacks|XIMStatusNothing,
        XIMPreeditCallbacks|XIMStatusNone,
        XIMPreeditCallbacks|XIMStatusCallbacks ,
#endif
        XIMPreeditPosition|XIMStatusArea,
        XIMPreeditPosition|XIMStatusNothing,
        XIMPreeditPosition|XIMStatusNone,
#ifdef CALLBACK_SUPPORT
        XIMPreeditPosition|XIMStatusCallbacks,
#endif
        XIMPreeditArea|XIMStatusArea,
        XIMPreeditArea|XIMStatusNothing,
        XIMPreeditArea|XIMStatusNone,
#ifdef CALLBACK_SUPPORT
        XIMPreeditArea|XIMStatusCallbacks,
#endif
        XIMPreeditNothing|XIMStatusArea,
        XIMPreeditNothing|XIMStatusNothing,
        XIMPreeditNothing|XIMStatusNone,
#ifdef CALLBACK_SUPPORT
        XIMPreeditNothing|XIMStatusCallbacks,
#endif
        XIMPreeditNone|XIMStatusArea,
        XIMPreeditNone|XIMStatusNothing,
        XIMPreeditNone|XIMStatusNone,
#ifdef CALLBACK_SUPPORT
```

**Example 6-11:** Creating an IC  (continued)

```
          XIMPreeditNone|XIMStatusCallbacks,
#endif
          NULL
    } ;
    if(!style){
        /*
         * _DetermineStyle() function chooses the best style from
         * the combination of the application's prefered style,
         * the locale-specific system's preferred style, and the input
         * method's prefered style.
         */
        style = _DetermineStyle(im, rdb, res_name, res_class, supported_styles);
    }
    if((ic = XCreateIC(im,
                    XNInputStyle, style,
                    XNClientWindow, client_window,
                    NULL)) == NULL){
        (void)printf("%s: Cannot create an IC\n", program_name);
    }
    return(ic);
}
```

Example 6-12 shows a procedure that determines the best style from twenty possible input styles.

**Example 6-12:** Choosing the Best Input Style

```
/*
 * DetermineStyle() returns the best input style from 20 possible
 * input styles, by taking user's preference priority, system default
 * priority per locale if it exists and the supported styles
 * queried by XGetIMValues().
 *
 */
#include <stdio.h>
#include <fcntl.h>
#include <sys/types.h>
#include <sys/mman.h>
#include <sys/stat.h>
#include <string.h>
#include <X11/Xlocale.h>
#include <X11/Xlib.h>
#include <X11/Xresource.h>
#ifndef XLOCALEDIR
#define XLOCALEDIR "/usr/X11R6/lib/X11/locale"
#endif
#define STYLEFILEPATHSZMAX 30
/*
 * In order to cache the multiple best style per locale, per IM, per
 * individual resource name and class, this complicated structure is needed.
 */
typedef struct _style_cache {
    struct _style_cache *next ;
    char *locale ;
    XIM   im ;
    XrmDatabase rdb;
```

**Example 6-12:** Choosing the Best Input Style (continued)

```
    char        *res_name ;
    char        *res_class ;
    XIMStyle    best_style ;
    XIMStyles   *user_styles ;
    XIMStyles   *im_dep_styles ;
    XIMStyles   *lc_dep_styles ;
} style_cache_t ;
/*
 * Fallback default
 */
#define DEFAULTStyle        (XIMPreeditNothing|XIMStatusNothing)
static XIMStyles *StrToIMStyles();
static XIMStyle BestStyle();
XIMStyle
DetermineStyle(im, rdb, res_name, res_class, supported_styles)
    XIM         im;
    XrmDatabase rdb;
    char        *res_name ;
    char        *res_class ;
    XIMStyles   *supported_styles ;
{
    static style_cache_t *p = 0 ;
    static XIMStyles *lc_dep_styles = 0 ;
    static XIMStyles ;
    char *rmtype ;
    XrmValue rmval ;
    if(!p){
        if((p = (style_cache_t *)calloc(sizeof(style_cache_t),1))==NULL) {
            return(DEFAULTStyle);
        }
    } else {
        /*
         * check the cache first
         */
        XIMStyles *lc_dep_styles = 0 ;
        char *locale = setlocale(LC_CTYPE, NULL);
        for(;;) {
            if(!strcmp(p->locale, locale)){
                if(p->im == im &&
                   p->rdb == rdb &&
                   !strcmp(p->res_name, res_name) &&
                   !strcmp(p->res_class, res_class)) {
                    return(p->best_style);
                }
                lc_dep_styles = p->lc_dep_styles ;
            }
            if (p->next){
                p = p->next ;
            } else {
                break ;
            }
        }
        if((p->next = (style_cache_t *)calloc(sizeof(style_cache_t),1))
                ==NULL) {
            return(DEFAULTStyle);
        }
        p = p->next ;
```

*6. Internationalization*

**Example 6-12:** Choosing the Best Input Style  (continued)

```
        if(lc_dep_styles){
            p->lc_dep_styles = lc_dep_styles ;
        }
    }
    /*
     * first time for this combination
     */
    p->locale = strdup(setlocale(LC_CTYPE, NULL));
    p->im = im ;
    p->rdb = rdb ;
    p->res_name = strdup(res_name);
    p->res_class = strdup(res_class);
    XGetIMValues(im, XNQueryInputStyle, &p->im_dep_styles, NULL);
    if(XrmGetResource(rdb, res_name, res_class, &rmtype, &rmval)){
        /*
         * We should use user's priority list
         */
        p->user_styles = StrToIMStyles(rmval.size, rmval.addr);
        p->best_style = BestStyle(p->user_styles, p->im_dep_styles,
                supported_styles) ;
    } else {
        if(!p->lc_dep_styles){
        /*
         * An application typically defines its input style
         * preference priority order in its program. However, the input
         * style preference priory differs among locales.
         * The sample code listed inside #ifdef USESYSTEMDEFAULTSTYLE
         * shows one solution for an application to avoid hard-coding
         * the locale-specific input style preference priority.
         * The sample code suggests to have a priority order list
         * outside of the application program as a locale-specific file.
         */
#ifdef USESYSTEMDEFAULTSTYLE
        /*
         * The code in this block runs once per locale.
         */
        int fd ;
        static int size = 0 ;
        static char *fn ;
        char *s ;
        static char *xlocalehome=0 ;

        if(!size){
            size = getpagesize();
        }
        if(!xlocalehome){
            if(!(xlocalehome = (char *)getenv("XLOCALEDIR"))){
                xlocalehome = XLOCALEDIR ;
            }
            fn = (char *)malloc(strlen(xlocalehome)+strlen(p->locale)
                    +STYLEFILEPATHSZMAX) ;
            sprintf(fn, "%s/%s/InputStyles", xlocalehome, p->locale);
        }
        if( (fd = open(fn, O_RDONLY)) == -1 ){
            p->lc_dep_styles = p->im_dep_styles ;
        } else {
            struct stat buf ;
```

**Example 6-12:** Choosing the Best Input Style (continued)

```
                    fstat(fd, &buf) ;
                    size = ((buf.st_size+size)/size)*size ;
                    if((int)(s = mmap(0,size ,PROT_READ,MAP_SHARED,fd,0)) == -1){
                        p->lc_dep_styles = StrToIMStyles(buf.st_size, s);
                    }
                    close(fd);
                }
    #else
                p->lc_dep_styles = p->im_dep_styles ;
    #endif
                p->best_style= BestStyle(p->lc_dep_styles, p->im_dep_styles,
                        supported_styles) ;
            }
        }
        return(p->best_style);
    }
    #define MAXSTYLES 20
    /*
     * This structure maps the input style name that a user or a system
     * specifiy to the XIMStyle value.
     */
    static
    struct _XIMStyleRec {
        XIMStyle style ;
        char *name ;
        int namelen ;
    } XIMStyleRec[] = {
    XIMPreeditCallbacks|XIMStatusArea,"XIMPreeditCallbacks|XIMStatusArea",33,
    XIMPreeditCallbacks|XIMStatusNothing,
            "XIMPreeditCallbacks|XIMStatusNothing",36,
    XIMPreeditCallbacks|XIMStatusNone,"XIMPreeditCallbacks|XIMStatusNone",33,
    XIMPreeditCallbacks|XIMStatusCallbacks,
            "XIMPreeditCallbacks|XIMStatusCallbacks",38,
    XIMPreeditPosition|XIMStatusArea,"XIMPreeditPosition|XIMStatusArea",32,
    XIMPreeditPosition|XIMStatusNothing,
            "XIMPreeditPosition|XIMStatusNothing",35,
    XIMPreeditPosition|XIMStatusNone,"XIMPreeditPosition|XIMStatusNone",32,
    XIMPreeditPosition|XIMStatusCallbacks,
            "XIMPreeditPosition|XIMStatusCallbacks",37,
    XIMPreeditArea|XIMStatusArea,"XIMPreeditArea|XIMStatusArea",28,
    XIMPreeditArea|XIMStatusNothing,"XIMPreeditArea|XIMStatusNothing",31,
    XIMPreeditArea|XIMStatusNone,"XIMPreeditArea|XIMStatusNone",28,
    XIMPreeditArea|XIMStatusCallbacks,"XIMPreeditArea|XIMStatusCallbacks",33,
    XIMPreeditNothing|XIMStatusArea,"XIMPreeditNothing|XIMStatusArea",31,
    XIMPreeditNothing|XIMStatusNothing,"XIMPreeditNothing|XIMStatusNothing",34,
    XIMPreeditNothing|XIMStatusNone,"XIMPreeditNothing|XIMStatusNone",31,
    XIMPreeditNothing|XIMStatusCallbacks,
            "XIMPreeditNothing|XIMStatusCallbacks",36,
    XIMPreeditNone|XIMStatusArea,"XIMPreeditNone|XIMStatusArea",28,
    XIMPreeditNone|XIMStatusNothing,"XIMPreeditNone|XIMStatusNothing",31,
    XIMPreeditNone|XIMStatusNone,"XIMPreeditNone|XIMStatusNone",28,
    XIMPreeditNone|XIMStatusCallbacks,"XIMPreeditNone|XIMStatusCallbacks",33,
    } ;
    /*
     * Convert the string containing the input style priority list
     * in the format like
     *
```

**Example 6-12:** Choosing the Best Input Style (continued)

```
XIMPreeditPosition|XIMStatusArea
XIMPreeditPosition|XIMStatusNothing
XIMPreeditArea|XIMStatusArea
XIMPreeditArea|XIMStatusNothing    .
XIMPreeditNothing|XIMStatusArea
XIMPreeditNothing|XIMStatusNothing
 *
 * to the XIMStyles structure.
 */
static XIMStyles *
StrToIMStyles(size, s)
    int size ;
    char *s  ;
{
    XIMStyles *p = (XIMStyles *)calloc(sizeof(XIMStyles),1);
    register int i ;
    register char *c ;
    register char *end = s + size ;
    /*
     * assuming at least following 4 styles (Nothing * None)
     * are supported.
     */
    p->count_styles = 4 ;
    p->supported_styles = (XIMStyle *)calloc(sizeof(XIMStyle), MAXSTYLE+4);
    p->supported_styles[0] = XIMPreeditNothing|XIMStatusNothing ;
    p->supported_styles[1] = XIMPreeditNothing|XIMStatusNone ;
    p->supported_styles[2] = XIMPreeditNone|XIMStatusNothing ;
    p->supported_styles[3] = XIMPreeditNone|XIMStatusNone ;
    /*
     * The following routine assumes that the style name listed in
     * InputStyle file is identical with the programatic name of style.
     * For example, "XIMPreeditPosition|XIMStatusArea" means the
     * XIMPreeditPosition|XIMStatusArea value is specified. If the
     * style name is changed, such as "OverTheSpot|imDisplaysInClient",
     * the parsing logic below should be modified as well.
     */
    for(c = strchr(s, 'X') ; c < end ;){
        for(i=0;i<MAXSTYLES;i++){
            if(!strncmp(c, XIMStyleRec[i].name, XIMStyleRec[i].namelen)){
              p->count_styles++ ;
              p->supported_styles[p->count_styles-1] = XIMStyleRec[i].style ;
               c += XIMStyleRec[i].namelen ;
               break ;
              }
          }
        if(!(c = strchr(c, 'X'))){
            break ;
          }
      }
    return(p);
}
/*
 * Choose the best style
 */
static XIMStyle
BestStyle(prio_order, im_support, client_support)
    XIMStyles *prio_order ;
```

**Example 6-12:** Choosing the Best Input Style  (continued)

```
        XIMStyles *im_support ;
        XIMStyles *client_support ;
{
        register int i, j, k ;
        register XIMStyle best_style ;
        for (i = 0 ; i<prio_order->count_styles ; i++){
            best_style = prio_order->supported_styles[i];
            for (j = 0 ; j<im_support->count_styles ; j++){
                if(im_support->supported_styles[i] == best_style ){
                    for (k = 0 ; k<im_support->count_styles ; k++){
                        if(client_support->supported_styles[i] == best_style ){
                            return(best_style);
                        }
                    }
                }
            }
        }
        return(DEFAULTStyle);
}
_XGetIMInputStyleError(){
        fprintf(stderr, "%s: Warning: Cannot determine inputstyle\n",
                program_name);
}
```

## 6.8.5   String Conversion

The String Conversion facility provides a general framework for manipulating text residing in the client buffer. With String Conversion, an input method can retrieve text from a client, as if it were XEvents sent from the X Server, and manipulate it as its input. Because String Conversion is a multi-purpose framework, it can be used differently depending on the language needs. Typical usage of String Conversion includes: composition without using pre-editing, re-conversion of a previously committed string, or context-sensitive composition.

Composition with String Conversion is an alternative to pre-editing in some languages; it is often called *post-editing*. Unlike pre-editing, which hides an intermediate composition process from a client, a post-editing exposes the intermediate composition process to a client by directly manipulating the text residing in the client buffer.

Re-conversion of a previously committed text or a selected text which resides within the client buffer is one of the long-awaited convenient features for languages that require a complex input method, such as Japanese. Re-conversion is very common in commercial word processors in such languages. With a re-conversion facility, a user can save a significant number of keystrokes to compose text. Re-conversion can typically work as an *undo* operation of the text previously pre-edited. If an input method does not have a re-conversion facility, a user needs to redo the whole pre-editing sequence from the beginning when he mistypes text. However, with the re-conversion facility, a user can undo the commit operation and go back to the middle of the pre-editing stage, with just a small number of key strokes (for example, *cntl-/*) to designate the re-conversion operation.

Context-sensitive conversion with String Conversion is also an alternative method of pre-editing in languages that require context-sensitive composition, such as Thai. While in composition, an input method needs to retrieve the text surrounding the current insertion point of the client's buffer in order to compose complete and meaningful characters by checking the input sequence.

String Conversion can be initiated from either a client or an input method. Client-initiated String Conversion needs to be implemented in the client side. A client-initiated String Conversion is typically used for re-conversion of the selected text in the client's buffer. A client initiates String Conversion by calling `XSetICValues` with `XNStringConversion` XIC value with an argument of type `XIMStringConversion-Text`, containing the text to be converted. How to select the text and how to trigger String Conversion depends on the client's implementation.

The structure of type `XIMStringConversionText` is shown in Example 6-13.

**Example 6-13:** The XIMStringConversionText

```
typedef struct _XIMStringConversionText {
        unsigned short length;
        XIMStringConversionFeedback *feedback;
        Bool encoding_is_wchar;
        union {
                char    *mbs;
                wchar_t *wcs;
        } string;
} XIMStringConversionText;
typedef unsigned long XIMStringConversionFeedback;
```

Input method-initiated String Conversion requires a client to provide a String Conversion Callback function that the input method will use to retrieve the text from the client's buffer. A client needs to register a String Conversion Callback function as an argument of the `XNStringConversionCallback` XIC value via `XSetICValues()`. The input method-initiated String Conversion is often bound to the input method key sequence. A String Conversion Callback is a structure of type `XIMCallback`. The callback prototype is shown in Example 6-14.

**Example 6-14:** String Conversion Callback

```
void
StringConversionCallback(ic, client_data, call_data)
    XIC ic;
    XPointer client_data;
    XIMStringConversionCallbackStruct *call_data;
```

The call_data passed to the string conversion callback is a pointer to a structure of type `XIMStringConversionCallbackStruct`. This structure carries the data not only from the input method to the callback, but also from the callback to the input method. The `XIMStringConversionCallbackStruct` structure and the definitions of its members are shown in Example 6-15.

**Example 6-15:** XIMStringConversionCallbackStruct and Its Members

```
typedef struct _XIMStringConversionCallbackStruct {
        XIMStringConversionPosition position;
        XIMCaretDirection direction;
        short factor;
        XIMStringConversionOperation operation;
        XIMStringConversionText *text;
} XIMStringConversionCallbackStruct;
typedef short XIMStringConversionPosition;
typedef unsigned short XIMStringConversionOperation;
#define XIMStringConversionSubstitution (0x0001)
#define XIMStringConversionRetrieval    (0x0002)
typedef enum {
        XIMForwardChar, XIMBackwardChar,
        XIMForwardWord, XIMBackwardWord,
        XIMCaretUp, XIMCaretDown,
        XIMNextLine, XIMPreviousLine,
        XIMLineStart, XIMLineEnd,
        XIMAbsolutePosition,
        XIMDontChange,
} XIMCaretDirection;
```

XIMStringConversionPosition specifies the starting position of the text to be returned in the XIMStringConversionText structure. The value identifies a position, in units of characters, relative to the client's insertion point in the client's buffer. The direction specifies the extent to which string conversion takes effect. The factor specifies the number of times direction will be applied.

XIMStringConversionOperation specifies whether the string to be converted should be deleted by the client (when XIMStringConversionOperation is XIMStringConversionSubstitution) or copied by the client (when XIMStringConversionOperation is XIMStringConversionRetrieval). The substitute operation is typically used for re-conversion and transliteration conversion (for example, converting between locale-specific phonetic characters and the corresponding romanized characters), while the retrieval operation is typically used for context-sensitive conversion.

## 6.8.6    Hot Keys

In X11R5, the XIM architecture assumed that an input method always takes precedence over a client, while an input method is performing pre-editing. In X11R6, XIM enhances this approach by introducing a facility for temporary escape from and return to pre-editing. An application that requires a special key operation regardless of the input method state, such as moving input focus with a special key, or a client-specific help key (until a help session is finished, the pre-editing session needs to be suspended), can register a set of keys as *Hot Keys*. Hot Keys are guaranteed by an input method not to be processed even during pre-editing. When the Hot Keys specified conflict with the key bindings of the input method, hot keys take precedence. Resolving the conflicts is left to the key binding of the input method and the application.

To register Hot Keys, set the hot key list (which is a pointer to a structure of type `XIMHotKeyTriggers`) to the `XNHotKey` attribute via `XSetICValues()`. The structure `XIMHotKeyTriggers` is shown in Example 6-16.

**Example 6-16:** The XIMHotKeyTriggers

```
typedef struct {
        int num_hot_key;
        XIMHotKeyTrigger key;
} XIMHotKeyTriggers;
typedef struct {
        KeySym keysym;
        unsigned int modifier;
        unsigned int modifier_mask;
} XIMHotKeyTrigger;
```

Once a Hot Key is found by an input method during pre-editing, the input method suspends itself and passes control temporarily back to a client. A client is responsible for returning control back to the input method by setting `XNHotKeyState` to `XIMHotKeyStateOFF` via `XSetICValues()`. The possible values of type `XIMHotKeyState` are as shown in Example 6-17.

**Example 6-17:** The XIMHotKeyState

```
typedef unsigned long XIMHotKeyState;
#define XIMHotKeyStateON  (0x0001L)
#define XIMHotKeyStateOFF (0x0002L)
```

## 6.8.7    Visible Position Indication

The X11R5 *on-the-spot* input style has a deficiency when attempting to draw pre-edit strings that are longer than the available space. Once the display area is exceeded, a pre-edit string could be displayed randomly by the client. X11R5 *on-the-spot* input style uses the type `XIMText`, which contains a member of type `XIMFeedback` to indicate the attribute per character, to exchange the text data between an input method and an application.

X11R6 introduces three new `XIMFeedback` values, `XIMVisibleToForward`, `XIMVisibleToBackward`, and `XIMVisibleCenter`. These new values allow the IM to give hints on the priority of displaying a particular character within a pre-edit string, should the display length of the pre-edit string exceed the length of the display area. The type `XIMText` in X11R6 is shown in Example 6-18:

**Example 6-18:** The Visible Position Indication in XIMText

```
typedef unsigned long XIMFeedback;
#define XIMReverse        1L
#define XIMUnderline      (1L<<1)
#define XIMHighlight      (1L<<2)
#define XIMPrimary        (1L<<3)
#define XIMSecondary      (1L<<4)
```

**Example 6-18:** The Visible Position Indication in XIMText (continued)

```
#define XIMTertiary           (1L<<5)
#define XIMVisibleToForward    (1L<<8)
#define XIMVisibleToBackward   (1L<<9)
#define XIMVisibleCenter       (1L<<10)
typedef struct _XIMText {
    unsigned short length;
    XIMFeedback *feedback;
    Bool encoding_is_wchar;
    union {
        char * multi_byte;
        wchar_t * wide_char;
    } string;
} XIMText;
```

These three new values are mutually exclusive (behavior is undefined if multiple values are specified), in the feedback of XIMText, but they may be OR'ed with the original X11R5 XIMFeedback bit values. At most, one character within the string can be set to one of the three visible position values by the input method. If no character has XIMVisibleToForward, XIMVisibleToBackward, or XIMVisibleCenter set then the client can display the pre-edit as in the Release 5 implementation.

XIMVisibleToForward indicates the drawing of the associated pre-edit character should be started at the left-most position of the display area. XIMVisibleToBackward indicates drawing of the associated pre-edit character should be started at the right-most position of the display area. XIMVisibleCenter indicates drawing of the associated pre-edit character should be started at the middle of the display area.

When visible position is specified, the insertion point of the pre-edit string could exist outside of the visible area.

Figure 6-11 shows a pre-edit area of 5 characters being used to edit a string of 10 characters, using each of the feedback values.

Example 6-19 shows code that handles visible position feedback in a PreeditDrawCallback.

**Example 6-19:** Visible Position Handling in PreeditDrawCallback

```
#include <X11/Xlib.h>

/*
 * The local functions to perform the real work
 * which you need to implement.
 */
static void update_buffers();
static void scroll_visible_area_forward();
static void scroll_visible_area_backward();
static void scroll_visible_area_center();
static void delete_from_buffer();
/*
 * In some releases of X11R6, there are bugs in Xlib.h
 * The specification defines XIMVisibleToBackward but
 * Xlib.h defines XIMVisibleToBackword. Also the
```

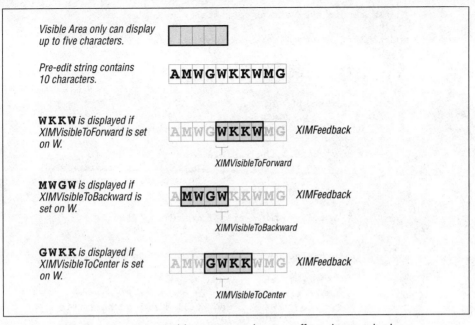

**Figure 6-11:** How visible position indication affects the text display

**Example 6-19:** Visible Position Handling in PreeditDrawCallback (continued)

```
 * specification defines XIMVisibleCenter but
 * Xlib.h defines XIMVisibleToCenter.
 */
#ifdef XIMVisibleToBackword
#undef XIMVisibleToBackword
#define XIMVisibleToBackward (1L<<9)
#endif
#ifdef XIMVisibleToCenter
#undef XIMVisibleToCenter
#define XIMVisibleCenter (1L<<10)
#endif
/*
 * Sample X11R6 Preedit Draw Callback.
 */
static XIMProc
narrow_area_preedit_draw_cb(xic, client_data, call_data)
    XIC xic;
    XPointer client_data;
    XIMPreeditDrawCallbackStruct *call_data;
{
    XIMText *text      = call_data->text;
    int     chg_first  = call_data->chg_first;
    int     chg_length = call_data->chg_length;
    int     i;
    if (text && text->length > 0){ /* text/feedback substitution */
        /*
         * update the buffer accordingly.
         * The functionality of update_buffer() function
```

```
                    * can remain the same as X11R5 callback.
                    */
                   update_buffers(chg_first, chg_length, text);
                   /*
                    * X11R6 specific operation
                    * Update the text position in the visible area
                    */
                   if(text->feedback){
                       for(i = 0 ; i < text->length ; i++){
                           if(text->feedback[i] | XIMVisibleToForward){
                               /*
                                * Scroll the visible area
                                * so that character in the buffer position
                                * chg_first + i and the preceding characters
                                * are displayed
                                */
                               scroll_visible_area_forward(chg_first + i);
                               break ;
                           }
                           if(text->feedback[i] | XIMVisibleToBackward){
                               /*
                                * Scroll the visible area
                                * so that character in the buffer position
                                * chg_first + i and the following characters
                                * are displayed
                                */
                               scroll_visible_area_backward(chg_first + i);
                               break ;
                           }
                           if(text->feedback[i] | XIMVisibleCenter){
                               /*
                                * Scroll the visible area backward
                                * so that character in the buffer position
                                * chg_first + i and the surrounding characters
                                * are displayed
                                */
                               scroll_visible_area_center(chg_first + i);
                               break ;
                           }
                       }
                   }
               } else { /* text deletion */
                   /*
                    * delete the length chg_length of text starting from
                    * character position chg_fitst of the buffer
                    */
                   delete_from_buffer(chg_first, chg_length);
               }
           }
```

## 6.8.8    PreeditState

The XNPreeditState XIC value specifies or retrieves the preedit state, indicating whether the input method is currently performing a pre-editing operation. An input method may have several internal states, depending on its implementation and the locale. Because the internal state of an input method is implementation-dependent and locale-dependent, in X11R6 the `XNPreeditState` XIC value specifies or retrieves only whether the input method is currently performing a pre-editing operation, which is considered a locale-independent concept. The `XNPreeditState` XIC value is of type `XIMPreeditState`. The possible values are as shown in Example 6-20 and described below.

**Example 6-20:** The XIMPreeditState

```
typedef unsigned long XIMPreeditState;

#define XIMPreeditUnknown 0L
#define XIMPreeditEnable  1L
#define XIMPreeditDisable (1L<<1)
```

`XIMPreeditUnknown`

If a value of `XIMPreeditUnknown` is returned from `XGetICValues()`, then the pre-editing state of the input method is unknown.

`XIMPreeditEnable`

If a value of `XIMPreeditEnable` is set by `XSetICValues()`, then input pre-editing is turned on by the input method. If a value of `XIMPreeditEnable` is returned from `XGetICValues()`, then the input method is currently performing input pre-editing.

`XIMPreeditDisable`

If a value of `XIMPreeditDisable` is set by `XSetICValues()`, then input pre-editing is turned off by the input method. If a value of `XIMPreeditEnable` is returned from `XGetICValues()`, then the input method is currently performing input pre-editing.

## 6.8.9    PreeditStateCallback

The `XNPreeditStateCallback` XIC attribute registers a pre-edit state notify callback to an input context. When the pre-editing state of the specified input context is changed, the pre-edit state notify callback is invoked by the input method. A use of pre-edit state notify callback for checking a pre-edit state of an input context may be less expensive than frequently querying a pre-editing state of an input context by using `XGetICValues()` with `XNPreeditState`.

The `XNPreeditStateCallback` is passed a *call_data* of type `XIMPreeditStateCallbackStruct`, which is shown in Example 6-21.

**Example 6-21:** The XIMPreeditStateCallbackStruct

```
typedef unsigned long XIMPreeditState;

#define XIMPreeditUnknown 0L
#define XIMPreeditEnable  1L
#define XIMPreeditDisable (1L<<1)


typedef struct _XIMPreeditStateNotifyCallbackStruct {
       XIMPreeditState state;
} XIMPreeditStateNotifyCallbackStruct;
```

### 6.8.10    Reset State

In X11R5, the input context returns to the initial state after you call XmbResetIC() or
XwcResetIC(). X11R6 allows you to specify whether the input context preserves the
current state or returns to the initial state after such a reset. The XNResetState XIC
value specifies which state the input context returns to after calling XmbResetIC() or
XwcResetIC(). The XNResetState XIC value is of type XIMResetState. The possible
values are XIMInitialState or XIMPreserveState.

If XIMPreserveState is set, an input context retains the current state after XmbRe-
setIC() or XwcResetState().

If XIMInitialState is specified, or XNResetState is left unspecified, an input context will return to the initial state after you call XmbResetIC() or XwcResetState().

## 6.9    Complete X i18n Example Program

Example 6-22 is the complete code of a program that performs simple internationalized text input and output. Many of the examples in this chapter are fragments of this
program. This program demonstrates some of the Release 6 internationalized Xlib
functions. It creates a very simple window, connects to an input method, and displays
composed text obtained by calling XwcLookupString. It backspaces when it receives
the Backspace or Delete keysyms. Example 6-22 shows the program running.

**Example 6-22:** Complete X i18n Sample Program

```
#include <stdio.h>
#include <malloc.h>
#include <X11/Xlib.h>
#include <X11/Xutil.h>
#include <X11/keysym.h>
#include <X11/Xresource.h>
#include <string.h>
/*
 * Xlocale.h includes <locale.h> or the non-standard X substitutes
 * depending on the X_LOCALE compilation flag.
 */
#include <X11/Xlocale.h>
/*
```

**Example 6-22:** Complete X il8n Sample Program (continued)

```
 * For error messages
 */
char *program_name ;
char* class_name ;
/*
 * Whether Xlib performs directional dependent drawing or not.
 * Assume Xlib does not perform as default.
 */
Bool is_implicit_ddd = False;
/*
 * Whether Xlib performs contextual dependent drawing or not.
 * Assume Xlib does not perform as default.
 */
Bool is_implicit_cdd = False;
/*
 * Default Orientation.
 */
XOMOrientation *orientation ;
/*
 * Supported im/ic values list.
 */
XIMValuesList im_values_list ;
XIMValuesList ic_values_list ;
/*
 * Private convenient functions
 */
static XOM open_om(/*display, ProgramName, ClassName*/) ;
static XOC create_oc(/*om, ProgramName, ClassName*/) ;
static XIC create_ic(/*im, client_window, rdb, res_name, res_class*/);
static void initializeXIM(/*display, app_im_init*/) ;
static void app_im_init(/* display */);
static XIMStyle _DetermineStyle(/* im, rdb, res_name, res_class,
        supported_styles*/);
static void GetPreferredGeometry(/* ic, name, area */) ;
static void SetGeometry(/* ic, name, area */) ;
XOM om;
XOC oc;
XIM im;
XIC ic;
int screen;
Window win;
int
main(argc, argv)
int argc;
char *argv[];
{
    Display *display ;
    GC gc;
    XGCValues gcv;
    XEvent event;
    XIMStyles *im_supported_styles;
    XIMStyle app_supported_styles;
    XIMStyle style;
    XIMStyle best_style;
    XVaNestedList list;
    long im_event_mask;
    XRectangle preedit_area;
```

**Example 6-22:** Complete X i18n Sample Program (continued)

```
XRectangle status_area;
char **missing_charsets;
int num_missing_charsets = 0;
char *default_string;
wchar_t string[200];
int str_len = 0;
int i;
XWMHints hints;
unsigned long  mask;
program_name = strdup(argv[0]);
class_name = strdup(argv[0]);
/*
 * The error messages in this program are all in English.
 * In a truly internationalized program, they would not
 * be hardcoded; they would be looked up in a database of
 * some sort.
 */
if (setlocale(LC_ALL, "") == NULL) {
    (void) fprintf(stderr, "%s: cannot set locale.\n",program_name);
    exit(1);
}
if ((display = XOpenDisplay(NULL)) == NULL) {
    (void) fprintf(stderr, "%s: cannot open Display.\n", program_name);
    exit(1);
}
if (!XSupportsLocale()) {
    (void) fprintf(stderr, "%s: X does not support locale \"%s\".\n",
                program_name, setlocale(LC_ALL, NULL));
    exit(1);
}
if (XSetLocaleModifiers("") == NULL) {
    (void) fprintf(stderr, "%s: Warning: cannot set locale
                            modifiers.\n", program_name);

    /*
     * Try setting the local IM as fallback
     */
    if (XSetLocaleModifiers("@im=none") == NULL) {
        (void) fprintf(stderr,
            "%s: Warning: cannot set fallback locale modifiers.\n",
                    program_name);
    }
}
/*
 * Opening an output method
 */
if((om = open_om(display, program_name, class_name)) == NULL){
    (void) fprintf(stderr,
            "%s: Cannot open XOM for the locale \"%s\".\n",
                    program_name, setlocale(LC_ALL, NULL));
    exit(1);
}
/*
 * Creating an output context
 */
if((oc = create_oc(om, program_name, class_name)) == NULL){
    (void) fprintf(stderr,
```

**Example 6-22:** Complete X i18n Sample Program (continued)

```
                       "%s: Cannot create XOC for the locale \"%s\".\n",
                           program_name, setlocale(LC_ALL, NULL));
        exit(1);
    }

    screen = DefaultScreen(display);
    win = XCreateSimpleWindow(display, RootWindow(display, screen), 0, 0,
            400, 100, 2, WhitePixel(display,screen),
            BlackPixel(display,screen));
    gc = XCreateGC(display,win,0,&gcv);
    XSetForeground(display,gc,WhitePixel(display,screen));
    XSetBackground(display,gc,BlackPixel(display,screen));
    hints.flags = InputHint;
    hints.input = True;
    XSetWMHints(display, win, &hints);
    mask = StructureNotifyMask | FocusChangeMask | ExposureMask;
    XSelectInput(display, win, mask);
    /*
     * Register XIM instantiate callback if IM Server is not running,
     * otherwise call application's IM initialize routine
     */
    initializeXIM(display, program_name, class_name, app_im_init);
    XMapWindow(display,win);
    while(1) {
        int buf_len = 10;
        wchar_t *buffer = (wchar_t *)malloc(buf_len * sizeof(wchar_t));
        int len;
        KeySym keysym;
        Status status;
        Bool redraw = False;
        XNextEvent(display, &event);
        if (XFilterEvent(&event, None))
            continue;
        switch (event.type) {
        case Expose:
            /* draw the string at a hard-coded location */
            if (event.xexpose.count == 0)
                XwcDrawString(display, win, (XFontSet)oc, gc, 10, 50,
                        string, str_len);
            break;
        case KeyPress:
            if(ic){
                len = XwcLookupString(ic, (XKeyPressedEvent*)&event, buffer,
                                    buf_len, &keysym, &status);
                if (status == XBufferOverflow) {
                    buf_len = len;
                    buffer = (wchar_t *)realloc((char *)buffer,
                                        buf_len * sizeof(wchar_t));
                    len = XwcLookupString(ic, (XKeyPressedEvent*)&event,
                                        buffer,buf_len, &keysym, &status);
                }

                redraw = False;

                switch (status) {
                  case XLookupNone:
                    break;
```

**Example 6-22:** Complete X i18n Sample Program  (continued)

```
                case XLookupKeySym:
                case XLookupBoth:
                    /* Handle backspacing, and <Return> to exit */
                    if ((keysym == XK_Delete) || (keysym == XK_BackSpace)) {
                        if (str_len > 0) str_len--;
                        redraw = True;
                        break;
                    }
                    if (keysym == XK_Return) exit(0);
                    if (status == XLookupKeySym) break;
                case XLookupChars:
                    for(i=0; i < len; i++)
                        string[str_len++] = buffer[i];
                    redraw = True;
                    break;
                }
            } else {
                /*
                 * Until ic is created, behave as C locale client.
                 */
                len = XLookupString(&event, buffer, buf_len,
                                    &keysym, NULL);
            }
            /* do a very simple-minded redraw, if needed */
            if (redraw) {
                XClearWindow(display, win);
                XwcDrawString(display, win, (XFontSet)om, gc, 10, 50, string,
                        str_len);
            }
            break;
        case ConfigureNotify:
            /*
             * When the window is resized, we should re-negotiate the
             * geometry of the Preedit and Status area, if they are used
             * in the interaction style.
             */
            if (best_style & XIMPreeditArea) {
                preedit_area.width = event.xconfigure.width*4/5;
                preedit_area.height = 0;
                GetPreferredGeometry(ic, XNPreeditAttributes,
                        &preedit_area);
                preedit_area.x = event.xconfigure.width -
                        preedit_area.width;
                preedit_area.y = event.xconfigure.height -
                        preedit_area.height;
                SetGeometry(ic, XNPreeditAttributes, &preedit_area);
            }
            if (best_style & XIMStatusArea) {
                status_area.width = event.xconfigure.width/5;
                status_area.height = 0;
                GetPreferredGeometry(ic, XNStatusAttributes,
                        &status_area);
                status_area.x = 0;
                status_area.y = event.xconfigure.height -
                        status_area.height;
                SetGeometry(ic, XNStatusAttributes, &status_area);
            }
```

```
                break;
            case FocusIn:
                if (event.xany.window == win) {
                    if(ic)
                        XSetICFocus(ic);
                }
                break;
            case FocusOut:
                if (event.xany.window == win) {
                    if(ic)
                        XUnsetICFocus(ic);
                }
                break;
        }
    }
}
XOM
open_om(display, ProgramName, ClassName)
    Display *display;
    char *ProgramName;
    char *ClassName;
{
    XOM om ;
    XrmDatabaserdb = XrmGetDatabase(display);

    if((om = XOpenOM(display, rdb, ProgramName, ClassName)) == NULL){
        (void)fprintf(stderr, "%s: Cannot open Output Method\n",
                    program_name);
        return (XOM)NULL ;
    }
    if(XGetOMValues(om, XNOrientation, &orientation, NULL)){
        /*
         * Assume Left to Right, Top to Bottom as fallback.
         */
        orientation = (XOMOrientation *)malloc(sizeof(XOMOrientation));
#ifdef BUGFIX
        /*
         * As this book goes to press, there are bugs in Xlib.h.
         * The specification defines num_orientation and orientation
         * as members of XOMOrientation, but Xlib.h defines them
         * as num_orient and orient
         */
        orientation->num_orientation = 1 ;
        orientation->orientation = (XOrientation *)malloc(sizeof
                (XOrientation));
        *orientation->orientation = XOMOrientation_LTR_TTB ;
#else
        orientation->num_orient = 1 ;
        orientation->orient = (XOrientation *)malloc(sizeof(XOrientation));
        *orientation->orient = XOMOrientation_LTR_TTB ;
#endif
    }
    XGetOMValues(om, XNDirectionalDependentDrawing, &is_implicit_ddd, NULL);
    XGetOMValues(om, XNContextualDrawing, &is_implicit_cdd, NULL);

    return om ;
}
```

**Example 6-22:** Complete X i18n Sample Program (continued)

```
#define DEFAULT_BASE_FONT "-misc-fixed-*-*-*-*-*-130-75-75-*-*-*-*"
XOC
create_oc(om, ProgramName, ClassName)
    XOM om ;
    char *ProgramName;
    char *ClassName;
{
    int i ;
    char    *base_font_name = DEFAULT_BASE_FONT ;
    XOC oc;
    XOMCharSetList list;

    if ((oc = XCreateOC(om, XNBaseFontName, base_font_name, NULL)) == NULL){
        (void)fprintf(stderr, "%s: Cannot create Output Context\n",
                    program_name);
        return (XOC)NULL ;
    }

    if(!XGetOCValues(oc, XNMissingCharSet, &list, NULL)){
        if( list.charset_count > 0){
            (void)fprintf(stderr,
                "%s: Warning: the following charsets are missing\n",
                program_name);
            for(i=0; i < list.charset_count ; i++){
                (void)fprintf(stderr,
                    "%s:        %s\n", program_name, list.charset_list[i]);
            }
        }
    }
    return oc;
}
/*
 * Callback to instantiate an input method on demand.
 * invoke input method related application initialization routine.
 */
static void
im_instantiate_callback(display, client_data, call_data)
    Display *display;
    XPointer client_data;
    XPointer call_data;
{
    XIMProc app_im_init = (XIMProc)client_data ;

    (*app_im_init)(display); /* invoke application im initialize routine */
}
/*
 * Register im instantiate callback.
 * If IM Server is already runnning, im_instantiate_callback
 * is immediately invoked from here.
 */
void
initializeXIM(display, program_name, class_name, app_im_init)
    Display *display;
    char *program_name;
    char * class_name;
    XIMProc app_im_init ; /* Client data */
{
```

*6. Internationalization*

**Example 6-22:** Complete X il8n Sample Program (continued)

```
        XrmDatabaserdb = XrmGetDatabase(display);
        XRegisterIMInstantiateCallback(display, rdb,
                                program_name, class_name,
                                im_instantiate_callback,
                                (XPointer*)app_im_init);
}
static void
destroy_callback(ic, client_data, call_data )
    XIC        ic;
    XPointer   client_data;
    XPointer   *call_data;
{
    im = NULL;
    ic = NULL;
}
static
is_supported(val, val_list)
    char *val ;
    XIMValuesList *val_list ;
{
    unsigned short i ;
    for(i = 0 ; i < val_list->count_values ; i++){
        /*
         * Workarround: double check
         */
        if(!val_list->supported_values)
            return False ;
        if(!strcmp(val, val_list->supported_values[i])){
            return True;
        }
    }
    return False;
}
/*
 * Application specific XIM initialization
 */
void app_im_init(display)
    Display *display;
{
    XIMCallback destroy;
    XrmDatabaserdb = XrmGetDatabase(display);
    if(!(im = XOpenIM(display, rdb, program_name, class_name))){
        return;
    }
    /*
     * Retrieve supported XIM velues list and XIC values list
     * for later usage.
     */
    if(XGetIMValues(im, XNQueryIMValuesList, &im_values_list, NULL)){
        fprintf(stderr, "%s: Warning: XNQueryIMValuesList failed\n",
                program_name);
    }

    /*
     * Check XNDestroyCallback is supported or not by using the
     * just retrieved im values list
     */
```

**Example 6-22:** Complete X i18n Sample Program (continued)

```
            if(is_supported(XNDestroyCallback, &im_values_list)){
                destroy.callback = destroy_callback;
                destroy.client_data = NULL;
                XSetIMValues(im, XNDestroyCallback, &destroy, NULL );
            } else {
                fprintf(stderr, "%s: Warning: Xlib does not support destroy
                        callback\n",program_name);
            }
            if(is_supported(XNQueryICValuesList, &im_values_list)){
                /*
                 * Retrieve supported XIC velues list and XIC values list
                 * for later usage.
                 */
                if(XGetIMValues(im, XNQueryICValuesList, &ic_values_list, NULL)){
                    fprintf(stderr, "%s: Warning: XNQueryICValuesList failed\n",
                            program_name);
                }
            }
            /*
             * Creating an input context
             */
            if((ic = create_ic(im, win, rdb, program_name, class_name)) == NULL){
                (void) fprintf(stderr,
                        "%s: Cannot create XOC for the locale \"%s\".\n",
                            program_name, setlocale(LC_ALL, NULL));
                exit(1);
            }
    }
    /*
     * Create an IC with best input style in given environment.
     */
    XIC
    create_ic(im, client_window, rdb, res_name, res_class)
    XIM im;
    Window client_window ;
    XrmDatabase rdb;
    char        *res_name ;
    char        *res_class ;
    {
        XIMStyles supported_list ;
        XIC ic ;
        static XIMStyle style ;
        /*
         * The input styles supported by this application.
         */
        static XIMStyle supported_styles[] = {
    #ifdef CALLBACK_SUPPORT
            XIMPreeditCallbacks|XIMStatusArea,
            XIMPreeditCallbacks|XIMStatusNothing,
            XIMPreeditCallbacks|XIMStatusNone,
            XIMPreeditCallbacks|XIMStatusCallbacks ,
    #endif
            XIMPreeditPosition|XIMStatusArea,
            XIMPreeditPosition|XIMStatusNothing,
            XIMPreeditPosition|XIMStatusNone,
    #ifdef CALLBACK_SUPPORT
            XIMPreeditPosition|XIMStatusCallbacks,
```

**Example 6-22:** Complete X il8n Sample Program (continued)

```
#endif
        XIMPreeditArea|XIMStatusArea,
        XIMPreeditArea|XIMStatusNothing,
        XIMPreeditArea|XIMStatusNone,
#ifdef CALLBACK_SUPPORT
        XIMPreeditArea|XIMStatusCallbacks,
#endif
        XIMPreeditNothing|XIMStatusArea,
        XIMPreeditNothing|XIMStatusNothing,
        XIMPreeditNothing|XIMStatusNone,
#ifdef CALLBACK_SUPPORT
        XIMPreeditNothing|XIMStatusCallbacks,
#endif
        XIMPreeditNone|XIMStatusArea,
        XIMPreeditNone|XIMStatusNothing,
        XIMPreeditNone|XIMStatusNone,
#ifdef CALLBACK_SUPPORT
        XIMPreeditNone|XIMStatusCallbacks,
#endif
           0
     } ;
     if(!style){
        style = _DetermineStyle(im, rdb, res_name, res_class,
                supported_styles);
     }
     if((ic = XCreateIC(im,
                   XNInputStyle, style,
                   XNClientWindow, client_window,
                   XNFocusWindow, client_window,
                   NULL)) == NULL){
        (void)printf("%s: Cannot create an IC\n", program_name);
     }
     return(ic);
}
/*
 * _DetermineStyle() returns a best input style from 20 possible
 * input styles, by taking user's preference priority, system default
 * priority per locale if exist and the suppoted styles which is queried
 * by XGetIMValues().
 *
 */
#ifndef XLOCALEDIR
#define XLOCALEDIR "/usr/X11R6/lib/X11/locale"
#endif
#define STYLEFILEPATHSZMAX 30
/*
 * In order to cache the multiple best style per locale, per IM, per
 * individual resource name and class, this complicated structure
 * is needed.
 */
typedef struct _style_cache {
    struct _style_cache *next ;
    char *locale ;         •
    XIM   im ;
    XrmDatabase rdb;
    char      *res_name ;
    char      *res_class ;
```

**Example 6-22:** Complete X i18n Sample Program (continued)

```
    XIMStyle     best_style ;
    XIMStyles   *user_styles ;
    XIMStyles   *im_dep_styles ;
    XIMStyles   *lc_dep_styles ;
} style_cache_t ;
/*
 * Fallback default
 */
#define DEFAULTStyle      (XIMPreeditNothing|XIMStatusNothing)
static XIMStyles *StrToIMStyles();
static XIMStyle BestStyle();
static XIMStyle
_DetermineStyle(im, rdb, res_name, res_class, supported_styles)
    XIM          im;
    XrmDatabase rdb;
    char        *res_name ;
    char        *res_class ;
    XIMStyles   *supported_styles ;
{
    static style_cache_t *p = 0 ;
    static XIMStyles *lc_dep_styles = 0 ;
    char *rmtype ;
    XrmValue rmval ;
    if(!p){
        if((p = (style_cache_t *)calloc(sizeof(style_cache_t),1))==NULL) {
            return(DEFAULTStyle);
        }
    } else {
        /*
         * check the cache first
         */
        XIMStyles *lc_dep_styles = 0 ;
        char *locale = setlocale(LC_CTYPE, NULL);
        for(;;) {
            if(!strcmp(p->locale, locale)){
                if(p->im == im &&
                    p->rdb == rdb &&
                    !strcmp(p->res_name, res_name) &&
                    !strcmp(p->res_class, res_class)) {
                     return(p->best_style);
                }
                lc_dep_styles = p->lc_dep_styles ;
            }
            if (p->next){
                p = p->next ;
            } else {
                break ;
            }
        }
        if((p->next = (style_cache_t *)calloc(sizeof(style_cache_t),1))
               ==NULL) {
            return(DEFAULTStyle);
        }
        p = p->next ;
        if(lc_dep_styles){
            p->lc_dep_styles = lc_dep_styles ;
        }
```

```
      }
      /*
       * first time for this combination
       */
      p->locale = strdup(setlocale(LC_CTYPE, NULL));
      p->im = im ;
      p->rdb = rdb ;
      p->res_name = strdup(res_name);
      p->res_class = strdup(res_class);
      XGetIMValues(im, XNQueryInputStyle, &p->im_dep_styles, NULL);
      if(XrmGetResource(rdb, res_name, res_class, &rmtype, &rmval)){
          /*
           * We should use user's priority list
           */
          p->user_styles = StrToIMStyles(rmval.size, rmval.addr);
          p->best_style = BestStyle(p->user_styles, p->im_dep_styles,
                  supported_styles) ;
      } else {
          /*
           * We will use system's per-locale priority list
           */
          if(!p->lc_dep_styles){
#ifdef USESYSTEMDEFAULTSTYLE
              /*
               * The code in this block runs once per locale.
               */
              int fd ;
              static int size = 0 ;
              static char *fn ;
              char *s ;
              static char *xlocalehome=0 ;

              if(!size){
                  size = getpagesize();
              }
              if(!xlocalehome){
                  if(!(xlocalehome = (char *)getenv("XLOCALEDIR"))){
                      xlocalehome = XLOCALEDIR ;
                  }
                  fn = (char *)malloc(strlen(xlocalehome)+strlen(p->locale)
                          +STYLEFILEPATHSZMAX) ;
                  sprintf(fn, "%s/%s/InputStyles", xlocalehome, p->locale);
              }
              if( (fd = open(fn, O_RDONLY)) == -1 ){
                  p->lc_dep_styles = p->im_dep_styles ;
              } else {
                  struct stat buf ;
                  fstat(fd, &buf) ;
                  size = ((buf.st_size+size)/size)*size ;
                  if((int)(s = mmap(0,size ,PROT_READ,MAP_SHARED,fd,0)) == -1){
                      p->lc_dep_styles = StrToIMStyles(buf.st_size, s);
                  }
                  close(fd);
              }
#else
              p->lc_dep_styles = p->im_dep_styles ;
#endif
```

**Example 6-22:** Complete X i18n Sample Program (continued)

```
                 p->best_style= BestStyle(p->lc_dep_styles, p->im_dep_styles,
                          supported_styles) ;
         }
     }
     return(p->best_style);
}
#define MAXSTYLES 20
/*
 * This structure maps the input style name that a user or a system
 * specifiy to the XIMStyle value.
 */
static
struct _XIMStyleRec {
    XIMStyle style ;
    char *name ;
    int namelen ;
} XIMStyleRec[] = {
XIMPreeditCallbacks|XIMStatusArea,"XIMPreeditCallbacks|XIMStatusArea",33,
XIMPreeditCallbacks|XIMStatusNothing,
        "XIMPreeditCallbacks|XIMStatusNothing",36,
XIMPreeditCallbacks|XIMStatusNone,"XIMPreeditCallbacks|XIMStatusNone",33,
XIMPreeditCallbacks|XIMStatusCallbacks,
        "XIMPreeditCallbacks|XIMStatusCallbacks",38,
XIMPreeditPosition|XIMStatusArea,"XIMPreeditPosition|XIMStatusArea",32,
XIMPreeditPosition|XIMStatusNothing,
        "XIMPreeditPosition|XIMStatusNothing",35,
XIMPreeditPosition|XIMStatusNone,"XIMPreeditPosition|XIMStatusNone",32,
XIMPreeditPosition|XIMStatusCallbacks,
        "XIMPreeditPosition|XIMStatusCallbacks",37,
XIMPreeditArea|XIMStatusArea,"XIMPreeditArea|XIMStatusArea",28,
XIMPreeditArea|XIMStatusNothing,"XIMPreeditArea|XIMStatusNothing",31,
XIMPreeditArea|XIMStatusNone,"XIMPreeditArea|XIMStatusNone",28,
XIMPreeditArea|XIMStatusCallbacks,"XIMPreeditArea|XIMStatusCallbacks",33,
XIMPreeditNothing|XIMStatusArea,"XIMPreeditNothing|XIMStatusArea",31,
XIMPreeditNothing|XIMStatusNothing,"XIMPreeditNothing|XIMStatusNothing",34,
XIMPreeditNothing|XIMStatusNone,"XIMPreeditNothing|XIMStatusNone",31,
XIMPreeditNothing|XIMStatusCallbacks,
        "XIMPreeditNothing|XIMStatusCallbacks",36,
XIMPreeditNone|XIMStatusArea,"XIMPreeditNone|XIMStatusArea",28,
XIMPreeditNone|XIMStatusNothing,"XIMPreeditNone|XIMStatusNothing",31,
XIMPreeditNone|XIMStatusNone,"XIMPreeditNone|XIMStatusNone",28,
XIMPreeditNone|XIMStatusCallbacks,"XIMPreeditNone|XIMStatusCallbacks",33,
} ;
/*
 * Convert the string containing the input style priority list
 * in the format like
 *
XIMPreeditPosition|XIMStatusArea
XIMPreeditPosition|XIMStatusNothing
XIMPreeditArea|XIMStatusArea
XIMPreeditArea|XIMStatusNothing
XIMPreeditNothing|XIMStatusArea
XIMPreeditNothing|XIMStatusNothing
 *
 * to the XIMStyles structure.
 *
 */
```

**Example 6-22:** Complete X il8n Sample Program  (continued)

```
static XIMStyles *
StrToIMStyles(size, s)
    int size ;
    char *s  ;
{
    XIMStyles *p = (XIMStyles *)calloc(sizeof(XIMStyles),1);
    register int i ;
    register char *c ;
    register char *end = s + size ;
    /*
     * assuming at least following 4 styles (Nothing * None)
     * are supported.
     */
    p->count_styles = 4 ;
    p->supported_styles = (XIMStyle *)calloc(sizeof(XIMStyle),
            MAXSTYLES+4);
    p->supported_styles[0] = XIMPreeditNothing|XIMStatusNothing ;
    p->supported_styles[1] = XIMPreeditNothing|XIMStatusNone ;
    p->supported_styles[2] = XIMPreeditNone|XIMStatusNothing ;
    p->supported_styles[3] = XIMPreeditNone|XIMStatusNone ;
    /*
     * The following routine assumes that the style name listed in
     * InputStyle file is identical with the programatic name of style.
     * for example, "XIMPreeditPosition|XIMStatusArea" means the
     * XIMPreeditPosition|XIMStatusArea value is specified. If the
     * style name is changed, such as "OverTheSpot|imDisplaysInClient",
     * the parsing logic below should be modified as well.
     */
    for(c = strchr(s, 'X') ; c < end ;){
        for(i=0;i<MAXSTYLES;i++){
            if(!strncmp(c, XIMStyleRec[i].name, XIMStyleRec[i].namelen)){
              p->count_styles++ ;
              p->supported_styles[p->count_styles-1] = XIMStyleRec[i].style ;
              c += XIMStyleRec[i].namelen ;
              break ;
            }
        }
        if(!(c = strchr(c, 'X'))){
            break ;
        }
    }
    return(p);
}
/*
 * Choose the best style
 */
static XIMStyle
BestStyle(prio_order, im_support, client_support)
    XIMStyles *prio_order ;
    XIMStyles *im_support ;
    XIMStyles *client_support ;
{
    register unsigned short i, j, k ;
    register XIMStyle best_style ;
    for (i = 0 ; i<prio_order->count_styles ; i++){
        best_style = prio_order->supported_styles[i];
        for (j = 0 ; j<im_support->count_styles ; j++){
```

**Example 6-22:** Complete X il8n Sample Program (continued)

```
            if(im_support->supported_styles[i] == best_style ){
                for (k = 0 ; k<im_support->count_styles ; k++){
                    if(client_support->supported_styles[i] == best_style ){
                        return(best_style);
                    }
                }
            }
        }
    }
    return(DEFAULTStyle);
}
_XGetIMInputStyleError(){
        fprintf(stderr, "%s: Warning: Cannot determine inputstyle\n",
                program_name);
}
static void
GetPreferredGeometry(ic, name, area)
XIC ic;
char *name;             /* XNPreEditAttributes or XNStatusAttributes */
XRectangle *area;       /* the constraints on the area */
{
    XVaNestedList list;
    list = XVaCreateNestedList(0, XNAreaNeeded, area, NULL);
    /* set the constraints */
    XSetICValues(ic, name, list, NULL);
    /* Now query the preferred size */
    XGetICValues(ic, name, list, NULL);
    XFree(list);
}
static void
SetGeometry(ic, name, area)
XIC ic;
char *name;             /* XNPreEditAttributes or XNStatusAttributes */
XRectangle *area;       /* the actual area to set */
{
    XVaNestedList list;
    list = XVaCreateNestedList(0, XNArea, area, NULL);
    XSetICValues(ic, name, list, NULL);
    XFree(list);
}
```

# CHAPTER 7

# Other Changes in X11R6

*Paula Ferguson*

The preceding chapters have covered the major changes in X11R6: support for session management, in Xt multithreading in Xt and Xlib, internationalization in Xlib, and new font capabilities. This chapter describes other changes in Release 6, including changes to Xlib and the *Inter-Client Communications Conventions Manual* (ICCCM). It also introduces the new protocols, extensions, and authorization schemes provided with X11R6.

The remaining changes in Release 6 are listed below:

- Xlib has been modified so that it provides a form of asynchronous replies.

- The Display and GC structures are opaque.

- Xlib supports multithreaded access to a single display connection.

- Transparent extensions to Xlib support protocol requests of $2^{32}$ bytes in length and allow long-running X clients to request additional resource identifiers.

- The ICCCM has been updated to clarify a number of window management, selection, resource sharing, and session management issues.

- A new *Inter-Client Exchange* protocol provides a framework for building other protocols.

- The *X Session Management Protocol* provides a way for session managers to communicate with applications.

- The Synchronization extension is now a standard of the X Consortium. This extension allows clients to synchronize via the X server.

**Paula Ferguson** is author of the *Motif Programming Manual* and *Motif Reference Manual* and editor of *The X Resource*, all published by O'Reilly & Associates, Inc.

- Kerberos is supported as another authorization protocol.

- The client-side X code runs on Microsoft Windows NT.

- The Athena widget set has been internationalized.

- Many X clients have been moved from the core distribution to contributed software.

- The X11R6 source tree has been reorganized.

- Several components of X11R6, including Fresco, Low Bandwidth X, the X Keyboard extension, and the Record extension, are provided as snapshots of work in progress.

# 7.1    Miscellaneous Xlib Changes

The Display and GC structures in Xlib are supposed to be opaque, but in previous releases the structures were fully declared in *Xlib.h*, which made it easy for applications to depend inadvertently on implementation-dependent features. In Release 6, *Xlib.h* has been changed to hide the internals of these structures, so programmers are forced to use the defined, portable interfaces. If a program references a private field, it results in a compile-time error. Although an application can work around some of these errors by compiling with the *–DXLIB_ILLEGAL_ACCESS* flag, it is better to fix the illegal references.

The Xlib implementation has also been changed to support a form of asynchronous replies. Now, a request can be sent to the server, and then other requests can be generated without waiting for the first reply to come back. This feature is used to advantage in two new functions, XInternAtoms() and XGetAtomNames(). These routines reduce what would otherwise require multiple round trips to the server down to a single round trip. Asynchronous replies are also used in some existing functions, such as XGetWindowAttributes(), to reduce two round trips to just one.

In Release 6, Xlib supports a new authorization scheme for X clients, MIT-KERBEROS-5. This scheme uses MIT's Kerberos Version 5 user-to-user authentication.

## 7.1.1    Multithreaded Xlib

In Chapter 4, we described how to write a multithreaded Xt application. Since most programs are developed at the Xt level, using multiple threads in an Xt application can increase interactivity and concurrency. However, many Xt applications need to call Xlib routines. If these calls are made from multiple threads, Xlib needs to be thread-safe as well. Fortunately, Release 6 Xlib supports multithreaded access to a display connection.

The original library API design was done with multithreading in mind, but the macros `LockDisplay()` and `UnlockDisplay()` used in most of the Xlib code had inadequate implementations prior to X11R6. Now Xlib functions lock the display structure, which causes other threads calling Xlib functions to be suspended until the first thread unlocks. Threads inside Xlib that are waiting to read to or write from the X server do not keep the display locked, so for example a thread hanging on `XNextEvent()` does not prevent other threads from performing output to the server.

The new routine `XInitThreads()` must be the first Xlib function a multithreaded application calls. This function declares that multiple threads will be using Xlib, so that at link-time it can be determined whether to include threads-related Xlib internal routines. These internal routines in turn force inclusion of the necessary threads library routines. The advantage of this approach is that non-threaded applications can use the thread-capable Xlib without incurring the time and space overhead of locking support.

While it is presumably a rare requirement, there are some situations where an application needs to keep a display locked across several Xlib calls. The `XLockDisplay()` and `XUnlockDisplay()` functions have been provided to handle this requirement. For example, an application needs to use `XLockDisplay()` immediately before it calls `XNextRequest()` to learn the sequence number of the next request. The lock is necessary to ensure that no other thread steals the sequence number by sending its own request first.

## 7.1.2　The XC-MISC Extension

Xlib typically allocates $2^{22}$ resource identifiers to an X client. While this may seem like a lot, some clients run for so long, and allocate and free so many resources, that they run out of resource IDs. In previous implementations, when a client ran out of IDs, it would die with a protocol error. To allow clients to continue running, the XC-MISC protocol extension has been added to the X server. This extension allows Xlib to ask the server for a new range of IDs; the server responds with a range of IDs that had been allocated previously but have since been freed by the client. Xlib uses this extension automatically behind the scenes, so getting additional IDs does not require application intervention.

## 7.1.3　The BIG-REQUESTS Extension

The standard X protocol only allows requests up to $2^{18}$ bytes in length. While it is possible to generate longer requests with the core X protocol, this is more likely to be a problem with PEX and other extensions that transmit complex information to the server. To solve this problem, the BIG-REQUESTS protocol extension has been added. This extension allows a client to extend the length field in protocol requests to be a 32-bit value. The trick is to use a length of zero, which is normally illegal in the core protocol, to indicate that an extra 32-bit length field has been inserted in the request. Again, Xlib handles this extension automatically, without application intervention.

## 7.2 Inter-Client Communication Conventions Manual Changes

The *Inter-Client Communication Conventions Manual* (ICCCM) has been updated to Version 2.0 in X11R6. This version contains a large number of minor, but significant, changes in the areas of window management, selections, resource sharing, and session management. The document also includes a large number of editorial and typographical changes to make it easier to read and more useful to application developers. The complete Version 2 ICCCM is reprinted in O'Reilly's *X Programmers' Handbook,* [†] and is available for ftp from the X Consortium (*ftp.x.org*).

### 7.2.1 Window Management

ICCCM 2.0 clarifies the definition of a "top-level window." A client's top-level window is a window whose override-redirect attribute is `False`. The window must either be a child of the root window, or it must have been a child of the root window immediately before it was reparented by the window manager. If the client reparents the window away from root, the window is no longer a top-level window. It can become a top-level window again if the client reparents it back to root.

With prior versions of the ICCCM, it was difficult for a client to track its absolute location on the screen. A client could always use the TranslateCoordinates protocol request, but this is expensive because it requires a server round trip. To remedy this problem, Version 2.0 clarifies the circumstances under which the window manager is required to send synthetic `ConfigureNotify` events. These clarifications ensure that any ConfigureWindow request issued by the client results in a `ConfigureNotify` event, either from the server or from the window manager.

The document also contains advice about how a client that wants to keep track of its absolute position should inspect events so it can minimize its need to use the `Trans-lateCoordinates` request. When a client receives a synthetic `ConfigureNotify` event, the coordinates in the event are relative to the root window, so they give the absolute position of the window. However, the coordinates in real `ConfigureNotify` events are relative to the window's parent, which may not be the root window if the window has been reparented by a window manager. If the client receives another event that specifies both absolute and relative coordinates (e.g., `ButtonPress`), the client can calculate the position of the top-level window from the differences between the absolute and relative coordinates of the different events. Only when these techniques fail does a client need to use the TranslateCoordinates request.

Window manager decorations have also been problematic because when the window manager reparents a window, it shifts the window as specified by the `win_gravity` field of WM_NORMAL_HINTS. ICCCM 2.0 defines a new value for this field, `Static-Gravity`. This value specifies that the window manager should not shift a client win-

---

† To be published in Winter 1996.

dow's location when reparenting the window. The meanings of all of the other values for win_gravity have been clarified in the new document.

The aspect ratio hints of the WM_NORMAL_HINTS property are useful for an application to say that it would like the width-to-height ratio of its window to fall within a certain range. For example, a page previewer might use these hints to request that its image area have the same aspect ratio as a sheet of letter-sized paper. Unfortunately, most applications need additional space in their window (such as for a menu bar) that should not be included in the aspect ratio calculation. Version 2.0 fixes this problem by specifying that the base size property in WM_NORMAL_HINTS is included in the aspect ratio calculation. Window managers that honor aspect ratios should subtract the base size from the window size before checking that the aspect ratio falls within the specified range.

Note that window managers still have the prerogative of disregarding geometry hints. However, many popular window managers do honor geometry hints most of the time, so it makes sense to enhance the flexibility of these hints.

The WM_HINTS property has a new flag, UrgencyHint. A client can set this flag to indicate that the window contents are urgent and require a timely response by the user. The window manager must make an effort to draw the user's attention to this window while the flag is set. The window manager supporting virtual screens, for example, could switch to the screen where the urgent window is displayed. The window manager must also monitor this flag and take appropriate action when the state of the flag changes. This mechanism is useful for alarm dialog boxes or reminder windows. For example, the window manager could attract attention to an urgent window by adding an indicator to its title bar or its icon. When a window is newly urgent, the window manager could take an additional action, such as flashing its icon or raising it to the top of the stack.

In Version 2.0, window managers are explicitly prohibited from using the value CurrentTime in the timestamp field of WM_TAKE_FOCUS messages. The ClientMessage event must contain a valid timestamp that can be used by the client.

The definition of the WM_STATE property is perhaps the most significant window management change in ICCCM 2.0. Earlier versions of the ICCCM mentioned the WM_STATE property but gave only suggested contents. This property was meant to be used for private communication between the window manager and session manager; clients were forbidden to read the property, but many did so anyway. With the new session management protocol in Release 6, the original intent of WM_STATE is no longer relevant. The suggested contents have been turned into a formal definition in Version 2.0.

The window manager places a WM_STATE property on each top-level window that is not in the withdrawn state. Top-level windows in the withdrawn state may or may not have the WM_STATE property. The WM_STATE property contains state and icon fields, where the state field can have one of the following values: WithdrawnState, NormalState, or IconicState. The definitions of these different states have been clarified in Version 2.0, and the description of window state changes has been made more consistent.

The ICCCM no longer contains any prohibition against clients reading the WM_STATE property. In fact, clients are now encouraged to read the property in certain cases. For example, a client might want to withdraw a window and then re-use it for another purpose. In this situation, a problem would arise if the client remapped the window before the window manager finished withdrawing the window. The ICCCM now specifies that clients should wait for the window manager to change the WM_STATE property before proceeding. Another example involves clients that ask the user to click on a window, such as *xprop*. The intent is typically for the window to be a top-level window. The client can find a top-level window by searching the window hierarchy beneath the selected location for a window with the WM_STATE property.

## 7.2.2　Selections

ICCCM 2.0 contains a number of small improvements in the selection conventions area. For instance, the uses of the CLIENT_WINDOW, LENGTH, MULTIPLE, and PIXMAP targets have been clarified. In particular, the use of the LENGTH target is now discouraged, since its definition is ambiguous. When a selection can be converted to multiple targets, each of which may return a different amount of data, the requesting client has no way to know which length it is getting. Earlier versions of the ICCCM specified that the PIXMAP target returned a property of type DRAWABLE. In Version 2.0, this target has been revised to return a property of type PIXMAP.

Version 2.0 also contains a number of new targets for Encapsulated PostScript and for the Apple Macintosh PICT structured graphics format. These new targets are: ADOBE_PORTABLE_DOCUMENT_FORMAT, APPLE_PICT, ENCAPSULATED_POSTSCRIPT, ENCAPSULATED_POSTSCRIPT_INTERCHANGE, and POSTSCRIPT.

The new selection property type, C_STRING, is simply a string of non-zero bytes. This is in contrast to the STRING type, which excludes many control characters. The C_STRING type is meant to be used when there is no specific character set for the text. One use of C_STRING would be to transfer the names of files, since many operating systems do not interpret filenames as having a character set.

Another new feature in Version 2.0 is the ability for a selection requestor to pass parameters with the request. The selection owner then finds the parameters in a property named by the requestor. This facility was actually already in use by the MULTIPLE target. In version 2.0, the mechanism has been generalized so that new targets can be defined to take parameters. The target definition specifies the type, format, and contents of the property used to store the parameters. The selection mechanisms in Xt have been modified to support parameterized targets, as described in Section 3.4.

Version 2.0 now specifies that if a selection owner receives more than one `Selection-Request` event with the same requestor, selection, target, and timestamp, it must respond to the requests in the same order in which they were received. This requirement is necessary for the requestor, so that it can determine which request failed.

Another new requirement for the selection owner concerns changing the value of the selection, while the owner remains the same. For example, the user could select a completely different piece of text in the same *xterm* window. In this case, the selection owner should reacquire the selection as if he or she was not the owner, thereby providing a new timestamp. However, if the selection value is modified, but can still reasonably be viewed as the same selected object, the owner does not have to take any action.

The concept of manager selections is another new feature in ICCCM 2.0. Certain clients, called *managers*, take on responsibilities for managing shared resources for other clients. The window manager and session manager are the two most common types of managers. A client that manages a shared resource should take ownership of an appropriate selection. The manager may support conversion of various targets for that selection. Managers are encouraged to use this technique as the primary means by which clients interact with the managed resource, as described in the ICCCM.

The one actual use of manager selections described by the ICCCM involves window managers. For each screen that it manages, a window manager is required to acquire ownership of a selection named WM_S*n*, where *n* is the screen number. The intent is for clients to be able to request a variety of information or services by issuing conversion requests on this selection. At present, the only service defined for window managers is to report the ICCCM version number with which the window manager complies. However, now that this mechanism is in place, additional services can be added in the future.

### 7.2.3    Resource Sharing

A prominent new addition in Version 2.0 is the ability of clients to take control of colormap installation under certain circumstances. Earlier versions of the ICCCM specified that the window manager had exclusive control over colormap installation. This proves to be inconvenient for certain situations, such as when a client has the server grabbed. ICCCM 2.0 allows a client to install colormaps itself after having informed the window manager. A client must hold a pointer grab for the entire time it is doing its own colormap installation.

Version 2.0 also clarifies a number of rules about how clients can exchange resources. These rules are important when a client places a resource ID into a window manager property or passes a resource ID through the selection mechanism. When a window manager property contains a resource ID, the client that specified the property should ensure that the resource exists for at least as long as the window on which the property resides. When a selection property contains a resource ID, the selection owner should ensure that the resource is not destroyed and that its contents are not changed until after the selection transfer is complete. A requestor that relies on the resource must operate on it before deleting the selection property. For example, the requestor might copy the contents of a pixmap.

### 7.2.4 Session Management

Although the new *X Session Management Protocol* (XSMP) is not part of the ICCCM, it does affect the ICCCM. Section 5 of Version 1.1 of the ICCCM contained definitions of a number of window properties and protocols for session management. Most of these have been made obsolete by the new session management protocol, so they have been moved into an appendix. The use for session management purposes of the WM_COMMAND and WM_CLIENT_MACHINE properties, as well as the protocol called WM_SAVE_YOURSELF, is obsolete in ICCCM 2.0.

The ICCCM now defines some new properties related to the XSMP in Section 5. According to the XSMP, each session participant obtains a unique client identifier from the session manager. The client must identify one of its top-level windows as the client leader. The client leader window must have a SM_CLIENT_ID property, which specifies the client ID obtained from the session manager. All of the top-level windows for a client must have a WM_CLIENT_LEADER property, which specifies the window ID of the client leader. Top-level windows can also have an optional WM_WINDOW_ROLE property that can be used to uniquely identify a window across sessions. As described in Chapter 2, the new SessionShell widget class in Xt handles all of these properties for an application.

### 7.2.5 Editorial Changes

One of the common criticisms of earlier versions of the ICCCM was that it was hard to read. In some cases, the wording was unclear, and the specifications were not always consistent. There were also times when the document fell short of readers' needs. For instance, when a rule was stated, there was often no recommendation for how clients ought to proceed and no reasoning behind the formulation of the rule. To remedy this problem, ICCCM 2.0 now contains a number of commentary paragraphs labeled "Advice to Implementors" and "Rationale" that provide additional information for readers.

Earlier versions of the ICCCM also contained references to a document called the *Window and Session Manager Conventions Manual* (WSMCM). The intent of this document was to describe conventions from the point of view of window and session managers, while the ICCCM itself was to describe the conventions from the point of view of ordinary clients. This distinction has not proven useful, and in any case the WSMCM has never been written, so the references to the WSMCM have been removed and material that covers both points of view is included in the ICCCM.

## 7.3    The Inter-Client Exchange Protocol

As the work on Release 6 progressed at the X Consortium, many of the discussions of proposed projects seemed to be leading towards the design of special-purpose protocols. At this time, it was noted that these protocols would have many elements in common. Most protocols need mechanisms for authentication, for version negotiation, and for setting up and taking down connections. There are also cases where the same two parties need to talk to each other using multiple protocols. For example, an embedding relationship between two parties is likely to require the simultaneous use of session management, data transfer, focus negotiation, and command notification protocols. While these are logically separate protocols, it is desirable for them to share as many pieces of implementation as possible.

The *Inter-Client Exchange* (ICE) protocol provides a generic framework for building protocols on top of reliable, byte-stream transport connections. ICE supplies basic mechanisms for setting up and shutting down connections, for performing authentication, for negotiating versions, and for reporting errors. The protocols running within an ICE connection are referred to as *subprotocols*. ICE provides facilities for each subprotocol to do its own version negotiation, authentication, and error reporting. In addition, if two parties are communicating using several different subprotocols, ICE allows them to share the same transport layer connection. ICElib provides a common interface to these mechanisms so that protocol implementors need not reinvent them.

The *X Session Management Protocol* is the first protocol to make use of ICE. Several other protocols that use ICE are being designed or considered by the X Consortium, however. These possible protocols include a drag-and-drop protocol, a high-volume selection transfer mechanism, a customization protocol, and support for screen readers for the blind.

Note that ICE does not go through the X server, so it can be used with non-X programs. For example, non-X programs can be managed by a session manager.

For complete information about ICElib, including a tutorial and reference pages, see the book *X Programmer's Handbook*, published by O'Reilly & Associates, Inc.

## 7.4    Session Management

The *X Session Management Protocol* (XSMP) provides a uniform mechanism for users to save and restore their sessions using the services of a network-based session manager. This protocol enables session managers to communicate with client applications, so that the session manager can save the state of the applications, as well as start and restart them automatically on both local and remote systems. The XSMP is built on top of ICE; SMlib is the C language interface to the protocol.

Xt has been modified to support XSMP in Release 6. The SessionShell widget class encapsulates the requirements of the protocol. Chapter 2 describes the session management features in Xt and demonstrates the creation of a session-aware Xt application.

The Release 6 distribution provides a sample session manager, called *xsm*, in *xc/workInProgress/xsm*. This session manager is meant to test the protocol, but the user interface is rather crude. While *xsm* does have enough functionality to be useful for programmers, it needs more work before it would be appropriate for non-technical users.

For complete information about SMlib, including a tutorial and reference pages, see the book *X Programmer's Handbook*, published by O'Reilly & Associates, Inc.

In order for session management to work over a network, a session manager needs to be able to start and restart clients on remote systems. X11R6 provides a new program, *rstart*, that simplifies this task. This protocol is built on top of existing remote execution programs such as *rsh*. However, it adds important features such as the ability to pass environment variables and authentication data to the applications that are being started remotely.

## 7.5    The Synchronization Extension

The Synchronization extension is a new X Consortium standard in Release 6 that allows clients to synchronize with each other via the X server.

Without this extension, multiple clients using independent connections to an X server have no guarantees about the relative order in which the server will execute their requests. If one client wants to make sure that its protocol requests are executed after those of some other client, the clients have to synchronize in an operating system-dependent manner on the client side, and either rely on specific knowledge of how the X server works or incur expensive round trips to the server to ensure synchronization. A client that wants to do time-based animation has no way to express that synchronization in terms of the server's clock. Instead, it has to rely on trying to turn time delays in the client into corresponding time delays in the server, which is difficult given unpredictable network delays, server request scheduling, and operating system scheduling.

By permitting clients to synchronize within the X server, the Synchronization extension eliminates the problems related to network delays, as well as the differences in synchronization primitives between operating systems. The extension provides a general Counter resource maintained by the server; only clients can alter the value of a Counter, and can block their execution until a Counter reaches a specific threshold. Thus, for example, two clients can draw into one window. One client would create a

Counter initialized to zero, draw some graphics, and then increment the Counter, while the other client can block until the Counter reaches a value of one and then draw some additional graphics.

The extension also provides system Counters; the values of these Counters are automatically set by the server. One such Counter gives the server time in milliseconds. A client that wants to do time-based animation can block on this Counter between drawing frames to achieve a constant frame rate.

The trigger for resuming execution after blocking can be made more complicated than a threshold on a single Counter. The client can wait for any of several Counters to reach a threshold. Additionally, a threshold can be specified in terms of a positive or negative transition, with comparison against either an absolute value or a value relative to the value of the Counter at the time the client blocked. For example, a client could wait for either a Counter to exceed a value of 10 or system time to progress by five seconds.

Asynchronous alarms are also provided in the extension. An alarm is set by specifying the same kind of trigger as for a blocking operation. However, when the trigger is satisfied, an `AlarmNotify` event is sent to the client. Finally, the extension provides a simple priority scheduling mechanism, with integer-valued priority levels that can be assigned on a per-client basis.

For more information on using the Synchronization extension, see the book *X Programmer's Handbook*, published by O'Reilly & Associates, Inc.

# 7.6    New Authorization Protocol

Release 6 adds a new authorization scheme, MIT-KERBEROS-5, for controlling clients' access to the X server. Kerberos code is available from MIT and needs to be built and installed separately from X.

Kerberos is a network-based authorization scheme developed by MIT for Project Athena. Kerberos allows mutually suspicious principals to authenticate each other as long as each trusts a third party, Kerberos. Each principal has a secret key known only to it and Kerberos. Principals includes servers, such as an FTP server or an X server, and human users, whose key is their password. However, since a public workstation is not secure, and thus has no place to store a secret key, X uses a variation of Kerberos called user-to-user authentication. In this scheme, the X server is not a separate principal, but instead shares keys with the user who is logging in.

Since Kerberos is a user-based authorization protocol, like the SUN-DES-1 protocol introduced in Release 5, the owner of an X server can enable and disable specific users or Kerberos principals. This feature provides finer-grained access control than enabling access based only on the host name. The *xhost* client is still used to enable or disable authorization.

As with other authentication protocols, *xdm* sets Kerberos up at login time, and Xlib uses it to authenticate the client to the X server. Support for Kerberos is only built into X when the `HadKrb5` configuration option is set; systems that have Kerberos Version 5 should make sure to build X with this option.

## 7.7    Microsoft Windows NT

The client-side X code (Xlib, Xt, etc.) now runs on Microsoft Windows NT. All of the base libraries are supported, including multithreading in Xlib and Xt. Only a few of the libraries are built as dynamic-link libraries (DLLs), because of deficient DLL semantics.

Some of the more complicated applications, specifically *xterm* and *xdm*, are not supported. There are also some other rough edges in the implementation. For example, there is no support for non-socket file descriptors as Xt alternate inputs. In addition, the implementation does not use the Registry for configurable parameters like system filenames and search paths.

## 7.8    Athena Widget Set Changes

The most significant change to the Athena widgets in Release 6 is the addition of internationalization support. Xaw uses native wide character support when it is available, otherwise it uses the Xlib wide character routines. In order to use the Xaw internationalization features, an application needs to call `XtSetLanguageProc()`, as decribed in Chapter 6.

The Command, Label, List, MenuButton, Repeater, SmeBSB, and Toggle widgets all have new `XtNinternational` and `XtNfontSet` resources. If `XtNinternational` is set to `True`, the widget displays its text using the specified font set.

The AsciiText widget has also been internationalized, so the name is now a misnomer, but it has been retained for backward compatibility. If the new `XtNinternational` resource is `False`, the widget creates AsciiSrc and AsciiSink source and sink widgets and behaves as it did in Release 5. However, if the resource is `True`, the widget creates `MultiSrc` and `MultiSink` source and sink widgets instead. The `MultiSrc` widget connects to an Input Method server if one is available. Otherwise it uses an Xlib internal input method that, at a minimum, does compose processing.

## 7.9    Client Modifications in X11R6

There are no new clients in X11R6 (except *xsm* and *xsmclient*, a client used only for testing *xsm*). Moreover, many programs that were supported in Release 5 are no longer supported, so the clients have been moved to the contributed software area. These programs include: *ico, listres, maze, puzzle, showfont, viewres, xbiff, xcalc, xedit, xev, xeyes, xfontsel, xgc, xload, xman,* and *xpr*.

The *lndir* utility now has an alternative called *mkshadow*, which is available in *xc/config/util.*

The *xhost* client has been modified to support two new families: LocalHost, for connections over a non-network transport, and Krb5Principal, for Kerberos principals. Because the growing number of authorization protocols makes it difficult to determine what family a name belongs to, family prefixes have been added to the *xhost* syntax. A complete name has the syntax *family:name,* where the families are as follows:

inet
>Internet host

dnet
>DECnet host

nis
>Secure RPC network name

krb
>Kerberos 5 principal

local
>Contains only one name, the empty string

The format of the name varies with the family and uses the same syntax as before. If a name does not contain a colon, the family is determined as in Release 5.

## 7.10   New Fonts

Besides the new font capabilities described in Chapter 5, X11R6 provides three new Chinese bdf fonts in *xc/fonts/bdf/misc.* In addition, the Type 1 fonts contributed by Bitstream, IBM, and Adobe that shipped as contributed software in Release 5 have been moved into the core release in Release 6.

## 7.11   Source Tree Reorganization

The top-level source directory for the core X distribution has been renamed *xc/* (from *mit/*) in Release 6. Many of the directories under *xc/* have also been reorganized. The general layout under *xc/* is now as follows:

*config/*
>Configuration files, *imake, makedepend,* and build utilities

*doc/*
> All documentation other than per-program manual pages

*fonts/*
> BDF, Speedo, and Type 1 fonts

*include/*
> Include files shared by multiple directories

*lib/*
> All libraries

*nls/*
> Localization files

*programs/*
> All programs, including the X server (was *clients/* and *server/*)

*test/*
> X Test Suite and other test suites

*util/*
> *patch, compress,* and other utilities

*workInProgress/*
> Shapshots of work in progress

This reorganization has simplified dependencies in the build process. A few other changes are that the *xc/config/* directory now has subdirectories and there is no longer a top-level extensions directory. Extension libraries are now under *xc/lib/*, server extension code is under *xc/programs/Xserver/Xext/*, and extension header files are under *xc/include/extensions/*.

## 7.12   Work in Progress in X11R6

X11R6 includes a number of components that are considered work-in-progress by the X Consortium. Fresco, Low Bandwidth X (LBX), the Record extension, and the X Keyboard (XKB) extension are neither standards nor draft standards and are discussed in subsequent sections. These components are known to need design and/or implementation work, are still evolving, and will not be compatible with any final standard should such a standard eventually be agreed upon. The X Consortium is making these technologies available in an early form in order to gather broader experimentation and feedback from those who are willing to invest the time and energy to help produce better standards.

## 7.12.1 Fresco

Fresco is a new user interface technology in X11R6 that supports *graphical embedding* by combining the traditional areas of structured graphics and application embedding into a simple, uniform architectural framework. The graphical embedding framework provides a way to compose both graphical objects, such as circles and polygons found in a drawing editor, and application-level editors, like word processors and spreadsheets connected with Microsoft's OLE, using a single mechanism. Embedded application objects can appear within graphical scenes and can be transformed appropriately.

Another distinguishing feature of Fresco is its use of the Interface Definition Language (IDL) that is part of the Common Object Request Broker Architecture (CORBA) defined by the Object Management Group (OMG). The use of CORBA means that Fresco objects may be distributed across a network. The ability to distribute IDL-specified objects is particularly important for application embedding, where it is desirable to run relatively large applications as several independent processes.

IDL also has several advantages over other alternatives. While IDL is more abstract than object-oriented programming languages, it is concrete enough to be translated automatically into source code. IDL can also be mapped to several programming languages, so it is not tied to a particular language. OMG has defined a standard binding to C and is in the process of standardizing mappings for C++ and Smalltalk.

The Fresco application programming interface provides functionality that is handled by both Xlib and Xt, with additional features for graphical embedding. As part of its support for graphical objects, Fresco operations are resolution-independent. Coordinates are translated from application-defined units to pixels automatically by the implementation, so that an application's appearance is the same on different screens or printers without the programmer having to write any special code. Fresco also supports multithreaded applications by locking access to shared data and by spawning an independent thread to handle screen redraw.

The Fresco 0.7 sample implementation in Release 6 is a work-in-progress; it is neither an X Consortium standard nor a draft standard. The sample implementation is written entirely in C++ and includes a set of C++ include files, and a library that implements the Fresco classes. In this first release of Fresco, the emphasis has been to define an API for structured graphics, although the sample implementation does provide additional features in preparation for supporting graphical embedding. The current implementation does not completely support distribution, although extensions to the runtime library would make that possible.

Fresco has been distributed as a work-in-progress in Release 6 to demonstrate the current direction of the system, as well as to gather feedback on requirements for a Fresco standard. Fresco releases are now separate from X releases, and there have been updated Fresco release since R6.

## 7.12.2    Low Bandwidth X

With the ever-declining prices of high-speed modems, deployment of ISDN networks, and dramatic coverage of the potential for running applications over information "super highways," the need for a standard for running X applications over serial lines and other "slow" links has become clear. Members of the X Consortium, led by NCD, are working together to add sophisticated caching and data compression techniques to NCD's XRemote technology. This effort, called Low Bandwidth LBX, draws on experience gained over the last four years to dramatically improve application startup time and interactive responsiveness.

With LBX, applications connect to a pseudoserver (called the LBX proxy) that converts the LAN-oriented X protocol into the more compact LBX protocol for transmission over phone lines or other slow links. The proxy caches data flowing between the server and the clients, merges the X protocol streams, and compresses the data. The X server at the other end uncompresses the data and splits it back out into separate request streams, automatically converting the LBX protocol back into the original X requests, events, replies, and errors. All of this is handled transparently to the application; LBX is binary compatible with all existing applications. The goal is to make X applications transparently usable over 9600 bps modems.

LBX provides significantly better performance over slow links through two means. First, it compresses information that is transmitted to and from the X server by squeezing unused bits out of the X protocol. In particular, this reduces the amount of data that has to be transmitted for font metrics, window properties, bitmaps, pixmaps, events, and text strings. Second, the proxy caches certain X data to minimize the number of times that the data needs to be transmitted to and from the server. Large data objects, such as font metrics, window properties, and keysym tables are only sent the first time they are used; after that, the proxy simply reuses the data. In certain situations, such as interning atom names and allocating read-only color cells, the proxy can even bypass the X server completely.

The snapshot of LBX provided in Release 6 contains the following features:

- LZW compression of the binary data stream. Since commercial use of LZW requires licensing patented technology, the X Consortium is also looking for an unencumbered algorithm and implementation to provide as well.

- Delta compression of X packets, so that packets are represented as differences from previously sent packets.

- Re-encoding of some graphics requests, such as points, lines, segments, rectangles, and arcs.

- Motion event throttling to keep motion events from flooding the wire.

- Caching of data in the proxy for large data objects that would otherwise be transmitted multiple times, such as keyboard mappings and font metrics.

- Short-circuiting of requests for constant data, such as atoms and color mappings.

However, there are still several items that have not been implemented. For example, a number of requests still need to be re-encoded. The LBX implementation also needs a non-networked serial protocol for environments that cannot support operating-system-level networking over serial lines. The full specification that describes the network protocol used between the proxy and the server still needs to be written. Some of this work has been done in releases since R6.

The X Consortium is continuing to work on both the LBX implementation and the full specification, so that it can go out for public review in the near future. Since the specification will definitely change, the prototype LBX provided with X11R6 should not be incorporated into a product.

## 7.12.3   The X Keyboard Extension

The core X protocol specifies the ways that the Shift, Mode_switch, Control, and Lock modifiers interact to generate keysyms and characters. Core X also allows users to specify that a key affects one or more modifiers. This behavior is simple and fairly flexible, but it has a number of limitations that make it difficult or impossible to properly support many common kinds of keyboard behavior.

The X Keyboard (XKB) extension makes it possible to specify most aspects of keyboard behavior clearly and explicitly on a global or per-key basis. XKB adds mechanisms to track the logical and physical state of the keyboard more closely. For keyboard control and layout clients, XKB also provides descriptions and symbolic names for many aspects of keyboard appearance and behavior. XKB incorporates controls designed to make keyboards more accessible to people with movement impairments.

The capabilities of the X Keyboard extension include:

- Multiple keyboard groups, with explicit support for up to eight keyboard groups.

- Control of symbol lookup on a per-key basis. The rules for looking up the symbol associated with a key event can vary from key to key.

- Explicit control of modifier key behavior. Users can specify locking or latching behavior for any modifier key, regardless of the modifier it affects.

- Controls to make keyboards usable by the movement impaired.

- Keyboard control of the core pointer. MouseKeys make it possible to simulate mouse events from the keyboard.

- Keyboard control of server behavior. Optional actions control virtual screens, kill the server, or activate other server controls.

- Bell events and named bells. Clients can ask to receive an event whenever a bell is rung and can attach symbolic names to the bells they ring. This simplifies clients that provide audible or visible feedback.

- An indicator map. The map controls the way the X server lights or extinguishes keyboard indicators in response to changes in keyboard state.

- Keyboard geometry that can be used to describe the physical appearance of a keyboard.

- Alternate symbols that allow locale-specific keyboard layouts on a per-client basis.

A keyboard description is more complex with XKB than with the core protocol, but much of that complexity is hidden from the casual user by a compatibility mapping mechanism. Most capabilities can be enabled simply by assigning new keysyms to the keys that should invoke the desired behavior.

When the X Keyboard extension becomes a standard, it will be available to all clients because it is meant to replace the core protocol definition of a keyboard. Unlike most extensions, XKB is invoked automatically by core X library keyboard functions. When a client opens a display, the X library will determine whether or not the server supports the extension. If the server does support XKB, the library will enable the extension and use versions of XLookupString() and other keyboard functions that use the new capabilities of XKB; if the server does not support XKB, the library will use functions that rely only on the core protocol.

In Release 6, support for XKB is not compiled into Xlib by default. It is not compiled into the X server by default either, except on Sun and Omron Luna machines. To compile the X server and Xlib with XKB support, set the BuildXKB and BuildXKBLib configuration options. The XKB support in Xlib is still at an early stage of formal review, so it could change.

## 7.12.4   The Record Extension

Over the last few years, several attempts have been made to standardize record and playback, or journaling, in X. Although input synthesis, or playback, has been recently standardized by the X Consortium in the XTEST extension, no standard yet exists for recording. As a result, server vendors have been required by their customers to support a variety of recording extensions and methodologies. The Record extension is an X protocol extension, developed by members of the XTEST working group, that supports the recording of all core X protocol and arbitrary X extension protocol.

Although the requirement to provide synchronization of contextual information comes from the playback mechanism, contextual information must be captured during recording so that device or user events can be interleaved with their consequences. The Record extension takes a "broad brush" approach to synchronization, making no assumptions about the intended use of the recorded data, since it is impossible to predict in advance what synchronization information is required by a particular application. Therefore, Record does not enforce a specific synchronization methodology, such as window mapping/unmapping or cursor changes.

The Record extension intercepts all core X protocol and arbitrary X extension protocol entirely within the X server itself. The extension provides a mechanism for capturing all events, including input device events that go to no clients. This mechanism is analogous to a client expressing interest in all events, in all windows, including the root window. There are two possible event-filtering models that Record could use:

- User input actions are copied, with one copy sent to the server for normal processing and one copy going to a client.

- User input actions are diverted to a client before being processed by the server, the effect being as if the user had performed no input action.

Record supports the first model. The assumption is that the second model will be provided in a later version of the extension or in another extension altogether.

A recording client can specify, or express interest in, the range of protocol values that are intercepted by the extension. These values can include core X protocol requests and replies, extension requests and replies, core X protocol and extension events, and core X protocol and extension errors. These ranges can be specified for only one client or a set of clients, including all currently existing and future clients. When the extension has been set up to intercept specific protocol by one or more clients, the protocol data is formatted and returned to the recording clients.

Record uses a client model whereby a recording client opens two connections to the server: a control connection and a data connection. Protocol data intercepted on behalf of the recording client is returned to the recording client via multiple replies to a single protocol request. The control connection is used by the recording client to:

- Obtain information about the supported protocol version

- Create and destroy configurations

- Specify protocol ranges to be intercepted

- Query the current state of a configuration

- Stop interception and reporting of protocol data

The data connection is used by the recording client to:

- Request the start of interception and reporting for a particular configuration
- Receive intercepted protocol data as replies to that request

Inside Xlib, the data connection uses the asynchronous reply mechanism that has been implemented in Release 6. At a higher level, since the Xt model supports a single application context with multiple display connections, the application can simply register both connections within a single application context. In this case, Xt automatically handles the processing of replies on the data connection. A callback procedure can then be executed when input is available on the data connection.

# An Introduction to the X Image Extension

*Ben Fahy*

The X Image Extension (XIE) is the biggest and most important extension developed and standardized for R6. This chapter cannot document all of XIE because that would take a book bigger than this one. Instead, we'll concentrate on an introduction that will get you started.[†]

## 8.1 Introduction to XIE

The fundamental design goal of XIE was to facilitate image display of virtually any image type on virtually any X-capable hardware. A secondary goal was to expand the hardware model of the server, in order to accommodate the use of hardware accelerators for simple image enhancement. The goals of XIE stop short of defining a full image processing standard; this functionality is left to other standards on the client side, such as ISO's IPI/PIKS.[‡]

There are at least three fundamental problems associated with image display using only the Core X protocol: image transfer, image representation, and image rendition. The image transfer problem refers to the excessive amount of time it can take to send raw image data from the client to the server. For example, an 8½ by 11 inch FAX image digitized at 300 dpi is 2550 by 3300 bits, or a little over 1 Mbyte. Most ethernet-based networks are incapable of reaching 1 Mbyte/sec transfer rates between machines, even with no load. An office making heavy use of document imaging software will quickly saturate all network bandwidth, with the result that transfer throughout may fall as low as 50-100 Kbyte/sec. At this point, images begin taking an unacceptably long time to

---

**Ben Fahy** was involved in design and development of XIE at AGE logic, though he has now left.
† This chapter is based on the paper "Experience with XIE: Server and Client, Past, Present and Future" which is copyright 1993-94 © AGE Logic, Inc. All Rights Reserved. Used by permission.
‡ Image Processing and Interchange Functional Specification, Part 2: Programmers Imaging Kernel System Application Program Interface. ISO Draft International Standard (DIS) 12087-2, August 1993.

213

display (10-20 seconds). The problem can be somewhat alleviated by pre-formatting the 300 dpi image down to a smaller size on the host prior to transfer; this may be necessary to scale the image to a window anyway.

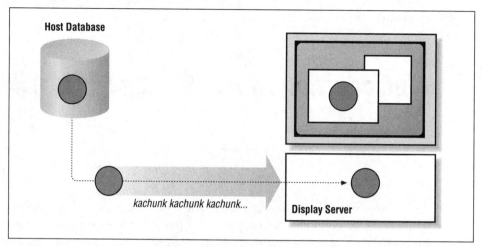

**Figure 8-1:** Transporting millions of raw pixels across the network can be unacceptably slow.

XIE supports the transport across the network of compressed image data. XIE servers are capable of reading in the compressed data and decompressing it on demand. Since FAX images tend to be largely white (the background paper), high compression ratios can often be obtained simply through runlength encoding. Adding Huffman coding of the runlengths gains additional compression at the expense of more complicated (and usually more time-consuming) decompression. Taking advantage of similarities between consecutive image lines (called vertical coding) can give more compression still, again at the expense of requiring more time-consuming and more complex decompression. XIE can accommodate any or all of these classes of compression schemes.

By transferring full-resolution compressed data to the server and decompressing it there, XIE enables display server CPU time to be traded for increased network bandwidth. XIE also allows the image to be scaled by the server, so that the original image only needs to be transferred once, with all subsequent processing done on the server side. This is an effective trade because whereas the network is usually overloaded by enterprise-wide imaging applications, the server often represents an underutilized resource, largely idle and waiting for something to do. By asking the server to do a little more, network traffic can be reduced by an order of magnitude, making installation of an imaging system much more cost-effective (avoiding the need to lay parallel links or fiber-optic cable between stations). Also, the load on the host CPU is reduced, because with XIE doing almost all of the work, the only job of the host is to find and transport the (highest-resolution) compressed image.

*8. An Introduction to the X Image Extension*

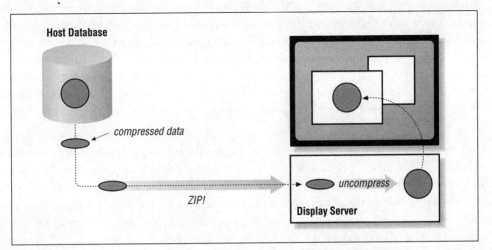

**Figure 8-2:** XIE sends a small amount of compressed data to the server and decompresses it there.

The second problem with using Core X to do imaging is the inability to adequately store a robust set of image types in the server, referred to above as the image representation problem. In medical imaging, for example, various imaging modalities, such as Computed Tomography (CT) and Magnetic Resonance Imaging (MRI), produce high-depth images, requiring as many as 12 or 14 bits per pixel to represent the analog data. Very few DACs are capable of displaying more than 8 bits at a time, and it is not acceptable to simply truncate the pixel depths and throw away the extra bits, due to legal and medical ethics ramifications: a patient's pathology may only be evident in the bits that were thrown away.

Because only 8 bits can physically be shown at a time even though it is potentially necessary for the physician to examine all 12 or 14, the best solution possible is to allow the physician to interactively control which pixel intensities are simultaneously displayed and which are not. It is considered to be a clinically acceptable method of viewing 12-bit data if the physician can examine all "important" mappings from 12 to 8 bits quickly and easily. Therefore, a standard paradigm has evolved in which a "window" (range of intensities to map to 8 bits) and "level" (center of the window) is controlled by moving a trackball or mouse. The companies which build CT and MRI machines routinely provide this capability in all the machines they sell, accelerated by relatively simple hardware tricks.

Recently, there has been a movement in the medical industry to install digital imaging networks in hospitals, so that after diagnosis is made on an image by a radiologist, that image can be quickly transferred to the referring physician, who is probably working in another part of the hospital. If both doctors can view the images simultaneously (at different viewing stations), then they can discuss the diagnosis over the phone instead of having to waste precious time walking back and forth through a large building. The general idea is called installing a Picture Archiving and Communications System (PACS).[†] Beside the convenience benefit described here, there are many other associated benefits, including the ability to use database technology to accelerate retrieval of images, reducing the possibility of physically losing films, and reducing the expense of storing patient images for long periods of time (which is required by law).

Unfortunately, X has up to now proven unsuitable for PACS application, except for expensive, dedicated workstations[‡] because it is not possible to load and do window and leveling operations on a conventional X terminal. The vast majority of these devices are limited to 8 bits per pixel, and therefore the full-depth image cannot be maintained resident in the server. Instead, it must reside on the client side, and after any operation is performed on the image, it must then be converted to 8 bits and transferred across the wire to the server using XPutImage. Even on an unloaded network, a 1K by 1K image can be transferred at most once per second, which implies that reaching interactive rates (5-10 enhancements per second) is clearly impossible.

XIE allows images to be stored at depths up to 16 bits per pixel in the server (even if the server display hardware supports less than 16 bits). This process implies that the full-depth image can be transferred once from client to display, and after that, all window and leveling operations may take place locally. Real-time rates can be achieved on images as large as 2K by 2K, assuming lookup table hardware is available in the server. Even without acceleration, the Motorola 88110-based IBM Xstation 150 (with XIE software installed) has been found capable of delivering interactive performance for images as large as 1K by 1K. This performance is clinically acceptable for remote viewing stations, and represents a potential breakthrough for the use of X in PACS environments.[§]

As an example of an image rendition problem, consider displaying a 24-bit YCC color image on an 8-bit pseudocolor display (YCC is a standard color space). Rendition in XIE is defined as the process of changing the format of an image in order to make it compatible with the server's frame buffer, its associated lookup table(s), and other limitations. Once an image has been rendered, it may be transferred directly to the hardware and viewed on the screen.

---

[†] D.F. Leotta and Y. Kim, Requirements for Picture Archiving and Communications Systems, IEEE Engineering in Medicine and Biology Magazine, Vol. 12, pp. 62-69, March 1993.
[‡] D.K. Yee, D.R. Haynor, H.S. Choi, S.W. Milton, and Y. Kim, Development of a Prototypical PACS Workstation Based on the IBM RS/6000 and the X Window System, SPIE Medical Imaging VI, Vol. 1653, pp. 337-348, 1992.
[§] J.B. Fahy, R. Masse, Y. Kim, and D.R. Haynor, The Role of the X Window Image Extension in Medical Imaging Workstations, SPIE Medical Imaging VII: Image Capture, Formatting, and Display, Vol. 1897, pp. 350-362, 1993.

XIE contains primitives to allow the image to be:

- Received in compressed (JPEG) format from the client

- Decompressed by the server

- Converted from YCC to RGB color space

- Dithered from 8 bits per pixel to 6 levels per band (216 possible colors)

- Converted from a `TripleBand` to a `SingleBand` data type

- Passed through a lookup table to produce colormap indexes

- Exported to a Core X drawable

If the image is displayed on a grayscale or bitonal display, XIE contains additional operations to compute the luminance of the image (giving "intensity" without "color"). XIE's Geometry operator allows the image to be scaled to any size and also flipped, rotated or skewed. Other operators exist for doing other display-oriented processing.

In summary, XIE solves the three basic problems associated with trying to do imaging with Core X alone. The transfer problem is solved by allowing compressed images to be sent across the wire and decompressed in the server, trading display server processing cycles for greater network bandwidth and less host load. Expanding the pixmap concept to allow storing color, deep, or compressed images solves an image representation problem. Finally, XIE contains an entire set of primitives designed to allow the client to solve arbitrarily complex rendering problems.

Not all X servers have the memory and performance to handle full XIE, and not all imaging applications require full XIE. Therefore, the XIE standard defines a Document Imaging Subset (DIS) that provides just the features necessary to handle monochrome images like FAX. DIS is a subset of XIE. XIElib provides a call to find out whether an X server supports DIS, full XIE, or no XIE at all.

XIElib is the standard C language interface to the XIE protocol, like Xlib is to the X protocol. This chapter gives a simple example of XIElib programming.

## 8.2 The XIE Computational Model

XIE defines six new resources, or data types. The ones involved in computation are:

- Photomaps, which store images. A photomap is analogous to a pixmap.

- Lookup Tables (LUTs), which define point operations on images.

- Rectangles of Interest (ROIs), which define processing regions.

XIE can also use Core X drawables and colormaps as read/write data types. XIE uses graphics contexts in a read-only fashion. XIE Color Lists are write-only; they remember which colors are allocated from a colormap by XIE's `ConvertToIndex` element. Those colors can be queried later by a specific protocol request.

All data flowing to or from the client and to or from resources must flow through a computational engine called a photoflo. The client defines a photoflo out of smaller units called elements. Import elements bring data into the photoflo, either from a resource or from the client. Process elements work on data within the flow. Export elements take data out of the flow, and put it into a resource (e.g., a Photomap or drawable) or send it back to the client. The smallest possible photoflo that can be built consists of two elements, one import element and one export element. For example, the photoflo depicted in Figure 8-3 accepts image data from the client and exports it to a Core X drawable.

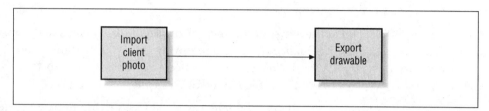

**Figure 8-3:** This photoflo accepts image data from the client and draws it in a Core X drawable.

Note that merely defining a photoflo doesn't necessarily get it to start doing anything. In the case of the photoflo shown in Figure 8-3, execution of the photoflo merely puts it in a state of waiting for data to arrive from the client. XIE's Photoflo Manager contains a scheduler that monitors the readiness state of each element in the photoflo. It knows ExportDrawable can't begin to export data until it receives something from ImportClientPhoto. ImportClientPhoto in turn needs to wait until the X server receives some data from the client. The data arrives via a PutClientData request and the client may deliver it at any time, thus execution of photoflos is generally asynchronous. The PutClientData request, which contains the raw data, is routed from Core X to XIE's dispatcher, and from there to XIE's scheduler, which delivers the data to the ImportClientPhoto element. Figure 8-4 below depicts this path along with other elements of the architecture.

The work done by ImportClientPhoto is not necessarily trivial. In defining the parameters of the ImportClientPhoto element when specifying the photoflo, the client must describe the format of the data to be received. If the ImportClientPhoto element is configured to receive compressed data such as JPEG or CCITT image data, then it must decompress the input data and produce uncompressed output data. The output data is passed by XIE's dataflo manager to the ExportDrawable element, where it is received as input. Decompression is also done by an ImportPhotomap element. Compression is done by the ExportClientPhoto and ExportPhotomap elements.

There is no limit to how complex a photoflo can be constructed, beyond the simple convention that it has to make sense. Any Directed Acyclic Graph (DAG) is legal except graphs containing cycles in them, as depicted in Figure 8-5. These are illegal because the source data for at least one element must be undefined in the presence of cycles.

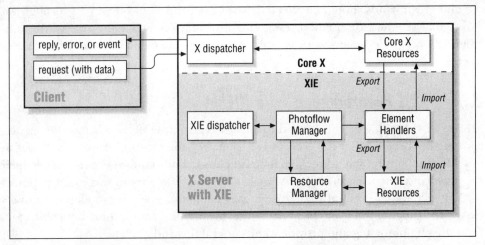

**Figure 8-4:** High-level view of an X server containing XIE support

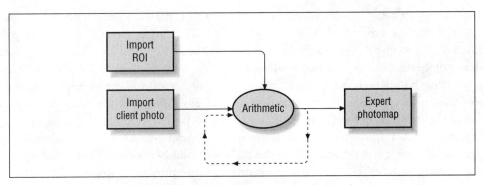

**Figure 8-5:** An illegal photoflo (arithmetic output fed back as a source)

Image pixel data within XIE can be either SingleBand or TripleBand, and must be either constrained or unconstrained. SingleBand data represent grayscale or bitonal images. TripleBand data is used for color images. The constraint model determines whether the number of levels represented by the pixel values is known (and discrete) or unknown (not discrete). Constrained data is integer data, whereas unconstrained data should be thought of as floating point or scaled fractions. Generally, working with unconstrained data should yield more accurate results, at a possible loss of speed. Errors can be generated if trying to pass the wrong data type to an element. For example, export elements can only accept constrained data.

The behavior of many elements in XIE is modifiable according to a "technique" specifier which the client passes in the definition of the element. For example, Import-ClientPhoto takes a technique parameter that specifies whether the data is compressed or not, and if so, how to decompress it. Behavior may also be altered by band-mask and processing domain parameters. If a TripleBand image is passed to the

Geometry element, for example, the band mask may be used to specify that only the red and green bands should be affected. The blue band would then pass through with its original size and orientation, even if it no longer matches the size of the other bands. Processing domains work to restrict action of the element to specified areas of interest.

## 8.3    XIE Programming with XIElib

XIElib is a C binding of the XIE protocol. It is very low-level, which has the virtue of allowing the programmer full access to all aspects of the protocol. However, it does not provide much in the way of convenience functions, and requires expert knowledge of the protocol to be used properly. As such it can be difficult and somewhat tedious to use for beginners. It is anticipated that eventually there will be toolkits available to make XIE programming easier, but in the meantime, this section is meant to cut through a bit of the fog and provide some general tips and guidance.

### 8.3.1    Initialization

The extension must be initialized with a call to `XieInitialize()` before any other XIElib functions are called. `XieInitialize()` calls `XInitExtension()` looking for XIE, and if successful then queries the extension for service class (full XIE or DIS), version numbers, and other miscellaneous information. It also sets up error and event conversion handlers, records the extension op code, error and event codes, and registers known client-side technique handlers. All of this information is stored in an `Xie-ExtensionInfo` structure, a pointer to which was passed to `XieInitialize()` as an argument. It's important to hold onto this information, because it is needed to decode XIE event types. Specifically, the XIE event number is computed by subtracting the X event number of the first XIE event from the number returned in the `XEvent` structure.

### 8.3.2    Keeping it Simple

It's probably best to write one photoflo per module, and try to write photoflos so you can conveniently change parameters, so that they can be re-used as part of a toolkit, which you will naturally build up over time. You will also probably want to start out always using immediate-mode photoflos, which are specified and started executing in a single request, and which are destroyed immediately upon termination of processing. Immediate photoflos only require one X resource for all the immediate photoflos you define. Permanent photoflos, on the other hand, require one resource per photoflo, and have to be executed and destroyed explicitly, so you have to be more careful when using them.

All photoflos are identified by a pair of IDs, a name space and a flo-id. For immediate-mode photoflos, the name space is a resource called a photospace, which is created by calling `XieCreatePhotospace()` once, with the display parameter. The best place to do this is usually right after calling `XieInitialize()`. The flo-id is simply a CARD32 number, which you can create any way you want. The only thing you need to understand is that two different immediate-mode photoflos with the same photospace are differentiated by their flo-ids, so you need to use a different number to distinguish them. The easiest strategy is to simply define the flo-id of the first photoflo you create to be 1, define the next one to be 2, and so on. Thus a typical XIE program might include code segments similar to Example 8-1:

```
XieExtensionInfo *xieInfo;
Status status;
XiePhotospace photospace;
XiePhotoflo flo_id=1;

status = XieInitialize(display,&xieInfo);
if (!status)   ...    /* complain */

photospace = XieCreatePhotospace(display);

...

LoadAnImage(photospace,flo_id++,... /* other parameters */ );
...
EnhanceAnImage(photospace,flo_id++,... /* other parameters */
);
```

### 8.3.3   General Paradigms

Typical XIE programs load an image into a server photomap, simultaneously rendering and displaying the image in a window, using a photoflo which looks like Figure 8-6:

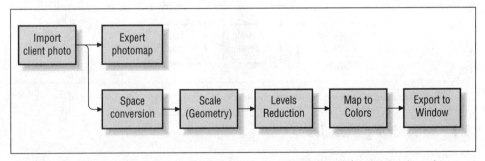

**Figure 8-6:**   A generalized photoflo that stores an image in a photomap and renders it

Here, the "Space Conversion" element might be converting from bitonal to grayscale, color to grayscale, from a non-RGB colorspace to RGB, etc. Levels reduction can be accomplished by dithering or re-constraining. Mapping to colors can be achieved by using `ConvertToIndex`, Point, or combinations of other elements. Exporting to a window is done by using `ExportDrawable` or `ExportDrawablePlane`, depending on the final data type.

Note that there is no explicit element to do decompression. As was mentioned above, all image data within a flow is uncompressed. The `ImportClientPhoto` element can take in either compressed or uncompressed data, but always produces uncompressed data. The `ExportPhotomap` element may be used to compress the data before storing the image in a photomap.

Once an image has been initially displayed, an application may choose to let the user alter the rendering strategy. Thus a set of callbacks would be registered which change the parameters passed to the rendering function. Optionally, the image might be immediately re-rendered, with a photoflo similar to Figure 8-7:

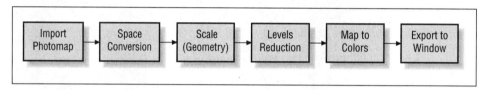

**Figure 8-7:**   Re-rendering of an image stored in the server

Note that if the image is stored compressed in a photomap, it will be automatically decompressed by the `ImportPhotomap` element. For maximum speed, it is usually better to store images in photomaps uncompressed. You can also gain speed by saving intermediate results in photomaps, instead of the original image. For example, in an application mainly concerned with fast interactive contrast enhancement, the photo flo in Figure 8-8 might be used instead of those in Figure 8-7:

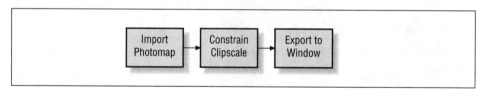

**Figure 8-8:**   Saving intermediate results to speed subsequent operations

## 8.3.4    Specifying Photoflos

A photoflo is created in XIElib by:

- Allocating an empty graph large enough to contain all the elements in the photoflo.

- For each element in the photoflo, define the techniques used by the element with a convenience function and insert the element at some position in the graph.

Since allocating the photoflo graph (often called flograph for short) requires knowing the total number of elements in advance, an application writer should generally sketch out the photoflo graph in advance on paper before sitting down to write any code. A flograph is created using the XIElib function `XieAllocatePhotofloGraph()` as illustrated here:

```
XiePhotoElement *flograph;
int n_els = 7;

flograph = XieAllocatePhotofloGraph(n_els);
```

Notice that no display parameter is passed to `XieAllocatePhotofloGraph()`. This implies (correctly) that you can use the same flograph for multiple displays.

As an example of defining an element, consider using a Constrain element with the `ClipScale` technique for the fourth element in the graph of Figure 8-7. XIElib provides the `XieTecClipScale` convenience function, which takes as arguments the parameters which specify how the input intensities of each band are to map to output levels. It stores that information into an XIElib-defined structure. To map 12-bit grayscale data values from the range (100,2936) to the range (0,255), one could write:

```
XieClipScaleParam *tech_parms;
XieConstant in_low,in_high;
XieLTriplet
out_low,out_high;

in_low[0] = 100; in_high[0] = 2936; out_low[0] = 0;
out_high[0] = 255;
        /* for grayscale images, always use the first band */

in_low[1] = 0;  in_high[1] = 0; out_low[1] = 0;  out_high[1] =
0; in_low[2] = 0;  in_high[2] = 0; out_low[2] = 0;  out_high[2]
= 0;

tech_parms = XieTecClipScale(in_low,in_high,out_low,out_high);
```

`XieConstant` and `XieLTriplet` are typedef'd as arrays of 3 elements. The input to a Constrain element may be floating point data, so the input ranges need to be specified with the `XieConstant` (floating point) data type, whereas the outputs are always constrained and are specified with the `XieLTriplet` (long triplet) data type.

`XieTecClipScale()` returns a pointer to the XIElib structure for holding `ClipScale` data. This information will then be passed along with the other parameters which define the Constrain element:

```
XieLTriplet levels;

levels[0] = 8;
levels[1] = 0;
levels[2] = 0;

XieFloConstrain( &flograph[3],
```

```
      3,                 /* source image phototag */
      levels,            /* output levels per band  */
      xieValConstrainClipScale, tech_parms );
```

The result of the above code is that a Constrain element is created as the fourth element in the flograph, taking input from the third element. The elements do not have to be specified in order: the next section of code could legally define the second element, followed by the fifth, etc. All that matters is that when all of the positions of the allocated flograph are filled, their connections (as specified by the source phototag parameters) should correspond to your hand drawing of the photoflo.

Once the photoflo is completely specified, you can tell the server to start it executing with the `XieExecuteImmediate()` function. It takes as arguments the display, the photospace, flo-id, flograph, number of elements, and a Boolean flag that indicates whether an event should be sent when the photoflo is done. This flag should always be set to True, in the author's opinion.

### 8.3.4.1    Sending Data to a Photoflo

Once a photoflo is running, if it needs data it will block until the client sends it a `Put-ClientData` request. Typically, a program will contain a loop which reads data from the image source (e.g., disk) and streams it to the server:

```
final = False;
while (bytes_left > 0) {
        nbytes = ...;    /* calculate how many bytes to send */
        if (nbytes == bytes_left)
                    final = True;

        ....;                   /* get the image data */

        XiePutClientData(display,
                photospace,flo_id,phototag,final,band_number,data,nbytes);

        bytes_left -= nbytes;
}
```

Notice that it is up to the client to specify when the final packet of image data is being sent by setting the final parameter to 1. The photospace and `flo_id` parameters specify the photoflo (a server may run multiple photoflos simultaneously). The phototag parameter indicates which element of the photoflo is receiving the data. If the element was placed in position $n$ in the flograph (in the element definition call), then the phototag should be specified as +1.

# 8.4    Some Tips

The fastest way to convert from grayscale image intensities to colormap indexes is to allocate contiguous color entries in the colormap, then use Constrain/ClipScale to map intensities directly to indexes. This order can save the use of a Point operation, which requires sending a lookup table over the network.

For color images, try to stick with standard colormaps. Look into using the Dither element to reduce the number of colors in the image to what the standard colormap will holds, then use `BandExtract` to remap all the colors to indice directly. This process is much faster in general than methods based on `ConvertToIndex`.

For bitonal images, keep them bitonal (unless you want to do anti-aliasing) and use `ExportDrawablePlane` instead of `ExportDrawable`. You will need to set the foreground and background of the graphics context for `ExportDrawablePlane` in order to get the white/black polarity right.

An Introduction to the X Image Extension

# Release 6 Release Notes

## A.1    Easy Build Instructions

This quick summary is no substitute for reading the full build instructions later in this document.

Edit *xc/config/cf/site.def* for local preferences. If you want to build with *gcc*, uncomment the `HasGcc2` line. If you want to install somewhere other than */usr/X11R6*, change `ProjectRoot`. (Do *not* use DESTDIR.)

If any fixes have been released by the X Consortium, stop here and follow the instructions at the top of each patch, but don't do any of the *make* commands suggested in the patches. Then continue here.

Check the appropriate *xc/config/cf/vendor.cf* file (where *vendor* is "sun," "bin," etc.) to make sure that `OSMajorVersion` and `OSMinorVersion` are set correctly for your system (change them if necessary).

See if there is a `BootstrapCFlags` mentioned in the comments in the *vendor.cf* file. If there isn't one, *cd* to the **xc** directory and type:

```
make World >& world.log
```

If there is a `BootstrapCFlags`, take its value and type:

```
make World BOOTSTRAPCFLAGS="value" >& world.log
```

Do not call the output file "make.log". If the build is successful, you can install most of it with:

```
make install >& install.log
```

You can install manual pages with:

```
make install.man >& man.log
```

While the system is building (or if things fail), read the rest of these Release Notes.

# A.2  What Is Release 6

This is the sixth release of X Window System software from the X Consortium.

The X Consortium is an independent, not-for-profit corporation, and the successor to the MIT X Consortium, which was part of the MIT Laboratory for Computer Science. See the *XConsortium* manual page for details.

## A.2.1  Overview of the X Consortium Release

There are two parts to Release 6: X Consortium software and documentation, and user-contributed software and documentation. The X Consortium part contains the following:

X Consortium Standards

> The X Consortium produces standards: documents which define network protocols, programming interfaces, and other aspects of the X environment. See the `XStandards` manual page for a list of standards.

Sample Implementations

> For most of our standards, we provide *sample* implementations to demonstrate proof of concept. These are not *reference* implementations; the written specifications define the standards.

Fonts

A collection of bitmap and outline fonts are included in the distribution, contributed by various individuals and companies.

Utility Libraries

A number of libraries, such as the *Athena Widget Set*, are included. These are not standards, but are used in building X Consortium applications and may be useful in building other applications.

Sample Programs

We also provide a number of application programs. A few of these programs, such as *xdm*, should be considered essential in almost all environments. The rest of the applications carry no special status; they are simply programs that have been developed and/or maintained by X Consortium staff. In some cases, you will find better substitutes for these programs in the user-contributed part.

The user-contributed part consists of people's contributions. You'll find a variety of software and documentation here: programs, demos, games, libraries, X server extensions, etc.

## A.2.2    Supported Systems

We built and tested this release on the following systems:

```
A/UX 3.0.1
AIX 3.2.5
BSD/386 1.0
HP-UX 9.1
IRIX 5.2
Mach 2.5 Vers 2.00.1
Microsoft Windows NT 3.1
NCR Unix System V Release 4/MP-RAS
NEWS-OS 6.0
OSF/1 1.3
OSF/1 1.0
SunOS 4.1.3
SunOS 5.3
UNICOS 8.0
UNIX System V/386 Release 4.2 Version 1
Unix System V/860 Release 4.0 Version 3
Ultrix-32 4.3
```

## A.2.3    The XC Tree

The first thing you may notice is that you can't find anything. The source tree has undergone a major reorganization since Release 5. The top-level directory has been renamed from *mit/* to *xc/*.

The general layout under *xc/* is now as follows:

```
config/         config files, imake, makedepend, build utilities
doc/            all documentation other than per-program manual pages
fonts/          BDF, Speedo, Type1 fonts
```

```
include/           include files shared by multiple directories
lib/               all libraries
nls/               localization files
programs/          all programs, including the X server and rgb
test/              X Test Suite and other test suites
util/              patch, compress, other utilities
workInProgress/    snapshots of work in progress
bug-report/        bug reporting template
registry/          X Registry
```

### A.2.3.1    config/

The *xc/config* directory now has subdirectories:

```
config/cf/            all the config files: Imake.tmpl, Project.tmpl, etc.
config/imake/         the imake program
config/makedepend/    the makedepend program
config/util/          other configuration utility programs and scripts
```

### A.2.3.2    lib/

Xlib sources are in *xc/lib/X11*; we've renamed directories to match the lib*name*.a names.

### A.2.3.3    doc/

```
doc/specs/     X Consortium standards and other specifications
doc/man/       manual pages for libraries and general manual pages
doc/util/      macro packages and utilities for formatting
doc/hardcopy/  PostScript versions of the documentation
```

The *xc/doc/hardcopy* directory contains compressed, pre-formatted, PostScript versions of documentation elsewhere in the **doc** tree and the program manual pages, which are in each program's source directory. These files can be uncompressed with the *compress* program, which is included in *xc/util/compress*.

### A.2.3.4    extensions

There is no longer a top-level extensions directory. Extension libraries are now under *xc/lib/*, server extension code is under *xc/programs/Xserver/Xext/*, and extension header files are under *xc/include/extensions/*.

## A.2.4    Extensions Supported

The core distribution includes the following extensions: BIG-REQUESTS, LBX, MIT-SHM, MIT-SUNDRY-NONSTANDARD, Multi-Buffering, RECORD, SHAPE, SYNC, X3D-PEX, XC-MISC, XIE, XInputExtension, XKEYBOARD, XTEST, and XTestExtension1.

## A.2.5    Implementation Parameters

Some of the specifications define some behavior as implementation-dependent. Implementations of X Consortium standards need to document how those parameters are implemented; this section does so.

XFILESEARCHPATH default

    This default can be set at build time by setting the *imake* variables XAppLoadDir, XFileSearchPathDefault, XAppLoadDir, XFileSearchPathBase, and Project-Root in *site.def*. See *xc/config/cf/Project.tmpl* for how they are used.

    By default, XFILESEARCHPATH has these components:

```
/usr/X11R6/lib/X11/%L/%T/%N%C%S
/usr/X11R6/lib/X11/%l/%T/%N%C%S
/usr/X11R6/lib/X11/%T/%N%C%S
/usr/X11R6/lib/X11/%L/%T/%N%S
/usr/X11R6/lib/X11/%l/%T/%N%S
/usr/X11R6/lib/X11/%T/%N%S
```

XUSERFILESEARCHPATH default

    If the environment variable XAPPLRESDIR is defined, the default value of XUSER-FILESEARCHPATH has the following components:

```
$XAPPLRESDIR/%L/%N%C
$XAPPLRESDIR/%l/%N%C
$XAPPLRESDIR/%N%C
$HOME/%N%C
$XAPPLRESDIR/%L/%N
$XAPPLRESDIR/%l/%N
$XAPPLRESDIR/%N
$HOME/%N
```

Otherwise it has these components:

```
$HOME/%L/%N%C
$HOME/%l/%N%C
$HOME/%N%C
$HOME/%L/%N
$HOME/%l/%N
$HOME/%N
```

XKEYSYMDB default

    Defaults to  */usr/X11R6/lib/X11/XKeysymDB*, assuming ProjectRoot is set to */usr/X11R6*.

XCMSDB default

    Defaults to  */usr/X11R6/lib/X11/Xcms.txt*, assuming ProjectRoot is set to */usr/X11R6*.

XLOCALEDIR default

Defaults to the directory */usr/X11R6/lib/X11/locale*, assuming `ProjectRoot` is set to */usr/X11R6*.

XErrorDB location

The Xlib error database file is */usr/X11R6/lib/X11/XErrorDB*, assuming `Project-Root` is set to */usr/X11r6*.

XtErrorDB location

The Xt error database file is */usr/X11R6/lib/X11/XtErrorDB*`ProjectRoot`, assuming is set to */usr/X11R6*.

Supported Locales

For a list of locales supported, see the files *locale.dir* and *locale.alias* in the *xc/nls/X11/locale/* directory.

Input Methods supported

The core distribution does not include any input methods servers. However, in Latin-1 locales, a default method that supports European compose processing is enabled. See *xc/nls/X11/locale/Compose/iso8859-1* for the supported compositions. There are input method servers in contrib.

# A.3    Building X

This section gives detailed instructions for building Release 6: getting it off the distribution medium, configuring, compiling, installing, running, and updating.

## A.3.1    Unpacking the Distribution

The distribution normally comes as multiple tar files, either on tape or across a network, or as a CD-ROM.

If you are unpacking tar files, you will need about 150 megabytes to hold the *xc/* part.

### A.3.1.1    Unpacking a Compressed FTP Distribution

If you have obtained compressed tar files over the network, create a directory to hold the sources and *cd* into it:

```
mkdir sourcedir
cd sourcedir
```

Then for each tar file *xc-\*.tar.Z*, execute this:

```
zcat ftp-dir/xc-N.tar.Z | tar xpf-
```

For each tar file *contrib-\*.tar.Z*, execute this:

```
zcat ftp-dir/contrib-N.tar.Z | tar xpf -
```

### A.3.1.2    Unpacking a gzipped FTP Distribution

If you have obtained gzipped tar files over the network, create a directory to hold the sources and *cd* into it:

```
mkdir sourcedir
cd sourcedir
```

Then for each tar file *xc-\*.tar.gz*, execute this:

```
gunzip -c ftp-dir/xc-N.tar.gz | tar xpf -
```

For each tar file *contrib-\*.tar.gz*, execute this:

```
gunzip -c ftp-dir/contrib-N.tar.gz | tar xpf -
```

### A.3.1.3    Unpacking a Split Compressed FTP Distribution

If you have obtained compressed and split tar files over the network, create a directory to hold the sources:

```
mkdir sourcedir
```

Then for each directory *xc-\**:

```
cd ftp-dir/xc-N
cat xc-N.?? | uncompress | (cd sourcedir\; tar xpf -
```

For each directory *contrib-\**, execute this:

```
cd ftp-dir/contrib-N
cat contrib-N.?? | uncompress | (cd sourcedir\; tar xpf -
```

### A.3.1.4    Unpacking the Tape Distribution

If you have obtained a tape, create a directory to hold the sources and untar everything into that directory:

```
mkdir sourcedir
cd sourcedir
tar xpf tape-device
```

### A.3.1.5    Using the CD-ROM

If you have obtained a CD-ROM, you don't have to do anything to unpack it. However, you will have to create a symbolic link tree to build X. See the next section.

## A.3.2    Apply Patches

If there are fixes released, apply them now. Follow the instructions at the top of each patch, but don't do any *make* commands. Then continue here. See section A.6 for how to get the patches.

## A.3.3 Symbolic Link Trees

If you expect to build the distribution on more than one machine using a shared source tree, or you are building from CD-ROM, or you just want to keep the source tree pure, you may want to use the program *xc/config/util/lndir.c* to create a symbolic link tree on each build machine. The links may use an additional ten megabytes, which is cheaper than having multiple copies of the source tree.

It may be tricky to compile *lndir* before the distribution is built. If you have a copy from Release 5, use that. *Makefile.ini* can be used for building *lndir* the first time. You may have to specify OSFLAGS-D*something* to get it to compile. What you would pass as BOOT-STRAPCFLAGS might work. The command line looks something like this:

```
make -f Makefile.ini OSFLAGS=-Dflag
```

To use a symbolic link tree, create a directory for the build, *cd* to it, and type this:

```
lndir sourcedir
```

where *sourcedir* is the pathname of the directory where you stored the sources. All of the build instructions given below should then be done in the build directory on each machine, rather than in the source directory.

*xc/config/util/mkshadow/* contains *mkshadow*, an alternative program to *lndir*.

## A.3.4 Configuration Parameters

Build information for each source directory is in files called *Imakefile*. An *Imakefile*, along with local configuration information in *xc/config/cf/*, is used by the program *imake* to generate a *Makefile*.

Most of the configuration work prior to building the release is to set parameters so that *imake* will generate correct files. Most of those parameters are set in *xc/config/cf/site.def*. You will also need to check the appropriate *xc/config/cf/vendor.cf* file to make sure that OSMajorVersion, OSMinorVersion, and OSTeenyVersion are set correctly for your system (change them if necessary).

The *site.def* file has two parts, one protected with #ifdef BeforeVendorCF and one with #ifdef AfterVendorCF. The file is actually processed twice, once before the *.cf* file and once after. About the only thing you need to set in the "before" section is Has-Gcc2; just about everything else can be set in the "after" section.

The sample *site.def* also has commented out support to include another file, *host.def*. This scheme may be useful if you want to set most parameters site-wide, but some parameters vary from machine to machine. If you use a symbolic link tree, you can share *site.def* across all machines and give each machine its own copy of *host.def*.

The config parameters are listed in *xc/config/cf/README*, but here are some of the more common parameters that you may wish to set in *site.def*.

`ProjectRoot`

> The destination where X will be installed. This variable needs to be set before you build, as some programs that read files at run-time have the installation directory compiled in to them. Assuming you have set the variable to some value */path*, files will be installed into */path*/bin, */path*/include/X11, */path*/lib, and */path*/man.

`HasGcc`

> Set to **YES** to build with *gcc* version 1.

`HasGcc2`

> Set to **YES** to build with *gcc* version 2. Both this option and `HasGcc` look for a compiler named *gcc*, but `HasGcc2` will cause the build to use more features of *gcc* 2, such as the ability to compile shared libraries.

`HasCplusplus`

> Declares the system has a C++ compiler. C++ is necessary to build *Fresco*. On some systems, you may also have to set additional variables to say what C++ compiler you have.

`DefaultUsrBin`

> This is a directory where programs will be found even if PATH is not set in the environment. It is independent of ProjectRoot and defaults to */usr/bin*. It is used, for example, when connecting from a remote system via *rsh*. The *rstart* program installs its server in this directory.

`InstallServerSetUID`

> Some systems require the X server to run as root to access the devices it needs. If you are on such a system and will not be using *xdm*, you can set this variable to **YES** to install the X server `setuid` to root. Note that the X server has not been analyzed by the X Consortium for security in such an installation; talk to your system manager before setting this variable.

`MotifBC`

> Causes Xlib and Xt to work around some bugs in older versions of Motif. Set to **YES** only if you will be linking with Motif version 1.1.1, 1.1.2, or 1.1.3.

`GetValuesBC`

> Setting this variable to **YES** allows illegal `XtGetValues` requests with NULL `ArgVal` to usually succeed, as Release 5 did. Some applications erroneously rely on this behavior. Support for this will be removed in a future release.

The following *vendor*.**cf** files are in the release but have not been tested recently and hence probably need changes to work: *DGUX.cf*, *Mips.cf*, *apollo.cf*, *bsd.cf*, *convex.cf*, *moto.cf*, *pegasus.cf*, and *x386.cf*. *Amoeba.cf* is known to require additional patches.

The file *xc/lib/Xdmcp/Wraphelp.c*, for XDM-AUTHORIZATION-1, is not included in this release. The file is available within the US; for details get */pub/R6/xdm-auth/README* from *ftp.x.org* via anonymous FTP.

## A.3.5    System Notes

This section contains hints on building X with specific compilers and operating systems.

### A.3.5.1    gcc

*gcc* version 2 is in regular use at the X Consortium. You should have no problems using it to build. Set the variable `HasGcc2`. X will not compile on some systems with *gcc* version 2.5, 2.5.1, or 2.5.2 because of an incorrect declaration of memmove() in a *gcc* include file.

### A.3.5.2    SparcWorks 2.0

If you have a non-threaded program and want to debug it with the old SparcWorks 2.0 dbx, you will need to use the thread stubs library in *xc/util/misc/thr_stubs.c*. Compile it as follows:

```
cc -c thr_stubs.c
ar cq libthr_stubs.a thr_stubs.o
ranlib libthr_stubs.a
```

Install the file libthr_stubs.a in the same directory with your X libraries (e.g., */usr/X11R6/lib/libthr_stubs.a*). Add the following line to *site.def*:

```
#define ExtraLibraries -lsocket -lnsl $(CDEBUGFLAGS:-g=-lthr_stubs)
```

This example uses a *make* macro substitution; not all *make* implementations support this feature.

### A.3.5.3    CenterLine C Under Solaris 2.3

If you are using the CenterLine C compiler to compile the distribution under Solaris 2.3, place the following line in your *site.def*:

```
#define HasCenterLineC YES
```

If *clcc* is not in your default search path, add this line to *site.def*:

```
#define CcCmd /path/to/your/clcc
```

If you are using `CodeCenter` 4.0.4 or earlier, the following files trigger bugs in the *clcc* optimizer:

```
xc/programs/Xserver/cfb16/cfbgetsp.c
xc/programs/Xserver/cfb16/cfbfillsp.c
xc/programs/Xserver/cfb/cfbgetsp.c
```

Thus to build the server, you will have to compile these files by hand with the **-g** flag:

```
% cd xc/programs/Xserver/cfb16
% make CDEBUGFLAGS="-g" cfbgetsp.o cfbfillsp.o
% cd ../cfb
% make CDEBUGFLAGS="-g" cfbgetsp.o
```

This optimizer bug appears to be fixed in `CodeCenter` 4.0.6.

### A.3.5.4    Microsoft Windows NT

The set of operating systems that the client-side code will run on has been expanded to include Microsoft Windows NT 3.1. All of the base libraries are supported, including multithreading in Xlib and Xt, but some of the more complicated applications, specifically *xterm* and *xdm*, are not supported.

There are also some other rough edges in the implementation, such as lack of support for non-socket file descriptors as Xt alternate inputs and not using the registry for configurable parameters like the system filenames and search paths.

## A.3.6    The Build

On NT, type:

```
nmake World.Win32 > world.log
```

On other systems, find the `BootstrapCFlags` line, if any, in the *vendor.cf* file. If there isn't one, type:

```
make World >& world.log
```

otherwise type:

```
make World BOOTSTRAPCFLAGS="value" >& world.log
```

You can call the output file something other than "world.log," but do not call it "make.log" because files with this name are automatically deleted during the "cleaning" stage of the build.

Because the build can take several hours to complete, you will probably want to run it in the background and keep a watch on the output. For example:

```
make World >& world.log &
tail -f world.log
```

If something goes wrong, the easiest thing is to just start over (typing "make World" again) once you have corrected the problem. It is possible that a failure will corrupt the top-level *Makefile*. If that happens, simply delete the file and recreate a workable substitute:

```
cp Makefile.ini Makefile
```

Release 6
Release Notes

### A.3.7    Installing X

If everything is built successfully, you can install the software by typing the following as root:

```
make install >& install.log
```

Again, you might want to run this in the background and use *tail* to watch the progress.

You can install the manual pages by typing the following as root:

```
make install.man >& man.log
```

## A.3.8    Shared Libraries

Except on SunOS 4, the version number of all the shared libraries has changed to **6.0**. If you want programs linked against previous versions of the libraries to use the Release 6 libraries, create a link from the old name to the new name.

## A.3.9    Setting Up xterm

If your */etc/termcap* and */usr/lib/terminfo* databases do not have correct entries for *xterm*, use the sample entries provided in the directory *xc/programs/xterm/*. System V users may need to compile and install the *terminfo* entry with the *tic* utility.

Since each *xterm* will need a separate pseudoterminal, you need a reasonable number of them for normal execution. You probably will want at least 32 on a small, multiuser system. On most systems, each pty has two devices, a master and a slave, which are usually named /dev/tty[pqrstu][0-f] and /dev/pty[pqrstu][0-f]. If you don't have at least the "p" and "q" sets configured (try typing *ls /dev/?ty??*), you should have your system administrator add them. This is commonly done by running the MAKEDEV script in the */dev* directory with appropriate arguments.

## A.3.10    Starting Servers at System Boot

The *xfs* and *xdm* programs are designed to be run automatically at system startup. Please read the manual pages for details on setting up configuration files; reasonable sample files are in *xc/programs/xdm/config/* and *xc/programs/xfs/*.

If your system uses an */etc/rc* file at boot time, you can usually enable these programs by placing the following at or near the end of the file:

```
if [ -f /usr/X11R6/bin/xfs ]; then
        /usr/X11R6/bin/xfs &; echo -n ' xfs'
fi

if [ -f /usr/X11R6/bin/xdm ]; then
        /usr/X11R6/bin/xdm; echo -n ' xdm'
fi
```

Since *xfs* can serve fonts over the network, you do not need to run a font server on every machine with an X display. You should start *xfs* before *xdm*, since *xdm* may start an X server which is a client of the font server.

The examples here use */usr/X11R6/bin*, but if you have installed into a different directory by setting (or unsetting) `ProjectRoot` then you need to substitute the correct directory.

If you are unsure about how system boot works, or if your system does not use */etc/rc*, consult your system administrator for help.

## A.3.11  Using OPEN LOOK Applications

You can use the X11R6 Xsun server with OPEN LOOK applications, but you must pass the new **-swapLkeys** flag to the server on startup, or the OPEN LOOK Undo, Copy, Paste, Find, and Cut keys may not work correctly. For example, to run Sun's `OpenWindows` 3.3 desktop environment with an X11R6 server, use the command:

```
% openwin -server /usr/X11R6/bin/Xsun -swapLkeys
```

The keysyms reported by keys on the numeric keypad have also changed since X11R5; if you find that `OpenWindows` applications do not respond to keypad keys and cursor control keys when using the Release 6 server, you can remap the keypad to generate Release 5 style keysyms using the following *xmodmap* commands:

```
keysym Pause = F21
keysym Print = F22
keysym Break = F23
keysym KP_Equal = F24
keysym KP_Divide = F25
keysym KP_Multiply = F26
keysym KP_Home = F27
keysym KP_Up = Up
keysym KP_Prior = F29
keysym KP_Left = Left
keycode 100 = F31
keysym KP_Right = Right
keysym KP_End = F33
keysym KP_Down = Down
keysym KP_Next = F35 .
keysym KP_Insert = Insert
keysym KP_Delete = Delete
```

## A.3.12  Rebuilding After Patches

You shouldn't need to rebuild after patches right away, but eventually you are probably going to make changes to the sources, for example by applying X Consortium public patches.

Each patch comes with explicit instructions at the top of it saying what to do. Thus the procedure here is only an overview of the types of commands that might be necessary to rebuild X after changing it.

If you are building from CD-ROM, apply the patches to the symbolic link tree. The links to changed files will be replaced with a local file containing the new contents.

If only source files are changed, you should be able to rebuild just by going to the **xc** directory in your build tree and typing:

```
make >& make.log
```

If configuration files are changed, the safest thing to do is type:

```
make Everything >& every.log
```

"Everything" is similar to "World" in that it rebuilds every *Makefile*, but unlike "World" it does not delete the existing objects, libraries, and executables, and only rebuilds what is out of date.

Note that in both kinds of rebuilds you do not need to supply the `BootstrapCFlags` value any more; the information is already recorded.

### A.3.13    Building Contributed Software

The software in *contrib* is not set up to have everything built automatically. It is assumed that you will build individual pieces as you find the desire, time, and/or disk space. You need to have the X Consortium part built and installed before building the contributed software. To build a program or library in *contrib*, look in its directory for any special build instructions (for example, a *README* file). If there are none, and there is an *Imakefile*, *cd* to the directory and type:

```
xmkmf -a
make >& make.log
```

This will build a *Makefile* in the directory and all subdirectories, and then build the software. If the build is successful, you should be able to install it using the same commands used for the **xc** software:

```
make install >& install.log
make install.man >& man.log
```

## A.4    *What Is New in Release 6*

This section describes changes in the X Consortium distribution since Release 5. Release 6 contains much new functionality in many areas. In addition, many bugs have been fixed. However, in the effort to develop the new technology in this release, some bugs, particularly in client programs, did not get fixed.

Except where noted, all libraries, protocols, and servers are upward compatible with Release 5. That is, Release 5 clients and applications should continue to work with Release 6 libraries and servers.

## A.4.1    New Standards

The following are new X Consortium standards in Release 6. Each is described in its own section below.

```
X Image Extension
Inter-Client Communications Conventions Manual (update)
Inter-Client Exchange Protocol
Inter-Client Exchange Library
X Session Management Protocol
X Session Management Library
Input Method Protocol
X Logical Font Descriptions (update)
SYNC extension
XTEST extension
PEX 5.1 Protocol (released after Release 5)
PEXlib (released after Release 5)
BIG-REQUESTS extension
XC-MISC extension
```

## A.4.2    XIE (X Image Extension)

The sample implementation in Release 6 is a complete implementation of full XIE 5.0 protocol, except for the following techniques that are excluded from the SI:

```
ColorAlloc:    Match, Requantize
Convolve:      Replicate
Decode:        JPEG lossless
Encode:        JPEG lossless
Geometry:      AntialiasByArea, AntialiasByLowpass
```

*xieperf* exercises the server functionality; it provides unit testing and a reasonable measure of multi-element photoflo testing.

A draft standard of the XIElib specification is included in this release and is open for Public Review. The XIElib code matches the 5.0 protocol.

The JPEG compression and decompression code is based on the Independent JPEG Group's (IJG) JPEG software, Release 4. This software provides baseline Huffman DCT encoding as defined by ISO/IEC DIS 10918-1, "Digital Compression and Coding of Continuous-tone Still Images, Part 1: Requirements and guidelines", and was chosen as a basis for our implementation of JPEG compression and decompression primarily because the IJG's design goals matched ours for the implementation of the XIE SI: achieve portability and flexibility without sacrificing performance. Less than half of the files distributed by the IJG have been incorporated into the XIE SI. The Independent JPEG Group's software is made available with restrictions; see *xc/ programs/Xserver/XIE/mixie/jpeg/README*.

### A.4.3    Inter-Client Communications Conventions Manual

Release 6 includes version 2.0 of the ICCCM. This version contains a large number of changes and clarifications in the areas of window management, selections, session management, and resource sharing.

#### A.4.3.1    Window Management

The circumstances under which the window manager is required to send synthetic `ConfigureNotify` events have been clarified to ensure that any `ConfigureWindow` request issued by the client will result in a `ConfigureNotify` event, either from the server or from the window manager. We have also added advice about how a client should inspect events so as to minimize the number of situations where it is necessary to use the `TranslateCoordinates` request.

The window_gravity field of WM_NORMAL_HINTS has a new value, `StaticGravity`, which specifies that the window manager should not shift the client window's location when reparenting the window.

The base size in the **WM_NORMAL_HINTS** property is now to be included in the aspect ratio calculation.

The WM_STATE property now has a formal definition (it was previously only suggested).

#### A.4.3.2    Selections

We have clarified the CLIENT_WINDOW, LENGTH, and MULTIPLE targets. We have also added a number of new targets for Encapsulated PostScript and for the Apple Macintosh PICT structured graphics format. We have also defined a new selection property type C_STRING, which is a string of non-zero bytes. (This is in contrast to the STRING type, which excludes many control characters.)

A selection requester can now pass parameters in with the request.

Another new facility is manager selections. This use of the selection mechanism is not to transfer data, but to allow clients known as *managers* to provide services to other clients. Version 2.0 also specifies that window managers should hold a manager selection. At present, the only service defined for window managers is to report the ICCCM version number to which the window manager complies. Now that this facility is in place, additional services can be added in the future.

#### A.4.3.3    Resource Sharing

A prominent new addition in version 2.0 is the ability of clients to take control of colormap installation under certain circumstances. Earlier versions of the ICCCM specified that the window manager had exclusive control over colormap installation. This proves to be inconvenient for certain situations, such as when a client has the server grabbed. Version 2.0 allows clients to install colormaps themselves after having informed the window manager. Clients must hold a pointer grab for the entire time they are doing their own colormap installation.

Version 2.0 also clarifies a number of rules about how clients can exchange resources. These rules are important when a client places a resource ID into a hints property or passes a resource ID through the selection mechanism.

### A.4.3.4  Session Management

Some of the properties in section 5 of ICCCM 1.1 are now obsolete, and new properties for session management have been defined.

## A.4.4    ICE (Inter-Client Exchange)

ICE provides a common framework on which to build protocols. It supplies authentication, byte order negotiation, version negotiation, and error reporting conventions. It supports multiplexing multiple protocols over a single transport connection. ICElib provides a common interface to these mechanisms so that protocol implementors need not reinvent them.

An *iceauth* program was written to manipulate an ICE authority file; it is very similar to the *xauth* program.

## A.4.5    SM (Session Management)

The X Session Management Protocol (XSMP) provides a uniform mechanism for users to save and restore their sessions using the services of a network-based session manager. It is built on ICE. SMlib is the C interface to the protocol. There is also support for XSMP in Xt.

A simple session manager, *xsm*, is included in *xc/workInProgress/xsm*.

A new protocol, *rstart*, greatly simplifies the task of starting applications on remote machines. It is built upon already existing remote execution protocols such as *rsh*. The most important feature that it adds is the ability to pass environment variables and authentication data to the applications being started.

## A.4.6    Input Method Protocol

Some languages need complex pre-editing input methods, and such an input method may be implemented separately from applications in a process called an Input Method (IM) Server. The IM Server handles the display of pre-edit text and the user's input operation. The Input Method (IM) Protocol standardizes the communication between the IM Server and the IM library linked with the application.

The IM protocol is a completely new protocol, based on experience with Release 5's sample implementations. The following new features are added, beyond the mechanisms in the Release 5 sample implementations:

- The IM Server can support any of several transports for connection with the IM library.

- Both the IM Server and clients can authenticate each other for security.

- A client can connect to an IM Server without restarting even if it starts up before the IM Server.

- A client can initiate string conversion to the IM Server for re-conversion of text.

- A client can specify some keys as hot keys, which can be used to escape from the normal input method processing regardless of the input method state.

The Release 6 sample implementation for the internationalization support in Xlib has a new pluggable framework, with the capability of loading and switching locale object modules dynamically. For backward compatibility, the Release 6 sample implementation can support the Release 5 protocols by switching to IM modules supporting those protocols. In addition, the framework provides the following new functions and mechanisms:

X   An X Locale database format is defined, and the subset of a user's environment dependent on language is provided as a plain ASCII text file. You can customize the behavior of Xlib without changing Xlib itself.

*ANSI C and non-ANSI C bindings*
The common set of methods and structures are defined, which bind the X locale to the system locales within *libc*, and a framework for implementing this common set under non-ANSI C base system is provided.

*Converters*
The sample implementation has a mechanism to support various encodings by pluggable converters and provides the following converters:

- Light weight converter for C and ISO 8859

- Generic converter (relatively slow) for other encoding

- High performance converter for Shift-JIS and EUC

- Converter for UCS-2 defined in ISO/IEC 10646-1

You can add your converter using this mechanism for your specific performance requirement.

*Locale modules*

The library is implemented such that input methods and output methods are separated and are independent of each other. Therefore, an output-only client does not link with the IM code, and an input-only client does not link with the OM code. Locale modules can be loaded on demand if the platform supports dynamic loading.

*Transport Layer*

There are several kinds of transports for connection between the IM library and the IM Server. The IM protocol is independent of a specific transport layer protocol, and the sample implementation has a mechanism to permit an IM Server to define the transports which the IM Server is willing to use. The sample implementation supports transport over the X protocol, TCP/IP and DECnet.

There are IM Servers and an IM Server developer's kit in *contrib* for Japanese and for Korean internationalized clients using IM services. The IM Server developer's kit hides the details of the IM protocol and the transport layer protocols. It also hides the differences between the Release 5 and Release 6 protocols from the IM Server developer, so that an IM developer has an easier task in developing new IM Servers.

## A.4.7    X Logical Font Description

The X Logical Font Description has been enhanced to include general 2D linear transformations, character set subsets, and support for polymorphic fonts. See *xc/doc/specs/XLFD/xlfd.tbl.ms* for details.

## A.4.8    SYNC Extension

The Synchronization extension lets clients synchronize via the X server. This process eliminates the network delays and the differences in synchronization primitives between operating systems. The extension provides a general Counter resource; clients can alter the value of a Counter and can block their execution until a Counter reaches a specific threshold. For example, two clients can share a Counter initialized to zero, one client can draw some graphics and then increment the Counter, and the other client can block until the Counter reaches a value of one and then draw some additional graphics.

## A.4.9    BIG-REQUESTS Extension

The standard X protocol only allows requests up to $2^{18}$ bytes long. A new protocol extension, BIG-REQUESTS, has been added that allows a client to extend the length of the field in protocol requests to be a 32-bit value. This is useful for PEX and other extensions that transmit complex information to the server.

## A.4.10    XC-MISC Extension

A new extension, XC-MISC, allows clients to get back ID ranges from the server. Xlib handles this automatically. Obtaining ID ranges can be useful for a long-running application that uses many IDs over its lifetime.

## A.4.11    XTEST Extension

The XTEST extension, which first shipped as a patch to Release 5, is included.

## A.4.12    Tree Reorganization

Many of the directories under *xc/* (renamed from *mit/*) have been moved. See the section **The XC Tree** for the new layout. The reorganization has simplified dependencies in the build process. Once you get used to the new layout, things will be easier to find.

Various filenames have been changed to minimize name conflicts on systems that limit file names to eight characters, a period, and three more characters. Conflicts remain for various header (.h) files.

## A.4.13    Configuration Files

The configuration files have changed quite a bit, we hope in a mostly compatible fashion. The main config files are now in *xc/config/cf*, imake sources are in *xc/config/imake*, and makedepend sources are in *xc/config/makedepend*. The *lndir* program (for creating link trees) is in *xc/config/util*; there is a *Makefile.ini* in that directory that may be useful to get *lndir* built the first time (before you build the rest of the tree).

The rules for building libraries have changed a lot; it is now much easier to add a new library to the system.

The selection of *vendor.cf* file has moved from *Imake.tmpl* to a new *Imake.cf*.

The config variable that was called ServerOSDefines in Release 5 has been renamed to ServerExtraDefines and applies globally to all X server sources. The variable ServerOSDefines now applies just to the *os* directory of the server.

There are a number of new config variables dealing with C++, all of which have "Cplusplus" in their names.

# should no longer be thought of as a valid comment character in Imakefiles; use \*QXCOMM instead.

There are new variables HasPoll, HasBSD44Sockets, ThreadedX) and new rules (SpecialCObjectRule). Read *xc/config/cf/README* for details.

The way libraries get built has changed: the unshared library .o's are now placed in a subdirectory rather than with the shared library .o's.

Multithreaded programs can often just include *Threads.tmpl* in their *Imakefile* to get the correct compile-time defines and libraries.

## A.4.14    Kerberos

There is a new authorization scheme for X clients, MIT-KERBEROS-5. It implements MIT's Kerberos Version 5 user-to-user authentication. See the *Xsecurity* manual page for details on how Kerberos works in X. As with any other authentication protocol, *xdm* sets it up at login time, and Xlib uses it to authenticate the client to the X server.

If you have Kerberos 5 on your system, set the HasKrb5 config variable in *site.def* to YES to enable Kerberos support.

## A.4.15    X Transport Library (xtrans)

The X Transport Library is intended to combine all system and transport specific code into a single place in the source tree. This API should be used by all libraries, clients, and servers of the X Window System. Note that this API is *not* an X Consortium standard; it is merely in internal part of our implementation. Use of this API should allow the addition of new types of transports and support for new platforms without making any changes to the source except in the X Transport Interface code.

The following areas have been updated to use xtrans:

```
lib/X11 (including the Input Method code)
lib/ICE
lib/font/fc
lib/FS
XServer/os
xfs/os
```

The XDMCP code in *xdm* and in the X server has not been modified to use *xtrans*.

No testing has been done for DECnet.

## A.4.16    Xlib

Xlib now supports multithreaded access to a single display connection. Xlib functions lock the display structure, causing other threads calling Xlib functions to be suspended until the first thread unlocks. Threads inside Xlib waiting to read to or write from the X server do not keep the display locked, so for example a thread hanging on XNextEvent will not prevent other threads from doing output to the server.

Multithreaded Xlib runs on SunOS 5.3, DEC OSF/1 1.3, Mach 2.5 Vers 2.00.1, AIX 3.2.5 with DCE threads, and Microsoft Windows NT 3.1. Locking for Xcms and i18n support has not been reviewed. A version of *ico* that can be compiled to use threads is located in *contrib/programs/ico*.

The Display and GC structures have been made opaque to normal application code; references to private fields will get compiler errors. You can work around some of these by compiling with -DXLIB_ILLEGAL_ACCESS, but fixing the offending code is better.

The side tab text

Release 6
Release Notes

The Xlib implementation has been changed to support a form of asynchronous replies, meaning that a request can be sent off to the server, and then other requests can be generated without waiting for the first reply to come back. This is used to advantage in two new functions, XInternAtoms and XGetAtomNames, which reduce what would otherwise require multiple round trips to the server down to a single round trip. It is also used in some existing functions, such as XGetWindowAttributes, to reduce two round trips to just one.

Lots of Xlib source files were renamed to fit better on systems with short filenames. The "X" prefix was dropped from most file names, and "TekHVC" prefixes were dropped.

Support for using poll() rather than select() is implemented, selected by the HasPoll config option.

The BIG-REQUESTS extension is supported.

The following Xlib functions are new in Release 6:

```
XInternAtoms, XGetAtomNames
XExtendedMaxRequestSize
XInitImage
XReadBitmapFileData
IsPrivateKeypadKey
XConvertCase
XAddConnectionWatch, XRemoveConnectionWatch, XProcessInternalConnection
XInternalConnectionNumbers
XInitThreads, XLockDisplay, XUnlockDisplay

XOpenOM, XCloseOM
XSetOMValues, XGetOMValues
XDisplayOfOM, XLocaleOfOM
XCreateOC, XDestroyOC
XOMOfOC
XSetOCValues, XGetOCValues
XDirectionalDependentDrawing, XContextualDrawing
XRegisterIMInstantiateCallback, XUnregisterIMInstantiateCallback
XSetIMValues

XAllocIDs
XESetBeforeFlush
_XAllocTemp, _XFreeTemp
```

Support for MIT-KERBEROS-5 has been added.

## A.4.17    Internationalization

Internationalization (also known as i18n, there being 18 letters between the *i* and *n*) of the X Window System, which was originally introduced in Release 5, has been significantly improved in Release 6. The Release 6 i18n architecture follows that in Release 5, and is based on the locale model used in ANSI C and POSIX, with most of the i18n capability provided by Xlib. Release 5 introduced a fundamental framework for internationalized input and output. It could enable basic localization for left-to-right, non-context sensitive, 8-bit or multi-byte codeset languages and cultural conventions. However, it did not deal with all possible languages and cultural conventions. Release 6 also does not cover all possible languages and cultural conventions, but Release 6 contains substantial new Xlib interfaces to support i18n enhancements, in order to enable additional language support and more practical localization.

The additional support is mainly in the area of text display. In order to support multi-byte encodings, the concept of a `FontSet` was introduced in Release 5. In Release 6, Xlib enhances this concept to a more generalized notion of output methods and output contexts. Just as input methods and input contexts support complex text input, output methods and output contexts support complex and more intelligent text display, dealing not only with multiple fonts but also with context dependencies. The result is a general framework to enable bi-directional text and context sensitive text display.

## A.4.18    Xt

- Support has been added for participation in session management, with callbacks to application functionality in response to messages from the session manager.

- The entire library is now thread-safe, allowing one thread at a time to enter the library and protecting global data as necessary from concurrent use.

- Support is provided for registering event handlers for events generated by X protocol extensions and for dispatching those events to the appropriate widget.

- A mechanism has also been added for dispatching events for non-widget drawables (such as pixmaps used within a widget) to a widget.

- Two new widget methods for instance allocation and deallocation allow widgets to be treated as C++ objects in a C++ environment.

- A new interface allows bundled changes to the managed set of children of a Composite, reducing the visual disruption of multiple changes to geometry layout.

- Several new resources have been added to Shell widgets, making the library compliant with the Release 6 ICCCM. Parameterized targets of selections (new in Release 6) and the MULTIPLE target are supported with new APIs.

- Safe handling of POSIX signals and other asynchronous notifications is now provided.

- A hook has been added to give notification of blocking in the event manager.

- The client will be able to register callbacks on a per-display basis for notification of a large variety of operations in the X Toolkit. This feature is useful to external agents such as screen readers.

- `XtStringToGravity` and `XtCvtStringToRestartStyle` are new string resource converters.

- The file search path syntax has a new %D substitution that inserts the default search path, making it easy to prepend and append to the default search path.

- The Xt implementation allows a configuration choice of poll or select for I/O multiplexing, selectable at compile time by the `HasPoll` config option.

The Release 6 Xt implementation requires Release 6 Xlib. Specifically, it uses the following new Xlib features: `XInternAtoms` instead of multiple `XInternAtom` calls where possible, input method support (Xlib internal connections), and tests for the `XVisibleHint` in the flags of `XWMHints`.

When linking with Xt, you now need to link also with SMlib and ICElib. This procedure is automatic if you use the XTOOLLIB make variable or `XawClientLibs` *imake* variable in your **Imakefiles**. This implementation no longer allows NULL to be passed as the value in the name/value pair in a request to `XtGetValues`. The default behavior is to print the error message "NULL `ArgVal` In `XtGetValues`" and exit. To restore the Release 5 behavior, set the *config* variable `GetValuesBC` in *site.def*. The old behavior was never part of the Xt specification, but some applications erroneously rely on it.

Motif 1.2 defines the types `XtTypedArg` and `XtTypedArgList` in `VaSimpleP.h`. These types are now defined in `IntrinsicP.h`. To work around the conflict, in Motif `VaSimple.c`, if `IntrinsicP.h` is not already included before `VaSimpleP.h` then include it. In `VaSimpleP.h`, fence off the type declarations with #if (XT_REVISION < 6) and #endif.

See Chapter 13 of the Xt specification for more details.

## A.4.19    Xaw

Some minor bugs have been fixed. Please note that the Athena Widgets have been and continue to be low on our priority list; therefore, many bugs remain and many requests for enhancements have not been implemented.

Text and Panner widget translations have been augmented to include keypad cursor keysyms in addition to the normal cursor keysyms.

The Clock, Logo, and Mailbox widgets have moved to their respective applications.

Internationalization support is now included. Xaw uses native widechar support when available, otherwise it uses the Xlib widechar routines. Per system specifics are set in Xawi18n.h.

The shared library major version number on SunOS 4 has been incremented because of these changes.

### A.4.19.1    AsciiText

The name AsciiText is now a misnomer, but has been retained for backward compatibility. A new resource, XtNinternational, has been added. If the value of the XtNinternational resource is False (the default) AsciiSrc and AsciiSink source and sink widgets are created, and the widget behaves as it did for Release 5. If the value is True, MultiSrc and MultiSink source and sink widgets are created. The MultiSrc widget will connect to an Input Method Server if one is available, or if one isn't available, it will use an Xlib internal pseudo-input method that, at a minimum, does compose processing. Application programmers who wish to use this feature will need to add a call to XtSetLanguageProc to their programs.

The symbolic constant FMT8BIT has been changed to XawFmt8Bit to be consistent with the new symbolic constant XawFmtWide. FMT8BIT remains for backwards compatibility, however its use is discouraged as it will eventually be removed from the implementation. See the Xaw manual for details.

### A.4.19.2    Command, Label, List, MenuButton, Repeater, SmeBSB, and Toggle

Two new resources have been added: XtNinternational and XtNfontSet. If XtNinternational is set to True, the widget displays its text using the specified fontset. See the Xaw manual for details.

## A.4.20    PEX

In discussing PEX it is important to understand the nature of 3D graphics and the purpose of the existence of the PEX SI. The type of graphics for which PEX provides support, while capable of being done in software, is most commonly found in high performance hardware. Creation and maintenance of software rendering code is costly and resource-consumptive. The original Sample Implementation for the PEX Protocol 5.0 was primarily intended for consumption by vendors of the X Consortium who intended to provide PEX products for sale. This implementation was intended to be fairly complete; however, it was understood that vendors who intended to commercialize it would dispose of portions of it, often fairly substantial ones. It was therefore understood that functionality most likely to be disposed of by them might be neglected in the development of a Sample Implementation. As PEX is now a fairly mature standard distributed by most if not all major vendors, and the standard itself has evolved from the 5.0 protocol level to the 5.1 protocol level, the X Consortium and its supporting vendors have recognized a need to focus on certain portions of the PEX technology while deemphasizing others.

This release incorporates PEX functionality based upon the PEX 5.1 level protocol. The PEX Sample Implementation (SI) is composed of several parts. The major components are the extension to the X Server, which implements the PEX 5.1 protocol, and the client side API, which provides a mechanism by which clients can generate PEX protocol.

The API now provided with the PEX-SI is called PEXlib. This is a change from Release 5 which shipped an API based upon the ISO IS PHIGS and PHIGS PLUS Bindings. That API has been moved to *contrib* in favor of the PEXlib API based upon the PEXlib 5.1 binding, which itself is an X Consortium standard. The PEXlib binding is a lower-level interface than the previous PHIGS binding was and maps more closely to the PEX protocol itself. It supports immediate mode rendering functionality as well as the previous PHIGS workstation modes and is therefore suited to a wider range of applications. It is also suited for the development of higher level APIs. There are, in fact, commercial implementations of the PHIGS API that utilize the PEXlib API.

The PHIGS API-based verification tool called InsPEX is moved to *contrib*. A prototype of a possible new tool called suspex is in the directory *contrib/test/suspex*. Suspex is PEXlib based.

Demo programs are no longer supported and have moved to *contrib*.

### A.4.20.1  PEX Standards and Functionality

This release conforms to the PEX Protocol Specification 5.1 though it does not implement all the functionality specified therein.

The release comes with 2 fonts, Roman and Roman_M (see the *User's Guide* for more details).

As discussed briefly above, certain functionality is not implemented in this Sample Implementation. Most notably Hidden Line, Hidden Surface Removal (HLHSR) is not implemented, which is a result of both architectural decisions and the fact that it surely would have been replaced by vendors with proprietary code. A contributed implementation that supports some of the HLHSR functionality utilizing a Z buffer based technique is available for ftp from **ftp.x.org** in the directory *contrib/PEX_HLHSR*.

This release does not support monochrome displays, though it does support 8 bit and 24 bit color.

Other functionality not complete in this release is:

- Backface Attributes and Distinguish Flag

- Font sharing between clients

- Patterns, Hatches and associated attributes

- Transparency

- Depth Cueing for Markers

Double Buffering is available for the PHIGS Workstation subsets directly through the workstation. The buffer mode should be set on when creating the workstation. For immediate mode users, double buffering is achieved via the Multi Buffering Extension (aka MBX) found in the directory *xc/lib/Xext*.

PEX 5.1 protocol adds certain functionality to the PEX server extension, accessible directly via the PEXlib API. The most important features of this functionality include Picking via the Immediate Mode Renderer (Render Elements and Accumulate State commands in Chapter 6, all of Chapter 7, of the PEX protocol specification); new Escape requests to allow vendors to support optional functionality; a Match Rendering Targets request to return information about visuals, depth, and drawables the server can support; a noop Output command; Hierarchical HLHSR control (i.e., during traversals); and renderer clearing controls.

## A.4.21 Header Files

Two new macros are defined in *Xos.h*: X_GETTIMEOFDAY and *strerror*. X_GETTIMEOFDAY is like `gettimeofday()` but takes one argument on all systems. *strerror* is defined only on systems that don't already have it.

A new header file *Xthreads.h* provides a platform-independent interface to threads functions on various systems. Include it instead of the system threads header file. Use the macros defined in it instead of the system threads functions.

## A.4.22 Fonts

There are three new Chinese bdf fonts in *xc/fonts/bdf/misc* (*gb16fs.bdf, gb16st.bdf, gb24st.bdf*).

Bitmap Charter fonts that are identical to the output generated from the outline font have been moved to *xc/fonts/bdf/unnec_{75,100}dpi*.

The Type 1 fonts contributed by Bitstream, IBM, and Adobe that shipped in *contrib* in Release 5 have been moved into the core.

Some of the *misc* fonts, mostly in the *Clean* family, have only the ASCII characters, but were incorrectly labeled \*QISO8859-1". These fonts have been renamed to be \*QISO646.1991-IRV". Aliases have been provided for the Release 5 names.

The **9×15** font has new shapes for some characters. The **6×10** font has the entire ISO 8859-1 character set.

## A.4.23    Font Library

The Type1 rasterizer that shipped in *contrib* in Release 5 is now part of the core.

There is an option to have the X server request glyphs only as it needs them. The X server then caches the glyphs for future use.

Aliases in a *fonts.alias* file can allow one scalable alias name to match all instances of another font. The "!" character introduces a comment line in *fonts.alias* files.

A sample font authorization protocol, "hp-hostname-1" has been added. It is based on host names and is non-authenticating. The client requesting a font from a font server provides (or passes through from its client) the host name of the ultimate client of the font. There is no check that this host name is accurate, as this is a sample protocol only.

The Speedo rasterizer can now read fonts with retail encryption. This means that fonts bought over-the-counter at a computer store can be used by the font server and X server.

Many, many font-related bugs have been fixed.

## A.4.24    Font Server

The font server has been renamed from *fs* to *xfs* to avoid confusion with an AFS program. The default port has changed from 7000 (used by AFS) to 7100 and has been registered with the Internet Assigned Numbers Authority.

The font server now implements a new major protocol version, version 2. This change was made only to correct errors in the implementation of version 1. Version 1 is still accepted by *xfs*.

You can now connect to *xfs* using the *local/* transport.

Many, many bugs have been fixed.

## A.4.25    X Server

The server sources have moved to *xc/programs/Xserver*. Server-side extension code exists as subdirectories. The *ddx* directory is gone; *mi*, *cfb*, and *mfb* are at the top level, and an *hw* (hardware) subdirectory now exists for holding vendor-specific ddx code. Note: the absence of a ddx directory does not imply that the conceptual split between dix and ddx is gone.

Function prototypes have been added to header files in the directories called *xc/programs/Xserver/include*, *cfb*, *mfb*, *mi*, and *os*.

Support for pixmap privates has been added. It is turned off by default, but can be activated by putting -DPIXPRIV in the `ServerExtraDefines` parameter in your *vendor.cf* file. See the porting layer document for details.

New screen functions, called primarily by code in *window.c*, have been added to make life easier for vendors with multi-layered framebuffers. Several functions and some pieces of functions have moved from *window.c* to *miwindow.c*. See the porting layer document for details. Also, the contents of union `_Validate` (validate.h) are now device dependent; *mivalidate.h* contains a sample definition.

An implementation of the SYNC extension is in *xc/programs/Xserver/Xext/sync.c*. As part of this work, client priorities have also been implemented; see the tail end of `WaitFor-Something()` in *WaitFor.c*. The priority scheme is *strict* in that the client(s) with the highest priority always runs. *twm* has been modified to provide simple facilities for setting client priorities.

The server can now fetch font glyphs on demand instead of loading them all at once (see the directories *xc/programs/Xserver/dix/dixfonts.c*, *xc/lib/font/fc/fserve.c*, and *xc/lib/font/fc/fsconvert.c*). A new X server command line option, **-deferglyphs**, controls which types of fonts (8 bit vs. 16 bit) to demand load; see the X manual page for details.

The *os* layer now uses sigaction on POSIX systems; a new function, OsSignal, was added for convenience, which you should use in your *ddx* code.

A new timer interface has been added to the *os* layer; see the functions in *os/WaitFor.c*. This interface is used by XKB, but we haven't tried to use it anywhere else (such as *Xext/sleepuntil.c*) yet.

Redundant code for GC funcs was moved from *cfbgc.c* and *mfbgc.c* to *migc.c*. This file also contains a few utility functions such as `ComputeCompositeClip`, which replaces the chunk of code that used to appear near the top of most versions of `ValidateGC`.

The *cfb* code can now be compiled multiple times to provide support for multiple depths in the same server, e.g., 8, 12, and 24. See *Imakefile* and *cfb/cfbmskbits.h* under the *xc/programs/Xserver/* directory for starters.

The *cfb* and *mfb* code have been modified to perform 64 bit reads and writes of the framebuffer on the Alpha AXP. These modifications should be usable on other 64 bit architectures as well, though we have not tested it on any others. There are a few hacks in *dix*, notably `ProcPutImage` and `ProcGetImage`, to work around the fact that the protocol doesn't allow you to specify 64 bit padding. Note that the server will still not run on a machine such as a Cray that does not have a 32 bit data type.

For performance, all region operations are now invoked via macros which by default make direct calls to the appropriate *mi* functions. You can conditionally compile them to continue calling through the screen structure. The following change was made throughout the server:

```
"(*pScreen->RegionOp)(...)" changes to "REGION_OP(pScreen, ...)"
```

Some of the trivial region ops have been inlined in the macros. For compatibility, the region function pointers remain in the screen structure even if the server is compiled to make direct calls to *mi*. See *include/regionstr.h*.

A generic callback manager is included and can be used to add notification-style hooks anywhere in the server. See *dixutils.c*. The callback manager is now being used to provide notification of when the server is grabbed/ungrabbed, when a client's state changes, and when an event is sent to a client. The latter two are used by the RECORD extension.

A new option has been added, *-config filename*. This lets you put server options in a file. See *os/utils.c*.

Xtrans has been installed into the os layer. See *os/connection.c*, *io.c*, and *transport.c*. As a result, the server now supports the many flavors of SVR4 local connections.

The client structure now has privates like windows, pixmaps, and GCs. See *include/dixstruct.h*, *dix/privates.c*, and *dispatch.c*.

Thin line pixelization is now consistent across *cfb*, *mfb*, and *mi*. It is also reversible, meaning the same pixels are touched when drawing from point A to point B as are touched when drawing from point B to point A. A new header file, *miline.h*, consolidates some miscellaneous line drawing utilities that had previously been duplicated in a number of places.

### A.4.25.1   Xnest

A new server, Xnest, uses Xlib to implement *ddx* rendering. See *xc/programs/Xserver/hw/xnest*. Xnest lets you run an X server in a window on another X server. Uses include testing *dix* and extensions, debugging client protocol errors, debugging grabs, and testing interactive programs in a hardware-starved environment.

### A.4.25.2   Xvfb

Another new server, Xvfb, uses *cfb* or *mfb* code to render into a framebuffer that is allocated in virtual memory. See *xc/programs/Xserver/hw/vfb*. The framebuffer can be allocated in normal memory, shared memory, or as a memory mapped file. Xvfb's screen is normally not visible; however, when allocated as a memory mapped file, *xwd* can display the screen by specifying the framebuffer file as its input.

### A.4.25.3   ddx

Sun *ddx*

> Expanded device probe table finds multiple frame buffers of the same type. Expanded keymap tables provide support for European and Asian keyboards. Added per-key autorepeat support. Considerable cleanup and duplicate code eliminated. Deletion of SunView support. GX source code now included.

HP *ddx*

> *cfb*-based sources included as *xc/programs/Xserver/hw/hp*.

svga *ddx*

> new svga *ddx* for SVR4 included as *xc/programs/Xserver/hw/svga*.

xfree86 *ddx*

> ddxen from XFree86, Inc. included as *xc/programs/Xserver/hw/xfree86*.

Amoeba *ddx*

> *ddx* for Sun server on the Amoeba operating system included as *xc/programs/Xserver/hw/sunAmoeba*. The server will require additional patches for this to be usable.

## A.4.26   New Programs

*xc/config/util/mkshadow/* a replacement for *lndir*.

## A.4.27   Old Software

We have dropped support for the following libraries and programs and have moved them to *contrib*. CLX library, PHIGS library, *MacFS, auto_box, beach_ball, gpc, ico, listres, maze, puzzle, showfont, viewres, xbiff, xcalc, xditview, xedit, xev, xeyes, xfontsel, xgas, xgc, xload, xman,* and *xpr*.

## A.4.28   xhost

Two new families have been registered: `LocalHost`, for connections over a non-network transport, and `Krb5Principal`, for Kerberos V5 principals.

To distinguish between different host families, a new xhost syntax "family:name" has been introduced. Names are as before; families are as follows:

```
inet:   Internet host
dnet:   DECnet host
nis:    Secure RPC network name
krb:    Kerberos V5 principal
local:  contains only one name, "\^"
```

The old-style syntax for names is still supported when the name does not contain a colon.

## A.4.29   xrdb

Many new symbols are defined to tell you what extensions and visual classes are available.

## A.4.30   twm

An interface for setting client priorities with the Sync extension has been added.

Many bugs have not been fixed yet.

## A.4.31   xdm

There is a new resource, `choiceTimeout`, that controls how long to wait for a display to respond after the user has selected a host from the chooser.

Support has been added for a modular, dynamically-loaded greeter library. This feature allows different dynamic libraries to be loaded by *xdm* at run-time to provide different login window interfaces without access to the *xdm* sources. It works on DEC OSF/1 and SVR4. The name of the greeter library is controlled by another new resource, `greeterLib`.

When you log in via *xdm*, *xdm* will use your password to obtain the initial Kerberos tickets and store them in a local credentials cache file. The credentials cache is destroyed when the session ends.

## A.4.32   xterm

Release 6 supports a few escape sequences from HP terminals, such as memory locking. See *xc/doc/specs/xterm/ctlseqs.ms* for details.

The *termcap* and *terminfo* files have been updated.

*ctlseqs.ms* has moved out of the xterm source directory into *xc/doc/specs/xterm*.

The logging mis-feature of xterm is removed. This change first appeared as a public patch to Release 5.

Many bugs have not been fixed yet.

## A.4.33   xset

The screen saver control option has two new sub-options to immediately activate or deactivate the screen saver: **xset s activate** and **xset s reset**.

## A.4.34   X Test Suite

The X Test Suite, shipped separately from Release 5, is now part of the core distribution in Release 6.

The code has been fixed to work on Alpha AXP. The Xi tests contributed by HP and XIM tests contributed by Sun are integrated.

## A.4.35    Work in Progress

Everything under *xc/workInProgress* represents a work in progress of the X Consortium.

Fresco, Low Bandwidth X (LBX), the Record extension, and the X Keyboard extension (XKB, which logically belongs here but was too tightly coupled into Xlib and the server to extract) are neither standards nor draft standards, are known to need design and/or implementation work, are still evolving, and will not be compatible with any final standard should such a standard eventually be agreed upon. We are making them available in early form in order to gather broader experimentation and feedback from those willing to invest the time and energy to help us produce better standards.

Any use of these interfaces in commercial products runs the risk of later source and binary incompatibilities.

### A.4.35.1    Fresco

Release 6 includes the first sample implementation of Fresco, a user interface system specified using CORBA IDL and implemented in C++. Fresco is not yet a Consortium standard or draft standard, but is being distributed as a work in progress to demonstrate our current directions and to gather feedback on requirements for a Fresco standard.

The Fresco Sample Implementation has been integrated into the X11R6 build process and will be built automatically if you have a C++ compiler available. Documentation on Fresco can be found in *xc/doc/specs/Fresco*. The Fresco and Xtf libraries are found in *xc/workInProgress/Fresco* and *xc/workInProgress/Xtf*, respectively. There are some simple Fresco example programs in *contrib/examples/Fresco* and a number of related programs in *contrib/programs*, including:

*ixx*  An IDL to C++ translator

*i2mif*
> A program to generate FrameMaker MIF documents from comments in an IDL specification

*fdraw*
> A simple Fresco drawing editor

*dish*
> A TCL interpreter with hooks to Fresco

Working Imakefiles are provided for all of the utilities and examples.

A demo program (*dish*) is included that shows how a scripting language (Tcl) can rather easily be bound to Fresco through the CORBA dynamic invocation mechanism. A copy of Tcl is included in *contrib/lib/tcl*.

To build Fresco you must define HasCplusplus in *site.def*; in addition, you may have to set CplusplusCmd and/or CplusplusDependIncludes to invoke the appropriate C++ compiler and find the required header files during make depend. Finally, you should check the *vendor.cf* to see if there are any other configuration variables you should set to provide information about your C++ compiler.

Fresco requires a C++ compiler that implements version 3 of the C++ language (as approximately defined by USL cfront version 3). While Fresco does not currently use templates or exceptions, it does make extensive use of nested types, which were inadequately supported in earlier versions of the language.

Fresco has been built with the following platforms and C++ compilers:

```
SPARCstation    SunOS 4.1.3     CenterLine C++
SPARCstation    Solaris 2.3     CenterLine C++ (requires v2.0.6)
SPARCstation    Solaris 2.3     SPARCCompiler C++ v4.0
HP 9000/700     HPUX 9.0.1      CenterLine C++
SGI Indy        IRIX 5.2        SGI C++
IBM RS/6000     AIX 3.2.5       IBM xlC
Sony NEWS       NEWSOS 6.0      Sony C++
```

Fresco has also been compiled on the DEC Alpha under OSF/1 version 2.0 using a beta test version of DEC C++ 1.3. Fresco cannot be built with the Gnu C++ compiler (version 2.5.8 or earlier) due to bugs and limitations in g++.

Building Fresco with CenterLine C++ requires that you pass the **-Xa** flag to the C++ compiler. Place the following lines in your *site.def*:

```
#define HasCenterLineCplusplus YES
#define CplusplusOptions -Xa
```

If CC is not in your default search path, add this line to *site.def*:

```
#define CplusplusCmd /path/to/your/CC
```

If you are building under Solaris 2, you must use ObjectCenter version 2.0.6 or later; the C++ compiler in ObjectCenter 2.0.4 will produce Fresco applications that dump core on startup.

Fresco does not yet build under Microsoft Windows/NT.

### A.4.35.2    XKB (X Keyboard Extension)

Support for XKB is not compiled into Xlib by default. It is compiled in the X server by default only on Sun and Omron Luna machines. You can compile it in by setting

```
#define BuildXKB YES        /* for support in the X server */
#define BuildXKBLib YES     /* for support in the X library */
```

in the file *xc/config/cf/site.def*. Note that enabling XKB in the X server is a pervasive change; you need to clean the server and rebuild everything if you change this option.

Turning on XKB in the X server usually requires changes to the vendor *ddx* keyboard handling. There is currently support only in the Sun and Omron *ddx*.

If you turn on `BuildXKBLib`, additional functions are added to Xlib. Since the resulting library is non-standard, it is given a different name: libX11kb instead of libX11. All Makefiles produced by *imake* will use **-lX11kb** to link Xlib.

The library changes for XKB are known not to work on the Cray; many other systems have been tested, including the Alpha AXP.

There are some XKB test programs in *contrib/test/Xkb*.

The XKB support in Xlib is still at an early stage of formal review and could change. We expect some additions in an eventual standard, but few changes to the interfaces provided in this implementation. A working draft of the protocol is in */xc/doc/specs/Xkb/*.

### A.4.35.3   LBX (Low Bandwidth X)

The X Consortium is working to define a standard for running X applications over serial lines, wide area networks, and other slow links. This effort, called Low Bandwidth X (LBX), aims to improve the startup time, performance, and interactive feel of X applications run over low bandwidth transports.

LBX does this by interposing a *pseudo-server* (called the *proxy*) between the X clients and the X server. The proxy caches data flowing between the server and the clients, merges the X protocol streams, and compresses the data that is sent over the low bandwidth wire. The X server at the other end uncompresses the data and splits it back out into separate request streams. The target is to make many X applications transparently usable over 9600 bps modems.

A snapshot of the code for this effort is included in *xc/workInProgress/lbx/* for people to examine and begin experimenting with. It contains the following features:

*   LZW compression of the binary data stream. Since commercial use of LZW requires licensing patented technology, we are also looking for an unencumbered algorithm and implementation to provide as well.

*   Delta compression of X packets (representing packets as differences from previously sent packets).

*   Re-encoding of some graphics requests (points, lines, segments, rectangles, and arcs).

*   Motion event throttling (to keep from flooding the wire).

*   Caching of data in the proxy for large data objects that otherwise would be transmitted over the wire multiple times (e.g., properties, font metrics, keyboard mappings, connection startup data, etc.).

- Short-circuiting of requests for constant data (e.g., atoms, colorname/rgb mappings, and read-only color cells).

However, the following items have yet to be implemented (which is why it isn't a standard yet):

- Re-encoding of a number of requests (e.g., `QueryFont`), events, etc.

- Support for BIG-REQUESTS extension.

- A non-networked serial protocol for environments which cannot support *os*-level networking over serial lines.

- A full specification needs to be written describing the network protocol used between the proxy and the server.

The X Consortium is continuing to work on both the implementation of the remaining items and the full specification. The goal is to have all of the pieces ready for public review later this year. Since the specification for LBX *will* change, we strongly recommend against anyone incorporating LBX into a product based on this prototype. But, they are encouraged to start looking at the code, examining the concepts, and providing feedback on its design.

### A.4.35.4    RECORD Extension

RECORD is an X protocol extension that supports the recording of all core X protocol and arbitrary X extension protocol.

A version of the extension is included in *xc/workInProgress/record*. The implementation does not quite match the version 1.2 draft specification, but the spec is going to change anyway; the version 1.3 draft is in *xc/doc/specs/Xext/record.ms*. The GetConfig request is not fully implemented. A test program is in *contrib/test/record*.

### A.4.35.5    Simple Session Manager

A simple session manager has been developed to test the new Session Management protocol. At the moment, it does not exercise the complete XSMP protocol, and the user interface is rather simple. While it does have enough functionality to make it useful, it needs more work before we would want people to depend on it or use it as a good example of how to implement the session protocol. The simple session manager performs the following tasks:

- Handles accepting connections from clients

- Handles graceful or unexpected termination of clients

- Maintains database of all properties set by clients

- Provides a way to issue checkpoint and shutdown messages to clients via a user interface.

- Manages client interaction with the user

- Can restart clients; handles clients running on remote machines by using the new *rstart* protocol

- Requires MIT-MAGIC-COOKIE-1 authentication from clients

We have not yet written a proxy for connecting ICCCM 1.0 clients to the session manager.

A sample client, *xsmclient*, has been written to demonstrate the session support in Xt.

### A.4.35.6    Multithreaded X Server

An attempt has been made to merge the multithreaded server source with the singlethreaded source. The result is in the *xc/workInProgress/MTXserver* directory. The sources here include only files that were changed from the singlethreaded server. The multithreaded server may not compile. Unfortunately, the singlethreaded server sources have continued to evolve since this snapshot of the MTXserver was produced, so there is work to be done to get the MTXserver sources back into a state where they can be compiled.

## A.4.36    ANSIfication

We've changed our sources to stop using the BSD function names index, rindex, bcopy, bcmp; we now use strchr, strrchr, memcpy/memmove, and memcmp. We still use the name bzero (because there is no BSD equivalent for the general case of memset) but it is translated to memset via a #define in <X11/Xfuncs.h>. The BSD function names are still supported in <X11/Xos.h> and <X11/Xfuncs.h>.

Most client-side uses of caddr_t should now be gone from our sources.

Explicit declarations of *errno* are now only used on non-ANSI systems.

The libraries use more standard POSIX *_t types.

## A.4.37    Miscellaneous

A new version of the *patch* program is in *xc/util/patch*; it understands the unified diff format produced by GNU *diff*.

## A.5    Filing Bug Reports

If you find a reproducible bug in software in the *xc* directory, or find bugs in the *xc* documentation, please send a bug report to the X Consortium using the form in the file *xc/bug-report* and this destination address:

```
xbugs@x.org
```

Please try to provide all of the information requested on the form if it is applicable; the little extra time you spend on the report will make it much easier for us to reproduce, find, and fix the bug. Receipt of bug reports is generally acknowledged, but sometimes it can be delayed by a few weeks.

Bugs in *contrib* software should not be reported to the X Consortium. Consult the documentation for the individual software to see where (if anywhere) to report the bug.

## A.6    Public Fixes

We occasionally put out patches to X Consortium software, to fix any serious problems that are discovered. Such fixes (if any) can be found on *ftp.x.org*, in the directory *pub/R6/fixes*, using anonymous FTP.

For those without FTP access, individual fixes can be obtained by electronic mail by sending a message to

```
xstuff@x.org
```

In the usual case, the message should have a subject line and no body, or a single-line body and no subject, in either case the line looking like:

```
send fixes number
```

where *number* is a decimal number, starting from one. To get a summary of available fixes, make the line:

```
index fixes
```

If you need help, make the line:

```
help
```

Some mailers produce mail headers that are unusable for extracting return addresses. If you use such a mailer, you won't get any response. If you happen to know an explicit return path, you can include one in the body of your message, and the daemon will use it. For example:

```
path user%host.bitnet@mitvma.mit.edu
```

## A.7    Acknowledgements

Release 6 of X Version 11 is brought to you by X Consortium, Inc: Bob Scheifler, Janet O'Halloran, Ralph Swick, Matt Landau, Donna Converse, Stephen Gildea, Jay Hersh, Kaleb Keithley, Ralph Mor, Dave Wiggins, and Gary Cutbill.

Many companies and individuals have cooperated and worked extremely hard to make this release a reality, and our thanks go out to them. You will find many of them listed in the acknowledgements in the individual specifications. Major implementation contributions come from Data General, Digital, Fujitsu, HP, NCD, NCR, Omron, SGI, Sony, SunSoft, and XFree86.

Contributions were received from the following people at various X Consortium member companies. Each X Window System release is the work of many, many people, and this list is surely incomplete.

Fresco

> Mark Linton (Silicon Graphics); Chuck Price (SunSoft); Charles Brauer (Fujitsu); Steve Churchill (Fujitsu); Steve Tang (Stanford University); Douglas Pan (Fujitsu); Jean-Daniel Fekete (2001 S.A.)

Xlib

> Courtney Loomis (Hewlett-Packard Company); Daniel Dardailler (Open Software Foundation)

Xlib internationalization

> The manager of the internationalization project is Masahiko Narita (Fujitsu). The principal authors of Input Method Protocol document are Hideki Hiura (SunSoft) and Masahiko Narita (Fujitsu). The principal authors of Xlib specification Chapter 13 are Hideki Hiura (SunSoft) and Shigeru Yamada (Fujitsu OSSI), The principal producers of the sample implementation of the internationalization facilities are Jeffrey Bloomfield (Fujitsu OSSI), Takashi Fujiwara (Fujitsu), Hideki Hiura (SunSoft), Yoshio Horiuchi (IBM), Makoto Inada (Digital), Hiromu Inukai (Nihon SunSoft), Song JaeKyung (KAIST), Riki Kawaguchi (Fujitsu), Franky Ling (Digital), Hiroyuki Miyamoto (Digital), Hidetoshi Tajima (HP), Toshimitsu Terazono (Fujitsu), Makoto Wakamatsu (Sony), Masaki Wakao (IBM), Shigeru Yamada (Fujitsu OSSI) and Katsuhisa Yano (Toshiba). The coordinators of the integration, testing, and release of this implementation are Nobuyuki Tanaka (Sony) and Makoto Wakamatsu (Sony). Others who have contributed on the architectural design or the testing of sample implementation are Hector Chan (Digital), Michael Kung (IBM), Joseph Kwok (Digital), Hiroyuki Machida (Sony), Nelson Ng (SunSoft), Frank Rojas (IBM), Yoshiyuki Segawa (Fujitsu OSSI), Makiko Shimamura (Fujitsu), Shoji Sugiyama (IBM), Lining Sun (SGI), Masaki Takeuchi (Sony), Jinsoo Yoon (KAIST), and Akiyasu Zen (HP).

Xt Intrinsics

Douglas Rand (Open Software Foundation), parameterized selections; Paul Asente (Adobe Systems Incorporated), extension event handling; Ajay Vohra (SunSoft), support for multithreading; Sam Chang (Novell), widget caching research; Larry Cable (SunSoft), object allocation and change managed set; Vania Joloboff (Open Software Foundation); Courtney Loomis (Hewlett-Packard Company); Daniel Dardailler (Open Software Foundation); and Ellis Cohen (Open Software Foundation). The following people at Georgia Tech contributed the extensions for disability access: Keith Edwards, Susan Liebeskind, Beth Mynatt, and Tom Rodriguez.

Athena Widget Set

Frank Sheeran (Omron Data General)

X Logical Font Description

Paul Asente (Adobe Systems Incorporated); Nathan Meyers (Hewlett-Packard Company); Jim Graham (Sun); Perry A. Caro (Adobe Systems Incorporated)

Font Support Enhancements

Nathan Meyers (Hewlett-Packard Company), implementation of matrix enhancement, glyph caching, scalable aliases, sample authorization protocol

X Transport Library

Stuart R. Anderson (AT&T Global Information Solutions)

X Keyboard Extension

Erik Fortune (Silicon Graphics), design and sample implementation; Jordan Brown (Quarterdeck Office Systems); Will Walker (Digital Equipment Corporation), AccessX portion; Mark Novak (Trace Center), AccessX portion

Low-Bandwidth X

Jim Fulton (Network Computing Devices); Dave Lemke (Network Computing Devices); Dale Tonogai (Network Computing Devices); Keith Packard (Network Computing Devices); Chris Kantarjiev (Xerox PARC)

X Image Extension

Bob Shelley (AGE Logic), protocol architect, lead implementation architect; Larry Hare (AGE Logic), server implementation; Dean Verheiden (AGE Logic), server implementation; Syd Logan (AGE Logic), xieperf; Gary Rogers (AGE Logic), JPEG code, XIElib documentation; Ben Fahy (AGE Logic), client and server implementation

ICCCM

Stuart Marks (SunSoft); Gabe Beged-Dov (Hewlett-Packard Company); Chan Benson (Hewlett-Packard Company); Jordan Brown (Quarterdeck Office Systems); Larry Cable (SunSoft); Ellis Cohen (Open Software Foundation); Brian Cripe (Hewlett-Packard Company); Susan Dahlberg (Silicon Graphics); Peter Daifuku (Silicon Graphics); Andrew deBlois (Open Software Foundation); Clive Feather

(IXI); Christian Jacobi (Xerox PARC); Bill Janssen (Xerox PARC); Vania Joloboff (Open Software Foundation); Phil Karlton (Silicon Graphics); Mark Manasse (Digital Equipment Corporation); Todd Newman (Silicon Graphics); Keith Taylor (Hewlett-Packard Company); Jim VanGilder (Digital Equipment Corporation); Mike Wexler (Kubota Pacific); Michael Yee (Apple Computer)

ICE

Jordan Brown (Quarterdeck Office Systems); Vania Joloboff (Open Software Foundation); Stuart Marks (SunSoft)

XSMP

Mike Wexler (Kubota Pacific); Jordan Brown (Quarterdeck Office Systems); Ellis Cohen (Open Software Foundation); Vania Joloboff (Open Software Foundation); Stuart Marks (SunSoft)

SYNC Extension

Tim Glauert (Olivetti Research Limited); Dave Carver (Digital Equipment Corporation); Jim Gettys (Digital Equipment Corporation); Pete Snider (Digital Equipment Corporation)

RECORD

Martha Zimet (Network Computing Devices); Robert Chesler (Absol-puter); Kieron Drake (UniSoft); Marc Evans (Synergytics); Jim Fulton (Network Computing Devices); Ken Miller (Digital Equipment Corporation)

X Input Extension tests

George Sachs (Hewlett-Packard Company)

PEX

Ken Garnett (Shographics); Cheryl Huntington (Sun Microsystems); Karl Schultz (IBM); Jeff Stevenson (Hewlett-Packard Company); Paula Womack (Digital Equipment Corporation)

Multi-Buffering Extension

Eng-Shien Wu (IBM); John Marks (Hewlett-Packard Company); Ian Elliott (Hewlett-Packard Company)

X server

Milind Pansare (SunSoft), pixmap privates; Peter Daifuku (SGI), layered window support; David Lister (Adobe Systems Incorporated), callback manager; Ken Whaley (Kubota Pacific), thin line pixelization; Joel McCormack (Digital Equipment Corporation), 64-bit *mfb* and *cfb*; Rob Lembree (Digital Equipment Corporation), 64-bit *mfb* and *cfb*; Davor Matic (MIT), xnest ddx; Nathan Meyers (Hewlett-Packard Company), font support; Jordan Brown (Quarterdeck Office Systems), -config option; Michael Brenner (Apple Computer), macII ddx; Thomas Roell, svga ddx

**Multithreaded X Server**

John A. Smith (while at Data General), team leader; H. Chiba (Omron), ddx; Akeio Harada (Omron), ddx; Mike Haynes (Data General), dix; Hidenobu Kanaoka (Omron), ddx; Paul Layne (Data General), dix and ddx; Takayuki Miyake (Omron), ddx; Keith Packard (Network Computing Devices), design; Richard Potts (Data General), dix; Sid Manning (IBM), integration with core server; Rob Chesler (Absol-puter), integration with core server

**xdm modular loadable greeter**

Peter Derr (Digital Equipment Corporation)

**x11perf**

Joel McCormack (Digital Equipment Corporation); Graeme Gill (Labtam Australia); Mark Martin (CETIA)

**config**

Stuart R. Anderson (AT&T Global Information Solutions); David Brooks (Open Software Foundation); Kendall Collett (Motorola); John Freeman (Cray); John Freitas (Digital Equipment Corporation); Patrick E. Kane (Motorola); Mark Kilgard (Silicon Graphics); Akira Kon (NEC); Masahiko Narita (Fujitsu); Paul Shearer (Sequent); Mark Snitily (SGCS)

**XFree86 port**

Stuart R. Anderson (AT&T Global Information Solutions); Doug Anson; Gertjan Akkerman; Mike Bernson; David Dawes; Marc Evans; Pascal Haible; Matthieu Herrb; Dirk Hohndel; David Holland; Alan Hourihane; Jeffrey Hsu; Glenn Lai; Ted Lemon; Rich Murphey; Hans Nasten; Mark Snitily; Randy Terbush; Jon Tombs; Kees Verstoep; Paul Vixie; Mark Weaver; David Wexelblat; Philip Wheatley; Thomas Wolfram; Orest Zborowski

**Fonts**

Under *xc/fonts/*, the *misc/* directory contains a family of fixed-width fonts from Dale Schumacher, several Kana fonts from Sony Corporation, two Hangul fonts from Daewoo Electronics, two Hebrew fonts from Joseph Friedman, two cursor fonts from Digital Equipment Corporation, and cursor and glyph fonts from Sun Microsystems. The *Speedo* directory contains outline fonts contributed by Bitstream, Inc. The **75dpi** and **100dpi** directories contain bitmap fonts contributed by Adobe Systems, Inc., Digital Equipment Corporation, Bitstream, Inc., Bigelow and Holmes, and Sun Microsystems, Inc.

# PART II

# Xlib Reference

This part consists of reference pages for all Xlib function and prototype procedures that are new in Release 6.

## Name

XAddConnectionWatch — tracks internal connections for a display.

## Synopsis

```
Status XAddConnectionWatch(display, procedure, client_data)
    Display *display;
    XConnectionWatchProc procedure;
    XPointer client_data;
```

### Arguments

display
> Specifies the connection to the X server.

procedure
> Specifies the procedure to be called.

client_data
> Specifies the client data to be passed to procedure.

### Returns

Nonzero status if the procedure is successfully registered; otherwise, zero.

## Availability

Release 6 or later.

## Description

XAddConnectionWatch() registers a procedure to be called each time Xlib opens or closes an internal connection for the specified display.

XAddConnectionWatch() can be called at any time after a display is opened. If internal connections already exist, the registered procedure will be called immediately for each of them, before XAddConnectionWatch() returns.

## See Also

*XConnectionWatchProc,*
*XInternalConnectionNumbers(),*
*XRemoveConnectionWatch()*

# ■ XCloseOM

## Name

XCloseOM — closes an output method.

## Synopsis

```
Status XCloseOM(om)
      XOM om;
```

### Arguments

om  Specifies the output method.

### Returns

Non-zero if the output method is successfully closed; otherwise zero.

## Availability

Release 6 or later.

## Description

XCloseOM() closes the specified output method.

## See Also

*XOpenOM()*

## Name

XConnectionWatchProc

## Synopsis

```
typedef void (*XConnectionWatchProc)(display, client_data, fd, opening,
        watch_data)
    Display *display;
    XPointer client_data;
    int fd;
    Bool opening;
    XPointer *watch_data;
```

### Arguments

*display*
Specifies the connection to the X server.

*client_data*
Specifies the *client_data* passed in XAddConnectionWatch().

*fd*  Specifies the file description for the server connection.

*opening*
Specifies whether the connection is being opened or closed.

*watch_data*
Specifies a location for private *watch_data*.

## Availability

Release 6 or later.

## Description

XConnectionWatchProc is the type of the procedure registered by XAddConnection-Watch(). This procedure is called each time Xlib opens or closes an internal connection to the specified X server.

If opening is True, the procedure can store a pointer to private data in the location pointed to by watch_data; when the procedure is later called for this same connection and opening is False, the location pointed to by watch_data will hold this same private data pointer.

The registered procedure should not call any Xlib functions. If the procedure directly or indirectly causes the state of internal connections or watch procedures to change, the result is not defined. If Xlib has been initialized for threads, the procedure is called with the display locked and the result of a call by the procedure to any Xlib

## XConnectionWatchProc *(continued)*

function that locks the display is not defined unless the executing thread has exter-
nally locked the display using XLockDisplay().

## See Also

*XAddConnectionWatch(),*
*XInternalConnectionNumbers()*

## Name

XContextualDrawing — finds out whether rendering can be context-dependent.

## Synopsis

```
Bool XContextualDrawing(font_set)
     XFontSet font_set;
```

### Arguments

    *font_set*
        Specifies the font set.

### Returns

True or False.

## Availability

Release 6 or later.

## Description

XContextualDrawing() returns True if text drawn with the font set might include context-dependent drawing; otherwise, it returns False.

## See Also

*XDirectionalDependentDrawing()*

# ◼ XConvertCase

XConvertCase — obtains the uppercase and lowercase forms of a KeySym.

## Synopsis

```
void XConvertCase(keysym, lower_return, upper_return)
    KeySym keysym;
    KeySym *lower_return;
    KeySym *upper_return;
```

### Arguments

*keysym*
> Specifies the KeySym that is to be converted.

*lower_return*
> Returns the lowercase form of *keysym*, or original *keysym*.

*upper_return*
> Returns the uppercase form of *keysym*, or original *keysym*.

## Availability

Release 6 or later.

## Description

XConvertCase() returns the uppercase and lowercase forms of the specified Keysym, if the KeySym is subject to case conversion; otherwise, the specified KeySym is returned to both lower_return and upper_return. Support for conversion of other than Latin and Cyrillic KeySyms is implementation dependent.

## Name

XCreateOC — creates an output context.

## Synopsis

```
XOC XCreateOC(om, ...NULL)
    XOM om;
```

### Arguments

om  Specifies the output method.

...NULL
· Specifies the variable length argument list to set XOC values.

### Returns

An opaque pointer to the created output context.

## Availability

Release 6 or later.

## Description

XCreateOC() creates an output context within the specified output method.

The base font names argument is mandatory at creation time, and the output context will not be created unless it is provided. All other output context values can be set later.

XCreateOC() returns NULL if no output context could be created. NULL can be returned for any of the following reasons:

- A required argument was not set.
- A read-only argument was set.
- An argument name was not recognized.
- The output method encountered an output method implementation-dependent error.

## Errors

BadAtom

## See Also

*XDestroyOC()*

# ■ XDestroyOC

## Name

XDestroyOC — destroys an output context.

## Synopsis

```
void XDestroyOC(oc)
    XOC oc;
```

### Arguments

oc   Specifies the output context.

## Availability

Release 6 or later.

## Description

XDestroyOC() destroys the specified output context.

## See Also

*XCreateOC()*

# XDirectionalDependentDrawing ■

## Name

XDirectionalDependentDrawing — finds out about direction-dependent rendering.

## Synopsis

```
Bool XDirectionalDependentDrawing(font_set)
    XFontSet font_set;
```

### Arguments

    *font_set*
        Specifies the font set.

### Returns

True or False

## Availability

Release 6 or later.

## Description

XDirectionalDependentDrawing() returns True if the drawing functions implement implicit text directionality; otherwise, it returns False.

## See Also

*XContextDependentDrawing()*

# ■ XDisplayOfIM

## Name

XDisplayOfIM — obtains the display associated with an input method.

## Synopsis

```
Display * XDisplayOfIM(im)
        XIM im;
```

### Arguments

im  Specifies the input method.

### Returns

A pointer to a display structure.

## Availability

Release 6 or later.

## Description

XDisplayOfIM() returns the display associated with the specified input method.

## See Also

*XDisplayOfOM()*

## Name

XDisplayOfOM — obtains the display associated with an output method.

## Synopsis

```
Display * XDisplayOfOM(om)
      XOM om;
```

### Arguments

    *om*  Specifies the output method.

### Returns

A pointer to a display structure.

## Availability

Release 6 or later.

## Description

XDisplayOfOM() returns the display associated with the specified output method.

## See Also

*XDisplayOfIM()*

# ■ XExtendedMaxRequestSize

## Name

XExtendedMaxRequestSize — finds out if the specified display supports extended-length protocol encoding.

## Synopsis

```
long XExtendedMaxRequestSize(display)
      Display *display;
```

### Arguments

*display*

Specifies the connection to the X server.

### Returns

Maximum request size (in four-byte units).

## Availability

Release 6 or later.

## Description

XExtendedMaxRequestSize() returns zero if the specified display does not support an extended-length protocol encoding; otherwise, it returns the maximum request size (in 4-byte units) supported by the server using the extended-length encoding. The Xlib functions XDrawLines(), XDrawArcs(), XFillPolygon(), XChangeProperty(), XSetClipRectangles(), and XSetRegion() will use the extended-length encoding as necessary, if supported by the server. Use of the extended-length encoding in other Xlib functions (for example, XDrawPoints(), XDrawRectangles(), XDrawSegments(), XFillArcs(), XFillRectangles(), XPutImage()) is permitted but not required; an Xlib implementation may choose to split the data across multiple smaller requests instead.

## Name

XGetAtomNames — returns the names for an array of atom identifiers.

## Synopsis

```
Status XGetAtomNames(display, atoms, count, names_return)
    Display *display;
    Atom *atoms;
    int count;
    char **names_return;
```

### Arguments

*display*

Specifies the connection to the X server.

*atoms*

Specifies the array of atoms.

*count*

Specifies the number of atoms in the array.

*names_return*

Returns the atom names.

### Returns

Non-zero if names are returned for all atoms; otherwise zero.

## Availability

Release 6 or later.

## Description

XGetAtomNames() returns the names associated with the specified atoms. The names are stored in the *names_return* array supplied by the caller. Calling this function is equivalent to calling XGetAtomName() for each of the atoms in turn, but this function minimizes the number of round trip protocol exchanges between the client and the X server.

This function returns a nonzero status if names are returned for all of the atoms; otherwise, it returns zero.

## Errors

BadAtom
    Undefined atom.

**XGetAtomNames** *(continued)*

## See Also

*XInternAtom()*,
*XInternAtoms()*

## Name

XGetOCValues — obtains XOC values.

## Synopsis

```
char * XGetOCValues(oc, ...)
    XOC oc;
```

### Arguments

oc  Specifies the output context.

...

Specifies the variable length argument list to get XOC values.

### Returns

NULL on success; otherwise, the name of the first value that couldn't be obtained

## Availability

Release 6 or later.

## Description

XGetOCValues() returns NULL if no error occurred; otherwise, it returns the name of the first argument that could not be obtained. An argument might not be obtained for neither of the following reasons:

- The argument name is not recognized.
- An implementation-dependent error occurs.

Each argument value following a name must point to a location where the value is to be stored.

## See Also

*XSetOCValues()*

# ◼ XGetOMValues

## Name

XGetOMValues — queries features of an output method.

## Synopsis

```
char * XGetOMValues(om, ...)
     XOM om;
```

### Arguments

om   Specifies the output method.

. . .

       Specifies the variable length argument list to get XOM values.

### Returns

NULL on success; otherwise, the name of the first argument not obtained

## Availability

Release 6 or later.

## Description

XGetOMValues() presents a variable argument list programming interface for query-ing properties or features of the specified output method. This function returns NULL if it succeeds; otherwise, it returns the name of the first argument that could not be obtained.

## See Also

*XSetOMValues()*

## Name

XIMProc — type of the procedure called when input method starts up.

## Synopsis

```
void XIMProc(display, client_data, call_data)
    Display *display;
    XPointer client_data;
    XPointer call_data;
```

### Arguments

*display*
> Specifies the connection to the X server.

*client_data*
> Specifies the additional client data.

*call_data*
> Not used for this callback and always passed as NULL.

## Availability

Release 6 or later.

## Description

XIMProc is the type of procedure registered with XRegisterIMInstantiateCall-back(). It is called when an input method server becomes available that matches the current locale and modifiers.

## See Also

*XRegisterIMInstantiateCallback()*,
*XUnregisterIMInstantiateCallback()*

# ■ XInitImage

## Name

XInitImage — initializes the image manipulation routines of an image structure.

## Synopsis

```
Status XInitImage(image)
    XImage *image;
```

### Arguments

*ximage*
> Specifies the image.

### Returns

Non-zero on success; zero if an error occurs

## Availability

Release 6 or later.

## Description

XInitImage() initializes the internal image manipulation routines of an image structure, based on the values of the various structure members. All fields other than the manipulation routines must already be initialized. If the *bytes_per_line* member is zero, XInitImage() will assume the image data is contiguous in memory and set the *bytes_per_line* member to an appropriate value based on the other members; otherwise, the value of *bytes_per_line* is not changed. All of the manipulation routines are initialized to functions that other Xlib image manipulation functions need to operate on the the type of image specified by the rest of the structure.

This function must be called for any image constructed by the client before passing it to any other Xlib function. Image structures created or returned by Xlib do not need to be initialized in this fashion.

This function returns a nonzero status if initialization of the structure is successful. It returns zero if it detected some error or inconsistency in the structure, in which case the image is not changed.

## See Also

*XCreateImage()*

## Name

XInitThreads — initializes support for concurrent threads.

## Synopsis

```
Status XInitThreads();
```

### Arguments
None

### Returns
Non-zero on success; zero on errors

## Availability

Release 6 or later.

## Description

`XInitThreads()` initializes Xlib support for concurrent threads. This function must be the first Xlib function a multithreaded program calls, and it must complete before any other Xlib call is made. This function returns a nonzero status if initialization was successful; otherwise, it returns zero. On systems that do not support threads, this function always returns zero.

It is only necessary to call this function if multiple threads might use Xlib concurrently. If all calls to Xlib functions are protected by some other access mechanism (for example, a mutual exclusion lock in a toolkit or through explicit client programming), Xlib thread initialization is not required. It is recommended that single-threaded programs not call this function.

# ■ XInternAtoms

## Name

XInternAtoms — returns atoms for an array of names.

## Synopsis

```
Status XInternAtoms(display, names, count, only_if_exists, atoms_return)
    Display *display;
    char **names;
    int count;
    Bool only_if_exists;
    Atom *atoms_return;
```

### Arguments

*display*

Specifies the connection to the X server.

*names*

Specifies the array of atom names.

*count*

Specifies the number of atom names in the array.

*only_if_exists*

Specifies a Boolean value: False if the atom must be created; True if the atom should be returned only if it already exists.

*atoms_return*

Returns the atoms.

### Returns

Non-zero if atoms returned for all names; otherwise zero

## Availability

Release 6 or later.

## Description

XInternAtoms() returns the atom identifiers associated with the specified names. The atoms are stored in the *atoms_return* array supplied by the caller. Calling this function is equivalent to calling XInternAtom() for each of the names in turn with the specified value of *only_if_exists*, but this function minimizes the number of round trip protocol exchanges between the client and the X server.

This function returns a nonzero status if atoms are returned for all of the names; otherwise, it returns zero.

## Errors

BadAlloc, BadValue

## See Also

*XInternAtom()*

# ■ XInternalConnectionNumbers

## Name

XInternalConnectionNumbers — obtains all of the current internal connections for a display.

## Synopsis

```
Status XInternalConnectionNumbers(display, fd_return, count_return)
    Display *display;
    int **fd_return;
    int *count_return;
```

### Arguments

*display*
> Specifies the connection to the X server.

*fd_return*
> Returns the file descriptors.

*count_return*
> Returns the number of file descriptors.

### Returns

Non-zero if list is successfully allocated; otherwise zero

## Availability

Release 6 or later.

## Description

XInternalConnectionNumbers() returns a list of the file descriptors for all internal connections currently open for the specified display. When the allocated list is no longer needed, free it by using XFree(). This function returns a nonzero status if the list is successfully allocated; otherwise, it returns zero.

## See Also

*XConnectionWatchProc(),*
*XAddConnectionWatch(),*
*XRemoveConnectionWatch(),*
*XProcessInternalConnection()*

## Name

XLocaleOfOM — gets the locale associated with an output method.

## Synopsis

```
char * XLocaleOfOM(om)
    XOM om;
```

### Arguments

om    Specifies the output method.

### Returns

Locale string.

## Availability

Release 6 or later.

## Description

XLocaleOfOM() returns the locale associated with the specified output method.

# ■ XLockDisplay

## Name

XLockDisplay — locks a display across several Xlib calls.

## Synopsis

```
void XLockDisplay(display)
     Display *display;
```

### Arguments

display
        Specifies the connection to the X server.

## Availability

Release 6 or later.

## Description

XLockDisplay() locks out all other threads from using the specified display. Other threads attempting to use the display will block until the display is unlocked by this thread. Nested calls to XLockDisplay() work correctly; the display will not actually be unlocked until XUnlockDisplay() has been called the same number of times as XLockDisplay(). This function has no effect unless Xlib was successfully initialized for threads using XInitThreads.

## See Also

*XInitThreads()*,
*XUnlockDisplay()*

## Name

XOMOfOC — gets the output method associated with an output context.

## Synopsis

```
XOM XOMOfOC(oc)
    XOC oc;
```

### Arguments

oc  Specifies the output context.

### Returns

An opaque handle for an output method.

## Availability

Release 6 or later.

## Description

XOMOfOC() returns the output method associated with the specified output context.

# ■ XOpenOM

## Name

XOpenOM — opens an output method.

## Synopsis

```
XOM XOpenOM(display, db, res_name, res_class)
    Display *display;
    XrmDatabase db;
    char *res_name;
    char *res_class;
```

### Arguments

*display*
> Specifies the connection to the X server.

*db*  Specifies a pointer to the resource database.

*res_name*
> Specifies the full resource name of the application.

*res_class*
> Specifies the full class name of the application.

### Returns

An opaque handle for an output method.

## Availability

Release 6 or later.

## Description

XOpenOM() opens an output method matching the current locale and modifiers specification. The current locale and modifiers are bound to the output method when XOpenOM() is called. The locale associated with an output method cannot be changed.

The specific output method to which this call will be routed is identified on the basis of the current locale and modifiers. XOpenOM() will identify a default output method corresponding to the current locale. That default can be modified using XSetLocale-Modifiers() to set the output method modifier.

The *db* argument is the resource database to be used by the output method for looking up resources that are private to the output method. It is not intended that this database be used to look up values that can be set as OC values in an output context. If *db* is NULL, no database is passed to the output method.

The *res_name* and *res_class* arguments specify the resource name and class of the application. They are intended to be used as prefixes by the output method when looking up resources that are common to all output contexts that may be created for this output method. The characters used for resource names and classes must be in the X Portable Character Set. The resources looked up are not fully specified if *res_name* or *res_class* is NULL.

The *res_name* and *res_class* arguments are not assumed to exist beyond the call to XOpenOM(). The specified resource database is assumed to exist for the lifetime of the output method.

XOpenOM() returns NULL if no output method could be opened.

## See Also

*XCloseOM()*

# ■ XProcessInternalConnection

## Name

XProcessInternalConnection — processes input on an internal connection.

## Synopsis

```
void XProcessInternalConnection(display, fd)
    Display *display;
    int fd;
```

### Arguments

display

Specifies the connection to the X server.

fd  Specifies the file descriptor.

## Availability

Release 6 or later.

## Description

XProcessInternalConnection() processes input available on an internal connection. This function should be called for an internal connection only after an operating system facility (for example, select or poll) has indicated that input is available; otherwise, the effect is not defined.

## See Also

*XInternalConnectionNumbers()*

## Name

XReadBitmapFileData — reads a bitmap from a file and return it as data.

## Synopsis

```
int XReadBitmapFileData(filename, width_return, height_return, data_return,
     x_hot_return, y_hot_return)
   char *filename;
   unsigned int *width_return, *height_return;
   unsigned char *data_return;
   int *x_hot_return, *y_hot_return;
```

### Arguments

*filename*

Specifies the filename to use. The format of the filename is operating-system dependent.

*width_return*

*height_return*

Return the width and height values of the read in bitmap file.

*data_return*

Returns the bitmap data.

*x_hot_return*

*y_hot_return*

Return the hotspot coordinates.

### Returns

BitmapSuccess on success. BitmapOpenFailed, BitmapFileInvalid, or BitmapNoMemory on failure.

## Availability

Release 6 or later.

## Description

XReadBitmapFileData() reads in a file containing a bitmap, in the same manner as XReadBitmapFile(), but returns the data directly rather than creating a pixmap in the server. The bitmap data is returned in *data_return*; the client must free this storage when finished with it by calling XFree(). The status and other return values are the same as for XReadBitmapFile().

# ◼ XRegisterIMInstantiateCallback

## Name

XRegisterIMInstantiateCallback — registers an input method instantiate callback.

## Synopsis

```
Bool XRegisterIMInstantiateCallback(display, db, res_name, res_class,
        callback, client_data)
    Display *display;
    XrmDatabase db;
    char *res_name;
    char *res_class;
    XIMProc   callback;
    XPointer *client_data;
```

### Arguments

*display*
    Specifies the connection to the X server.

*db*  Specifies a pointer to the resource database.

*res_name*
    Specifies the full resource name of the application.

*res_class*
    Specifies the full class name of the application.

*callback*
    Specifies a pointer to the input method instantiate callback.

*client_data*
    Specifies the additional client data.

### Returns

True if the function was able to register the callback; False otherwise.

## Availability

Release 6 or later.

## Description

XRegisterIMInstantiateCallback() registers a callback invoked when a new input method is available for the specified display that matches current locale and modifiers.

## See Also

*XIMProc,*
*XUnregisterIMInstantiateCallback()*

## Name

XRemoveConnectionWatch — stops tracking internal connections for a display.

## Synopsis

```
Status XRemoveConnectionWatch(display, procedure, client_data)
    Display *display;
    XConnectionWatchProc procedure;
    XPointer client_data;
```

### Arguments

*display*
> Specifies the connection to the X server.

*procedure*
> Specifies the procedure to be called.

*client_data*
> Specifies the additional client data.

### Returns

Non-zero on success; otherwise, zero.

## Availability

Release 6 or later.

## Description

XRemoveConnectionWatch() removes a previously registered connection watch procedure. The *client_data* must match the *client_data* used when the procedure was initially registered.

## See Also

*XAddConnectionWatch()*,
*XConnectionWatchProc()*,
*XInternalConnectionNumbers()*

# ■ XSetOCValues

## Name

XSetOCValues — sets XOC values.

## Synopsis

```
char * XSetOCValues(oc, ...)
    XOC oc;
```

### Arguments

oc  Specifies the output context.

...

Specifies the variable length argument list to set XOC values.

### Returns

Returns `NULL` if no error occurred; otherwise, it returns the name of the first argument that could not be set.

## Availability

Release 6 or later.

## Description

`XSetOCValues()` sets values in an output context. An argument might not be set for any of the following reasons:

- The argument is read-only.
- The argument name is not recognized.
- An implementation-dependent error occurs.

Each value to be set must be an appropriate datum, matching the data type imposed by the semantics of the argument.

## Errors

`BadAtom`

## See Also

*XGetOCValues()*

## Name

XSetOMValues — sets output method attributes.

## Synopsis

```
char * XSetOMValues(om, ...)
    XOM om;
```

### Arguments

om   Specifies the output method.

. . .

Specifies the variable length argument list to set XOM values.

### Returns

Returns NULL if it succeeds; otherwise, it returns the name of the first argument that could not be obtained.

## Availability

Release 6 or later.

## Description

XSetOMValues() presents a variable argument list programming interface for setting properties or features of the specified output method.

No standard arguments are currently defined by Xlib.

## See Also

*XGetOMValues()*

# ■ XUnlockDisplay

## Name

XUnlockDisplay — unlocks a display.

## Synopsis

```
void XUnlockDisplay(display)
    Display *display;
```

### Arguments

display

Specifies the connection to the X server.

## Availability

Release 6 or later.

## Description

`XUnlockDisplay()` allows other threads to use the specified display again. Any threads that have blocked on the display are allowed to continue. Nested locking works correctly; if `XLockDisplay()` has been called multiple times by a thread, then `XUnlock-Display()` must be called an equal number of times before the display is actually unlocked. This function has no effect unless Xlib was successfully initialized for threads using `XInitThreads()`.

## See Also

*XLockDisplay()*,
*XInitThreads()*

## Name

XUnregisterIMInstantiateCallback — unregisters an input method instantiation callback.

## Synopsis

```
Bool XUnregisterIMInstantiateCallback(display, db, res_name, res_class,
    callback, client_data)
    Display *display;
    XrmDatabase db;
    char *res_name;
    char *res_class;
    XIMProc callback;
    XPointer *client_data;
```

### Arguments

*display*
    Specifies the connection to the X server.

*db*  Specifies a pointer to the resource database.

*res_name*
    Specifies the full resource name of the application.

*res_class*
    Specifies the full class name of the application.

*callback*
    Specifies a pointer to the input method instantiate callback.

*client_data*
    Specifies the additional client data.

### Returns

True if the function was able to unregister the callback; false otherwise.

## Availability

Release 6 or later.

## Description

XUnregisterIMInstantiateCallback() removes an input method instantiation callback previously registered.

## See Also

*XRegisterIMInstantiateCallback()*

# PART III

# X Toolkit Reference

This part consists of reference pages for all Xt functions, objects, base widgets, and prototype procedures that are new in Release 6.

## Name

allocate — Object class extension method to allocate a widget instance record.

## Synopsis

```
typedef void (*XtAllocateProc)(WidgetClass, Cardinal*, Cardinal*, ArgList,
        Cardinal*, XtTypedArgList, Cardinal*,
        Widget*, XtPointer*);
    WidgetClass widget_class;
    Cardinal* constraint_size;
    Cardinal* more_bytes;
    ArgList args;
    Cardinal* num_args;
    XtTypedArgList typed_args,
    Cardinal* num_typed_args;
    Widget* new_return;
    XtPointer* more_bytes_return;
```

### Inputs

widget_class

The class of the widget instance to allocate.

constraint_size

The size of the constraint record to allocate, or 0.

more_bytes

The number of auxiliary bytes of memory to allocate.

args

The resource argument list as given in the call to create the widget.

num_args

The number of elements in args.

typed_args

The list of typed arguments given in the call to create the widget.

num_typed_args

The number of elements in the typed_args array.

### Outputs

new_return

The address at which to store a pointer to the newly allocated instance. Store NULL at this address in case of error.

more_bytes_return

The address at which to store a pointer to the auxiliary memory if it was requested. Store NULL at this address if auxiliary memory was requested

**allocate** *(continued)*

and an error occurred. If no auxiliary memory was requested, leave the value at this address unchanged.

## Availability

Release 6 and later.

## Description

The allocate() method is the function pointed to by the allocate field of the Object class extension record, and is called by the Intrinsics to allocate a widget instance record and widget constraint record.

The allocate() method is not chained. A widget class can inherit the allocate() method of its superclass by specifying XtInheritAllocate for the allocate field of the Object class extension record, or simply by omitting the Object class extension record altogether. If the allocate field of the extension record is set to NULL, then this method is not inherited from the superclass; instead, the Intrinsics simply allocates the required memory internally. The Object class extension record should have its record_type field set to NULLQUARK. See Object(3) for more details on this extension record.

The allocate() method must perform the following steps:

* Allocate memory for the widget instance and return it in new_return. The memory must be at least wc->core_class.widget_size bytes in length, double word aligned. If an allocation error occurs, the allocate() method should return NULL in *new_return*.

* Initialize the core.constraints field in the newly allocated instance record to NULL if *constraint_size* is 0, or allocate *constraint_size* bytes, double word aligned, and initialize core.constraints field to point to this record.

* Allocate *more_bytes* of memory (if *more_bytes* is non-zero), double word aligned, and return this block of memory in *more_bytes_return*. If an allocation error occurs, the allocate() method should return NULL in *more_bytes_return*.

A class allocation procedure which envelops the allocation procedure of a superclass must rely on the enveloped procedure to perform the instance and constraint allocation. Allocation procedures are discouraged from initializing fields in the widget record, but if they choose to do so they should only initialize fields in the instance part record of their own class—they should not modify the instance part of any superclass.

## Usage

The `allocate()` method was added in X11R6 to allow widgets to be treated as C++ objects in the C++ environment. In order to do this, the widgets have to use a special C++ allocation function.

If you specify an `allocate()` method for a widget class, you should also specify a matching `deallocate()` method.

You generally do not need to use the *args* and *typed_args* arrays that are passed to this function, though some widget classes could conceivably optimize their allocation depending on resources that were specified when the widget was created. Note that these two arrays specify only hard-coded resources; they do not contain any resources that are specified through the resource database.

## Structures

The `Xttyped_args` argument to the `allocate()` method is an array of `XtTypedArg` structures, which have the following definition:

```
typedef struct {
        String name;     /* resource name */
        String type;     /* representation type of the value field */
        XtArgVal value;  /* the resource value; needs conversion */
        int size;        /* size in bytes of value */
} XtTypedArg, *XtTypedArgList;
```

The fields of this structure contain the `XtVaTypedArg` arguments specified in a call to `XtVaCreateWidget()` or a related function. See `XtVaSetValues()` for an explanation of how to specify typed arguments in a variable-length widget resource list.

## See Also

*XtVaSetValues*(1),
*Object*(3),
*deallocate*(4)

# ■ deallocate

## Name

deallocate — Object class extension method to deallocate a widget instance record.

## Synopsis

```
typedef void (*XtDeallocateProc)(Widget, XtPointer);
    Widget widget;
    XtPointer more_bytes;
```

### Inputs

widget

> The widget being destroyed.

more_bytes

> Auxiliary memory that was received from the allocate() method, or NULL.

## Availability

Release 6 and later.

## Description

The deallocate() method is the function pointed to by the deallocate field of the Object class extension record, and is called by the Intrinsics to free the memory of a widget instance record and widget constraint record.

The deallocate() method is not chained. A widget class can inherit the deallocate() method of its superclass by specifying XtInheritDeallocate for the deallocate field of the Object class extension record, or simply by omitting the Object class extension record altogether. If the deallocate field of the extension record is set to NULL, then this method will not be inherited from the superclass, and instead the Intrinsics will simply free the required memory internally. The Object class extension record should have its record_type field set to NULLQUARK. See Object(3) for more details on this extension record.

The responsibilities of the deallocate() method are to free the memory specified by more_bytes if it is not NULL, to free the constraint record as specified by the widget's core.constraints field if it is not NULL, and to free the widget instance itself.

## Usage

The deallocate() and the corresponding allocate() methods were added in X11R6 to allow widgets to be treated as C++ objects in the C++ environment. In order to do this, the widgets have to use a special C++ allocation function.

When you write a deallocate() method, be sure to pair it with an allocate() method that matches. If you allocate() method envelops the method of a superclass, it is generally safe to simply inherit the corresponding deallocate method of the superclass.

## See Also

*XtVaSetValues*(1),
*Object*(3),
*allocate*(4)

# ■ Hook Object

## Name

Hook Object — special object for registering Intrinsics hooks.

## Synopsis

Public Headers
  `<X11/StringDefs.h>`

Private Header
  none

Class Name
  unspecified

Class Hierarchy
  Object → Hook Object

Class Pointer
  unspecified

Instantiation
  One instance per display is automatically created by the Intrinsics.

Functions/Macros
  `XtHooksOfDisplay()`

## Availability

Release 6 and later.

## Description

The Hook Object provides callback lists that allow applications to register functions to be called at particular control points in the Intrinsics. These functions are intended to be used to provide notification of many kinds of "X Toolkit events"—widget creation, for example—to an external agent such as an interactive resource editor, a drag-and-drop server, or an aid for physically challenged users.

The Hook Object is a private, implementation-dependent, subclass of `Object`. It has no parent. To look up the Hook Object associated with a display, use `XtHooksOfDisplay()`. The Hook Object's resources are callback lists for hooks, and two read-only resources for getting a list of parentless shells and the list length. All of the callback lists are initially empty. When a display is closed the Hook Object associated with it is destroyed.

The following procedures can be called with the hook registration object as an argument:

- XtAddCallback(), XtAddCallbacks(), XtRemoveCallback(), XtRemoveCallbacks(), XtRemoveAllCallbacks(), XtCallCallbacks(), XtHasCallbacks(), XtCallCallbackList()

- XtClass(), XtSuperclass(), XtIsSubclass(), XtCheckSubclass(), XtIsObject(), XtIsRectObj(), XtIsWidget(), XtIsComposite(), XtIsConstraint(), XtIsShell(), XtIsOverrideShell(), XtIsWMShell(), XtIsVendorShell(), XtIsTransientShell(), XtIsToplevelShell(), XtIsApplicationShell(), XtIsSessionShell()

- XtWidgetToApplicationContext()

- XtName(), XtParent(), XtDisplayOfObject(), XtScreenOfObject()

- XtSetValues(), XtGetValues(), XtVaSetValues(), XtVaGetValues()

## Resources

The Hook Object has the following resources:

XtNshells and XtNnumShells are read-only resources. Querying XtNshells returns an array of all root shells that have been created on the display associated with the Hook Object. Querying XtNnumShells returns the number of elements in that array.

The remaining resources are the callback lists on which hooks may be registered. See the "Callbacks" section below for information on when each list is invoked, and the call_data that each is called with. Note that when you register procedures on these hook callbacks, you must exercise caution in calling Intrinsics functions in those callbacks in order to avoid recursion.

## Inherited Resources

The Hook Object inherits the XtNdestroyCallback resource from Object, its superclass.

## Class Structure

The Hook Object is private to the Intrinsics, and no information about its class structure is specified.

## Instance Structure

The Hook Object is private to the Intrinsics, and no information about its instance structure is specified.

## Hook Object *(continued)*

## *Callbacks*

The subsections below provide details about the hooks supported by the Intrinsics and about the callback lists that are invoked.

### *Widget Creation Hooks*

The XtNcreateHook callback list is called from: XtCreateWidget(), XtCreateManagedWidget(), XtCreatePopupShell(), XtAppCreateShell(), and their corresponding varargs versions.

The *call_data* parameter in a XtNcreateHook callback may be cast to type XtCreateHookData.

```
typedef struct {
        String type;
        Widget widget;
        ArgList args;
        Cardinal num_args;
} XtCreateHookDataRec, *XtCreateHookData;
```

The type field of this structure is set to XtHcreate, widget is the newly created widget, and args and num_args are the resources passed to the create function. The callbacks are called before returning from the the create function.

### *Widget Change Hooks*

The XtNchangeHook callback list is called from:

- XtSetValues(), XtVaSetValues()

- XtManageChild(), XtManageChildren(), XtUnmanageChild(), XtUnmanageChildren()

- XtRealizeWidget(), XtUnrealizeWidget()

- XtAddCallback(), XtRemoveCallback(), XtAddCallbacks() XtRemoveCallbacks(), XtRemoveAllCallbacks()

- XtAugmentTranslations(), XtOverrideTranslations(), XtUninstallTranslations()

- XtSetKeyboardFocus(), XtSetWMColormapWindows()

- XtSetMappedWhenManaged(), XtMapWidget(), XtUnmapWidget()

- XtPopup(), XtPopupSpringLoaded(), and XtPopdown()

The *call_data* parameter in a XtNchangeHook callback may be cast to type XtChangeHookData.

```
typedef struct {
        String type;
        Widget widget;
```

```
        XtPointer event_data;
        Cardinal num_event_data;
} XtChangeHookDataRec, *XtChangeHookData;
```

When the XtNchangeHook callbacks are called as a result of a call to XtSetVal-
ues() or XtVaSetValues(), type is set to XtHsetValues, widget is the new widget passed to the set_values() method, and event_data may be cast to type
XtChangeHookSetValuesData.

```
typedef struct {
        Widget old, req;
        ArgList args;
        Cardinal num_args;
} XtChangeHookSetValuesDataRec, *XtChangeHookSetValuesData;
```

The old, req, args, and num_args are the parameters passed to the
set_values() method. The callbacks are called after the set_values() and constraint set_values() methods have been called.

When the XtNchangeHook callbacks are called as a result of a call to XtMan-
ageChild() or XtManageChildren(), type is set to XtHmanageChildren, widget
is the parent, event_data may be cast to type WidgetList and is the list of children
being managed, and num_event_data is the length of the widget list. The callbacks are called after the children have been managed.

When the XtNchangeHook callbacks are called as a result of a call to XtUnman-
ageChild() or XtUnmanageChildren(), type is set to XtHunmanageChildren,
widget is the parent, event_data may be cast to type WidgetList and is a list of
the children being unmanaged, and num_event_data is the length of the widget
list. The callbacks are called after the children have been unmanaged.

The XtNchangeHook callbacks are called twice as a result of a call to XtChange-
ManagedSet(), once after unmanaging and again after managing. When the callbacks are called the first time, type is set to XtHunmanageSet, widget is the parent, event_data may be cast to type WidgetList and is a list of the children being
unmanaged, and num_event_data is the length of the widget list. When the callbacks are called the second time the type is set to XtHmanageSet, widget is the
parent, event_data may be cast to type WidgetList and is a list of the children
being managed, and num_event_data is the length of the widget list.

When the XtNchangeHook callbacks are called as a result of a call to XtReal-
izeWidget(), type is set to XtHrealizeWidget and widget is the widget being
realized. The callbacks are called after the widget has been realized.

When the XtNchangeHook callbacks are called as a result of a call to XtUnrealizeWidget(), type is set to XtHunrealizeWidget, and widget is the widget being unrealized. The callbacks are called after the widget has been unrealized.

When the XtNchangeHook callbacks are called as a result of a call to XtAddCallback(), type is set to XtHaddCallback, widget is the widget to which the callback is being added, and event_data may be cast to type String and is the name of the callback being added. The callbacks are called after the callback has been added to the widget.

When the XtNchangeHook callbacks are called as a result of a call to XtAddCallbacks(), type is set to XtHaddCallbacks, widget is the widget to which the callbacks are being added, and event_data may be cast to type String and is the name of the callbacks being added. The callbacks are called after the callbacks have been added to the widget.

When the XtNchangeHook callbacks are called as a result of a call to XtRemoveCallback(), type is set to XtHremoveCallback, widget is the widget from which the callback is being removed, and event_data may be cast to type String and is the name of the callback being removed. The callbacks are called after the callback has been removed from the widget.

When the XtNchangeHook callbacks are called as a result of a call to XtRemoveCallbacks(), type is set to XtHremoveCallbacks, widget is the widget from which the callbacks are being removed, and event_data may be cast to type String and is the name of the callbacks being removed. The callbacks are called after the callbacks have been removed from the widget.

When the XtNchangeHook callbacks are called as a result of a call to XtRemoveAllCallbacks(), type is set to XtHremoveAllCallbacks and widget is the widget from which the callbacks are being removed. The callbacks are called after the callbacks have been removed from the widget.

When the XtNchangeHook callbacks are called as a result of a call to XtAugmentTranslations(), type is set to XtHaugmentTranslations and widget is the widget whose translations are being modified. The callbacks are called after the widget's translations have been modified.

When the XtNchangeHook callbacks are called as a result of a call to XtOverrideTranslations(), type is set to XtHoverrideTranslations and widget is the widget whose translations are being modified. The callbacks are called after the widget's translations have been modified.

When the XtNchangeHook callbacks are called as a result of a call to XtUninstallTranslations(), type is XtHuninstallTranslations and widget is the widget whose translations are being uninstalled. The callbacks are called after the widget's translations have been uninstalled.

When the XtNchangeHook callbacks are called as a result of a call to XtSetKeyboardFocus(), type is set to XtHsetKeyboardFocus and event_data may be cast to type Widget and is the value of the descendant argument passed to XtSetKeyboardFocus(). The callbacks are called before returning from XtSetKeyboardFocus().

When the XtNchangeHook callbacks are called as a result of a call to XtSetWMColormapWindows(), type is set to XtHsetWMColormapWindows, event_data may be cast to type WidgetList and is the value of the list argument passed to XtSetWMColormapWindows(), and num_event_data is the length of the list. The callbacks are called before returning from XtSetWMColormapWindows().

When the XtNchangeHook callbacks are called as a result of a call to XtSetMappedWhenManaged(), type is set to XtHsetMappedWhenManaged and event_data may be cast to type Boolean and is the value of the mapped_when_managed argument passed to XtSetMappedWhenManaged(). The callbacks are called after setting the widget's mapped_when_managed field and before realizing or unrealizing the widget.

When the XtNchangeHook callbacks are called as a result of a call to XtMapWidget(), type is set to XtHmapWidget and widget is the widget being mapped. The callbacks are called after mapping the widget.

When the XtNchangeHook callbacks are called as a result of a call to XtUnmapWidget(), type is set to XtHunmapWidget and widget is the widget being unmapped. The callbacks are called after unmapping the widget.

When the XtNchangeHook callbacks are called as a result of a call to XtPopup(), type is set to XtHpopup, widget is the widget being popped up, and event_data may be cast to type XtGrabKind and is the value of the grab_kind argument passed to XtPopup(). The callbacks are called before returning from XtPopup().

When the XtNchangeHook callbacks are called as a result of a call to XtPopupSpringLoaded(), type is set to XtHpopupSpringLoaded and widget is the widget being popped up. The callbacks are called before returning from XtPopupSpringLoaded().

When the XtNchangeHook callbacks are called as a result of a call to XtPopdown(), type is set to XtHpopdown and widget is the widget being popped down. The callbacks are called before returning from XtPopdown().

A widget set that exports interfaces that change application state without employing the Intrinsics library should invoke the change hook itself. This is done by:

```
XtCallCallbacks(XtHooksOfDisplay(dpy), XtNchangeHook, call_data);
```

### Widget Configuration Hooks

The XtNconfigureHook callback list is called any time the Intrinsics move, resize, or configure a widget, and when XtResizeWindow() is called.

The *call_data* parameter may be cast to type XtConfigureHookData.

```
typedef struct {
        String type;
        Widget widget;
        XtGeometryMask changeMask;
        XWindowChanges changes;
} XtConfigureHookDataRec, *XtConfigureHookData;
```

When the XtNconfigureHook callbacks are called the type is XtHconfigure, widget is the widget being configured, changeMask and changes reflect the changes made to the widget. The callbacks are called after changes have been made to the widget.

### Geometry Negotiation Hooks

The XtNgeometryHook callback list is called from XtMakeGeometryRequest() and XtMakeResizeRequest() once before and once after geometry negotiation occurs.

The *call_data* parameter may be cast to type XtGeometryHookData.

```
typedef struct {
        String type;
        Widget widget;
        XtWidgetGeometry* request;
        XtWidgetGeometry* reply;
        XtGeometryResult result;
} XtGeometryHookDataRec, *XtGeometryHookData;
```

When the XtNgeometryHook callbacks are called prior to geometry negotiation, type is XtHpreGeometry, widget is the widget for which the request is being made, and request is the requested geometry. When the geometryHook callbacks are called after geometry negotiation, type is XtHpostGeometry, widget is the widget for which the request was made, request is the requested geometry, reply is the resulting geometry granted, and result is the value returned from the geometry negotiation.

### Widget Destruction Hooks

The XtNdestroyHook callback list is called when a widget is destroyed. The *call_data* parameter may be cast to type XtDestroyHookData.

```
typedef struct {
        String type;
        Widget widget;
} XtDestroyHookDataRec, *XtDestroyHookData;
```

When the `XtNdestroyHook` callbacks are called as a result of a call to `XtDestroy-Widget()`, type is `XtHdestroy` and widget is the widget being destroyed. The callbacks are called upon completion of phase one destroy for a widget.

## See Also

*Object*(3),
*XtHooksOfDisplay*(1)

# ■ SessionShell

## Name

SessionShell — root shell for an application that participates in session management.

## Synopsis

Public Headers
```
<X11/StringDefs.h> <X11/Shell.h>
```

Private Header
```
<X11/ShellP.h>
```

Class Name
SessionShell

Class Hierarchy
Core → Composite → Shell → WMShell → VendorShell → TopLevelShell →
ApplicationShell → SessionShell

Class Pointer
```
sessionShellWidgetClass
```

Instantiation
```
widget = XtOpenApplication(..., sessionShellWidgetClass, ...)
```

Functions/Macros
```
XtIsSessionShell()
```

## Availability

Release 6 and later; supersedes ApplicationShell for most applications.

## Description

A SessionShell provides the normal top-level window for an application. The Session-Shell interacts with both the window manager and the session manager and allows communication with the session manager through resources. A SessionShell is intended to be created by XtOpenApplication() or XtAppCreateShell() (or their XtVa analogs)—shells created in this way do not have a parent and are at the root of the widget tree.

The SessionShell supersedes its superclass, the ApplicationShell. In X11R6 and later, it is recommended that all Xt applications participate in session management by creating a root SessionShell widget with XtOpenApplication() instead of calling the super-seded initialization funcion XtAppInitialize().

An application should have only one SessionShell, unless the application is imple-mented as multiple logical applications which should appear separate to the session manager. Normally, an application should use TopLevelShell widgets for its auxiliary top-level windows.

## New Resources

The SessionShell defines the following resources:

| SessionShell Resource Set Name | Class | Type | Default |
|---|---|---|---|
| XtNcancelCallback | XtCCallback | XtRCallback | NULL |
| XtNcloneCommand | XtCCloneCommand | XtRCommandArgArray | See text |
| XtNconnection | XtCConnection | XtRSmcConn | NULL |
| XtNcurrentDirectory | XtCCurrentDirectory | XtRDirectoryString | NULL |
| XtNdieCallback | XtCCallback | XtRCallback | NULL |
| XtNdiscardCommand | XtCDiscardCommand | XtRCommandArgArray | NULL |
| XtNenvironment | XtCEnvironment | XtREnvironmentArray | NULL |
| XtNerrorCallback | XtCCallback | XtRCallback | NULL |
| XtNinteractCallback | XtCCallback | XtRCallback | NULL |
| XtNjoinSession | XtCJoinSession | XtRBoolean | True |
| XtNprogramPath | XtCProgramPath | XtRString | See text |
| XtNresignCommand | XtCResignCommand | XtRCommandArgArray | NULL |
| XtNrestartCommand | XtCRestartCommand | XtRCommandArgArray | See text |
| XtNrestartStyle | XtCRestartStyle | XtRRestartStyle | SmRestart-IfRunning |
| XtNsaveCallback | XtCCallback | XtRCallback | NULL |
| XtNsaveCompleteCallback | XtCCallback | XtRCallback | NULL |
| XtNsessionID | XtCSessionID | XtRString | NULL |
| XtNshutdownCommand | XtCShutdownCommand | XtRCommandArgArray | NULL |

All of these resources may be set at creation time of the session shell, or after creation, using `XtVaSetValues()`. `XtVaSetValues()` may be used for all of the SessionShell resources. Xt defines converters for `XtNcloneCommand`, `XtNrestartCommand`, `XtNcurrentDirectory`, and `XtNrestartStyles`. For more information on them, see the end of Section 3.5.

`XtNcancelCallback`
A list of callback procedures to be invoked when the SessionShell receives a `ShutdownCancelled` message from the session manager. This generally occurs when some client in the session has requested (at the behest of the user) that the pending session shutdown be cancelled. The *call_data* passed to this callback is NULL.

XtNcloneCommand

This resource specifies a command that the session manager can use to start a copy of the application. On POSIX systems, this command will be an argv-style array of strings. The XtNcloneCommand should be the same as the XtNrestartCommand, except without *–xtsessionID* argument.

If XtNcloneCommand is NULL when the SessionShell establishes its connection to the session manager, the value of the XtNrestartCommand resource will be copied and used for this resource. The *–xtsessionID* argument and its following session identifier will automaticallly be removed from this copy. Note that the XtNrestartCommand resource may itself be a copy of the argv array, with a *–xtsessionID* argument added.

XtNconnection

This resource specifies the connection between the SessionShell and the session manager. It is of type SmcConn, a type defined by the SmLib session management library. This connection is usually established (see XtNjoinSession) automatically when the SessionShell is created, and you generally do not need to set or query this resource. If your application has created its own connection to the session manager then it can set this resource to have the SessionShell use that existing session id. See "Joining a Session" and "Resigning from a Session" below.

XtNcurrentDirectory

A string that specifies the current directory that should be set up before the session manager restarts the client.

XtNdieCallback

A list of callback procedures that are invoked when the SessionShell receives a Die message from the session manager. They are passed NULL *client_data*, and the callbacks on this list should do whatever is appropriate to quit the application.

XtNdiscardCommand

This resource specifies a command that, when delivered to the host that the client is running on (determined from the connection), will cause the host to discard any information about the current state. If this resource is not specified, the session manager will assume that all of the client's state is encoded in the XtNrestartCommand resource. As with other command resources, this one should be an argv-style array of strings on POSIX systems.

XtNenvironment

This resource specifies the environment variables that should be set up before a command is restarted. On POSIX systems, this is an array of strings each in the form "name=value", where no '=' character appears in the name of an environment variable.

`XtNerrorCallback`

A list of callback procedures to be called if an unrecoverable communications error occurs between the SessionShell and the session manager. When this occurs, the SessionShell will close the connection and set `XtNconnection` to `NULL`. The `call_data` for these callbacks is `NULL`.

`XtNinteractCallback`

This resource is a callback list of a non-standard type. When a client wants to interact with a user before a session shutdown (to get user confirmation, for example), it must make a request to the session manager to do so. It makes the request by registering a callback on this `XtNinteractCallback` list. When the request is granted, the registered callback will be automatically removed from the callback list and invoked with a checkpoint token passed as its `call_data`. If there is more than one interaction callback registered on the list, then the first callback will be removed and called, and subsequent callbacks will not be removed or called until the previous callbacks return their checkpoint token by calling `XtSessionReturnToken()`. Because interaction through dialogs is asynchronous, the token is usually not returned until sometime after the callback itself has returned. See the sections "Requesting Interaction" and "Interacting with the User" below for more information.

`XtNjoinSession`

A `Boolean` resource that indicates whether the SessionShell should automatically establish a connection with the session manager. The default is `True`, so the SessionShell normally joins the session when it is created. If you set this resource to `False` when the SessionShell is created, then you can join the session later by setting it to `True`. Similarly, you can resign from a session by setting this resource to `False`. See "Joining a Session" and "Resigning from a Session" below.

`XtNprogramPath`

The name of the program that is running. This is a single string; not an array of strings. If this resource is `NULL` when the SessionShell establishes a connection with the session manager, the first element of the `XtNrestartCommand` resource will be copied and used. Note that the value of `XtNrestartCommand` may itself be a copy of the `argv` array.

`XtNresignCommand`

A client that sets `XtNrestartStyle` to `SmRestartAnyway` uses this resource to specify a command that undoes the effect of the client and removes any saved state. As an example, consider a session that runs *xmodmap*. *xmodmap* registers itself with the session manager, sets XtNrestartStyle to SmRestartAnyway, modifies the keyboard mapping and then exits. In order to allow the session manager (at the user's request) to remove *xmodmap* from the current session, *xmodmap* would specify a XtNresignCommand that restores the original keyboard mapping. On POSIX systems, this resource is an argv-style array of strings.

XtNrestartCommand

This resource contains a command that, when delivered to the host that the client is running on (determined from the connection), will cause the client to restart in its current state. On POSIX-based systems this command is an argv-style array of strings. This restart command should ensure that the client restarts with the client-id specified by XtNsessionID—it can do this by including a *–xtsessionID* argument in the command.

If XtNrestartCommand is NULL when the SessionShell establishes a connection to the session manager, the the client's argv array is copied and used for this resource.

Whether or not XtNrestartCommand was NULL, if the command-line arguments -xtsessionID *session-id* do not already appear in that command, they will be added at the beginning of the command. If the *–xtsessionID* argument already appears with an incorrect session identifier as its following argument, that argument will be replaced with the correct current session identifier.

XtNrestartStyle

This resource is a hint to the session manager that specifies how the client would like to be restarted. The possible values are SmRestartIfRunning, SmRestartAnyway, SmRestartImmediately, and SmRestartNever. A resource converter is registered for this resource—it recognizes the strings "RestartIfRunning", "RestartAnyway", "RestartImmediately" and "RestartNever". The meanings of these values are the following:

SmRestartIfRunning

Specifies that the client should be restarted in the next session if it was running at the end of the current session. This is the default value.

SmRestartAnyway

Specifies that the application should be restarted in the next session even if it exits before the current session is terminated. Noted that this is only a hint and the SM will follow the policies specified by its users in determining what applications to restart. A client that uses `SmRestartAnyway` should also set the `XtNresignCommand` and `XtNshutdownCommand` resources to commands that undo the state of the client after it exits.

`SmRestartImmediately`

Specifies that the client is meant to run continuously. If the client exits, the SM should try to restart it in the current session.

`SmRestartNever`

Specifies that the client does not wish to be restarted in the next session.

`XtNsaveCallback`

A list of callback procedures that will be invoked when the SessionShell receives a `SaveYourself` request from the session manager. The procedures will be called with a checkpoint token as their *call_data* argument and the procedures are responsible for saving the application's state. See "Saving Application State" below for more information.

`XtNsaveCompleteCallback`

A list of callback procedures that will be invoked when the SessionShell receives a `SaveComplete` message from the session manager. This will occur when all clients in a session have completed saving their state, and when the session manager will not be shutting down the session. This callback signals that no shutdown is impending. This means that clients may resume operation and allow changes to be made to their state. The procedures on this callback list will be invoked with *client_data* of `NULL`.

`XtNsessionID`

This resource identifies the session participant to the session manager. If it is `NULL` when the SessionShell joins the session, then the session manager will assign a session identifier, which the SessionShell will set on this resource. When a client is restored as part of a saved session, the value of this resource will come from the *–xtsessionID* command line argument, and the SessionShell will set it as the value of the `SM_CLIENT_ID` property so that the session manager can read it.

`XtNshutdownCommand`

This resource specifies a command that the session manager should execute at shutdown time to clean up after a client that is no longer running but which retained its state by setting `XtNrestartStyle` to `SmRestartAnyway`. This command should clean up after the client, but must not remove any saved state as the client is still part of the session. As an example, consider a client that turns on a camera at start up time. This client then exits. At session shutdown, the user wants the camera turned off. This client would set the `XtNrestartStyle` to SmRestartAnyway and would register a XtNshutdownCommand that would turn off the camera. As with the other command resources, this resource is an argv-style array of strings on POSIX systems.

## Inherited Resources

The SessionShell inherits the following resources. The resources are listed alphabetically, along with the superclass that defines them.

## Class Structure

The SessionShell class structure contains only an extension field. Its declaration is similar to those of the other shells:

```
typedef struct { XtPointer extension; } SessionShellClassPart;

typedef struct _SessionShellClassRec {
        CoreClassPart core_class;
        CompositeClassPart composite_class;
        ShellClassPart shell_class;
        WMShellClassPart wm_shell_class;
        VendorShellClassPart vendor_shell_class;
        TopLevelShellClassPart top_level_shell_class;
        ApplicationShellClassPart application_shell_class;
        SessionShellClassPart session_shell_class;
} SessionShellClassRec;

extern SessionShellClassRec sessionShellClassRec;
extern WidgetClass sessionShellWidgetClass;
```

There are no extensions currently defined for this class, and the extension field should be NULL.

## Instance Structure

The SessionShell instance structure contains at least the following fields (which need not be in this order):

```
typedef struct {
        SmcConn connection;
        String session_id;
        String * restart_command;
        String * clone_command;
        String * discard_command;
        String * resign_command;
        String * shutdown_command;
        String * environment;
        String current_dir;
        String program_path;
        unsigned char restart_style;
```

```
        Boolean join_session;
        XtCallbackList save_callbacks;
        XtCallbackList interact_callbacks;
        XtCallbackList cancel_callbacks;
        XtCallbackList save_complete_callbacks;
        XtCallbackList die_callbacks;
        XtCallbackList error_callbacks;
} SessionShellPart;

typedef  struct {
        CorePart core;
        CompositePart composite;
        ShellPart shell;
        WMShellPart wm;
        VendorShellPart vendor;
        TopLevelShellPart topLevel;
        ApplicationShellPart application;
        SessionShellPart session;
} SessionShellRec, *SessionShellWidget;
```

## Session Participation

Applications can participate in a user's session, exchanging messages with the session manager as described in the *X Session Management Protocol* and the *X Session Management Library*.

When a widget of `sessionShellWidgetClass` or a subclass is created, the widget provides support for the application as a session participant, and continues to provide support until the widget is destroyed.

### Joining a Session

When a SessionShell is created, if `XtNconnection` is `NULL`, and if `XtNjoinSession` is `True`, and if `XtNargv` or `XtNrestartCommand` is not `NULL`, and if in POSIX environments the `SESSION_MANAGER` environment variable is defined, the shell attempts to establish a new connection with the session manager.

To transfer management of an existing session connection from an application to the shell at widget creation time, pass the existing session connection ID as the `XtNconnection` resource value when creating the Session shell, and, if the other creation-time conditions on session participation are met, the widget will maintain the connection with the session manager. The application must ensure that only one SessionShell manages the connection.

In the SessionShell `set_values()` method, if `XtNjoinSession` changes from `False` to `True` and `XtNconnection` is `NULL` and when in POSIX environments the `SESSION_MANAGER` environment variable is defined, the shell attempts to open a connection to the session manager. If `XtNconnection` changes from `NULL` to non-`NULL`, the SessionShell will take over management of that session connection and will set XtNjoinSession to True. If XtNjoinSession changes from False to True and XtNconnection is not NULL, the SessionShell will take over management of the session connection.

When a successful connection has been established, XtNconnection contains the session connection ID for the session participant. When the shell begins to manage the connection, it will call XtAppAddInput to register the handler which watches for protocol messages from the session manager. When the attempt to connect fails, a warning message is issued and XtNconnection is set to NULL.

While the connection is being managed, if a SaveYourself, SaveYourself-Phase2, Interact, ShutdownCancelled, SaveComplete, or Die message is received from the session manager, the SessionShell will call out to application callback procedures registered on the respective callback list of the SessionShell, and will send SaveYourselfPhase2Request, InteractRequest, InteractDone, SaveYourselfDone, and ConnectionClosed messages as appropriate. Initially, all of the client's session properties are undefined. When any of the session property resource values are defined or change, the SessionShell initialize() and set_values() methods will update the client's session property value by a Set-Properties or a DeleteProperties message, as appropriate. The session ProcessID and UserID properties are always set by the shell when it is possible to determine the values of these properties.

### Resigning from a Session

When the SessionShell widget is destroyed, the destroy method will close the connection to the session manager by sending a ConnectionClosed protocol message, and will remove the input callback which was watching for session protocol messages.

When XtSetValues() is used to set XtNjoinSession to False, the set_values method of the SessionShell will close the connection to the session manager if, one exists, by sending a ConnectionClosed message, and XtNconnection will be set to NULL.

Applications which exit in response to user actions and which do not wait for phase 2 destroy to complete on the SessionShell should set XtNjoinSession to False before exiting.

When XtSetValues() is used to set XtNconnection to NULL, the SessionShell will stop managing the connection, if one exists. However, that session connection will not be closed.

Applications that wish to ensure continuation of a session connection beyond the destruction of the shell should first retrieve the XtNconnection resource value, then set the XtNconnection resource to NULL; then they may safely destroy the widget without losing control of the session connection.

The XtNerrorCallback list will be called if an unrecoverable communications error occurs while the shell is managing the connection. The shell will close the connection, set XtNconnection to NULL, remove the input callback, and call the procedures registered on the XtNerrorCallback list. The *call_data* for these callbacks is NULL.

### Saving Application State

The session manager instigates an application checkpoint by sending a Save-Yourself request. Applications are responsible for saving their state in response to the request.

When the SaveYourself request arrives, the procedures registered on the SessionShell's XtNsaveCallback list are called. If the application does not register any procedures on the XtNsaveCallback list, the shell will report to the session manager that the application failed to save its state. Each procedure on the XtNsaveCallback list receives a token in the *call_data* parameter.

The checkpoint token in the *call_data* parameter is of type XtCheckpointToken.

```
typedef struct {
    int save_type;
    int interact_style;
    Boolean shutdown;
    Boolean fast;
    Boolean cancel_shutdown
    int phase;
    int interact_dialog_type;    /* return */
    Boolean request_cancel;      /* return */
    Boolean request_next_phase;  /* return */
    Boolean save_success;        /* return */
} XtCheckpointTokenRec, *XtCheckpointToken;
```

The save_type, interact_style, shutdown, and fast fields of the token contain the parameters of the SaveYourself message. The possible values of save_type are SmSaveLocal, SmSaveGlobal, and SmSaveBoth; these indicate the type of information to be saved. The possible values of interact_style are SmInteractStyleNone, SmInteractStyleErrors, and SmInteractStyleAny; these indicate whether user interaction would be permitted and, if so, what kind of interaction. If shutdown is True, the checkpoint is being performed in preparation for the end of the session. If fast is True, the client should perform the checkpoint as quickly as possible. If cancel_shutdown is True, a ShutdownCancelled message has been received for the current save operation. (See

"Responding to a Shutdown Cancellation" below.) The phase is used by manager clients, such as a window manager, to distinguish between the first and second phase of a save operation. The phase will be either 1 or 2. The remaining fields in the checkpoint token structure are provided for the application to communicate with the shell.

Upon entry to the first application save callback procedure, the return fields in the token have the following initial values: interact_dialog_type is SmDialog-Normal; request_cancel is False; request_next_phase is False; and save_success is True. When a token is returned with any of the four return fields containing a non-initial value, and when the field is applicable, subsequent tokens passed to the application during the current save operation will always contain the non-initial value.

The purpose of the token's save_success field is to indicate the outcome of the entire operation to the session manager and, ultimately, to the user. Returning False indicates that some portion of the application state could not be successfully saved. If any token is returned to the shell with save_success False, tokens subsequently received by the application for the current save operation will show save_success as False. When the shell sends the final status of the checkpoint to the session manager, it will indicate failure to save application state if any token was returned with save_success False.

Session participants which manage and save the state of other clients should structure their save or interact callbacks to set request_next_phase to True when phase is 1, which will cause the shell to send the SaveYourselfPhase2Request when the first phase is complete. When the SaveYourselfPhase2 message is received, the shell will invoke the XtNsaveCallback list a second time with phase equal to 2. Manager clients should save the state of other clients when the callbacks are invoked the second time and phase equal to 2.

The application may request additional tokens while a checkpoint is under way; these additional tokens must be returned by an explicit call.

To request an additional token for a save callback response which has a deferred outcome, use XtSessionGetToken() —it returns NULL if no checkpoint operation is currently under way.

To indicate the completion of checkpoint processing, including user interaction, the application must signal the SessionShell by returning all tokens. To return a token, use XtSessionReturnToken().

Tokens passed as *call_data* to XtNsaveCallback procedures are implicitly returned when the save callback procedure returns. A save callback procedure should not call XtSessionReturnToken() on the token passed in its *call_data*.

### Requesting Interaction

When the token interact_style allows user interaction, the application may interact with the user during the checkpoint, but must wait for permission to interact. Applications request permission to interact with the user during the checkpointing operation by registering a procedure on the SessionShell's XtNinteractCallback list. When all save callback procedures have returned, and each time a token which was granted by a call to XtSessionGetToken() is returned, the SessionShell examines the XtNinteractCallback list. If interaction is permitted and the XtNinteractCallback list is not empty, the shell will send an InteractRequest to the session manager when an interact request is not already outstanding for the application.

The type of interaction dialog that will be requested is specified by the interact_dialog_type field in the checkpoint token. The possible values for interact_dialog_type are SmDialogError and SmDialogNormal. If a token is returned with interact_dialog_type containing SmDialogError, the interact request and any subsequent interact requests will be for an error dialog; otherwise, the request will be for a normal dialog with the user.

When a token is returned with save_success False or interact_dialog_type SmDialogError, tokens subsequently passed to callbacks during the same active SaveYourself response will reflect these changed values, indicating that an error condition has occurred during the checkpoint.

The request_cancel field is a return value for interact callbacks only. Upon return from a procedure on the save callback list, the value of the token's request_cancel field is not examined by the shell. This is also true of tokens received through a call to XtSessionGetToken().

### Interacting with the User

When the session manager grants the application's request for user interaction, the SessionShell receives an Interact message. The procedures registered on the XtNinteractCallback list are executed, but not as if executing a typical callback list. These procedures are individually executed in sequence, with a checkpoint token functioning as the sequencing mechanism. Each step in the sequence begins by removing a procedure from the XtNinteractCallback list and executing it with a token passed in the *call_data*. The interact callback will typically pop up a dialog box and return. When the user interaction and associated application checkpointing has completed, the application must return the token by calling

XtSessionReturnToken(). Returning the token completes the current step, and triggers the next step in the sequence.

During interaction the client may request cancellation of a shutdown. When a token passed as *call_data* to an interact procedure is returned, if shutdown is True and cancel_shutdown is False, request_cancel indicates whether the application requests that the pending shutdown be cancelled. If request_cancel is True, the field will also be True in any tokens subsequently granted during the checkpoint operation. When a token requesting cancellation of the session shutdown is returned, pending interact procedures will still be called by the Session shell. When all interact procedures have been removed from the XtNinteract-Callback list, executed, and the final interact token returned to the shell, an InteractDone message is sent to the session manager, indicating whether a pending session shutdown is requested to be cancelled.

### Responding to a Shutdown Cancellation

Callbacks registered on the XtNcancelCallback list are invoked when the SessionShell processes a ShutdownCancelled message from the session manager. This may occur during the processing of save callbacks, while waiting for interact permission, during user interaction, or after the save operation is complete and the application is expecting a SaveComplete or a Die message. The *call_data* for these callback procedures is NULL.

When the shell notices that a pending shutdown has been cancelled, the token cancel_shutdown field will be True in tokens subsequently given to the application.

Receiving notice of a shutdown cancellation does not cancel the pending execution of save callbacks or interact callbacks. After the cancel callbacks execute, if interact_style is not SmInteractStyleNone and the interact list is not empty, the procedures on the XtNinteractCallback list will be executed and passed a token with interact_style SmInteractStyleNone. The application should not interact with the user, and the SessionShell will not send an InteractDone message.

### Completing a Save

When there is no user interaction, the shell regards the application as having finished saving state when all callback procedures on the XtNsaveCallback list have returned, and any additional tokens passed out by XtSessionGetToken() have been returned by corresponding calls to XtSessionReturnToken(). If the save operation involved user interaction, the above completion conditions apply, and, in addition, all requests for interaction have been granted or cancelled, and all tokens passed to interact callbacks have been returned through calls to

`XtSessionReturnToken()`. If the save operation involved a manager client that requested the second phase, the above conditions apply to both the first and second phase of the save operation.

When the application has finished saving state, the Session Shell will report the result to the session manager by sending the `SaveYourselfDone` message. If the session is continuing, the shell will receive the `SaveComplete` message when all applications have completed saving state. This message indicates that applications may again allow changes to their state. The shell will execute the `XtNsaveCompleteCallback` list. The *call_data* for the callback procedures on this list is NULL.

### Responding to a Shutdown

Callbacks registered on the `XtNdieCallback` list are invoked when the session manager sends a `Die` message. The callbacks on this list should do whatever is appropriate to quit the application. Before executing procedures on the `XtNdieCallback` list, the SessionShell will close the connection to the session manager and will remove the handler which watches for protocol messages. The *call_data* for these callbacks is NULL.

## See Also

*ApplicationShell*(3),
*Shell*(3),
*TopLevelShell*(3),
*VendorShell*(3),
*WMShell*(3)
*XtIsSessionShell*(1)

# ■ XtAllocateProc

## Name

XtAllocateProc — interface definition for the allocate() method.

## Synopsis

```
typedef void (*XtAllocateProc)(WidgetClass, Cardinal*, Cardinal*, ArgList,
      Cardinal*,XtTypedArgList, Cardinal*,
      Widget*, XtPointer*);
   WidgetClass widget_class;
   Cardinal* constraint_size;
   Cardinal* more_bytes;
   ArgList args;
   Cardinal* num_args;
   XtTypedArgList typed_args,
   Cardinal* num_typed_args;
   Widget* new_return;
   XtPointer* more_bytes_return;
```

### Inputs

widget_class

> The class of the widget instance to allocate.

constraint_size

> The size of the constraint record to allocate, or 0.

more_bytes

> The number of auxiliary bytes of memory to allocate.

args

> The resource argument list as given in the call to create the widget.

num_args

> The number of elements in args.

typed_args

> The list of typed arguments given in the call to create the widget.

num_typed_args

> The number of elements in the typed_args array.

### Outputs

new_return

> The address at which to store a pointer to the newly allocated instance. Store NULL at this address in case of error.

more_bytes_return

> The address at which to store a pointer to the auxiliary memory if it was requested. Store NULL at this address if auxiliary memory was requested

and an error occurred. If no auxiliary memory was requested, leave the value at this address unchanged.

## Availability

Release 6 and later.

## Description

XtAllocateProc() is the type of the Object class extension allocate() method. See allocate(4) for complete details.

## See Also

*allocate*(4)

# XtAppAddBlockHook

## Name

XtAppAddBlockHook — register a procedure to be called before the Intrinsics block for input.

## Synopsis

```
XtBlockHookId
XtAppAddBlockHook(app_context, proc, client_data)
    XtAppContext app_context;
    XtBlockHookProc proc;
    XtPointer client_data;
```

### Inputs

*app_context*

    The application context that identifies the application.

*proc*

    The procedure to be called before blocking.

*client_data*

    The argument passed to *proc* when it is called.

### Returns

An identifier for the procedure/data pair. This value can be used with XtRemove-BlockHook() to remove the block hook.

## Availability

Release 6 and later.

## Description

XtAppAddBlockHook() registers the specified procedure *proc* and returns an identifier for it. The hook procedure *proc* will be called at any time in the future when the Intrisics are about to block and wait for input.

When *proc* is called, it will be passed *client_data* as its single argument.

XtAppAddBlockHook() returns a special "block hook id" value. You can un-register a "block hook" procedure by calling XtRemoveBlockHook() with this identifier.

## See Also

*XtRemoveBlockHook*(1),
*XtBlockHookProc*(2)

## Name

XtAppAddSignal — register a callback to be triggered from a signal handler.

## Synopsis

```
XtSignalId XtAppAddSignal(app_context, proc, client_data)
    XtAppContext app_context;
    XtSignalCallbackProc proc;
    XtPointer client_data;
```

### Inputs

> *app_context*
>> The application context that identifies the application.
>
> *proc*
>> The procedure to be called when the signal is noticed.
>
> *client_data*
>> An argument passed to *proc* when it is invoked.

### Returns

An `XtSignalId` identifier for the registered signal callback. This identifier is used by other signal handling functions.

## Availability

Release 6 and later.

## Description

`XtAppAddSignal()` registers the specified signal callback procedure *proc* and its associated *client_data* and returns an `XtSignalId` that identifies this procedure/data pair. The signal callback will be invoked when `XtNoticeSignal()` is called with that returned identifier.

## Usage

X Toolkit functions are not reentrant and cannot safely be called from a signal handler. (Signal handlers are registered with the `signal()` function, and because signals occur asynchronously, only a restricted set of standard C and POSIX functions may safely be called from such a handler.) The functions `XtAppAddSignal()` and `XtNoticeSignal()` provide a safe way for Xt programs to respond to asynchronous signals.

`XtAppAddSignal()` registers a signal callback (not the same as a signal handler) and returns an `XtSignalId` value that identifies that callback. When `XtNoticeSignal()` is called with this identifier, it causes the signal callback to be invoked.

XtNoticeSignal() is carefully written and is the only Xt function that may be safely called from an actual signal handler. Thus to respond to a signal in an Xt program, first register a callback for the signal with XtAppAddSignal() and save the returned identifier in some globally accessible location. Then establish a signal handler with signal() or some related routine. From this signal handler call XtNoticeSignal() and return. If the Intrinsics main loop is blocking for input at this point, then it will "wake up" and invoke the signal callback right away. Otherwise, if it is dispatching an event, then the signal callback will be invoked as soon as control returns to the main loop. The "Example" section below shows how you can respond to a signal in an Xt application.

Note that it is important to call XtAppAddSignal() to register a signal callback *before* you establish a signal handler. Otherwise a signal might occur and be caught before a callback is in place to handle it.

Because of the asynchronous nature of signals, multiple signals may occur before the signal callback is invoked. The Intrinsics do not maintain a count of the number of times a signal has occurred and may invoke the signal callback only once even when the signal handler is invoked multiple times in rapid succession. Generally this is not a problem—if a signal notifies your application of pending input, for example, a single call to the signal callback can read all pending input, even if that input has arrived in two batches (and caused two invocations of the signal handler). On the other hand, when the signal handler is invoked twice, the signal callback may be called and handle the pending input (or whatever) related to both signals, and then be called again and find no input pending. The implication is that you must design your signal callbacks to be flexible—when invoked, it may appear to them that the signal has occurred more than once, or it may appear that the signal has not occurred at all. See the "Background" section below for more details on these possibilities.

## Example

You could arrange for your Xt application to respond to a **Ctrl-C** (SIGINT signal) in the *xterm* that started it with code like the following:

```
/*
 * This value identifies the signal callback we registered.
 */
static XtSignalId sigint_id;

/*
 * This is the UNIX signal handler, registered with signal().
 * It uses XtNoticeSignal() to tell the Intrinsics to invoke
 * the signal callback associated with the signal id.
 * It is not allowed to make any other X or Xt calls.
```

```
    */
static void sigint_handler(int signal_number)
{
    XtNoticeSignal(sigint_id);
}


/*
 * This is the signal callback; the function we want to be called
 * in response to the signal. The Intrinsics will invoke this
 * callback when it safe to do so, so unlike the signal handler,
 * the signal callback can freely make X and Xt calls.
 * Since this callback is invoked when the user types Ctrl-C in the
 * controlling terminal, it calls a hypothetical function that pops
 * up a "Really Quit?" dialog box. This same function could be used
 * from the callback on an "Exit" button.
 */
static void sigint_callback(XtPointer data, XtSignalId *id)
{
    confirm_and_quit();
}


main(int argc, char **argv)
{
        .
        .
        .

    /*
     * Here we register the signal callback with Xt, and obtain
     * the signal id for use in the signal handler.
     */
    sigint_id = XtAppAddSignal(app_context, sigint_callback, NULL);

    /*
     * Here we register the signal handler with the operating system
     * Note that the signal callback was registered before the handler.
     */
    signal(SIGINT, sigint_handler);
        .
        .
        .

    XtAppMainLoop(app_context);
}
```

## Background

If XtNoticeSignal() is invoked multiple times before the Intrinsics are able to invoke the registered callback, the callback is only called once. Logically, the Intrinsics maintain a "pending" flag for each registered callback. This flag is initially False and is set to True by XtNoticeSignal(). When XtAppNextEvent() or XtAppProcessEvent() (with a mask including XtIMSignal) is called, all registered callbacks with the "pending" flag True are invoked and the flags are reset to False.

If the signal handler wants to track how many times the signal has been raised, it can keep its own private counter. Typically the handler would not do any other work; the callback does the actual processing for the signal. The Intrinsics never block signals from being raised, so a given signal can be raised multiple times before the Intrinsics can invoke the callback for that signal, and the callback must be designed to deal with this. In another case, a signal might be raised just after the Intrinsics set the pending flag to False but before the callback can get control, in which case the pending flag will still be True after the callback returns, and the Intrinsics will invoke the callback again, even though both of the signal raises were handled by the first invocation of the callback. The callback must also be prepared to handle this case.

## See Also

*XtNoticeSignal*(1),
*XtRemoveSignal*(1),
*XtSignalCallbackProc*(2)

## Name

XtAppGetExitFlag — check the state of the application-context exit flag.

## Synopsis

```
Boolean XtAppGetExitFlag(app_context)
    XtAppContext app_context;
```

### Inputs

> app_context
>> The application context whose exit flag is to be checked.

### Returns

True if the exit flag of the application context has been set; False otherwise.

## Availability

Release 6 and later.

## Description

XtAppGetExitFlag() checks the Intrinsics-internal exit flag for the specified application context. XtAppGetExitFlag() is intended to be used in event loops. Normally, this function returns False, indicating that event processing should continue. If XtAppSetExitFlag() has been called for the application context, however, XtAppGetExitFlag() returns True, and the event loop must terminate.

## Usage

XtAppMainLoop() uses XtAppGetExitFlag() internally. If you use that standard event loop, then you'll never have to use this function. The purpose of XtAppGetExitFlag() is to support multithreaded applications.

See XtAppSetExitFlag() for more information.

## See Also

*XtAppSetExitFlag*(1),
*XtAppMainLoop*(1)

# ▌ XtAppLock

XtAppLock — obtain exclusive access to application-context data structures.

## Synopsis

```
void XtAppLock(app_context)
    XtAppContext app_context;
```

### Inputs

> app_context
>> The application context to lock.

## Availability

Release 6 and later.

## Description

XtAppLock() is used in multithreaded applications to ensure that only one thread can access the state associated with an application context, including all displays and widgets associated with that application context.

XtAppLock() blocks until it is able to acquire the lock—i.e. if some other thread already has a lock on the application context, then the thread that called XtAppLock() stops executing until the lock is relinquished by the thread that owns it. Once XtAppLock() returns, the thread that called it owns the mutually-exclusive lock. A thread should relinquish its lock as soon as it no longer requires it.

Locking the application context also ensures that only the thread holding the lock makes Xlib calls from within Xt. An application which makes its own direct Xlib calls must either lock the application context around every call, or enable thread locking in Xlib.

A client may acquire a lock multiple times—the effect is cumulative. The client must then ensure that the lock is released an equal number of times in order for the lock to be acquired by another thread.

## Usage

Before writing a multithreaded application you should understand the need for mutual exclusion when there are multiple threads of execution. Mutual exclusion is required, for example, to prevent two threads from performing overlapping updates on the same data structure, and to prevent one thread from reading inconsistent data from a data structure that is being updated by another.

Any Xt application that uses multiple threads and locks must call the function `Xt-`
`ToolkitThreadInitialize()` before any other Xt functions.

Most application writers have little need to use locking as the Intrinsics performs the
necessary locking internally. An exception is resource type converters, which require
that the application context be locked before calling them directly.

Use `XtAppUnlock()` to release an application-context lock acquired by `XtAppLock()`.
Use `XtProcessLock()` and `XtProcessUnlock()` for mutually-exclusive access to process global data, such as widget class fields.

## Example

The following examples show how you might use `XtAppLock()` and `XtAppUnlock()`.

Application writers who write their own utility functions, retrieving the
`being_destroyed` field from a widget instance, for example, must lock the application
context before accessing widget internal data:

```
#include <X11/CoreP.h>
Boolean BeingDestroyed (widget)
Widget widget;
{
    Boolean ret;
    XtAppLock(XtWidgetToApplicationContext(widget));
    ret = widget->core.being_destroyed;
    XtAppUnlock(XtWidgetToApplicationContext(widget));
    return ret;
}
```

A client that wishes to atomically call two or more Intrinsics functions must lock the
application context:

```
    ...
    XtAppLock(XtWidgetToApplicationContext(widget));
    XtUnmanageChild (widget1);
    XtManageChild (widget2);
    XtAppUnlock(XtWidgetToApplicationContext(widget));
    ...
```

You must lock the application context before calling a resource converter directly:

```
    ...
    XtAppLock(app_context);
    XtCvtStringToPixel(dpy, args, num_args, fromVal, toVal, closure_ret);
    XtAppUnlock(app_context);
    ...
```

**XtAppLock** *(continued)*

## See Also

*XtAppUnlock*(1),
*XtProcessLock*(1),
*XtProcessUnlock*(1),
*XtToolkitThreadInitialize*(1)

## Name

XtAppSetExitFlag — terminate an event loop..

## Synopsis

```
void XtAppSetExitFlag(app_context)
    XtAppContext app_context;
```

### Inputs

app_context
> The application context that is to have its event loop terminated.

## Availability

Release 6 and later.

## Description

`XtAppSetExitFlag()` sets an internal termination flag for the specified application context. When the current event dispatch is complete, `XtAppMainLoop()` tests the value of this internal flag and returns if it has been set. Note that prior to X11R6, `XtAppMainLoop()` would never return.

## Usage

`XtAppSetExitFlag()` is useful in multithreaded applications in which you may want to cease event-processing in one thread without terminating other threads of the application.

If you want to use `XtAppSetExitFlag()` with your own custom event loops in an application, use `XtAppGetExitFlag()` in those loops.

## See Also

*XtAppGetExitFlag*(1),
*XtAppMainLoop*(1)

# ■ XtAppUnlock

## Name

XtAppUnlock — release a lock for an application context..

## Synopsis

```
void XtAppUnlock(app_context)
    XtAppContext app_context;
```

### Inputs

    *app_context*
        The application context which was previously locked.

## Availability

Release 6 and later.

## Description

XtAppUnlock() releases an application context mutual-exclusion lock acquired by XtAppLock().

See XtAppLock() for more information, and for examples of locking and unlocking an application context.

## See Also

*XtAppLock*(1),
*XtProcessLock*(1),
*XtProcessUnlock*(1),
*XtToolkitThreadInitialize*(1)

## Name

XtBlockHookProc — interface definition for a block hook callback procedure.

## Synopsis

```
typedef void (*XtBlockHookProc)(XtPointer);
    XtPointer client_data;
```

### Inputs

*client_data*

The client data argument that was registered for this procedure with `XtAppAddBlockHook()`.

## Availability

Release 6 and later.

## Description

An `XtBlockHookProc()` is registered, with its *client_data* value, in a call to `XtApp-pAddBlockHook()`. It is invoked immediately before the Intrinsics block to wait for input events.

See `XtAppAddBlockHook()` for more information.

## See Also

*XtAppAddBlockHook()*(1),
*XtRemoveBlockHook()*(1)

# ■ XtCancelSelectionRequest

## Name

XtCancelSelectionRequest — discard a bundle of deferred selection requests without sending them.

## Synopsis

```
void XtCancelSelectionRequest(requestor, selection)
    Widget requestor;
    Atom selection;
```

### Inputs

*requestor*
> The widget making the request. Must be of class Core or a subclass.

*selection*
> The particular selection desired. Usually XA_PRIMARY.

## Availability

Release 6 and later.

## Description

XtCancelSelectionRequest() discards any selection requests queued since the last call to XtCreateSelectionRequest() for the same *requestor* and *selection* and releases any associated resources. A subsequent call to XtSendSelectionRequest() will not result in any request being made. Subsequent calls to XtGetSelectionValue, XtGetSelectionValues, XtGetSelectionValueIncremental or XtGetSelection-ValuesIncremental will not be deferred.

See XtCreateSelectionRequest() and XtSendSelectionRequest() for a full discussion of bundling deferred selection requests into a single MULTIPLE target request.

## See Also

*XtCreateSelectionRequest*(1),
*XtGetSelectionValue*(1),
*XtGetSelectionValueIncremental*(1),
*XtGetSelectionValues*(1),
*XtGetSelectionValuesIncremental*(1),
*XtSendSelectionRequest*(1)

## Name

XtChangeManagedSet — simultaneously manage and unmanage children.

## Synopsis

```
void XtChangeManagedSet(unmanage_children, num_unmanage_children,
        do_change_proc, client_data, manage_children, num_manage_children)
    WidgetList unmanage_children;
    Cardinal num_unmanage_children;
    XtDoChangeProc do_change_proc;
    XtPointer client_data;
    WidgetList manage_children;
    Cardinal num_manage_children;
```

### Inputs

*unmanage_children*
> The list of widget children to initially remove from the managed set.

*num_unmanage_children*
> The number of entries in the *unmanage_children* list.

*do_change_proc*
> A procedure to invoke between unmanaging and managing the children, or NULL.

*client_data*
> Arbitrary data to be passed to the *do_change_proc*.

*manage_children*
> The list of widget children to add to the managed set.

*num_manage_children*
> The number of entries in the *manage_children* list.

## Availability

Release 6 and later.

## Description

XtChangeManagedSet() unmanages a specified group of children widgets, calls a specified procedure, and then manages a specified group of children widgets. It is equivalent to, but may be more efficient than, the following calls:

```
XtUnmanageChildren(unmanage_children, num_unmanage_children);
if (do_change_proc)
    (*do_change_proc)(XtParent(unmanage_children[0]),
                    unmanage_children, num_unmanage_children,
                    manage_children, num_manage_children,
```

```
                        client_data);
XtManageChildren(manage_children, num_manage_children);
```

If these function are called individually, then the parent composite widget's change_managed() method will be invoked twice—once when the widgets are unmanaged, and once when they are managed again. This is inefficient because the layout of the widgets is computed by the parent widget and then immediately recomputed. With XtChangeManagedSet(), however, some composite widgets allow the changes to be made efficiently with only a single call to the change_managed() method.

The specified do_change_proc procedure may make arbitrary updates to the children widgets. It is usually used in a more specific way, however, as explained in the "Usage" section below.

## Usage

There are two main uses for XtChangeManagedSet(). The first is simply to unmanage one set of widgets and manage a different set efficiently. To do this you'll specify non-overlapping sets of widgets for unmanage_children and manage_children, and specify a NULL do_change_proc. All composite widgets in X11R6 and later can handle this kind of simultaneous update with no do_change_proc.

The second important use of XtChangeManagedSet() is to perform multiple geometry requests efficiently for a set of widgets. When you want to update the geometry of several widgets at once, (i.e. change the size or position of the widgets, or set resources that affect their size or position) it is most efficient to do this while the widgets are unmanaged. Geometry changes are more efficient this way because changes can be made to unmanaged widgets without geometry negotiation. Managing the widgets again effectively batches the geometry changes into a single round of geometry negotiation.

To do this kind of batched geometry update efficiently with XtChangeManagedSet() you pass the same array of widgets for unmanage_children and manage_children, and specify a do_change_proc procedure that makes the required geometry changes to those widgets—the widgets are unmanaged, updated, and managed again by a single call to XtChangeManagedSet(). For certain widgets (those widgets in X11R6 and later that have their allows_change_managed_set field set to True in their Composite class extension record) the unmanaging, geometry updates, and managing can be performed in a single step with only one call to the parent's change_managed() method. For other widgets, the managing and unmanaging will have to be performed in two separate steps, with two calls to change_managed(), but this will usually still be more efficient than making the geometry changes to the children while they are managed.

Note that these two common uses for XtChangeManagedSet() are not mutually exclusive, and can be combined—you might use this function to unmanage four children, change the geometry of three of them, and then re-manage those three children along with two others that were previously unmanaged.

See XtDoChangeProc(2) for information on how to write a callback procedure suitable for use as the *do_change_proc* argument to XtChangeManagedSet().

Not all composite widgets can handle XtChangeManagedSet() requests efficiently. See Composite(3) for information on how to write a widget that can efficiently handle simultaneous unmanage, update, and manage requests for its children widgets. Composite(3) also explains how such a widget uses an extension record to notify the Intrinsics that it can handle these simultaneous updates.

## Algorithm

XtChangeManagedSet() performs the following steps:

* Returns immediately if *num_unmanage_children* and *num_manage_children* are both 0.

* Issues a warning and returns if the widgets specified in the *manage_children* and the *unmanage_children* lists do not all have the same parent, or if that parent is not a subclass of compositeWidgetClass.

* Returns immediately if the common parent is being destroyed.

* If *do_change_proc* is not NULL and the parent's CompositeClassExtension allows_change_managed_set field is False then XtChangeManagedSet performs the following:

* Calls XtUnmanageChildren(*unmanage_children, num_unmanage_children*).

* Calls the *do_change_proc*.

* Calls XtManageChildren (*manage_children, num_manage_children*).

* Otherwise, the following is performed:

* For each child on the *unmanage_children* list if the child is already unmanaged it is ignored, otherwise it is marked as unmanaged and if it is realized and its map_when_managed field is True, it is unmapped.

* If *do_change_proc* is non-NULL the procedure is invoked.

* For each child on the *manage_children* list if the child is already managed or is being destroyed it is ignored, otherwise it is marked as managed.

* If the parent is realized and after all children have been marked, the

change_managed method of the parent is invoked and subsequently some of the newly managed children are made viewable by calling `XtRealizeWidget()` on each previously unmanaged child that is unrealized and mapping each previously unmanaged child that has `map_when_managed True`.

## See Also

*XtManageChildren*(1),
*XtUnmanageChildren*(1),
*XtDoChangeProc*(2),
*Composite*(3),
*change_managed*(4)

## Name

XtCreateSelectionRequest — begin bundling selection request calls.

## Synopsis

```
void XtCreateSelectionRequest(requestor, selection)
    Widget requestor;
    Atom selection;
```

### Inputs

*requestor*
>    The widget making the request. Must be of class Core or a subclass.

*selection*
>    The particular selection desired; usually XA_PRIMARY.

## Availability

Release 6 and later.

## Description

To have the Intrinsics bundle multiple calls to make selection requests into a single request using a MULTIPLE target, use XtCreateSelectionRequest() and XtSendSelectionRequest().

When XtCreateSelectionRequest() is called, subsequent calls to XtGetSelectionValue(), XtGetSelectionValueIncremental(), XtGetSelectionValues() and XtGetSelectionValuesIncremental() with the same values for *requestor* and *selection* are deferred and bundled into a single selection request with multiple targets. The bundled request is sent as a single MULTIPLE request when XtSendSelectionRequest() is called.

The individual selection target requests made between calls to XtCreateSelectionRequest() and XtSendSelectionRequest() can be given parameters by preceding the request with a call to XtSetSelectionParameters(), just as if it were an individual request.

See the *Inter-Client Communications Conventions Manual, Version 2.0* for an explaination of how the MULTIPLE selection target uses parameters to group individual selection requests into a single request.

## Usage

XtGetSelectionValues() and XtGetSelectionValuesIncremental() can also be used to create MULTIPLE target requests. Using these functions may be easier than

## XtCreateSelectionRequest (continued)

using XtCreateSelectionRequest() and XtSendSelectionRequest() in some cases. Note, though, that XtGetSelectionValues() and XtGetSelectionValuesIncremental() do not allow parameters to be specified for the individual targets within the MULTIPLE request.

To cancel the creation of a MULTIPLE selection request without sending any of the individual deferred requests, call XtCancelSelectionRequest().

## See Also

*XtCancelSelectionRequest*(1),
*XtGetSelectionValue*(1),
*XtGetSelectionValueIncremental*(1),
*XtGetSelectionValues*(1),
*XtGetSelectionValuesIncremental*(1),
*XtSendSelectionRequest*(1),
*XtSetSelectionParameters*(1)

## Name

XtDeallocateProc — interface definition for the deallocate() method.

## Synopsis

```
typedef void (*XtDeallocateProc)(Widget, XtPointer);
    Widget widget;
    XtPointer more_bytes;
```

### Inputs

*widget*
> The widget being destroyed.

*more_bytes*
> Auxiliary memory that was received from the allocate() method, or NULL.

## Availability

Release 6 and later.

## Description

XtDeallocateProc is the type of the Object class extension deallocate() method. See deallocate(4).

## See Also

*deallocate*(4)

# ■ XtDispatchEventToWidget

## Name

XtDispatchEventToWidget — dispatch an event directly to a specified widget.

## Synopsis

```
Boolean XtDispatchEventToWidget (widget, event)
    Widget widget;
    XEvent* event;
```

### Inputs

*widget*
> The widget to which to dispatch the event.

*event*
> A pointer to the event to be dispatched.

### Returns

`True` if the event was dispatched to any event handler; `False` otherwise.

## Availability

Release 6 and later.

## Description

`XtDispatchEventToWidget()` scans the list of event handlers registered for the specified widget and calls each handler that has been registered to handle the type of the specified event, subject to the *continue_to_dispatch* value returned by each handler (see `XtEventHandler(2)`).

The Intrinsics behave as if event handlers were registered at the head of the list for `Expose`, `NoExpose`, `GraphicsExpose`, and `VisibilityNotify` events to invoke the widget's expose method according to the exposure compression rules (see `expose(4)`) and to update the widget's `visible` field if `visible_interest` is `True`. These internal event handlers never set *continue_to_dispatch* to `False`.

`XtDispatchEventToWidget()` returns `True` if any event handler was called and `False` otherwise.

## Usage

`XtDispatchEventToWidget()` is intended for use in low-level event dispatcher procedures registered with `XtSetEventDispatcher()`. Event dispatchers are usually used when handling extension events in an Xt program.

Do not confuse `XtDispatchEventToWidget()` with `XtDispatchEvent()`. `XtDispatchEvent()` is a high-level function that first invokes an appropriate event dispatcher based on the type of the event. This event dispatcher then determines the widget that the event should be dispatched to and calls the low-level XtDispatchEventToWidget().

See XtDispatchEvent() for a description of how the default event dispatcher decides which widget to direct events to.

## See Also

*XtDispatchEvent()(1)*,
*XtSetEventDispatcher(1)*,
*XtGetKeyboardFocusWidget(1)*,
*XtWindowToWidget(1)*,
*XtEventDispatchProc(2)*,
*XtEventHandler(2)*,
*expose(4)*

# ■ XtDoChangeProc

## Name

XtDoChangeProc — interface definition for the procedure invoked by XtChange-ManagedSet().

## Synopsis

```
typedef void (XtDoChangeProc*)(Widget, WidgetList, Cardinal*, WidgetList,
     Cardinal*, XtPointer);
  Widget composite_parent;
  WidgetList unmange_children;
  Cardinal *num_unmanage_children;
  WidgetList manage_children;
  Cardinal *num_manage_children;
  XtPointer client_data;
```

### Inputs

*composite_parent*
> The composite parent whose managed set is being altered.

*unmanage_children*
> The list of children just removed from the managed set.

*num_unmanage_children*
> The number of entries in the *unmanage_children* list.

*manage_children*
> The list of children about to be added to the managed set.

*num_manage_children*
> The number of entries in the *manage_children* list.

*client_data*
> The client data value passed to XtChangeManagedSet().

## Availability

Release 6 and later.

## Description

An XtDoChangeProc() is specified in a call to XtChangeManagedSet() and is invoked by XtChangeManagedSet() after it has unmanaged one list of widgets and before it has managed the other list of widgets.

The purpose of passing an XtDoChangeProc() to XtChangeManagedSet() is to provide a way to modify the geometries of widgets while they are unmanaged, thus avoiding the overhead of geometry negotiation. See XtChangeManagedSet() for more details.

## See Also

*XtChangeManagedSet*(1)

# XtEventDispatchProc

## Name

XtEventDispatchProc — interface definition for an extension event dispatch procedure.

## Synopsis

```
typedef Boolean (*XtEventDispatchProc)(XEvent*)
    XEvent *event;
```

### Inputs

*event*
> Passes the event to be dispatched.

### Returns

True if the event could be dispatched to a widget, or False otherwise.

## Availability

Release 6 and later.

## Description

An XtEventDispatchProc() is registered with XtSetEventDispatcher() and is invoked by XtDispatchEvent() when an event of the specified type and specified display arrives. The job of an XtEventDispatchProc() is to dispatch the event to a widget or elsewhere as appropriate for the event type.

An event dispatcher should perform the following steps:

- Determine whether the event is to be dispatched or discarded.

- If the event is to be dispatched, determine whether the event is to be dispatched to a widget or to elsewhere.

- If the event is to be dispatched to a widget, determine which widget it should be dispatched to.

- Call XFilterEvent() to give any running X Input Method the opportunity to process the event. If the event is to be dispatched to a widget, pass the window of the widget in this call. If the event will be discarded, call XFilterEvent() with a window of None. If the event will be dispatched to some other object with an associated window, pass that associated window.

- If `XFilterEvent()` returns `True`, then an active input method has dispatched the event, and the `XtEventDispatchProc` should return `True` without dispatching the event any further.

- If `XFilterEvent()` returns `False`, then the event should be dispatched or discarded as appropriate. If the event is to be dispatched to a widget, the procedure should call `XtDispatchEventToWidget()`. If the event is to be dispatched elsewhere, the `XtEventDispatchProc` should attempt to do that.

- The procedure should return `True` if the event was successfully dispatched and `False` if it was discarded or unsuccessfully dispatched. If the procedure calls `XtDispatchEventToWidget()` then it should return `True` if that procedure returned `True` and `False` if that procedure returned `False`.

## Usage

In practice, writing an event dispatch procedure is not as complicated as the description above makes it seem. For most event types, or for most sets of extension events, you will just call `XtWindowToWidget()` to determine the widget to dispatch the event to (based on the `window` field of the event structure) and call `XtDispatchEvent-ToWidget()` to dispatch the event to that widget. In these cases you need not worry about dispatching to other objects or about discarding events. For proper internationalization, note that it is important that you call `XFilterEvent()`, however.

Some dispatchers for extension events may wish to forward events according to the Intrinsics' keyboard focus mechanism. To determine which widget is the end result of keyboard event forwarding, use `XtGetKeyboardFocusWidget()` in conjunction with `XtWindowToWidget()`.

## See Also

*XtAddEventHandler*(1),
*XtDispatchEventToWidget*(1),
*XtGetKeyboardFocusWidget*(1),
*XtInsertEventHandler*(1),
*XtInsertEventTypeHandler*(1),
*XtRegisterExtensionSelector*(1),
*XtRemoveEventHandler*(1),
*XtRemoveEventTypeHandler*(1),
*XtSetEventDispatcher*(1),
*XtEventHandler*(2),
*XtExtensionSelectProc*(2)

# XtExtensionSelectProc

## Name

XtExtensionSelectProc — interface definition for an extension event selector procedure.

## Synopsis

```
typedef void (*XtExtensionSelectProc)(Widget, int *, XtPointer *, int,
    XtPointer);
    Widget widget;
    int *event_types;
    XtPointer *select_data;
    int count;
    XtPointer client_data;
```

### Inputs

*widget*

The widget that is being realized or is having an event handler added or removed.

*event_types*

An array of event types that the widget has registered event handlers for.

*select_data*

An array of the select_data parameters specified in XtInsertEventType-Handler().

*count*

The number of entries in the *event_types* and *select_data* arrays.

*client_data*

Arbitrary data specified when the procedure was registered.

## Availability

Release 6 and later.

## Description

An XtExtensionSelectProc() is registered with XtRegisterExtensionSelector().
It is called by the Intrinsics in order to request delivery of appropriate extension events
from the X server. It is called when a widget with extension event handlers is realized,
or when a realized widget has extension event handlers added or removed with XtIn-
sertEventTypeHandler() or XtRemoveEventTypeHandler().

The *widget* argument specifies the widget for which events are to be selected. You will
usually use the window of the widget to select events, though for some extensions you

might select events on some other X server object, such as a Buffer in the XMB multi-buffering extension.

The *event_types* and *select_data* arrays both contain *count* elements and specify the types of events that should be selected. The elements of *event_types* are integers that specify the numerical event number—the value of the type field in the event structure. The elements of the *select_data* array are the *select_data* values passed in the calls to XtInsertEventTypeHandler() when each of the extension events was selected. These values will often be event masks of some sort (or pointers to event masks) that correspond to each of the event types in the *event_types* array and are used to select events from the server.

X protocol extensions generally do not allow you to add and remove individual events from the list of selected events; instead, they provide a single protocol request that allows you to specify a complete list or bitfield that specifies all the desired event types. To request or remove an event, simply update the list or bitfield to match the new desired set of events. Thus, when an XtExtensionSelectProc is called, it is not passed a single event to add or remove; it is passed an array of all events (within its registered range of events) that should be selected. If three events from a particular extension are selected for a realized widget, and XtInsertEventTypeHandler() is called to add a handler for another one, the event selector procedure will be called with a *count* argument of four. Then if XtRemoveEventTypeHandler() is called to remove one of those handlers, the selector procedure will be called again with a *count* of three, and the *select_data* for the three event types that should remain selected.

## Usage

For simple extensions, an XtExtensionSelectProc will generally loop through the *select_data* array and combine the individual values to produce a single event mask that it can pass to an event selector function. For the SHAPE or MBX extensions, for example, it would pass the combined mask to XShapeSelectInput() or XmbufChangeBufferAttributes().

Other extensions may handle events in a different way. The X Input extension supports more than 32 event types, for example, so using traditional event masks is awkward. Instead, this extension would have you pass a pointer to an XEventClass structure as your *select_data* argument to XtInsertEventTypeHandler(), and then in the event selector procedure copy those XEventClass structures into an array and pass the array to the X Input extension function XSelectExtensionEvent().

**XtExtensionSelectProc** *(continued)*

## See Also

*XtAddEventHandler*(1),
*XtDispatchEventToWidget*(1),
*XtGetKeyboardFocusWidget*(1),
*XtInsertEventHandler*(1),
*XtInsertEventTypeHandler*(1),
*XtRegisterExtensionSelector*(1),
*XtRemoveEventHandler*(1),
*XtRemoveEventTypeHandler*(1),
*XtSetEventDispatcher*(1),
*XtEventDispatchProc*(2),
*XtEventHandler*(2)

## Name

XtGetClassExtension — obtain a class extension record for a widget class.

## Synopsis

```
XtPointer XtGetClassExtension(object_class, byte_offset,
type, version, record_size);
    WidgetClass object_class;
    Cardinal byte_offset;
    XrmQuark type;
    long version;
    Cardinal record_size;
```

### Inputs

*object_class*
> The object class containing the extension list to be searched.

*byte_offset*
> The offset, in bytes from the base of the class record, of the extension field to be searched. Use XtOffsetOf().

*type*
> The record_type of the class extension to be located.

*version*
> The minimum acceptable version of the class extension required for a match.

*record_size*
> The minimum acceptable length of the class extension record required for a match, or 0.

### Returns

A pointer to a matching extension record, or NULL if no match is found.

## Availability

Release 6 and later.

## Description

XtGetClassExtension() searches the list of extension records at the specified offset in the specified object class for an extension record with specified *type*, a version greater than or equal to the specified *version*, and a record size greater than or equal to the specified *record_size*, if that argument is nonzero.

XtGetClassExtension returns a pointer to a matching extension record or NULL if no match is found. The returned extension record must not be modified or freed by the caller if the caller is not the object class owner.

## Usage

Only widget writers should need to use this function.

Class extension records provide a way of adding additional fields to a class structure while maintaining backward binary compatability with older versions of the widget. See the "Background" section for a complete explanation of extension records.

## Background

It may be necessary at times to add new fields to already existing widget class structures. To permit this to be done without requiring recompilation of all subclasses, the last field in a class part structure should be an extension pointer (and is usually named extension). If no extension fields for a class have yet been defined, subclasses should initialize the value of the extension pointer to NULL.

If extension fields exist, as is the case with the Composite, Constraint and Shell classes, subclasses can provide values for these fields by setting the extension pointer for the appropriate part in their class structure to point to a statically declared extension record containing the additional fields. Setting the extension pointer is never mandatory; code that uses fields in the extension record must always check the extension pointer and take some appropriate default action if it is NULL.

In order to permit multiple subclasses and libraries to chain extension records from a single extension field, extension records should be declared as a linked list and each extension record definition should contain the following four fields at the beginning of the structure declaration:

```
struct {
    XtPointer next_extension;
    XrmQuark record_type;
    long version;
    Cardinal record_size;
};
```

next_extension
> Specifies the next record in the linked list, or NULL if this record is the last one in the list.

record_type
> Specifies the particular structure declaration to which each extension record instance conforms.

version

> Specifies a version number for the extension record. This is generally a symbolic constant supplied by the definer of the structure.

record_size

> Specifies the total number of bytes allocated for the extension record, including the bytes used by these four required fields.

The record_type field of an extension record is an XrmQuark that identifies the contents of the extension record and is used by the definer of the record to locate the record in a list of extension records. The record_type field is normally set to the result of calling XrmStringToQuark() for a standard string constant (registered with the X Consortium Registry). The Intrinsics reserve all record type strings beginning with the two characters "XT" for future standard uses. The value NULLQUARK may also be used by the class part owner in extension records attached to its own class part extension field to identify the extension record unique to that particular class.

The version field is an owner-defined constant that may be used to identify binary files that have been compiled with alternate definitions of the remainder of the extension record data structure. The private header file for a widget class should provide a symbolic constant for subclasses to use to initialize this field. The record_size field value is the size of the extension structure including the four required header fields and should normally be initialized with sizeof().

## See Also

*XrmStringToQuark*(1),
*XtOffsetOf*(1)

# ■ XtGetDisplays

## Name

XtGetDisplays — return a list of displays in an application context.

## Synopsis

```
void XtGetDisplays(app_context, dpy_return, num_dpy_return)
    XtAppContext app_context;
    Display ***dpy_return;
    Cardinal *num_dpy_return;
```

### Inputs

*app_context*

    The application context to have its display list queried.

### Outputs

*dpy_return*

    The address of a `Display **` at which an allocated array of `Display *` pointers should be stored.

*num_dpy_return*

    The address of a `Cardinal` in which the number of open displays in *app_context* will be returned.

## Availability

Release 6 and later.

## Description

`XtGetDisplays()` retreives a list of the displays associated with the specified application context.

The returned array is in allocated memory and should be freed when no longer needed with `XtFree()`.

## Usage

`XtGetDisplays()` may be used by an external agent to query the list of open displays that belong to an application context. Once the list of displays is obtained, `XtHooksOfDisplay()` allows an external agent to specify hooks for each display and to obtain a complete list of root shells on each display.

This function can also be useful in other contexts as well—when writing utility routines that work for single and multi-display applications, for example.

If you do not have the application context value to use with `XtGetDisplays()`, you can obtain it from a widget with `XtWidgetToApplicationContext()`.

## See Also

*XtHooksOfDisplay*(1),
*XtWidgetToApplicationContext*(1)

# ■ XtGetKeyboardFocusWidget

## Name

XtGetKeyboardFocusWidget — get the target of keyboard event forwarding.

## Synopsis

```
Widget XtGetKeyboardFocusWidget(widget)
    Widget widget;
```

### Inputs

    *widget*

        The widget to get forwarding information for.

### Returns

The widget that would be the end result of keyboard event forward for a keyboard event for *widget*.

## Availability

Release 6 and later.

## Description

XtGetKeyboardFocusWidget() takes the Intrinsics modal cascade and keyboard focus mechanisms into account and returns the widget that would receive a keyboard event directed to the specified *widget*. See XtDispatchEvent() for a detailed description of how these mechanisms affect the delivery of events.

## Usage

XtGetKeyboardFocusWidget() is intended for use in event dispatch procedures for extension events or for custom event handling. See XtSetEventDispatcher() and XtEventDispatchProc(2). You may also find this function useful for querying keyboard focus in an application so that it can be temporarily changed and restored with XtSetKeyboardFocus().

## See Also

*XtDispatchEventToWidget*(1),
*XtSetEventDispatcher*(1),
*XtSetKeyboardFocus*(1),
*XtWindowToWidget*(1),
*XtEventDispatchProc*(2)

## Name

XtGetSelectionParameters — query parameters associated with a selection conversion request.

## Synopsis

```
void
XtGetSelectionParameters(owner, selection, request_id, type_return,
        value_return, length_return, format_return)
    Widget owner;
    Atom selection;
    XtRequestId request_id;
    Atom *type_return;
    XtPointer *value_return;
    unsigned long *length_return;
    int *format_return;
```

### Inputs

*owner*

> The widget that owns the specified selection.

*selection*

> The selection being processed.

*request_id*

> The requestor id for incremental selections, or NULL for atomic transfers.

### Outputs

*type_return*

> The address of an atom in which the property type of the parameters are stored.

*value_return*

> The address at which a pointer to the parameters are to be stored. A NULL is stored if no parameters accompany the request.

*length_return*

> The address at which the number of data elements in *value_return* are stored.

*format_return*

> The address at which the size in bits of each of the elements of *value* is stored.

**XtGetSelectionParameters** *(continued)*

## Availability

Release 6 and later.

## Description

XtGetSelectionParameters() returns the type, contents, length, and format of a property associated with a pending selection request specified by *selection*. The contents of this property are the parameters specified by the selection requestor—for certain selection target types, these parameters specify additional information to be used in the selection conversion.

XtGetSelectionParameters() may only be called from within an XtConvertSelectionProc or from within the first call to an XtConvertSelectionIncrProc with a new *request_id*.

The particular parameters passed with a selection request, and the type, length, and format of the property are arbitrary and will be defined by the convention that governs the particular type of data target that has been requested. See XtSetSelectionParameters() for more information.

## Usage

None of the common selection target types use parameters, so you will rarely have to call this function.

## See Also

*XtOwnSelection*(1),
*XtSetSelectionParameters*(1),
*XtConvertSelectionProc*(2),
*XtConvertSelectionIncrProc*(2)

## Name

XtHooksOfDisplay — obtain the "hook registration object" for a display.

## Synopsis

```
Widget XtHooksOfDisplay(display)
    Display *display;
```

### Inputs

*display*
> The display for which the hook object is to be returned.

### Returns

The hook object of the specified display.

## Availability

Release 6 and later.

## Description

XtHooksOfDisplay() returns the "hook object" for a display. This object has callback resources that provide hooks at many important points in the Intrinsics. The object also has resources that can be queried to return a counted array of all the root shells of an application. See Hook Object(3) for a complete description of the hook object widget class and its callbacks and resources.

## Background

Applications may register functions which are called at a particular control points in the Intrinsics. These functions are intended to be used to provide notification of an "X Toolkit event"—widget creation, for example—to an external agent such as an interactive resource editor, drag-and-drop server, or an aid for physically challenged users. The control points containing such registration hooks are identified in a "hook registration" object.

The hook object is a private, implementation-dependent subclass of Object. The hook object has no parent. Its resources are callback lists for hooks, and two read-only resources for getting a list of parentless shells. All of the callback lists are initially empty. When a display is closed the hook object associated with it is destroyed.

The following procedures can be called with the hook registration object as an argument:

- `XtAddCallback()`, `XtAddCallbacks()`, `XtRemoveCallback()`, `XtRemoveCallbacks()`, `XtRemoveAllCallbacks()`, `XtCallCallbacks()`, `XtHasCallbacks()`, `XtCallCallbackList()`

- `XtClass()`, `XtSuperclass()`, `XtIsSubclass()`, `XtCheckSubclass()`, `XtIsObject()`, `XtIsRectObj()`, `XtIsWidget()`, `XtIsComposite()`, `XtIsConstraint()`, `XtIsShell()`, `XtIsOverrideShell()`, `XtIsWMShell()`, `XtIsVendorShell()`, `XtIsTransientShell()`, `XtIsToplevelShell()`, `XtIsApplicationShell()`, `XtIsSessionShell()`

- `XtWidgetToApplicationContext()`

- `XtName()`, `XtParent()`, `XtDisplayOfObject()`, `XtScreenOfObject()`

- `XtSetValues()`, `XtGetValues()`, `XtVaSetValues()`, `XtVaGetValues()`

## See Also

*XtGetDisplays*(1),
*Hook Object*(3)

## Name

XtInsertEventTypeHandler — register an event handler for a core or extension event..

## Synopsis

```
void XtInsertEventTypeHandler(widget, event_type, select_data, proc,
     client_data, position)
   Widget widget;
   int event_type;
   XtPointer select_data;
   XtEventHandler proc;
   XtPointer client_data;
   XtListPosition position;
```

### Inputs

*widget*

> The widget for which this event handler is being registered. This must be a windowed widget—a widget of class Core or a subclass.

*event_type*

> The event type for which to call this event handler; may specify a core protocol event or an extension event.

*select_data*

> Data used to request events of the specified type from the server, or NULL. Pointed at data must remain valid as long as the event handler is registered.

*proc*

> The event handler to be called when an event of the specified type for the specified widget is received.

*client_data*

> Arbitrary data to be passed to the event handler.

*position*

> Where the event handler should be inserted in the list of previously registered event handlers for the widget. Specify either XtListHead or XtListTail.

## Availability

Release 6 and later.

## Description

XtInsertEventTypeHandler() registers a procedure, *proc*, that is to be called when an event that matches the specified *event_type* is dispatched to the specified *widget*.

*event_type* is an integer that appears in the type field of all event structures. For core X Protocol events, there are pre-defined constants for each type of event (e.g. KeyPress). For extension events, this *event_type* value will be the sum of a constant defined by the extension and the *first_event_return* value returned by your call to XQueryExtension(). Some extensions will have custom functions to query the extension, and you may use these functions instead of XQueryExtension(). If the extension defines new event types, this function should return the event type value for the first event type it defines. For example, for the MBX multibuffering extension, you might specify an *event_type*:

```
mbx_first_event + MultibufferUpdateNotify.
```

The *select_data* argument specifies data that will be used to tell the X server that the widget is interested in receiving events of the specified type. If *event_type* specifies one of the core X protocol events then *select_data* must be a pointer to a value of type EventMask, indicating the event mask to be used to select for the desired event. This event mask is included in the value returned by XtBuildEventMask(). For core event types, if the widget is realized, XtInsertEventTypeHandler() calls XSelectInput() if necessary. Specifying NULL for *select_data* is equivalent to specifying a pointer to an event mask containing 0—the event handler will still be registered, but the event type will not be requested from the server; this is similar to the behavior of XtInsertRawEventHandler().

If, on the other hand, *event_type* specifies an extension event type then the Intrinsics cannot simply select the event by passing an event mask to XSelectInput(). Extension events are requested from the server in an extension-specific way. In order to tell the Intrinsics how to request extension event types, you must register a "selector procedure" of type XtExtensionSelectProc by calling XtRegisterExtensionSelector(). Assuming an extension selector has been registered, XtInsertEventTypeHandler() will call the selector and pass it the specified *select_data*. The value you pass for *select_data* will thus depend on the implementation of the selector procedure. See XtRegisterExtensionSelector() for more information. If you do not register a selector procedure for an extension, you can still register event handlers for events from that extension, but the Intrinsics will not be able to automatically request those events from the server. Instead, you should pass NULL for *select_data*, and explicitly request the events for the appropriate windows in your application code.

Note that whether a core or extension event is to be selected, the Intrinsics are not required to copy the data pointed to by *select_data*, so the caller must ensure that

that data remains valid as long as the event handler remains registered with this value of `select_data`.

The `proc` argument is the event hander that is to be registered. It is of type `XtEventHandler`, the standard event handler registered for core events with `XtAddEventHandler()` and `XtInsertEventHandler()`. See `XtEventHandler(2)` for an explanation of how to write an event handler. The specified event handler, `proc`, will be invoked with the specified `client_data` value as one of its arguments.

Each widget has a single registered event handler list, which will contain any procedure/client data pair exactly once if it is registered with `XtInsertEventTypeHandler()`, regardless of the manner in which it is which it is registered, and regardless of the value(s) of `select_data`. If the procedure is already registered with the same `client_data` value, the specified mask augments the existing mask and the procedure is repositioned in the list.

The `position` argument allows the client to control the order of invocation of event handlers registered for the event type. If you do not care about the order, you should specify `XtListTail`, which registers this event handler after any previously registered handlers for this event type. You can also specify `XtListHead` which will place the event handler at the head of the list, where it will be called before any previously registered handlers.

## Usage

To register an event handler for normal core protocol X events, you can use the simpler `XtAddEventHandler()` or other related functions.

You can remove an event handler registered with `XtInsertEventTypeHandler()` with `XtRemoveEventTypeHandler()`.

The discussion above explains that you may need to register an extension event selector procedure for each extension that you use. In order to use extension events in your Xt programs, there is one additional step you must take—you must register an event dispatcher procedure with `XtSetEventDispatcher()`. You have to do this because the default Xt event dispatcher discards all extension events, and because extension events may require special computation to determine which widget they should be dispatched to. See `XtSetEventDispatcher()` and `XtEventDispatchProc(2)` for more information.

## See Also

*XtAddEventHandler*(1),
*XtDispatchEventToWidget*(1),

*XtGetKeyboardFocusWidget*(1),
*XtInsertEventHandler*(1),
*XtRegisterExtensionSelector*(1),
*XtRemoveEventHandler*(1),
*XtRemoveEventTypeHandler*(1),
*XtSetEventDispatcher*(1),
*XtEventDispatchProc*(2),
*XtEventHandler*(2),
*XtExtensionSelectorProc*(2)

## Name

XtIsSessionShell — test whether a widget is a subclass of the SessionShell widget class.

## Synopsis

```
Boolean XtIsSessionShell(object)
    Widget object;
```

### Inputs

*object*

Specifies the object whose class is to be checked; may be of class Object or any subclass thereof.

### Returns

True if *object* is of class SessionShell or a subclass thereof; False otherwise.

## Availability

Release 6 and later.

## Description

XtIsSessionShell() tests whether *object* is a subclass of the SessionShell widget class. It may be defined as a macro or a function, and is equivalent to, but may be faster than, calling XtIsSubclass() for this class.

## See Also

*XtIsSubclass*(1)

# ■ XtLastEventProcessed

## Name

XtLastEventProcessed — obtain the most recently processed event.

## Synopsis

```
XEvent *XtLastEventProcessed(display)
    Display *display;
```

### Inputs

*display*
> The display connection from which to retrieve the event.

### Returns

The event most recently passed to `XtDispatchEvent()`, or NULL if no events have yet been processed for the specified display.

## Availability

Release 6 and later.

## Description

`XtLastEventProcessed()` returns the last event passed to `XtDispatchEvent()` for the specified display, or returns NULL if there is no such event.

You must not modify the contents of the returned event.

## See Also

*XtDispatchEvent*(1),
*XtLastTimestampProcessed*(1)

## Name

XtNoticeSignal — trigger a registered signal callback from a signal handler.

## Synopsis

```
void XtNoticeSignal(id)
    XtSignalId id;
```

### Inputs

*id*    The `XtSignalId` that identifies the signal callback to be invoked.

## Availability

Release 6 and later.

## Description

`XtNoticeSignal()` triggers the Intrinsics to invoke the signal callback associated with *id*. A signal callback is registered with `XtAppAddSignal()`, and *id* is the `XtSignalId` value returned when a signal callback and its client data are registered with that function.

## Usage

`XtNoticeSignal()` is the only Xt function that can be safely called from a signal handler on a POSIX-based system. It is used in signal handlers to notify the Intrinsics that a signal has occurred and the the signal callback specified by *id* should be invoked. The Intrinsics will not invoke the callback until it is safe to do so, and so it may contain arbitrary function calls; not the highly restricted set that are allowed in the signal handler itself.

See `XtAppAddSignal()` for a full discussion of signal handling in Xt applications.

## See Also

*XtAppAddSignal*(1),
*XtRemoveSignal*(1),
*XtSignalCallbackProc*(2)

# ■ XtOpenApplication

## Name

XtOpenApplication — initialize the X Toolkit internals, create an application context, open and initialize a display, and create the initial root shell instance.

## Synopsis

```
Widget XtOpenApplication(app_context_return,
application_class, options,
num_options, argc_in_out,
argv_in_out, fallback_resources,
widget_class
args, num_args)
      XtAppContext *app_context_return;
      String application_class;
      XrmOptionDescList options;
      Cardinal num_options;
      int *argc_in_out;
      String *argv_in_out;
      String *fallback_resources;
      WidgetClass widget_class;
      ArgList args;
      Cardinal num_args;
```

### Inputs

   application_class
      Specifies the class name of the application.

   options
      Specifies an array of XrmOptionDescRec which describe how to parse the command line.

   num_options
      Specifies the number of elements in options.

   argc_in_out
      Specifies the address of the number of command line arguments. This argument is of type int * in Release 5 and of type Cardinal * in Release 4.

   argv_in_out
      Specifies the array of command line arguments.

   fallback_resources
      Specifies a NULL-terminated array of resource specification strings to be used if the application class resource file cannot be opened or read, or NULL if no fallback resources are desired.

*widget_class*
> Specifies the class of the widget to be created. Must be shellWidgetClass or a subclass.

*args*
> Specifies an argument list to override any other resource specifications for the created shell widget.

*num_args*
> Specifies the number of elements in *args*.

**Outputs**

*app_context_return*
> Returns the newly created application context, if non-NULL.

*argc_in_out*
> Returns the number of command line arguments remaining after the command line is parsed by XtDisplayInitialize().

*argv_in_out*
> Returns the command line as modified by XtDisplayInitialize().

**Returns**

A root shell widget of the class specified by *widget_class*.

## Availability

Release 6 and later; supersedes XtAppInitialize().

## Description

XtOpenApplication() is a convenience procedure that most applications will use to initialize themselves. It does the following:

- Calls XtToolkitInitialize() to do Intrinsics internal initialization.

- Calls XtCreateApplicationContext() to create an application context for the application. If *app_context_return* is non-NULL, the newly created application context is stored at the address it points to.

- Calls XtAppSetFallbackResources() passing the application context and *fallback_resources*, unless that argument is NULL.

- Calls XtOpenDisplay() passing the application context, *application_class*, *options*, *num_options*, *argc_in_out*, and *argv_in_out*. XtOpenDisplay() determines the display name and the application name from the command line or environment variables, opens a connection to the display, and calls XtDisplayInitialize() to parse the command line and build the resource database. The command line as modified by XtDisplayInitialize() is returned in *argc_in_out* and argv_in_out.

- Calls XtAppCreateShell() to create a root shell of the class specified by *widget_class*, with *args* and *num_args* used to override any widget resources found in the database.

If the display cannot be opened, an error message is issued and XtOpenApplication() terminates the application.

## Usage

XtOpenApplication() is identical to XtAppInitialize(), except that it has an additional *widget_class* argument that allows you to specify the class of the root widget to be created. The recommended value for this argument is sessionShellWidgetClass so that clients can participate in session management. See XtAppInitialize() for detailed information on the application initialization procedure.

You can also use XtVaOpenApplication() to initialize an application. It is like XtOpenApplication() but takes a NULL-terminated variable-length argument list of resources instead of the *args* and *num_args* arguments.

## See Also

*XtAppCreateShell*(1),
*XtAppInitialize*(1),
*XtAppSetFallbackResources*(1),
*XtCreateApplicationContext*(1),
*XtDisplayInitialize*(1),
*XtOpenDisplay*(1),
*XtResolvePathname*(1),
*XtScreenDatabase*(1),
*XtSetLanguageProc*(1),
*XtToolkitInitialize*(1),
*XtVaOpenApplication*(1)

## Name

XtProcessLock — obtain exclusive access to global process data structures.

## Synopsis

```
void XtProcessLock()
```

### Inputs

None.

## Availability

Release 6 and later.

## Description

`XtProcessLock()` is used in multithreaded applications to ensure that only one thread at a time can access process-global data structures. `XtProcessLock()` blocks until it is able to acquire the lock—if some other thread owns the lock, then the thread that called `XtProcessLock()` will stop executing, and `XtProcessLock()` will not return until the lock has been relinquished by its previous owner and acquired by the calling thread. Once a process lock is acquired, it should be relinquished with `XtProcessUnlock()` as soon as it is no longer required.

A client may acquire a lock multiple times—the effect is cumulative—the client must ensure that the lock is released an equal number of times in order for the lock to be acquired by another thread.

To lock both an application context and the process at the same time, call `XtAppLock()` first and then `XtProcessLock()`. To release both locks, call `XtProcessUnlock()` first and then `XtAppUnlock()`. The order is important to avoid deadlock.

## Usage

Application writers will rarely need to use locking in their multithreaded applications. Widget writers will need to use locking, but it will usually be sufficient to simply lock application-context data with `XtAppLock()`. Widget writers might use `XtProcessLock()` to guarantee mutually exclusive access to a widget's static data, for example.

Any Xt application that uses multiple threads and locks must call the function `XtToolkitThreadInitialize()` before any other Xt functions.

See `XtAppLock()` for more information and examples about locking in Xt applications.

**XtProcessLock** *(continued)*

## See Also

*XtAppLock*(1),
*XtAppUnlock*(1),
*XtProcessUnlock*(1),
*XtToolkitThreadInitialize*(1)

## Name

XtProcessUnlock — relinquish a lock for process-global data structures.

## Synopsis

```
void XtProcessUnlock()
```

### Inputs

None.

## Availability

Release 6 and later.

## Description

XtProcessUnlock() relinquishes a mutual-exclusion lock on process-global data that was obtained with XtProcessLock().

See XtProcessLock() and XtAppLock() for more information.

## See Also

*XtAppLock*(1),
*XtAppUnlock*(1),
*XtProcessLock*(1),
*XtToolkitThreadInitialize*(1)

# ■ XtRegisterDrawable

## Name

XtRegisterDrawable — associate a window or pixmap with a widget..

## Synopsis

```
void XtRegisterDrawable(display, drawable, widget)
    Display *display;
    Drawable drawable;
    Widget widget;
```

### Inputs

*display*
> The drawable's display.

*drawable*
> The drawable to register.

*widget*
> The widget to register the drawable for. This must be a windowed widget—of class Core or a subclass.

## Availability

Release 6 and later.

## Description

XtRegisterDrawable() associates the *drawable* with *widget* so that future calls to XtWindowToWidget() for *drawable* will return *widget*. The default event dispatcher will dispatch future events that arrive for *drawable* to *widget* as though the event contained the widget's window, but the event itself will not be changed in any way when dispatched.

If the drawable is already registered with another widget, or if the drawable is the window of a widget in the client's widget tree, the results of calling XtRegisterDrawable() are undefined.

## Usage

Sometimes an application must handle events for drawables that are not associated with widgets in its widget tree. Examples include handling GraphicsExpose and NoExpose events on Pixmaps, and handling PropertyNotify events on the root window. XtRegisterDrawable() provides a way to do this.

XtRegisterDrawable() specifies that events on a given drawable should be delivered to a given widget. In order to actually handle those events, however, you will want to register an event handler or action procedure for the specific event type. You can use the window field of the event structure to determine whether the event actually occurred on the widget, or on one of the drawables registered for that widget.

Events from a drawable registered with XtRegisterDrawable() may be delivered even before the specified widget has been realized. Take care in your event handlers or action procedures not to assume that the widget has a valid window when events from other windows or pixmaps arrive.

Use XtUnregisterDrawable() to dissociate a drawable from a widget.

### See Also

*XtUnregisterDrawable*(1),
*XtWindowToWidget*(1)

# ■ XtRegisterExtensionSelector

## Name

XtRegisterExtensionSelector — register a procedure to select extension events.

## Synopsis

```
void XtRegisterExtensionSelector(display, min_event_type, max_event_type,
        proc, client_data)
    Display *display;
    int min_event_type;
    int max_event_type;
    XtExtensionSelectProc proc;
    XtPointer client_data;
```

### Inputs

*display*
> The display for which the extension selector is to be registered.

*min_event_type*
> The range of event types for which the selector will be used.

*max_event_type*
> The range of event types for which the selector will be used.

*proc*
> The extension selector procedure.

*client_data*
> Arbitrary data to be passed to the extension selector.

## Availability

Release 6 and later.

## Description

XtRegisterExtensionSelector() registers the procedure *proc* to be called with the specified client data, to arrange for the delivery of extension event types within the specified range to widgets.

If *min_event_type* and *max_event_type* match the parameters to a previous call to XtRegisterExtensionSelector() for the same *display*, then *proc* and *client_data* replace the previously registered values. If the range specified by *min_event_type* and *max_event_type* overlaps the range of the parameters to a previous call for the same display in any other way, an error results.

## Usage

Core X protocol events are requested with the Xlib function XSelectInput(), and the Intrinsics can automatically request these events from the X server when necessary. Extensions to the X protocol define their own methods for selecting extension events, however, and you must register an "event selector" procedure that the Intrinsics can call to request extension events from the server. See XtExtensionSelectProc(2) for information on how to write such a procedure.

The *min_event_type* and *max_event_type* arguments need not specify the complete range of events available for a given extension, but you will almost always want to write your event selectors so that they do work for all event types of an extension. This is because most extensions select and deselect events by passing an event mask to a single call that is analogous to XSelectInput(). With this model of event selection and deselection, it is not possible to write extension selector procedures that handle separate ranges of extension events.

Similarly, it is not possible to write an extension event selector procedure that handles events from multiple extensions. This is because extension event numbers are assigned dynamically by the server, and it is not possible to know in advance whether two given extensions will have a contiguous range of event numbers.

If you do not register an event selector for a particular extension event, then the Intrinsics will not be able to automatically select that event type, and you will have to select it explicitly in your application code.

In order to work with extension events, you must also perform two other steps. You must register an event dispatcher procedure for the event types that you are interested in, and you must register an event handler that will be called when the extension event of interest is dispatched to a widget. See XtSetEventDispatcher() and XtInsertEventTypeHandler() for more information.

## Background

An extension selector is called in the following circumstances:

* When a widget is realized, after the core.realize method is called, the Intrinsics check to see if any event handler specifies an event type within the range of a registered extension selector. If so, the Intrinsics call each such selector.

* If an event type handler is added or removed, the Intrinsics check to see if the event type falls within the range of a registered extension selector and if it does calls the selector.

## XtRegisterExtensionSelector *(continued)*

In either case, the Intrinsics pass a list of all the widget's event types that are within the selector's range. The corresponding select data are also passed.

### See Also

*XtAddEventHandler(1),*
*XtDispatchEventToWidget(1),*
*XtGetKeyboardFocusWidget(1),*
*XtInsertEventHandler(1),*
*XtInsertEventTypeHandler(1),*
*XtRemoveEventHandler(1),*
*XtRemoveEventTypeHandler(1),*
*XtSetEventDispatcher(1),*
*XtEventDispatchProc(2),*
*XtEventHandler(2),*
*XtExtensionSelectorProc(2)*

## Name

XtReleasePropertyAtom — release a temporary Property name for reuse.

## Synopsis

```
void XtReleasePropertyAtom(w, atom)
    Widget w;
    Atom atom;
```

### Inputs

*w*  The widget used to reserve the Atom.

*atom*

The Atom returned by `XtReservePropertyAtom()` that is to be released for reuse.

## Availability

Release 6 and later.

## Description

`XtReleasePropertyAtom()` marks the specified property name Atom as no longer in use and insures that any property having that name on the specified widget's window is deleted.

If *atom* does not specify a value returned by `XtReservePropertyAtom()` for the specified widget, the results are undefined.

## Usage

Unless you are performing particularly complicated work with selections, you will probably never need to use this function.

Certain uses of parameterized selections require clients to name other window properties within a selection parameter. To permit reuse of temporary property names in these circumstances and thereby reduce the number of unique Atoms created in the server, the Intrinsics maintains a cache of reusable "scratch" Atoms.

## See Also

*XtReservePropertyAtom*(1),
*XtSetSelectionParameters*(1)

# XtRemoveBlockHook

## Name

XtRemoveBlockHook — unregister a block hook callback procedure.

## Synopsis

```
void XtRemoveBlockHook(id)
    XtBlockHookId id;
```

### Inputs

    *id*  An identifier that specifies the "block hook" procedure to be unregistered. This identifier is returned by the call to XtAppAddBlockHook() that registered the procedure.

## Availability

Release 6 and later.

## Description

XtRemoveBlockHook() removes the procedure/data pair identified by *id* from the list of procedures which are called by the Intrinsics before blocking for input.

## See Also

*XtAppAddBlockHook*(1),
*XtBlockHookProc*(2)

## Name

XtRemoveEventTypeHandler — unregister an event handler for an extension or core event.

## Synopsis

```
void XtRemoveEventTypeHandler(widget, event_type, select_data, proc, client_data)
    Widget widget;
    int event_type;
    XtPointer select_data;
    XtEventHandler proc;
    XtPointer client_data;
```

### Inputs

*widget*

The widget for which the event handler was registered; must be of class Core or a subclass.

*event_type*

The event type for which the handler was registered.

*select_data*

Data used to deselect events of the specified type from the server, or NULL.

*proc*

The event handler to be removed.

*client_data*

The additional client data with which the procedure was registered.

## Availability

Release 6 and later.

## Description

XtRemoveEventTypeHandler() unregisters an event handler registered with XtInsertEventTypeHandler() for the specified widget and event type. The request is ignored if *client_data* does not match the value given when the handler was registered. *select_data* is used to tell the server to stop sending events of the specified type. For core protocol events, this is a pointer to an appropriate event mask.

See XtInsertEventTypeHandler() for more information on the use of the *select_data* argument, and for a detailed explanation of how to obtain extension events.

## XtRemoveEventTypeHandler *(continued)*

### Usage

For core protocol events, it is simpler to use register event handlers with XtAddEventHandler() or XtInsertEventHandler() and unregister them with XtRemoveEventHandler()

### See Also

*XtAddEventHandler*(1),
*XtDispatchEventToWidget*(1),
*XtGetKeyboardFocusWidget*(1),
*XtInsertEventHandler*(1),
*XtInsertEventTypeHandler*(1),
*XtRegisterExtensionSelector*(1),
*XtRemoveEventHandler*(1),
*XtSetEventDispatcher*(1),
*XtEventDispatchProc*(2),
*XtEventHandler*(2),
*XtExtensionSelectorProc*(2)

## Name

XtRemoveSignal — unregister a signal callback.

## Synopsis

```
XtRemoveSignal(id)
    XtSignalId id;
```

### Inputs

*id*  An identifier returned by a call to `XtAppAddSignal()`.

## Availability

Release 6 and later.

## Description

`XtRemoveSignal()` unregisters a signal callback and its associated client data. The procedure/data pair is specified by *id*—the value returned by the call to `XtAppAddSignal()` that registered them.

## Usage

Before you unregister a signal callback, be sure to remove any signal handlers that invoke the callback by calling `XtNoticeSignal()` with an argument of *id*. Otherwise, the signal might arrive asynchronously with no valid callback registered.

See `XtAppAddSignal()` for a thorough explaination of signal handling in Xt applications.

## See Also

*XtAppAddSignal*(1),
*XtNoticeSignal*(1),
*XtSignalCallbackProc*(2)

# ■ XtReservePropertyAtom

## Name

XtReservePropertyAtom — obtain a temporary Property name.

## Synopsis

```
Atom XtReservePropertyAtom(w)
    Widget w;
```

### Inputs

w    The widget making a selection request.

### Returns

An Atom suitable for use as the name of a temporary Property.

## Availability

Release 6 and later.

## Description

XtReservePropertyAtom() returns an Atom that may be used as a Property name during selection requests involving the specified widget. As long as the Atom remains reserved, it is unique with respect to all other reserved Atoms for the widget.

When the Atom is no longer required (e.g. when the Property it names is deleted) it should be relinquished, so that it can be reused, by calling XtReleaseProperty-Atom().

## Usage

Unless you are performing particularly complicated work with selections, you will probably never need to use this function.

Certain uses of parameterized selections require clients to name other window properties within a selection parameter. To permit reuse of temporary property names in these circumstances and thereby reduce the number of unique atoms created in the server, the Intrinsics maintains a cache of reusable "scratch" Atoms.

## See Also

*XtReleasePropertyAtom*(1),
*XtSetSelectionParameters*(1)

# XtSendSelectionRequest ■

## Name

XtSendSelectionRequest — send a bundle of deferred selection requests as a single
MULTIPLE request.

## Synopsis

```
void XtSendSelectionRequest(requestor, selection, time)
    Widget requestor;
    Atom selection;
    Time time;
```

### Inputs

*requestor*
> Specifies the widget making the request. Must be of class Core or a sub-
> class.

*selection*
> The particular selection desired. Usually XA_PRIMARY.

*time*
> The timestamp that indicates when the selection request was initiated.
> The value CurrentTime is not acceptable.

## Availability

Release 6 and later.

## Description

When XtSendSelectionRequest() is called with values of *requestor* and *selection*
matching those in a previous call to XtCreateSelectionRequest(), a selection
request is sent to the selection owner. If a single target request is queued, that request
is made. If multiple targets are queued, they are bundled into a single request with a
target of MULTIPLE and the specified timestamp. As the converted values are returned,
the callbacks specified in XtGetSelectionValue(), XtGetSelectionValueIncre-
mental(), XtGetSelectionValues() and XtGetSelectionValueIncremental() are
invoked.

Multi-threaded applications should lock the application context (see XtAppLock())
before calling XtCreateSelectionRequest() and release the lock (see XtAppUn-
lock()) after calling XtSendSelectionRequest() to ensure that the thread assembling the request is safe from interference by another thread assembling a different
request naming the same widget and selection.

You can discard a pending MULTIPLE request without sending by calling `XtCancelSelectionRequest()`. See `XtCreateSelectionRequest()` for further discussion of bundling individual requests into a single MULTIPLE target.

## See Also

*XtCancelSelectionRequest*(1),
*XtCreateSelectionRequest*(1),
*XtGetSelectionValue*(1),
*XtGetSelectionValueIncremental*(1),
*XtGetSelectionValues*(1),
*XtGetSelectionValuesIncremental*(1),
*XtSetSelectionParameters*(1)

## Name

XtSessionGetToken — defer the response to a SessionShell XtNsaveCallback request.

## Synopsis

```
XtCheckpointToken XtSessionGetToken(widget)
    Widget widget;
```

### Inputs

*widget*
> The Session shell widget which manages session participation.

### Returns

A checkpoint token that allows the response to the pending checkpoint operation to be deferred.

## Availability

Release 6 and later.

## Description

When a session manager asks a client to save its state, the SessionShell widget invokes the procedures on its XtNsaveCallback list. These procedures are passed a "checkpoint token" that indicates the status of the save, and which can be used to reply to the save request. When the callback procedure returns, the checkpoint token is "returned" to the SessionShell; this constitutes a response to the checkpoint request.

Sometimes, however, a XtNsaveCallback procedure will perform some sort of asynchronous operation and will not be ready to respond to the checkpoint request when the procedure itself returns. In this case, the callback can call XtSessionGetToken() to obtain an additional checkpoint token. When the callback procedure exits, the original token will be returned, but since the procedure has requested a new token, no response is issued to the checkpoint request.

When the callback procedure is ready to issue its deferred response to such a checkpoint request, it should return any outstanding tokens it obtained with XtSessionGetToken() by calling XtSessionReturnToken().

If you call XtSessionGetToken() when no checkpoint request is pending, it will return NULL.

See SessionShell(3) for a full description of the session management checkpoint protocol.

## See Also

*XtSessionReturnToken(1),*
*SessionShell(3)*

## Name

XtSessionReturnToken — indicate completion of deferred checkpoint processing or
user interaction.

## Synopsis

```
void XtSessionReturnToken(token)
    XtCheckpointToken token;
```

### Inputs

*token*

Specifies a token which was received as the `call_data` by a procedure on
a SessionShell `XtNinteractCallback` list, or a token which was received
by a call to `XtSessionGetToken()`.

## Availability

Release 6 and later.

## Description

`XtSessionReturnToken()` returns an outstanding token to tell the SessionShell widget that the client has completed a checkpoint request or a user interaction. There are
two uses for this function.

If a SessionShell `XtNsaveCallback` procedure cannot finish checkpoint processing
before it returns, it can defer its reply by calling `XtSessionGetToken()`. When the
client is finished with the checkpoint and ready to reply, it tells the SessionShell that it
is done and returns its status by returning the token with `XtSessionReturnToken()`.

When a client is given permission to interact with the user during a session shutdown,
the client is passed a token as the `call_data` of its SessionShell `XtNinteractCall-
back` procedure. Since interaction with the user is always asynchronous in Xt applica-
tions, this callback procedure will return before the interaction is complete. To tell the
session manager that the interaction is complete, return the token passed to the callback by calling `XtSessionReturnToken()`.

See SessionShell(3) for a complete description of the session management checkpoint
and shutdown protocols.

## See Also

*XtSessionGetToken*(1),
*SessionShell*(3)

# XtSetEventDispatcher

## Name

XtSetEventDispatcher — register a procedure to dispatch extension events.

## Synopsis

```
XtEventDispatchProc XtSetEventDispatcher(display, event_type,
proc)
    Display *display;
    int event_type;
    XtEventDispatchProc proc;
```

### Inputs

*display*
> The display for which the event dispatcher is to be registered.

*event_type*
> The event type for which the dispatcher should be invoked.

*proc*
> The event dispatcher procedure.

### Returns

The previously registered dispatcher, or the default dispatcher if no dispatcher was previously registered.

## Availability

Release 6 and later.

## Description

XtSetEventDispatcher() registers the event dispatcher procedure specified by *proc* for events with the type *event_type* that occur on the specified display. The previously registered dispatcher (or the default dispatcher if there was no previously registered dispatcher) is returned. If *proc* is NULL, the default procedure is restored for the specified type.

In the future, when XtDispatchEvent is called with an event type of *event_type*, the specified *proc* (or the default dispatcher) is invoked to determine a widget to which to dispatch the event.

See XtEventDispatchProc(2) for an explanation of the responsiblities of an event dispatcher.

## Usage

You can call `XtSetEventDispatcher()` to change the dispatching of core X protocol events, but you should never need to do this—the default dispatcher handles the Intrinsics modal cascade and keyboard focus mechanisms, handles the semantics of *compress_enterleave* and *compress_motion*, and discards all extension events.

The default dispatcher discards extension events because they often require special code to figure out how they should be delivered. Thus, in order to register event handlers for any extension events in your Xt programs, you will have to write a custom event dispatch procedure. See `XtEventDispatchProc(2)` for more information.

A single event dispatch procedure can often be written to handle all event types for a given extension. In this case, you would call `XtSetEventDispatcher()` once for each event type supported by the extension. If your application works with multiple displays, you may want to call `XtSetEventDispatcher()` once for each event type and for each display. See `XtGetDisplays()` to get all open displays associated with an application context.

In order to receive extension events in an Xt program, it is not sufficient to register an event dispatcher. You must also register an event handler which will be called when an extension event is dispatched to a widget. See `XtInsertEventTypeHandler()`. And you must usually also register an event selector procedure to request extension events from the server. See `XtRegisterExtensionSelector()`.

## See Also

*XtAddEventHandler*(1),
*XtDispatchEventToWidget*(1),
*XtGetKeyboardFocusWidget*(1),
*XtInsertEventHandler*(1),
*XtInsertEventTypeHandler*(1),
*XtRegisterExtensionSelector*(1),
*XtRemoveEventHandler*(1),
*XtRemoveEventTypeHandler*(1),
*XtEventDispatchProc*(2),
*XtEventHandler*(2),
*XtExtensionSelectProc*(2)

# ■ XtSetSelectionParameters

## Name

XtSetSelectionParameters — specify parameters for the following selection value request.

## Synopsis

```
void XtSetSelectionParameters(requestor, selection, type,
value, length, format)
    Widget requestor;
    Atom selection;
    Atom type;
    XtPointer value;
    unsigned long length;
    int format;
```

### Inputs

*requestor*
>    The widget making the request. Must be of class Core or any subclass.

*selection*
>    The Atom that names the selection. Usually XA_PRIMARY.

*type*
>    The type of the Property in which the parameters are passed.

*value*
>    A pointer to the parameters.

*length*
>    The number of data elements in *value*, where each element is of the size indicated by *format*.

*format*
>    Specifies the size in bits of the data in the elements of *value*. One of 8, 16, or 32.

## Availability

Release 6 and later.

## Description

When a client requests that the value of a selection be converted to a specific target type, it may also need to specify additional information to be used in the conversion. As specified in the *Inter-client Communications Conventions Manual, Version 2.0*, this additional information is stored in a property of the requestor's window. The type and format of the property will depend on the specific target type that is to be requested.

XtSetSelectionParameters() creates the appropriate Property on the requestor's window, using the specified *type*, *value*, *length* and *format*. *type* is an Atom that identifies the type of the Property. The appropriate value will be determined by the individual conventions for the parameterized selection request being made. *value* is an array with *length* elements. The size of each element is determined by *format*. If *format* is 8, then each element of *value* should be sizeof(char) bytes long. If *format* is 16, then each element should be sizeof(short). If *format* is 32, then each element should be sizeof(long). Again, the appropriate format, length, and contents of *value* will be determined by the conventions that govern whatever parameterized selection request is being made.

When data has been specified with a call to XtSetSelectionParameters(), that data will be used as parameters for any subsequent call to XtGetSelectionValue() or XtGetSelectionValueIncremental() that uses the same *requestor* widget and *selection* Atom

If XtSetSelectionParmeters() is called more than once with the same *requestor* and *selection* without an intervening call to make the selection request, the most recently specified parameters overwrite the earlier ones and are used in the subsequent request.

## Usage

None of the commonly used and standardized selection target types uses parameters (with the exception of the MULTIPLE target, which is handled internally by the Intrinsics) so you may never need to use this function. You might define your own private data transfer target types for use in communication between related clients.

Note that XtSetSelectionParameters() cannot be used to specify parameters for multiple targets requested with XtGetSelectionValues() or XtGetSelectionValuesIncremental(). To create multiple selection requests that include parameterized targets, use XtSetSelectionParameters() with XtGetSelectionValue() and XtGetSelectionValueIncremental(), and group those calls between calls to XtCreateSelectionRequest() and XtSendSelectionRequest().

The requestor of a selection specifies parameters with XtSetSelectionParameters(). The owner of the selection can retrieve these parameters by calling XtGetSelectionParameters() from within its XtConvertSelectionProc callback procedure. See XtGetSelectionParameters().

## XtSetSelectionParameters *(continued)*

### See Also

*XtCreateSelectionRequest*(1),
*XtGetSelectionParameters*(1),
*XtGetSelectionValue*(1),
*XtGetSelectionValueIncremental*(1),
*XtGetSelectionValues*(1),
*XtGetSelectionValuesIncremental*(1),
*XtOwnSelection*(1),
*XtSendSelectionRequest*(1)

## Name

XtSignalCallbackProc — interface definition for a signal callback procedure.

## Synopsis

```
typedef void (*XtSignalCallbackProc)(XtPointer, XtSignalId*);
    XtPointer client_data;
    XtSignalId *id;
```

### Inputs

client_data
: The client data value that was registered with this procedure in XtAppAddSignal().

id The signal callback identifier returned from the call to XtAppAddSignal() that registered this procedure.

## Availability

Release 6 and later.

## Description

An XtSignalCallbackProc() is registered, along with its *client_data*, in a call to XtAppAddSignal(). This registration call returns an XtSignalId identifier, and the registered XtSignalCallbackProc is invoked when that identifier is passed to XtNoticeSignal() (usually from within a signal handler function).

## Usage

Notice that the *id* argument to an XtSignalCallbackProc is a pointer to an XtSignalId identifier, not the identifier itself.

See XtAppAddSignal() and XtNoticeSignal() for more information about signal handling in Xt applications. Pay particular attention to the distinction between a signal handler registered with signal() and a signal callback (a XtSignalCallbackProc) registered with XtAppAddSignal().

## See Also

*XtAppAddSignal()*(1),
*XtNoticeSignal()*(1),
*XtRemoveSignal()*(1)

# ◼ XtToolkitThreadInitialize

## Name

XtToolkitThreadInitialize — initialize a threaded application.

## Synopsis

```
Boolean XtToolkitThreadInitialize()
```

### Inputs
None.

### Returns
True if the Intrinsics support threaded applications; False otherwise.

## Availability

Release 6 and later.

## Description

The Intrinsics may be used in environments which offer multiple threads of execution within the context of a single process. A multithreaded application using the Intrinsics must explicitly initialize the toolkit for mutually exclusive access by calling XtToolkit-ThreadInitialize(). This function returns True if the Intrinsics support mutually exclusive thread access, otherwise it returns False.

XtToolkitThreadInitialize() should be the first Xt function called in a multithreaded application—it must be called before XtCreateApplicationContext(), XtAppInitialize(), XtOpenApplication(), or XtSetLanguageProc() is called. Xt-ToolkitThreadInitialize() may be called more than once, but the application writer must ensure that it is not called simultaneously by two or more threads.

## Usage

XtToolkitThreadInitialize() simply initializes Xt multithreading support. You must still explicitly provide mutual exclusion where required—see XtAppLock(), XtAppUnlock(), XtProcessLock() and XtProcessUnlock().

## See Also

*XtAppLock*(1),
*XtAppUnlock*(1),
*XtProcessLock*(1),
*XtProcessUnlock*(1)

## Name

XtUnregisterDrawable — dissociate a window or pixmap from a widget.

## Synopsis

```
void XtUnregisterDrawable(display, drawable)
    Display *display;
    Drawable drawable;
```

### Inputs

*display*
> The drawable's display.

*drawable*
> The drawable to unregister.

## Availability

Release 6 and later.

## Description

XtUnregisterDrawable() removes an association created with XtRegisterDrawable(). Once XtUnregisterDrawable() has been called, events that occur on *drawable* will not be delivered to any widget.

If the *drawable* has not been associated with a widget, or is the window of a widget in the client's widget tree, the results of calling XtUnregisterDrawable() are undefined.

See XtRegisterDrawable() for more information.

## See Also

*XtRegisterDrawable*(1),
*XtWindowToWidget*(1)

# ■ XtVaOpenApplication

## Name

XtVaOpenApplication — initialize the X Toolkit internals, using varargs argument style.

## Synopsis

```
Widget XtVaOpenApplication(app_context_return, application_class,
options, num_options, argc_in_out, argv_in_out,
fallback_resources, widget_class, ..., NULL)
    XtAppContext *app_context_return;
    String application_class;
    XrmOptionDescList options;
    Cardinal num_options;
    int *argc_in_out;
    String *argv_in_out;
    String *fallback_resources;
    WidgetClass widget_class;
```

### Inputs

*app_context_return*

Returns the application context, if non-NULL.

*application_class*

Specifies the class name of the application.

*options*

Specifies the command line options table.

*num_options*

Specifies the number of entries in options.

*argc_in_out*

Specifies a pointer to the number of command line arguments. This argument was a Cardinal * in Release 4, and is an int * in Release 5.

*argv_in_out*

Specifies the command line arguments array.

*fallback_resources*

Specifies resource values to be used if the application class resource file cannot be opened, or NULL.

*widget_class*

Specifies the class of the widget to be created. Must be shellWidgetClass or a subclass.

*...NULL*

A NULL-terminated variable-length list of resource name/value pairs to override any other resource specifications for the created shell.

### Returns

A toplevel shell widget of the specified class.

## Availability

Release 6 and later; supercedes XtVaAppInitialize().

## Description

XtVaOpenApplication() initializes the Toolkit internals, creates an application context, opens and initializes a display, and creates the initial application shell. It is identical to XtOpenApplication() except that the *args* array of resource names and values and the *num_args* argument of that function are replaced with a NULL-terminated variable-length argument list.

XtVaOpenApplication() supercedes XtVaAppInitialize(); it is identical to that function except that it has a *widget_class* argument.

See XtOpenApplication() for more information on this function. See XtAppInitialize() for details on the application initialization process. See XtVaSetValues() for more information on using variable-length argument lists to specify resources.

## See Also

*XtAppInitialize*(1),
*XtOpenApplication*(1),
*XtVaSetValues*(1)

# Index

# BOOKS

*from*

# O'Reilly & Associates, Inc.

SUMMER 1995

"For programmers and people who like to understand the full gory detail of how things work, I must recommend the O'Reilly series of X books."

—Peter Collinson, *SunExpert*

---

## Motif Tools

*By David Flanagan*
*1st Edition August 1994*
*1024 pages (CD-ROM included), ISBN 1-56592-044-9*

*Motif Tools* and the Xmt programming library that accompanies it on CD-ROM offer resources that will empower Motif programmers and dramatically speed up application development with the X Toolkit and Motif. While the book is a complete programmer's guide and reference manual for the Xmt library, it is not just a dry volume about programming mechanics; it also describes a holistic philosophy of development of a complete application: from first conception, through design and implementation, and on to the finishing stylistic touches.

---

## X User Tools

*By Linda Mui & Valerie Quercia*
*1st Edition November 1994*
*856 pages, ISBN 1-56592-019-8*

*X User Tools* provides for X users what *UNIX Power Tools* provides for UNIX users: hundreds of tips, tricks, scripts, techniques, and programs—plus a CD-ROM—to make the X Window System more enjoyable, more powerful, and easier to use. This browser's book emphasizes useful programs culled from the network, offers tips for configuring individual and systemwide environments, and incudes a CD-ROM of source files for all—and binary files for some—of the programs.

---

FOR INFORMATION: **800-998-9938**, 707-829-0515; **TECH@ORA.COM**

# The X Window System Series

When it comes to X, think of these books as the ultimate owner's manuals. Because of its power and flexibility, X is also extremely complex. We help you sort through that complexity with books that show you, step-by-step, how to use, program, and administer the X Window System.

## Programmer's Supplement for Release 6

*Edited by Adrian Nye*
*1st Edition September 1995 (est.)*
*300 pages (est.), ISBN 1-56592-089-9*

This book is for programmers who are familiar with Release 5 of the X Window System and who want to know how to use the new features of Release 6. Intended as an update for owners of Volumes 1, 2, 4, and 5 of the X Window System series, it provides complete tutorial and reference information to all new Xlib and Xt toolkit functions. The book includes:

- An overview of the R6 changes as they affect application programming

- Preparing applications for Session Management

- New Xt features, including session management, signal handling, and C++ support

- Creating multi-threaded X applications

- Using transformed (rotated, scaled, or obliqued) fonts

- Internationalizing X applications

- An introduction to X image extensions

- Reference pages for all new Xlib and Xt functions

Together with Volumes 2 and 5, owners of the *Programmer's Supplement for Release 6* have a complete set of reference pages for the current X Consortium standards for Xlib and Xt.

## The X Companion CD for R6

*By O'Reilly & Associates*
*1st Edition January 1995*
*(Includes CD-ROM plus 126-page guide)*
*ISBN 1-56592-084-8*

Our new X11 R6 CD-ROM, a companion to our *X Window System Administrator's Guide* (Volume 8 of the X Window series), is a helpful resource for system administrators and programmers alike.

The CD features:

- X11 R6 binaries (compiled and supplied by Ready-to-Run Software) for all the major platforms: SUN4, Solaris, HP-UX on the HP700, DEC Alpha, DEC ULTRIX, and IBM RS6000

- X11 R6 sources and contrib directory

- X11 R5 sources directory

- Source files of the programming examples in our X Window System manuals

The accompanying booklet shows you how to install the software and briefly discusses new R6 material. Now you don't have to wait for your vendor's release of the software. It's all here, along with the latest patches from the X Consortium, on this handy CD.

## X Protocol Reference Manual

*Edited by Adrian Nye*
*4th Edition January 1995*
*458 pages, ISBN 1-56592-083-X*

This manual describes the X Network Protocol, which underlies all software for Version 11 of the X Window System. It not only provides a practical demonstration of what is involved in a client session, but also an extensive set of reference pages for each protocol request and event. Reference pages, alphabetized for easy access, include encoding of requests and replies. The fourth edition of *X Protocol Reference Manual* includes protocol clarifications of X11 Release 6, and can be used with any release of X. Note: This edition does not contain the Inter-Client Communication Conventions Manual (ICCCM) or the X Logical Font Description Convention (XLFD). This material will be included in an upcoming O'Reilly book.

## Xlib Programming Manual

**VOLUME 1**
*By Adrian Nye*
*3rd Edition July 1992*
*824 pages, ISBN 1-56592-002-3*

A complete programming guide to the X library (Xlib), the lowest level of programming interface to X. Covers X11 Release 5. Includes introductions to internationalization, device-independent color, font service, and scalable fonts.

## Xlib Reference Manual

**VOLUME 2**
*By Adrian Nye*
*3rd Edition June 1992*
*1138 pages, ISBN 1-56592-006-6*

Complete reference guide to the X library (Xlib), the lowest level of programming interface to X. Covers X11 R4 and R5.

## X Window System User's Guide

**VOLUME 3**
*Standard Edition*
*By Valerie Quercia & Tim O'Reilly*
*4th Edition May 1993*
*836 pages, ISBN 1-56592-014-7*

Orients the new user to window system concepts and provides detailed tutorials for many client programs, including the *xterm* terminal emulator and window managers. Later chapters explain how to customize the X environment. This popular manual is available in two editions, one for users of the MIT software, one for users of Motif. Revised for X11 Release 5.

## X Window System User's Guide

**VOLUME 3M**
*Motif Edition*
*By Valerie Quercia & Tim O'Reilly*
*2nd Edition January 1993*
*956 pages, ISBN 1-56592-015-5*

Highlights the Motif window manager and graphical interface, including new features such as tear-off menus and drag-and-drop. Revised for Motif 1.2 and X11 Release 5.

## X Toolkit Intrinsics Programming Manual

**VOLUME 4**
*Standard Edition*
*By Adrian Nye & Tim O'Reilly*
*3rd Edition April 1993*
*567 pages, ISBN 1-56592-003-1*

A complete guide to programming with Xt Intrinsics, the library of C language routines that facilitates the design of user interfaces with reusable components called widgets. Available in two editions. The *Standard Edition* uses Athena widgets in examples; the *Motif Edition* uses Motif widgets.

## X Toolkit Intrinsics Programming Manual

**VOLUME 4M**
*Motif Edition*
*By Adrian Nye & Tim O'Reilly*
*2nd Edition August 1992*
*674 pages, ISBN 1-56592-013-9*

The *Motif Edition* of Volume 4 uses the Motif 1.2 widgets set in examples and covers X11 Release 5.

## X Toolkit Intrinsics Reference Manual

**VOLUME 5**
*Edited by David Flanagan*
*3rd Edition April 1992*
*916 pages, ISBN 1-56592-007-4*

Complete programmer's reference for the X Toolkit, providing pages for each of the Xt functions, as well as the widget classes defined by Xt and the Athena widgets. This third edition has been reorganized and expanded for X11 Release 5.

## Motif Programming Manual

**VOLUME 6A**
*By Dan Heller, Paula Ferguson & David Brennan*
*2nd Edition February 1994*
*1016 pages, ISBN 1-56592-016-3*

A source for complete, accurate, and insightful guidance on Motif application programming. In addition to information on Motif, the book is full of tips about programming in general and about user-interface design. It includes material on using UIL, drag-and-drop, and tear-off menus and covers Motif Release 1.2 (while remaining usable with Motif 1.1). Complements Volume 6B, *Motif Reference Manual*.

## Motif Reference Manual

**VOLUME 6B**
*By Paula Ferguson & David Brennan*
*1st Edition June 1993*
*920 pages, ISBN 1-56592-038-4*

A complete programmer's reference for the Motif toolkit. This book provides reference pages for the Motif functions and macros, the Motif and Xt widget classes, the Mrm functions, the Motif clients, and the UIL file format, data types, and functions. The reference material has been expanded from the appendices of the first edition of Volume 6 and covers Motif 1.2. This manual is a companion to Volume 6A, *Motif Programming Manual*.

## XView Programming Manual

 **VOLUME 7A**

*By Dan Heller, Updated by Thomas Van Raalte*
*3rd Edition September 1991 (latest update August 1993)*
*770 pages, ISBN 0-937175-87-0*

The *XView Programming Manual* describes both the concepts and the technical approaches behind XView, the poor-man's object-oriented toolkit for building OPEN LOOK applications for X. Along with its companion volume, the *XView Reference Manual*, this book is perfect for the beginner breaking into X programming.

## XView Reference Manual

 **VOLUME 7B**

*Edited by Thomas Van Raalte*
*1st Edition September 1991 (latest update August 1993)*
*311 pages, ISBN 0-937175-88-9*

The XView toolkit provides extensive attribute-value pair combinations, convenience routines and object class hierarchies that are too voluminous to memorize without the aid of this comprehensive reference guide. A must-have companion for the *XView Programming Manual*.

## X Window System Administrator's Guide

 **VOLUME 8**

*By Linda Mui & Eric Pearce*
*1st Edition October 1992*
*372 pages, ISBN 0-937175-83-8*

This book is the first and only book devoted to the issues of system administration for X and X-based networks, written not just for UNIX system administrators, but for anyone faced with the job of administering X (including those running X on stand-alone workstations). Note: The CD that used to be offered with this book is now sold separately, (*The X Companion CD for R6*), allowing system administrators to purchase the book and the CD-ROM in quantities they choose.

"For…those system administrators wanting to set up X11 for the first time, this is the book for you. As an easy-to-use guide covering X administration, it doesn't get bogged down in too much detail…. This is not a book for bedtime reading or to generate an all-consuming interest in X windows, but a thoroughly good text to help you over the first hurdle or two." —*Sun UK User*

## The X Window System in a Nutshell

*Edited by Ellie Cutler, Daniel Gilly & Tim O'Reilly*
*2nd Edition April 1992*
*424 pages, ISBN 1-56592-017-1*

Indispensable companion to the X Window System series. Experienced X programmers can use this single-volume desktop companion for most common questions, keeping the full series of manuals for detailed reference. This book has been updated to cover R5, but is still useful for R4.

## The X Graphic Series

## PEXlib Programming Manual

*By Tom Gaskins*
*1st Edition December 1992*
*1154 pages, ISBN 1-56592-028-7*

The *PEXlib Programming Manual* is the definitive programmer's guide to PEXlib, covering both PEX versions 5.0 and 5.1. Containing over 200 illustrations and 19 color plates, it combines a thorough and gentle tutorial approach with valuable reference features. Includes numerous programming examples, as well as a library of helpful utility routines—all of which are available online. You do not need any prior graphics programming experience to use this manual.

## PEXlib Reference Manual

*Edited by Steve Talbott*
*1st Edition December 1992*
*577 pages, ISBN 1-56592-029-5*

The *PEXlib Reference Manual* is the definitive programmer's reference resource for PEXlib, containing complete and succinct reference pages for all the callable routines in PEXlib version 5.1. The content of the *PEXlib Reference Manual* stands, with relatively few changes, as it was created by the X Consortium.

## PHIGS Programming Manual

*By Tom Gaskins*
*1st Edition February 1992*
*Hardcover: 968 pages, ISBN 0-937175-92-7*

A complete and authoritative guide to PHIGS and PHIGS PLUS programming. Whether you are starting out in 3D graphics programming or are a seasoned veteran looking for an authoritative work on a fast-rising 3D graphics standard, this book will serve your purposes well.

## PHIGS Reference Manual

*Edited by Linda Kosko*
*1st Edition October 1992*
*1116 pages, ISBN 0-937175-91-9*

The definitive and exhaustive reference documentation for the PHIGS and PHIGS PLUS graphical programming language. Contains reference pages for all language functions. Together with the *PHIGS Programming Manual*, this book is the most complete and accessible documentation currently available for the PHIGS and PHIGS PLUS standards.

# The X Resource Journal

The X Resource, *a quarterly working journal for X programmers, provides practical, timely information about the programming, administration, and use of the X Window System.* The X Resource *is the official publisher of the X Consortium Technical Conference Proceedings. Issues are available separately or by subscription.*

" *The X Resource* is the only journal that I have ever come across which has a permanent place for every issue among the 'reference books in use' on my desk."

—*John Wexler,*
*Computing Services, Edinburgh University*

"I find the journal invaluable. It provides in-depth coverage of topics that are poorly documented elsewhere, or not documented at all."

—*Peter Nicklin,*
*Vice President R&D, Version Technology*

## The X Resource: Issue 15

*Edited by Paula Ferguson*
*Summer 1995*
*250 pages (est.), ISBN 1-56592-140-2*

## The X Resource: Issue 14

*Edited by Paula Ferguson*
*Spring 1995*
*208 pages, ISBN 1-56592-122-4*

Articles for Issue 14 include: WILLOW: The Washington Information Looker-Upper Layered Over Windows
• Tickling Fvwm: Extending Tk as an Fvwm Module
• The Knvas Widget: A 2D Graphics Framework
• Koalatalk: An ICE-based Lightweight Message Bus
• Hush: A C++ API for Tcl/Tk.

## The X Resource: Issue 13

*Edited by Paula Ferguson*
*Winter 1995*
*308 pages, ISBN 1-56592-121-6*

Articles for Issue 13, taken from the 9th Annual X Technical Conference, include: Help! There's a Spy in My Code
• Embedding of X Applications • OpenDoc and Its Architecture • A Pseudo-Root Extension: X Window System Nesting on a Budget • Common Desktop Environment Architectural Overview • The X Public Access Mechanism: Software Cooperation for Space Science and Beyond
• A Remote Access Protocol for the X Window System.

## The X Resource: Issue 12

*Edited by Paula M. Ferguson*
*Fall 1994*
*222 pages, ISBN 1-56592-069-4*

Articles for Issue 12 include:  The XPM Format and Library: A Tutorial and Reference • The Xmsg Library: An Application-Level Message-Reporting Facility
• Event-Free Structured Graphics in the X Environment
• An Object-oriented Approach to Motif 1.2 Drag and Drop • The X Administrator: Configuration and Administration of a Scalable X-based UNIX Service.

## The X Resource: Issue 11

*Edited by Paula M. Ferguson*
*Summer 1994*
*264 pages, ISBN 1-56592-068-6*

Articles for Issue 11 include: Writing Portable X Code
• xmove: A Pseudoserver for X Window Movement
• Interactive GUI Development Environments
• A Tutorial Introduction to Tcl and Tk • The XmtLayout Widget: A Tutorial.

## The X Resource: Issue 10

*Edited by Adrian Nye*
*Spring 1994*
*212 pages, ISBN 1-56592-067-8*

Articles for Issue 10 include:  What's New in R6
• The One Minute Manager: Custom Motif Layout Widgets Made Easy • The Motif 2.0 Uniform Transfer Model: Unifying Selection, Clipboard, and Drag and Drop
• Implementing Cut and Paste in the X Environment.

*Issues 0 (Fall 1991) through 9 (Winter 1994) are also available.*

*O'Reilly & Associates—*

# GLOBAL NETWORK NAVIGATOR™

The Global Network Navigator (GNN)™ is a unique kind of information service that makes the Internet easy and enjoyable to use. We organize access to the vast information resources of the Internet so that you can find what you want. We also help you understand the Internet and the many ways you can explore it.

## What you'll find in GNN

There are three main sections to GNN: Navigating the Net, Special GNN Publications, and Marketplace.
Here's a look at just some of what's contained in GNN:

### Navigating the Net

- The **WHOLE INTERNET USER'S GUIDE & CATALOG**, based on O'Reilly's bestselling book, is a collection of constantly updated links to 1000 of the best resources on the Internet, divided by subject areas.

- The **NCSA MOSAIC "WHAT'S NEW"** page is your best source for the latest Web listings. Browse it like you would a newspaper, then click on the new sites you're most interested in.

### Special GNN Publications

- **BOOK STORY**—GNN's newest publication, is the first Internet platform to provide an interactive forum for authors and readers to meet. Book Story serializes books, features author interviews and chats, and allows readers to contact authors with the ease of email.

- **TRAVELERS' CENTER**—This is a great place to visit before your trip begins. The Travelers' Resource Center takes advantage of information that's been on the Internet but hasn't been distilled and compiled in an easy-to-use format—until now. You'll also read feature stories and dispatches from fellow travelers.

- **PERSONAL FINANCE CENTER**—Here is where we bring you a broad spectrum of money management, investment, and financial planning resources on the Internet. There are original features and columns on personal finance, too.

- **GNN SPORTS**—Visit this center for Net coverage of your favorite professional and college teams. (It's better than waiting in line for tickets.) Every week we update the center with articles, interviews, stats, and links to sports resources on the Net.

### Marketplace

- **BUSINESS PAGES**—Here's where we've organized commercial resources on the Internet. Choose from a variety of categories like "Business Services," "Entertainment," and "Legal Financial Services."

- **GNN DIRECT**—This is the place to go to read about quality products and services in GNN's collection of catalogs. You can also order online using GNN Direct. Simply browse through product literature, do key word and text searches, and place an order at any time.

### Marketing Your Company on GNN

GNN is known as the premier interactive magazine and navigational guide on the Internet. With over 170,000 total subscribers and 8 million document hits every month, GNN attracts a large, dynamic, and growing audience. Because of this, GNN offers exciting opportunities for companies interested in creating a presence on the Internet. We currently offer two programs:

- **TRAFFIC LINKS**—We can link reader traffic from GNN to your Web site. Think of this option as an online form of direct response advertising. GNN staff will work with you to tailor a program to fit your needs. For details about this program, send email to **traffic-links@gnn.com** or call 1-510-883-7220 and ask for our Traffic Link sales representative.

- **BUSINESS PAGES**—Choose from a basic listing (up to 50 words), extended listing (up to 350 words), links from your listing in GNN to your server, or a FAQ (Frequently Asked Questions) document of up to 350 words that's coupled with either a basic or extended listing. For more information, send email to **market@gnn.com** or call 1-510-883-7220.

### Get Your Free Subscription to GNN Today

Come and browse GNN! A free subscription is available to anyone with access to the World Wide Web. To get complete information about subscribing, send email to **info@gnn.com**

If you have access to a World Wide Web browser such as Mosaic, Lynx, or NetScape, use the following URL to register online:
**http://gnn.com/**

If you use a browser that does not support online forms, you can retrieve an email version of the registration form automatically by sending email to **form@gnn.com** Fill this form out and send it back to us by email and we will confirm your registration.

## O'Reilly on the Net—
# ONLINE PROGRAM GUIDE

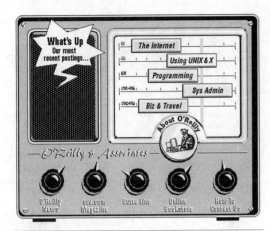

O'Reilly & Associates offers extensive information through various online resources. We invite you to come and explore our little neck-of-the-woods.

### Online Resource Center

Most comprehensive among our online offerings is the O'Reilly Resource Center. Here, you'll find detailed information on all O'Reilly products: titles, prices, tables of contents, indexes, author bios, software contents, reviews...you can even view images of the products themselves. With GNN Direct you can now order our products directly off the Net (GNN Direct is available on the Web site only; Gopher users can still use **order@ora.com**). We supply contact information along with a list of distributors and bookstores available worldwide. In addition, we provide informative literature in the field: articles, interviews, excerpts, and bibliographies that help you stay informed and abreast.

***To access ORA's Online Resource Center:***

Point your Web browser (e.g., `mosaic` or `lynx`) to:

`http://www.com.ora/`

or `http://gnn.com/ora/`

For the plaintext version, `telnet` or `gopher` to:

`gopher.ora.com`
(telnet login: `gopher`)

---

### FTP

The example files and programs in many of our books are available electronically via FTP.

***To obtain example files and programs from O'Reilly texts:***

`ftp` to:
`ftp.ora.com`

or `ftp.uu.net`
`cd published/oreilly`

### Ora-news

An easy way to stay informed of the latest projects and products from O'Reilly & Associates is to subscribe to "ora-news," our electronic news service. Subscribers receive email as soon as the information breaks.

***To subscribe to "ora-news":***

Send email to:
**listproc@online.ora.com**

and put the following information on the first line of your message (not in "Subject"):
**subscribe ora-news** "your name" **of** "your company"

For example enter:
`mail listproc@online.ora.com`

`subscribe ora-news Kris Webber of
    Mighty Fine Enterprises`

---

### Email

Many customer services are provided via email. Here are a few of the most popular and useful.

**tech@ora.com**
> For general questions and information.

**bookquestions@ora.com**
> For technical questions, or corrections, concerning book contents.

**order@ora.com**
> To order books online and for ordering questions.

**catalog@ora.com**
> To receive a free copy of our magazine/catalog, *ora.com* Please include a postal address.

---

### Snailmail and Phones

**O'Reilly & Associates, Inc.**
**103A Morris Street, Sebastopol, CA 95472**
Inquiries: **707-829-0515**, **800-998-9938**
Credit card orders: **800-889-8969** (Weekdays 6 A.M.- 5 P.M. PST)
FAX: **707-829-0104**

# O'Reilly & Associates—
# LISTING OF TITLES

## INTERNET

!%@:: A Directory of Electronic Mail
   Addressing & Networks
Connecting to the Internet:
   An O'Reilly Buyer's Guide
The Mosaic Handbook for
   Microsoft Windows
The Mosaic Handbook for
   the Macintosh
The Mosaic Handbook for
   the X Window System Smileys
The Whole Internet User's
   Guide & Catalog

## SOFTWARE

Internet In A Box™
WebSite™

## WHAT YOU NEED TO KNOW SERIES

Using Email Effectively
Marketing on the Internet
   (Summer 95 est.)
When You Can'T Find Your
   System Administrator

## WORKING & LIVING WITH COMPUTERS

Building a Successful Software Business
The Computer User's Survival Guide
   (Summer 95 est.)
The Future Does Not Compute
Love Your Job!

## AUDIOTAPES

### INTERNET TALK RADIO'S "GEEK OF THE WEEK" INTERVIEWS

The Future of the Internet Protocol,
   4 hours
Global Network Operations, 2 hours
Mobile IP Networking, 1 hour
Networked Information and
   Online Libraries, 1 hour
Security and Networks, 1 hour
European Networking, 1 hour

### NOTABLE SPEECHES OF THE INFORMATION AGE

John Perry Barlow, 1.5 hours

## USING UNIX

### BASICS

Learning the Bash Shell
Learning GNU Emacs
Learning the Korn Shell
Learning the UNIX Operating System
Learning the vi Editor
MH & xmh: Email for Users
   & Programmers
SCO UNIX in a Nutshell
The USENET Handbook (Summer 95 est.)
Using UUCP and Usenet
UNIX in a Nutshell: System V Edition

### ADVANCED

Exploring Expect
The Frame Handbook
Learning Perl
Making TeX Work
Programming perl
Running LINUX
sed & awk
UNIX Power Tools (with CD-ROM)

## SYSTEM ADMINISTRATION

Computer Security Basics
Computer Crime: A Crimefighter's
   Handbook (Summer 95 est.)
DNS and BIND
Essential System Administration
Linux Network Administrator's Guide
Managing Internet Information Services
Managing NFS and NIS
Managing UUCP and Usenet
Networking Personal Computers
   with TCP/IP (Summer 95 est.)
sendmail
Practical UNIX Security
PGP: Pretty Good Privacy
System Performance Tuning
TCP/IP Network Administration
termcap & terminfo
X Window System Administrator's
   Guide: Volume 8
The X Companion CD for R6

## PROGRAMMING

Applying RCS and SCCS
   (Summer 95 est.)
Checking C Programs with lint
DCE Security Programming
   (Summer 95 est.)
Distributing Applications Across DCE
   and Windows NT
Encyclopedia of Graphics File Formats
Guide to Writing DCE Applications
High Performance Computing
Managing Projects with make
Microsoft RPC Programming Guide
Migrating to Fortran 90
Multi-Platform Code Management
lex & yacc
ORACLE Performance Tuning
ORACLE PL/SQL Programming
   (Summer 95 est.)
Porting UNIX Software (Summer 95 est.)
POSIX Programmer's Guide
POSIX.4: Programming for
   the Real World
Power Programming with RPC
Practical C Programming
Practical C++ Programming
   (Summer 95 est.)
Programming with curses
Programming with GNU Software
   (Summer 95 est.)
Software Portability with imake
Understanding and Using COFF
Understanding DCE
Understanding Japanese Information
   Processing
UNIX for FORTRAN Programmers
Using C on the UNIX System
Using csh and tcsh (Summer 95 est.)

## BERKELEY 4.4 SOFTWARE DISTRIBUTION

4.4BSD System Manager's Manual
4.4BSD User's Reference Manual
4.4BSD User's Supplementary
   Documents
4.4BSD Programmer's
   Reference Manual
4.4BSD Programmer's
   Supplementary Documents
4.4BSD-Lite CD Companion
4.4BSD-Lite CD Companion:
   International Version

## X PROGRAMMING

Volume 0: X Protocol Reference
   Manual, R6
Volume 1: Xlib Programming Manual
Volume 2: Xlib Reference Manual:
Volume 3: X Window System
   User's Guide
Volume. 3M: X Window System
   User's Guide, Motif Ed
Volume. 4: X Toolkit Intrinsics
   Programming Manual
Volume 4M: X Toolkit Intrinsics
   Programming Manual, Motif Ed.
Volume 5: X Toolkit Intrinsics
   Reference Manual
Volume 6A: Motif Programming
   Manual
Volume 6B: Motif Reference Manual
Volume 7A: XView Programming
   Manual
Volume 7B: XView Reference Manual
   Motif Tools
Volume 8 : X Window System
   Administrator's Guide
PEXlib Programming Manual
PEXlib Reference Manual
PHIGS Programming Manual
   (soft or hard cover)
PHIGS Reference Manual
Programmer's Supplement for Release 6
   (Summer 95 est.)
The X Companion CD for R6
The X Window System in a Nutshell
X User Tools (with CD-ROM)

## THE X RESOURCE

### A QUARTERLY WORKING JOURNAL FOR X PROGRAMMERS

The X Resource: Issues 0 through 15
   (Issue 15 available 7/95)

## TRAVEL

Travelers' Tales Thailand
Travelers' Tales Mexico
Travelers' Tales India
Travelers' Tales: A Woman's World
Travelers' Tales France (6/95 est.)
Travelers' Tales Hong Kong (8/95 est.)
Travelers' Tales Spain (9/95 est.)

# *O'Reilly & Associates—*
# INTERNATIONAL DISTRIBUTORS

Customers outside North America can now order O'Reilly & Associates books through the following distributors. They offer our international customers faster order processing, more bookstores, increased representation at tradeshows worldwide, and the high-quality, responsive service our customers have come to expect.

## EUROPE, MIDDLE EAST, AND AFRICA

*(except Germany, Switzerland, and Austria)*

**INQUIRIES**

International Thomson Publishing Europe
Berkshire House
168-173 High Holborn
London WC1V 7AA, United Kingdom
Telephone: 44-71-497-1422
Fax: 44-71-497-1426
Email: itpint@itps.co.uk

**ORDERS**

International Thomson Publishing Services, Ltd.
Cheriton House, North Way
Andover, Hampshire SP10 5BE, United Kingdom
Telephone: 44-264-342-832 (UK orders)
Telephone: 44-264-342-806 (outside UK)
Fax: 44-264-364418 (UK orders)
Fax: 44-264-342761 (outside UK)

## GERMANY, SWITZERLAND, AND AUSTRIA

International Thomson Publishing GmbH
O'Reilly-International Thomson Verlag
Königswinterer Straße 418
53227 Bonn, Germany
Telephone: 49-228-97024 0
Fax: 49-228-441342
Email: anfragen@ora.de

## ASIA *(except Japan)*

**INQUIRIES**

International Thomson Publishing Asia
221 Henderson Road
#08-03 Henderson Industrial Park
Singapore 0315
Telephone: 65-272-6496
Fax: 65-272-6498

**ORDERS**

Telephone: 65-268-7867
Fax: 65-268-6727

## JAPAN

International Thomson Publishing Japan
Hirakawa-cho Kyowa Building 3F
2-2-1 Hirakawa-cho, Chiyoda-Ku
Tokyo, 102 Japan
Telephone: 81-3-3221-1428
Fax: 81-3-3237-1459

Toppan Publishing
Froebel Kan Bldg. 3-1, Kanda Ogawamachi Chiyoda-Ku
Tokyo 101 Japan
Telex: J 27317
Cable: Toppanbook, Tokyo
Telephone: 03-3295-3461
Fax: 03-3293-5963

## AUSTRALIA

WoodsLane Pty. Ltd.
7/5 Vuko Place, Warriewood NSW 2102
P.O. Box 935, Mona Vale NSW 2103
Australia
Telephone: 02-970-5111
Fax: 02-970-5002
Email: woods@tmx.mhs.oz.au

## NEW ZEALAND

WoodsLane New Zealand Ltd.
21 Cooks Street (P.O. Box 575)
Wanganui, New Zealand
Telephone: 64-6-347-6543
Fax: 64-6-345-4840
Email: woods@tmx.mhs.oz.au

## THE AMERICAS

O'Reilly & Associates, Inc.
103A Morris Street
Sebastopol, CA 95472 U.S.A.
Telephone: 707-829-0515
Telephone: 800-998-9938 (U.S. & Canada)
Fax: 707-829-0104
Email: order@ora.com

# Here's a page we encourage readers to tear out...

# O'REILLY WOULD LIKE TO HEAR FROM YOU

*Please send me the following:*

❏ *ora.com*
O'Reilly's magazine/catalog, containing behind-the-scenes articles and interviews on the technology we write about, and a complete listing of O'Reilly books and products.

❏ *Global Network Navigator*™
Information and subscription.

*Please print legibly*

Which book did this card come from?

_____

Where did you buy this book?
❏ Bookstore  ❏ Direct from O'Reilly
❏ Bundled with hardware/software  ❏ Class/seminar

Your job description:  ❏ SysAdmin  ❏ Programmer
❏ Other_____

What computer system do you use?  ❏ UNIX
❏ MAC  ❏ DOS(PC)  ❏ Other_____

| | |
|---|---|
| Name | Company/Organization Name |
| Address | |
| City | State | Zip/Postal Code | Country |
| Telephone | Internet or other email address (specify network) |

Nineteenth century wood engraving
of the horned owl from the O'Reilly
& Associates Nutshell Handbook®
*Learning the UNIX Operating System*

POST CARD

O'Reilly & Associates, Inc., 103A Morris Street, Sebastopol, CA 95472-9902

# BUSINESS REPLY MAIL
FIRST CLASS MAIL   PERMIT NO. 80   SEBASTOPOL, CA

*Postage will be paid by addressee*

## O'Reilly & Associates, Inc.
103A Morris Street
Sebastopol, CA  95472-9902